Ignored but Not Forgotten

ALSO BY LUCILLE H. CAMPEY

Seeking a Better Future:
The English Pioneers of Ontario and Quebec

Planters, Paupers, and Pioneers:
English Settlers in Atlantic Canada

An Unstoppable Force:
The Scottish Exodus to Canada

"A Very Fine Class of Immigrants":
Prince Edward Island's Scottish Pioneers 1770–1850

"Fast Sailing and Copper-Bottomed":
Aberdeen Sailing Ships and the Emigrant Scots
They Carried to Canada 1774–1855

The Silver Chief:
Lord Selkirk and the Scottish Pioneers of
Belfast, Baldoon and Red River

After the Hector*:*
The Scottish Pioneers of Nova Scotia and Cape Breton 1773–1852

The Scottish Pioneers of Upper Canada, 1784–1855:
Glengarry and Beyond

Les Écossais:
The Scottish Pioneers of Lower Canada, 1763–1855

With Axe and Bible:
The Scottish Pioneers of New Brunswick, 1784–1874

Lucille Campey has two websites:
www.englishtocanada.com
for her books on English emigration to Canada

www.scotstocanada.com
for her books on Scottish emigration to Canada

THE ENGLISH IN CANADA

Ignored but Not Forgotten

Canada's English Immigrants

Lucille H. Campey

DUNDURN
TORONTO

Editor: Allison Hirst
Design: Courtney Horner
Printer: Webcom
Cover design by Jennifer Scott
Front cover image courtesy the Tate Gallery, London, U.K.
Back cover photo by Geoff Campey.

Library and Archives Canada Cataloguing in Publication

Campey, Lucille H., author
Ignored but not forgotten : Canada's English immigrants / Lucille H. Campey.

(The English in Canada)
Includes bibliographical references and index.
Issued in print and electronic formats.
ISBN 978-1-4597-0961-4

1. English--Canada--History. 2. Immigrants--Canada--History. 3. Canada--Emigration and immigration. 4. England--Emigration and immigration. I. Title. II. Series: Campey, Lucille H. English in Canada.

FC106.B7C34 2014 325.2420971 C2014-902138-0
C2014-902139-9

1 2 3 4 5 18 17 16 15 14

We acknowledge the support of the **Canada Council for the Arts** and the **Ontario Arts Council** for our publishing program. We also acknowledge the financial support of the **Government of Canada** through the **Canada Book Fund** and **Livres Canada Books**, and the **Government of Ontario** through the **Ontario Book Publishing Tax Credit** and the **Ontario Media Development Corporation**.

Care has been taken to trace the ownership of copyright material used in this book. The author and the publisher welcome any information enabling them to rectify any references or credits in subsequent editions.
J. Kirk Howard, President

Cover image: *The Emigrant's Last Sight of Home, 1858.* This painting, by Richard Redgrave, depicts a carpenter, together with his wife and children, on their way to a new life abroad. While he appears to be optimistic about their future, his wife seems anxious and resentful that they should have had to leave their home in Surrey. The inhabitants on the opposite hill, including a boy on crutches, wish them well. It is a last farewell for them, since, at the time, it was prohibitively expensive for most immigrants to contemplate returning home.

The publisher is not responsible for websites or their content unless they are owned by the publisher.

Printed and bound in Canada.

VISIT US AT
Dundurn.com | @dundurnpress | Facebook.com/dundurnpress | Pinterest.com/Dundurnpress

Dundurn
3 Church Street, Suite 500
Toronto, Ontario, Canada
M5E 1M2

Gazelle Book Services Limited
White Cross Mills
High Town, Lancaster, England
LA1 4XS

Dundurn
2250 Military Road
Tonawanda, NY
U.S.A. 14150

To Geoff

CONTENTS

LIST OF MAPS

Note: All maps are © Geoff Campey, 2014

LIST OF TABLES

ACKNOWLEDGEMENTS

I am indebted to a great many people. First, I wish to gratefully thank the Foundation for Canadian Studies in the U.K. for their grant toward my research and travel costs.

I have relied on the wide-ranging primary sources to be found in English County Record Offices, the Canadian national and provincial archives, and in the Special Collections at English universities, especially the missionary reports of Anglican and Methodist missionaries. In carrying out this work, I am indebted to the many librarians and archivists on both sides of the Atlantic who helped me. In particular, I wish to thank Peter Nockles at the John Rylands Library in Manchester, Liz Sykes at the Manchester County Record Office, Renée Jackaman at the Devon Record Office, Kris Inwood at the Eccles Centre in the British Library, and Claire Skinner at the Wiltshire History Centre. I want to especially thank the archival and library staff at Library and Archives Canada, the Glenbow Archives, the City of Toronto Reference Library, the East Riding of Yorkshire Archives in Beverley, and the Manchester Archives.

I am grateful to the many people who helped me to locate and obtain illustrations. In particular, I thank Dominic R. Labbé, in McMasterville, Quebec, for providing me with photographs of Anglican and Methodist churches in southwestern Quebec and the Eastern Townships. I am indebted to Dr. Gordon Goldsborough of the Manitoba Historical Society for supplying a photograph of St. James Anglican Church in Winnipeg. I am very grateful to David Hill-Turner, curator of the Nanaimo Museum in British Columbia, for providing a photograph of one of the early Staffordshire miners who settled in Nanaimo and for sending me invaluable documentary material. I also thank Jane Hodkinson of the Manchester Library, Dorothy Clayton of the John Rylands Library (University of Manchester), Anna Butler of the Dorset County Museum, and Mrs. H. Clarke of the East Riding of Yorkshire Archives in Beverley. I also thank Alan Walker of the Special Collections Department at the Toronto Reference Library, Erin Strouth of the Archives of Ontario, Susan Kooyman of the Glenbow Archives, John Boylan of the Public Archives and Records Office of Prince Edward Island, and Theresa Sorel of the Ottawa Archives.

I offer a special thank you to my editor Allison Hirst for her painstaking work in checking my manuscript and in steering it to its publication. I also thank my stalwart friend Jean Lucas who has proofread this manuscript and as always has helped me greatly.

Finally, this book would not have been possible without my husband's help, encouragement, and strong belief in the value of the end product. This is our eleventh book. We are a team. He produced the tables and maps, located the illustrations, helped with the research, and kept me sane throughout. This, my third book on the English, is dedicated to him with all my love.

PREFACE

I had three objectives in writing this book. First, I wanted to build on my previous studies of English emigration to Atlantic Canada and Ontario and Quebec by also dealing with the English who settled in the Prairie provinces and British Columbia. These were essentially provincial analyses and their time scale extended from the seventeenth to the late nineteenth centuries. My second objective was to explore the great English influx of the early twentieth century, and for this I needed to take a national perspective. My third objective was to give the English a voice. Considering that they dominated the overall British influx to Canada, it seemed incredible to me that they should have been ignored so comprehensively by contemporary commentators and later by historians. There can be no doubt that their story deserves to be told.

The English have partly themselves to blame for seemingly fading into obscurity. When they arrived, they kept any feelings they had about their English identity to themselves. Coming as they did from the most powerful nation of the greatest Empire the world had ever seen, they felt that they had little need to explain who they were. They did not indulge in flag waving or march in parades. They simply merged into the background, adapted to new ways, and became Canadians. If they did attract attention it was for the wrong reasons. The British government's policy of offloading its surplus poor from the slums of the great English cities to parts of Canada was bound to annoy Canadians as did the grumbling and condescending tendencies of some of the English middle and upper classes. However, while great scorn has been poured on a few malcontents, the majority have been comprehensively ignored.

Emigration to Canada was driven partly by major economic changes taking place in England and partly by the lure of distinct opportunities that emigrants hoped to obtain in their chosen destinations. As can be seen in the evocative scene depicted on the front cover of this book, it was always going to be a gigantic leap of faith. The carpenter's final wave to the hillside speaks of optimism, while the sadness in the eyes of the children and the questioning look of his wife speak of despair. They were tearing themselves away from their loved ones in Surrey, would endure the horrors and discomfort of an Atlantic crossing, and would come to a country that was far less well-developed than their homeland. They did so because the carpenter believed that his prospects would be better in Canada. He could earn much higher wages if they went to a town or city and he might hope to prosper in time as a land-owning farmer. Given that the English influx grew steadily over many decades, one must conclude that the majority did experience a happy ending.

While using wide-ranging documentary sources in writing this book, I have placed particular importance on the emigrant letters, diaries, and journals that the English have left behind. These documents often reveal their homesickness and desire to associate with people who shared their geographical origins. Their immense determination to succeed also comes across. Nothing was ever handed to them on a silver platter. It took great courage, resilience, and an indomitable spirit to become a successful immigrant. Farming was often fraught with setbacks, back-breaking toil, and terrible hardships, while in the cities and towns many English struggled to obtain suitable jobs. Plenty of them began by working long hours in low-paying jobs, hoping for better times. Nevertheless, this is an enriching story of independent-minded and hard-working people who eventually reached their goals. Along the way they helped to people a nation and enhance it with their multi-faceted skills.

Emigration had begun in earnest in the early nineteenth century, primarily from the North of England, but later from both the north and south more equally. While most English emigrants were able to finance their own travel and other costs, a significant number were very poor and needed assistance. A major turning point was reached in the late nineteenth century when sailing ships gave way to steamships and Canada had at last built a transcontinental railway. This paved the way for the mass influx of the English that occurred in the early twentieth century. The growing preference for Empire destinations and the enthusiastically run promotional campaigns of the Canadian government, which focused attention on the agricultural potential of the Canadian West, had helped to swell the number of English who chose to emigrate. They scattered widely and the contribution they made to Canada's development was significant.

ABBREVIATIONS

AO	Archives of Ontario
BCL	Birmingham Central Library
BEA	Beverley (East Riding of Yorkshire) Archives
BL	British Library, London
BRO	Bedfordshire Record Office
CAS	Cumbria Archive Service
CKS	Centre for Kentish Studies
CRO	Cornwall Record Office
DCB	Dictionary of Canadian Biography
DHC	Dorset History Centre
DRO	Devon Record Office
ETRC	Eastern Townships Resource Centre
ERO	Essex Record Office
GLA	Glenbow Archives (Calgary)
GLRO	Greater London Record Office
GRO	Gloucestershire Record Office
HCA	Hull City Archives
HRO	Hertfordshire Record Office
JRL	John Rylands Library, University of Manchester

LAC	Library and Archives Canada
LARO	Lancashire Record Office (Preston)
LCA	Liverpool City Archives
LMA	London Metropolitan Archive
LRO	Lincolnshire Record Office
MAA	Manchester Archives
NAB	National Archives of Britain
NORO	Northamptonshire Record Office
NSARM	Nova Scotia Archives and Records Management
NTRO	Nottinghamshire Record Office
PANB	Public Archives of New Brunswick
PAPEI	Public Archives and Records Office of Prince Edward Island
PP	British Parliamentary Papers
RHL	Rhodes House Library, Oxford University
RIC	Royal Institution of Cornwall
SOAS	School of Oriental and African Studies, University of London,
SORO	Somerset Record Office
SPG	Society for the Propagation of the Gospel in Foreign Parts
SROI	Suffolk Record Office (Ipswich)
STRO	Staffordshire County Record Office
USPG	United Society for the Propagation of the Gospel
WHC	Wiltshire History Centre
WIA	Wirral Archives
WORO	Worcestershire Record Office
WYAS	West Yorkshire Archive Service

CHAPTER 1

Ignored but Not Forgotten

In my mind, I oftimes visit Rillington.[1]

Luke Harrison was desperately lonely. Having arrived in Nova Scotia from Rillington in the East Riding of Yorkshire in 1774, he was still pining for his native land in 1803, some twenty-nine years later. When he had first come, Luke had told his cousin back in Yorkshire, "[We] do not like it all, and a great many besides us [do not like it], and [we] are coming back to England;" but in his 1803 communication he could not "help but praise up Nova Scotia," the intervening period being the toughest of tests for the early arrivals.[2]

Luke and his family were among the nine hundred or so mainly Yorkshire people who came during the 1770s to Nova Scotia and what would later become the province of New Brunswick. Having the necessary skills to cultivate the tidal marshes of the Bay of Fundy, they flourished, although they needed time to adjust to the many new challenges. While he and the others yearned to be back in Yorkshire, those of their family and friends who remained behind soon forgot them. Despite being the first large contingent of colonizers to come directly from England to

Canada, the Yorkshire colonizers faded into obscurity. Yorkshire people were also very well represented in the early tide of emigration to come to Upper and Lower Canada, but they, too, escaped notice. And, when one considers the overall English influx to Canada, the sin of omission becomes much worse. Despite being the dominant group to immigrate to Canada during the late nineteenth and early twentieth centuries, their contribution to Canada's development has been largely ignored, both by contemporary observers and later historians.[3]

Why have the English been ignored? Part of the reason for this lies with the English themselves. In Canada, they were defined, together with the French, as forming one of its two "founding peoples." However, while the French were regarded as an ethnic group, the English were not. That is largely because the English did not regard themselves as having an ethnic identity. As the dominant culture in the former British Empire they saw no reason to define their distinguishing features to anyone. A further complication is that they could be English one minute and British the next. With either hat on, they could regard the Union Jack, the monarchy, and parliamentary institutions as symbols of their identity. In this confusion it is difficult to define what is meant by Englishness. If any categorization did register in Canada, it was their association with the elite, since they were very well represented in business and in the upper echelons of government. Another factor was the seeming disinterest in England over their departure. Unlike the Scots, who were associated with infamous clearances, and the Irish, who were associated with great famines, the English attracted little controversy and slipped away virtually unnoticed.

The French-speaking Acadians of Nova Scotia, who were expelled between 1755 and 1758; the New England Planters, who took their place shortly afterward; and the Highland Scots who came to the eastern Maritimes in the early 1770s, at the time when the Yorkshire settlers first arrived, have each been the subject of numerous histories. However, these publications pale into insignificance when compared with the voluminous accounts written about the many thousands of Americans of British descent who entered the Maritimes and the St. Lawrence region a decade later as Loyalists. While historians have considered the role played by the Acadians, Planters, Highland Scots, and Loyalists in Canada's early development, they have comprehensively ignored their near contemporary Yorkshire colonizers and have paid even less attention to the waves of English who followed them. Thus, the English have become the invisible and unsung heroes of Canada's immigration story.

English immigration was driven primarily by a desire for economic self-betterment. Its motivation was never solely a flight from poverty. In fact, the numbers emigrating rose with the advance of industrialization throughout Britain. The resulting higher living standards for those in work increased the number of people who could afford the costs of emigrating. Initially, most of the English sought farming opportunities, at first favouring mid Canada. But by the end of the nineteenth century, as the prairies were being opened up to settlers, they headed west. By then, however, a substantial number ended up in the towns and cities rather than in rural areas. In many ways the poor had the most to gain from moving

Courtesy Library and Archives Canada, C-075936.

Selling Canada to the British in 1905. Canadian produce was prominently displayed in horse-drawn wagons that were brought to agricultural shows and weekly markets across Britain. Immigration agents were on hand to distribute pamphlets and report favourably on Canada's prospects.

to Canada. The shortage of labour worked to their advantage since they could command much higher wages than the pittance they were paid in England. Also, the New World had no masters and no pecking order. No longer categorized as the subservient working class, the English working man could now be a free-thinking individual, seeking what was best for his family. Thus by emigrating, people could gain materially, while enjoying the freedom and benefits of a more egalitarian society.

The popular perception is that Canada was settled mainly by the Scots and Irish, but the English, in fact, outnumbered them. Although they were slow to arrive initially, constituting only around a quarter of the total British influx to Canada before Confederation,[4] the English actually dominated the much larger emigrant stream that arrived from Britain between 1867 and 1915.[5] By 1911 they formed 47 percent of that part of the Canadian population having British roots and 25 percent of the total Canadian population.[6] The English influx began as a North of England phenomenon, but by the 1830s people were being drawn equally from the north and south. Most English left as individuals or in small groups and chose their destinations primarily on economic grounds rather than on any desire to settle with other English. They were not clannish and had no wish to keep themselves apart from other ethnic groups.

After colonizing parts of Nova Scotia and New Brunswick during the 1770s, the English extended their territory across Canada after 1815, when the end of the Napoleonic Wars allowed for safe travel once again. They pursued timber trade and farming opportunities across the Maritimes and in southwestern Quebec, and beginning in the 1830s they headed in large numbers for Upper Canada (later Ontario), where they usually cultivated the best lands. They became concentrated primarily along the northwest side of Lake Ontario and parts of the southwestern peninsula.

While they came from the length and breadth of England, a striking proportion of those who arrived before 1850 originated from the three counties of Yorkshire, Devon, and Cornwall (Map 1). Meanwhile, the much larger English influx, which began in the late nineteenth century, brought thousands of English settlers to southwestern Manitoba, southern Saskatchewan, southern Alberta, and a smaller number to the Okanagan Valley of British Columbia.

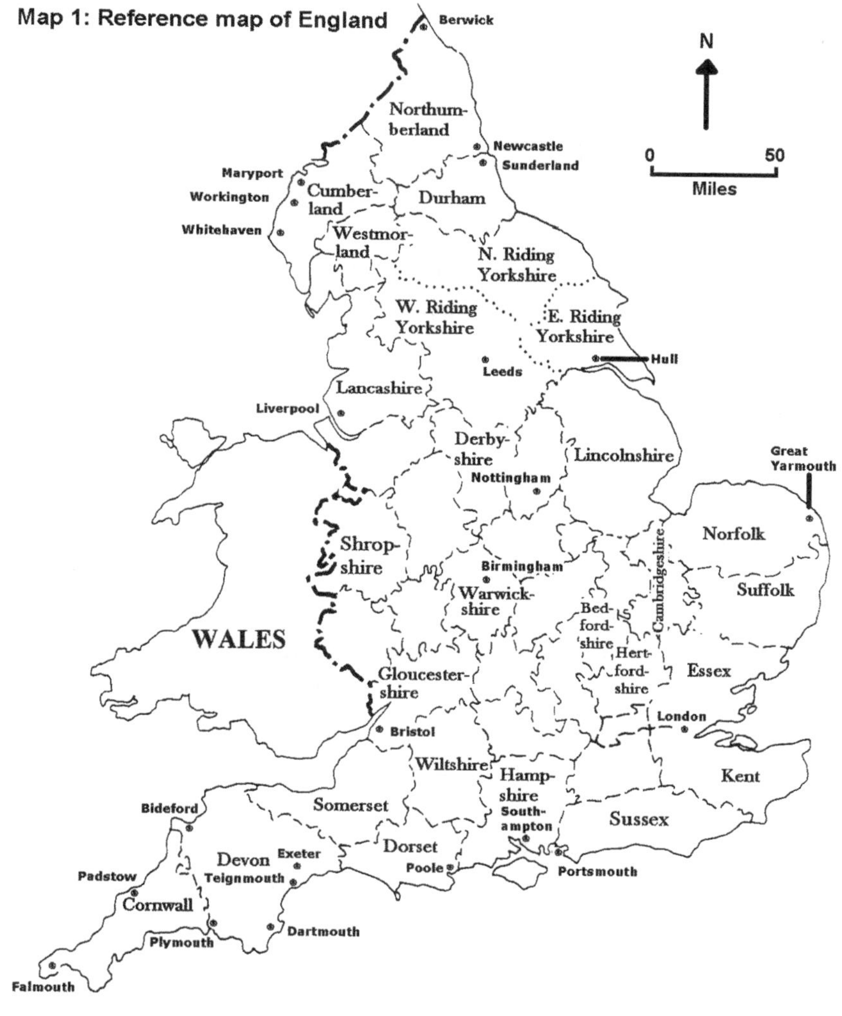

The English had an illusory presence in Nova Scotia and New Brunswick. The 1871 Census reveals that in each case they accounted for 29 percent of the population — a considerable feat given that relatively few English immigrants came to either province. The explanation for this apparent anomaly is that Census enumerators included descendents of the Planters and Loyalists, claiming distant English ancestry, in their overall tally of people who had originated from England. As was clear from the very beginning, Nova Scotia and New Brunswick could not measure up to the St. Lawrence region. The land there was poorer and the climate more adverse. In 1789 the Reverend Samuel Peters, a Connecticut Anglican minister, commented on their "barren shores and frozen climes [that] will forever prevent them any population and consequence,"[7] and Dr. Isaac Moseley, one of the agents employed in allocating land to Loyalists, agreed with his gloomy assessment. According to Moseley, those who went to Chaleur Bay in the Gaspé Peninsula found that it "did not answer their expectations and have chiefly returned. Those who went to the Upper Settlements [Upper Canada] are doing well.... I have reason to believe they are doing the best of any settlements that are yet made by the whole body of Loyalists, as the land and climate are preferable to Nova Scotia [and] New Brunswick."[8]

While Upper Canada undoubtedly had the greatest appeal, it only began to attract settlers in sizable numbers when its internal routes were opened up, and this only happened in the 1830s. At that time the Colonial Office went as far as advising intending immigrants to head for Upper Canada, since "Prince Edward Island, Newfoundland, Nova Scotia and Cape Breton ... do not contain the means either of affording employment at wages to a considerable number of emigrants or of settling them upon land."[9] This favouring of Upper Canada suited the British government's interests, since it wished to have a large English-speaking Protestant population to counterbalance the French-speaking Roman Catholic communities in Lower Canada. Meanwhile, by the mid nineteenth century the Maritime provinces were attracting relatively few immigrants, and, to make matters worse, they had to stand by and watch as their own populations drained away to Upper Canada and the United States.

Although most of the English who came to Canada were able to fund their own travel costs, the use of emigration as a solution for alleviating dire poverty is a recurring theme. For instance, the introduction of combine harvesters in England's rural south in the 1830s had calamitous consequences for agricultural workers, who were made redundant in their thousands. An unemployment crisis led to violent disturbances, which in turn led to calls for government action to assist the poor to emigrate. Aid did come, but not from national government. Instead, with the passing of the Poor Law Amendment Act of 1834, English parishes were allowed to raise funds locally for emigration schemes, which initially directed people to either Upper or Lower Canada.[10] However, such schemes were imperfect in that not everyone who was helped to emigrate wanted to remain on the land, let alone remain in Canada. A Yorkshireman complained to a local newspaper at the time that the area where he lived, two hundred miles from New York City, was being "inundated with English paupers. They are round us every day, some begging, some stealing and some working for their livelihood."[11] No doubt they had slipped away from the others and crossed the border in the hope of finding better-paid and less taxing jobs in the American towns and cities.

As Britain's industrialization intensified, the population continued to shift from the country to the towns and cities in ever greater numbers. With the country's surplus labour becoming concentrated in the city slums, a humanitarian crisis loomed. The British government came under increasing pressure by the late nineteenth century to provide state-assisted emigration schemes, but it resisted such calls, confining itself to unobtrusive help. Having accepted the argument that emigration offered the poor an escape from their poverty, it supported the fundraising work of philanthropic bodies and it also encouraged local government to play its part. Starting in the 1870s, various institutions and philanthropists organized the relocation of many thousands of orphaned and abandoned English children to Canada, although such schemes provoked considerable dismay on both sides of the Atlantic. The passing of the Unemployed Workmen Act of 1905 enabled English city councils to establish distress committees and raise funds to relocate their unemployed to Canada. However, while such schemes helped England to rid itself of its surplus labour, the new immigrants were of less benefit to Canada, which was crying out for agricultural workers and had little need for the skills of England's urban poor. Thus there was a serious mismatch between the needs of the donor and recipient countries. Moreover, the British government regularly came under fire for its apparent cynicism in using Canada as a dumping ground for its ne'er-do-wells and misfits.

Courtesy Library and Archives Canada, C-014658.

English immigrants arriving at Quebec in 1908. By this time immigrants had a considerably easier time reaching their destinations. They could travel in steamships in a fraction of the time taken by sailing ships, while the growing railway networks, on both sides of the Atlantic, provided them with an integrated service.

During the 1830s there were certainly plenty of middle- and upper-class people in England who welcomed the government's apparent desire to ship its paupers to Canada. An example was Miss Maude Davies, author of a history of Corsley, who regarded the poor in her community with utter contempt:

> In 1830, the parish of Corsley, Wiltshire, shipped off at its own cost [to Upper Canada] sixty-six of the least desirable of its inhabitants, about half being adults and half children....
>
> The emigrants consisted of several families of the very class one would wish to remove, men of suspected bad habits who brought up their children to wickedness, whilst there were several poachers amongst them, and other reputed bad characters.[12]

The same can be said of Henrietta Fielding, half sister of William Henry Fox-Talbot, squire of the Lacock estate in Wiltshire. She was equally disapproving of the contingent that was heading off to Upper Canada at this time, as was Lady Fielding, Fox-Talbot's mother:

> There are now 40 people going to America — Mr. Paley [the Vicar] says they remind him of the 40 thieves! — but so much the better riddance.... Mama has given clothes to the women, 10 of whom are going....[13]
>
> I do not intend to give anything till the last moment otherwise Mr. Spencer tells me they are very likely to sell it.[14]

However, what both ladies conveniently ignored was that they were at the top of a class system that left those at the bottom with few prospects and often dependent on charity. While the elite could dictate who had jobs and what they were paid, the poor had to make the best of what they were given. The top-down nature of the English class system essentially entrapped them in their poverty. Yet Canada's classless society was different. It gave them the freedom to sell their labour to the highest bidder in a highly competitive market, thus enabling workers to earn considerably higher wage rates than the pittances they were paid in England. When the new arrivals encountered this much more favourable environment, they blossomed and sang Canada's praises to friends and family back home, thus becoming major advocates for emigration.

The recipients of assisted emigration schemes clearly benefited from the opportunities that Canada had to offer. However, the British government did sanction one or two dubious schemes whose primary purpose was not to help the poor but rather to reduce welfare costs. For example, parishes in Dorset and Devon made savings by encouraging young men, dependent on poor relief, to take up employment in Newfoundland during the summer months with West Country merchants who ran the cod fishery. Examples include Isaac Peterson, "a poor child of the parish [of Poole]," who was packed off to Trinity Harbour in 1737, at the age of fourteen, to be apprenticed to the Reverend Robert Killpatrick until he turned twenty-one,[15] and Jack Ash of Puddletown (Dorset) who went thirty years later "if the parish will provide him with clothing."[16] Eighteen years later, Wimborne Parish (Dorset) paid the "expenses of apprenticing three poor boys of the [poor] house to Newfoundland," and later provided "clothes for Joshua Penny's boy and William Wheeler going to Newfoundland."[17] In 1801, George Penney of Wimborne Minster (Dorset), having been "a poor child of the parish," served his apprenticeship with two Fogo (Newfoundland) planters until he was twenty-one and ended up with just £5, together with his return passage to England.[18] These men had been used as cheap labour. An unexpected twist was that many remained in Newfoundland. The 1991 Census records that a staggering 82 percent of Newfoundland's population claimed to have some English ancestry, much of it attributable to the adventurous West Country fishermen who seized their opportunities in the province's distant past.

A much more despicable example of exploitation was the encouragement given in the 1830s to British Army war veterans, known as the Chelsea Pensioners, to commute their pensions to a lump sum. That money was then used to fund their relocation to Upper Canada. War veterans who had been wounded in battle and in advanced years were never going to succeed as pioneers in the Canadian wilderness and it was preposterous to think otherwise.[19] This was just a cynical attempt to reduce the War Office's pensions' bills. Eventually, Lord Durham decreed that something had to be done to relieve their suffering, but by the time he stepped in and arranged for them to receive aid, only a quarter of the original group of four thousand still survived. However, this was one isolated case. The many assisted emigration schemes that were administered by local government should not be tarred with the same brush. Britain was not just callously ridding itself of its poor.

However much the poor were despised by some people in England, the British government's approach to them was generally fair-minded and compassionate. With very few exceptions, assistance was well administered and adequately funded. English parishes could not skimp on the payments made to their paupers or on the quality of the ships that were used to take them to Canada. An elaborate bureaucracy overseen by the Poor Law commissioners in London kept a watchful eye over them.

The commissioners made certain that only those people judged to be of suitable age and in good health could be selected for emigration schemes. Parish files are bulging with the receipts for payments made for food, clothing, and household items, which were itemized down to the last bedpan, petticoat, and tin plate.

Given that English labourers and tradesmen were much in demand and could thus command far higher pay than was the case in England, they experienced considerable economic benefits in emigrating. They also found that, for the first time in their lives, they were treated as valued individuals. However, the transition to a levelling-down society was perplexing and often painful for their wealthier counterparts. Even the wealthy Loyalists who came to Canada with their slaves had to adjust to new ways. Thomas Peters, a Black Loyalist and former African-American slave who fled from North Carolina to Saint John, New Brunswick, with British Loyalists during the American War of Independence, alerted Granville Sharp, an English anti-slavery campaigner, to the fact that his city had twenty-one men who owned slaves. One of those named in Peters' list was Gabriel Ludlow, Saint John's first mayor. This meant that slavery was bound to be accepted in the city initially, although it was a short-lived abomination.[20]

When Mary Chaplin, a high-born Lincolnshire artist, visited the Eastern Townships in 1840 she was struck by the many Americans in the area and liked their "casual, easy and familiar manners."[21] When she was approached by a complete stranger in an inn, who then struck up a conversation, Mary realized that the lady "did not mean to be otherwise than civil; these manners arise from considering everybody on an equal footing." Similarly, when he toured New Brunswick in 1847, Abraham Gesner observed "a constant struggle between the aristocratic principle and the spirit of freedom and equality characteristic of the Americans." He noted that people rising from nothing to affluence and people "with advantages of birth and education" were disapproving of each other, just as they might have been back in England.[22]

Ten years earlier such tensions had sparked riots. Old-world patronage had crept into land grant policy, creating a cosy elitism at the heart of government. This practice flew in the face of the egalitarian society that settlers were seeking to create.[23] Rioting swept through parts of Upper and Lower Canada in 1837–38. Though this was quelled through military action, the point had been made.[24] In future, more would be done to meet the needs of ordinary people. These violent skirmishes brought a sudden halt to the influx from Britain and even prompted some English settlers to return home.[25]

The high cost of labour in Canada had dire consequences for any starry-eyed immigrants who thought that they could establish an English-style farm staffed by servants. Edmund Peel, an officer on leave from the British navy, and his wife, Lucy, tried to do this at Sherbrooke in the Eastern Townships in the 1830s. But the dream soon turned sour. Lucy declared that "Edmund is, after four years hard labour, convinced that nothing is to be done by farming in Canada; the land here produces too little to pay the labour requisite to cultivate it."[26] However, the issue was not poor land productivity, but rather that the Peels could not afford to pay for labour. They could have employed as many servants and labourers as they wanted in England, where wage rates were much lower, but not so in Lower Canada. Here the labour costs exceeded their means and, not wishing to do the land clearance work themselves, they had no option but to leave. Thus there were pitfalls for the unsuspecting and the ill-prepared.

Map 2: Reference Map of Canada in 1949

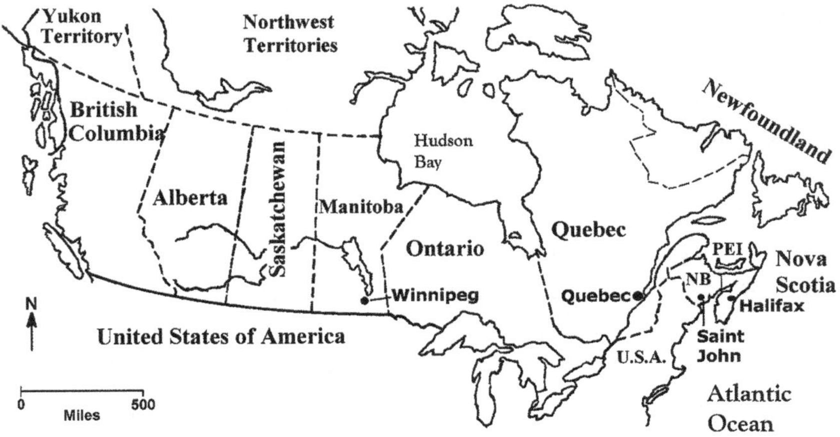

The English influx to Canada gathered pace very slowly. Before Confederation in 1867, most English had gone to the United States. However, with the opening up of the Prairie provinces for settlement from the 1870s, and a general improvement in Canada's economic

Courtesy Library and Archives Canada, e010779321-s1.

Western Canada: The New Eldorado, 1890–1920. Great quantities of glossy posters and pamphlets, produced by the Canadian government, promoted an idealized impression of the better prospects that awaited settlers in western Canada.

prospects, the trickle soon became a flood (Map 2). During the first three decades of the twentieth century, unprecedented numbers arrived from England, sometimes as many as 100,000 in a single year, with Canada being favoured far more than the United States.[27] The growing preference for Empire destinations and the growing scarcity of good land in the United States had helped to turn the immigrant stream toward Canada. Journey times had been transformed by the arrival of steamships and the completion of a transcontinental railway and enthusiastically run promotional campaigns focused attention on the agricultural potential of the Canadian West.

However, the expansion of agricultural settlement in the Prairies had stimulated industrial growth generally, thus creating new jobs in the towns and cities across Canada, jobs which the English were particularly keen to fill. The fact is that most of England's population at the time was urban. Thus, it is hardly surprising that when they came to Canada they headed for its towns and cities. This outcome upset Canada's labour unions, which feared that they would take jobs away from Canadians and depress wages. Nevertheless, they came. The true scale of the English preference for conurbations would be revealed in the 1921 Census, which showed their overwhelming presence in many towns and cities. For instance, they formed a substantial proportion of those employed in Ontario's growing industrial and service sectors and in Toronto alone the English accounted for half of the city's population.

Meanwhile, a large proportion of the wealthy English who arrived at this time headed for Alberta to try their luck as cattle ranchers, or to British Columbia, where they established fruit farms. Some were retired and others were often the younger sons of affluent families who hoped that their children would blossom as gentlemen farmers. However, their elitism often ruffled feathers, and many found it difficult to shake off the impression that they were upper-class misfits. Their reputation also suffered from their perceived association with the many upper-class remittance men living in both provinces, who received regular allowances from family or friends in England. Well-known for their "superior insolence," remittance men enjoyed a very leisurely lifestyle in which cricket bats, tennis rackets, and fishing rods were of prime importance.[28]

MONTREAL DAILY STAR—FRIDAY, NOVEMBER 15, 1901.

THE ENGLISHMAN IN CANADA—8.
He Goes on Board.

Courtesy Glenbow Archives, NA-3683-3.

A cartoonist's mocking impression of a wealthy Englishman making an entrance at Quebec in 1901 with his bulldog. He complains that "I feel quite lost you know without me top hat boxes, evening dwess [sic] cases and twouser [sic] stretchers, but I won't need them."

With the rising unemployment after the end of the First World War, the British government once again succumbed to the political attraction of assisting its poor to emigrate, only this time it committed millions of pounds per annum by way of loans and grants. Through the Empire Settlement Act of 1922, emigration was promoted both to alleviate unemployment in Britain and to bring British stock to the white dominions, where it was hoped they would boost their economies. However, by then Canada was at best a reluctant partner, since it had long grown tired of being landed with Britain's surplus urban poor. Most of the collaborative ventures carried out under this act were plagued by bad planning, high costs, and a failure to repay loans. A decade later, concerns over the rise of fascism prompted renewed interest in British Empire emigration schemes, but they, too, were short-lived and unsuccessful.[29]

Courtesy Glenbow Archives, NA-1687.

A. J. Wilkinson, an Anglican lay preacher on horseback in the snow somewhere in southern Alberta, circa 1913.

While Canada only gave grudging support to Empire settlement schemes, its people continued to embrace the concept of Empire. Loyalty to Empire is readily exemplified by the large numbers of Canadians who enrolled for the two world wars. Anglican and Methodist ministers and preachers tapped into this sense of patriotism to promote the special role of the church as a unifying force within the Empire.

The English were driven principally by the desire for economic self-betterment. Immigration to Canada stepped up a gear in the late nineteenth century with the coming of steamships and railways and, by the time they appeared, the focus had moved from east to west. The English who came in a great surge during the early twentieth century were principally being attracted by mid Canada's excellent industrial prospects and the agricultural opportunities of the western provinces. Canada was the recipient of their genes, culture, language, and wide-ranging skills. If they had defining features, they kept them to themselves and slipped into obscurity. Their story as one of Canada's major immigrant groups is told in the chapters that follow.

CHAPTER 2

The English Influx to Atlantic Canada

A baited line was dragged along ... and when it was hauled up it brought a codfish weighing 42 pounds and a half.[1]

Passengers sailing in the *Elizabeth* from London to Charlottetown in 1775 gazed with amazement at the enormous cod caught just off the Banks of Newfoundland. Most were Londoners who were on their way to the Island of St. John (now Prince Edward Island) to establish the future New London.[2] But there was certainly no question of any settlers from Britain making a similar attempt to found settlements in Newfoundland at this time. Having acquired exclusive sovereignty over Newfoundland in 1713, Britain had been exploiting the island primarily for its abundant codfish.[3] The island's agricultural potential was poor, the climate was harsh, jobs were badly paid and mainly limited to the fishery, and women were in short supply. A few of the Englishmen who had taken up seasonal employment in the fishery did remain and by so doing helped slowly to increase Newfoundland's resident population. However, while British Newfoundland was allowed to develop at its own pace, the rest of Atlantic Canada danced to a different tune.

When France surrendered Acadia (peninsular Nova Scotia) to the British in 1713, it handed over a colony that already had a substantial Roman Catholic, French-speaking population whose loyalties were with France.[4] Facing a possible threat to its interests, Britain decided to counterbalance the Acadian population with Protestant immigrants from England and Europe. In 1749, it took the unprecedented step of sanctioning public funds to finance the relocation to Nova Scotia of over 2,500 immigrants who came mainly from London. Governor Edward Cornwallis led the settlers across the Atlantic to the province and set them to work to build Halifax, the future capital. Many were ex-soldiers, ex-sailors, and tradesmen who, lacking farming experience, were ill-suited to the challenges that lay ahead.[5] Not surprisingly, the extremely tough conditions prompted many to leave.[6] Nevertheless, around 1,500 or so of the hardiest remained and founded the town, as was intended, and they were soon joined by large numbers of merchants and other settlers from New England who had correctly anticipated Halifax's potential as a future economic hub. Although there was much conflict between the immigrants from England and New England initially, both groups eventually came to live in harmony, since they shared common economic and political aspirations.

Shortly after establishing these English settlers in Halifax, the British government sought a fresh crop of immigrants, this time from mainland Europe. Up to 2,700 so-called "Foreign Protestants," chiefly Germans, Swiss, and French Huguenots, were recruited between 1750 and 1752, and they, too, received a free passage, land, and a year's subsistence.[7] But continuing hostilities with France and increasing doubts about the loyalty of Acadians caused Britain to take the much more drastic and cruel step of carrying out expulsions.[8] Almost 13,000 Acadians were expelled from Nova Scotia in two separate deportations carried out in 1755 and 1758.[9] In addition, the Native people of the area were systematically marginalized.[10] This ethnic cleansing paved the way for the arrival of around 8,000 New England Planters[11] between 1759 and 1762. They originated primarily from Massachusetts, Connecticut, and Rhode Island, but despite the fact that they were American-born, their ancestral roots were in England.

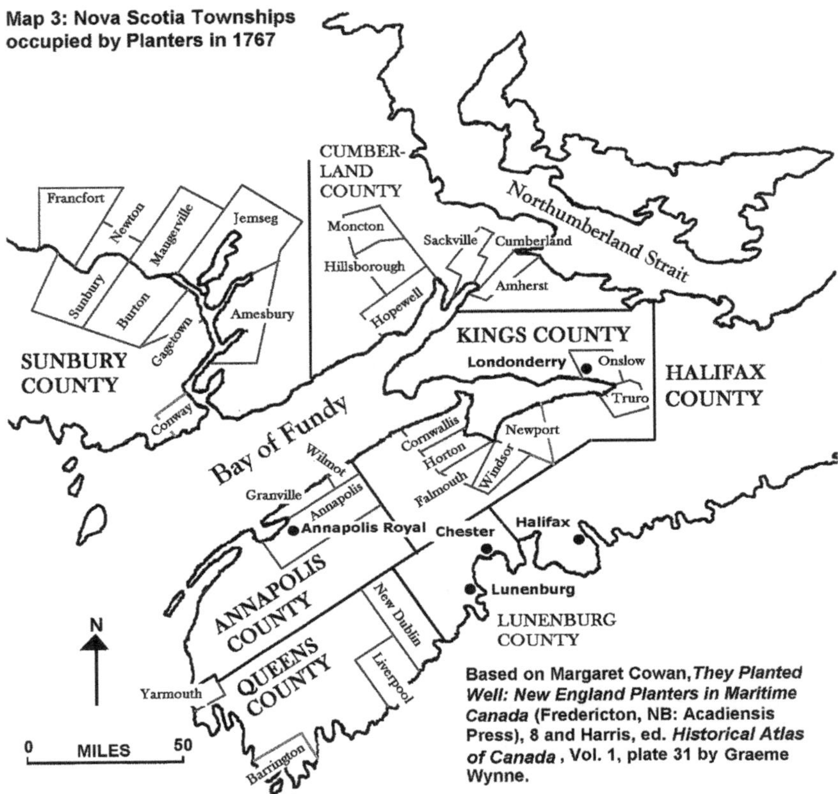

Map 3: Nova Scotia Townships occupied by Planters in 1767

Based on Margaret Cowan, *They Planted Well: New England Planters in Maritime Canada* (Fredericton, NB: Acadiensis Press), 8 and Harris, ed. *Historical Atlas of Canada*, Vol. 1, plate 31 by Graeme Wynne.

Given generous incentives by the British government to relocate to the Maritimes, and being enticed by the good agricultural land there, the Planters came in large family groups and occasionally as entire communities. Many settled on the former Acadian lands on the south side of the Bay of Fundy.[12] Farmers and tradesmen went mainly to the Annapolis Valley region and the Chignecto Isthmus, at the head of the Bay of Fundy, while fishermen headed for the rocky south shore. Some New Englanders also established settlements along the St. John River Valley in the future New Brunswick (Map 3). Being creatures of the New World, New Englanders refused to have anything to do with European-style leaseholds and insisted on having freeholds. While these aspirations were met, many were disappointed both with the quality of the land they received and the Nova Scotia government's unwillingness to tolerate a strong local democracy. They became dissatisfied and possibly half of the new arrivals left within a few years of the termination of subsidies. Few had brought much capital with them and, as a consequence, new communities progressed very slowly.

Immigration to the province reduced to a trickle during the mid 1760s, but increased dramatically between 1772 and 1775, when around 900 people from the North and East Ridings of Yorkshire and nearby parts of northern England took up residence in the Chignecto Isthmus. A combination of rent increases in Yorkshire and the desire to benefit from Nova Scotia's agricultural potential were the main driving forces that convinced them to leave England; but some were Methodists simply seeking a safe haven in which to practise their faith. Having been enticed to the Chignecto Isthmus by the availability of rich marsh land, they joined the New Englanders who had already established themselves at Amherst, Cumberland, and Sackville (Map 3).[13]

The Yorkshire settlers effectively doubled the population of the isthmus, and by bringing their more advanced farming techniques with them, they helped to stimulate the economic development of the area.[14] As John Salusbury had observed when he visited the area in 1750, "the country [is] not much cleared even though long inhabited; the people interest themselves with dyking out the Marsh ..."[15] Being accustomed to the fens of their homeland, which resembled the tidal marshes of the Bay of Fundy, Yorkshire immigrants knew precisely how to proceed. When Charles Dixon arrived in 1772, he immediately set to work building dikes and draining his land. By 1787, he had diked 104 acres of marshland and cleared thirty acres of upland on his 2,500-acre farm in Sackville, while Thomas Bowser had done the same for his 750-acre farm, a pattern that was repeated by the other settlers.[16]

The Yorkshire settlers had been recruited by no less a dignitary than Lieutenant Governor Michael Francklin. One of Halifax's leading merchants, Francklin had an enormous appetite for land speculation; but this proved to be his ruination, since it left him heavily in debt. He had failed to attract New England settlers to his choice tract of land in the Chignecto Isthmus, thus leaving himself with no revenue and a sizable bill in quit rents to pay to the Crown.[17] His solution was to seek settlers

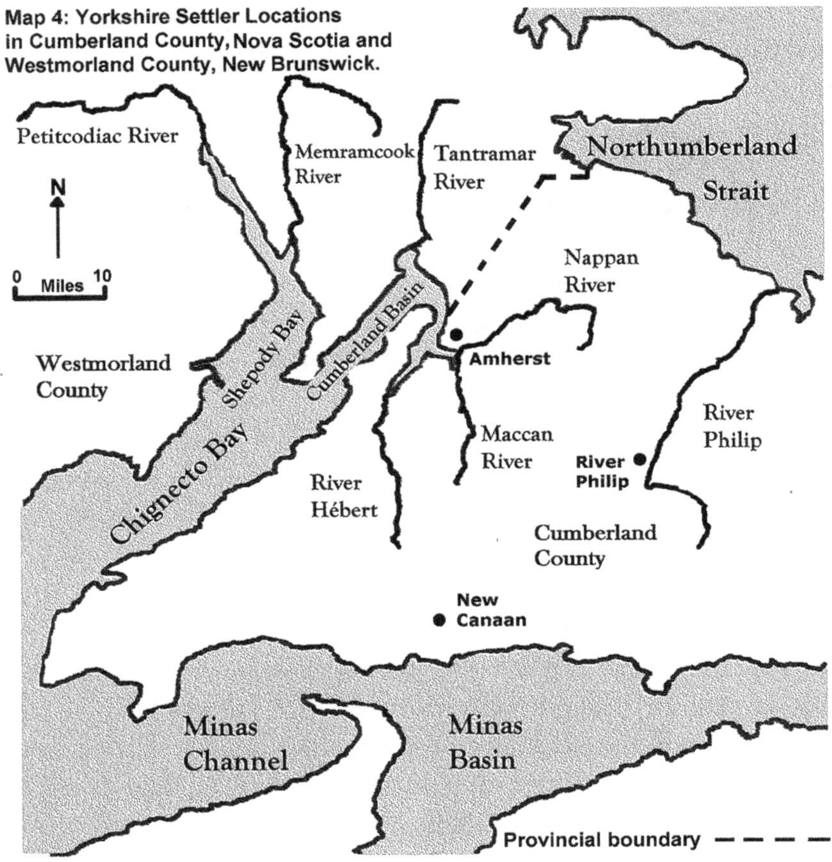

from overseas, concentrating his efforts in the North and East Ridings of Yorkshire, where there were people with the requisite skills and sufficient grievances to want to emigrate.

"Francklin Manor" offered prime sites along the rivers that empty into the Cumberland Basin, especially the Hébert, Maccan, and Nappan (Map 4), and there was icing on this cake. As Francklin made clear, "there are no game-laws, taxes on lands, or tithes in this province," thus offering settlers a welcome release from the feudal constraints and payments of the Old World.[18]

His sales pitch worked. Francklin's agents found plenty of receptive people and arranged for their sea crossings from Hull, Scarborough, Stockton-on-Tees, and Newcastle-upon-Tyne.[19] First to leave were sixty-two people who sailed in the *Duke of York*[20] in 1772 followed by the seven hundred who travelled between March and May, 1774, in the *Two Friends, Albion, Thomas and William, Prince George, Mary*, and *Providence*, and another eighty who came in the *Jenny* the following year.[21]

Meanwhile, the British government lamented the loss of Yorkshire people to Nova Scotia, despite needing loyal emigrants for its North American colonies. As the exodus grew, those departing had to withstand criticism from Britain's ruling classes, who feared that the loss of people would seriously deplete the country's workforce and armed services. Although parliamentary action to curb emigration was resisted, the government instructed customs officials at every port to record the numbers emigrating. This resulted in a set of passenger lists being produced for the period from 1773 to 1775, providing a rare instance when English immigration has been well-documented. The lists revealed that farmers and craftsmen and tradesmen were particularly well represented, while there were relatively few labourers and unskilled workers.

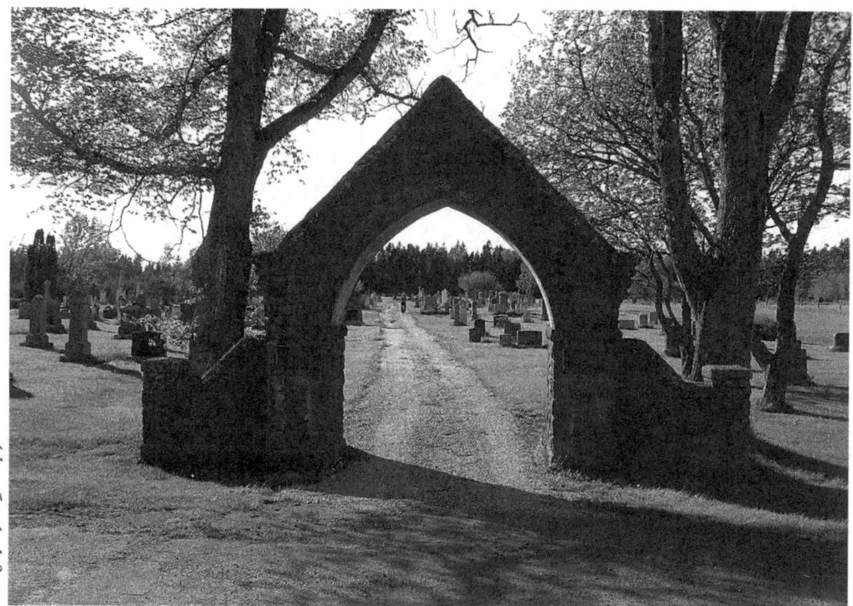

Photograph by Geoff Campey

Memorial stone archway at Pointe de Bute Cemetery, New Brunswick, dedicated to the early Yorkshire settlers. A bronze tablet commemorates the building in 1788 of the province's first Methodist church.

The Yorkshire settlers scattered far and wide, choosing their locations according to land and job availability.[22] Settling in a supportive community was often less important to them than ensuring they obtained the best opportunities they could. So, they mostly acted independently of each other. As Governor Francis Legge explained to Lord Dartmouth, Secretary of State for the American colonies, "some come to purchase [land], others perhaps to become tenants and some to labour."[23] Having rented substantial farms in Yorkshire, which had been handed down from father to son, they were accustomed to renting, so took their time before making the transition from renter to owner. And, when they finally bought farms from their New England predecessors, they became dispersed widely across the Chignecto Isthmus. Their territory extended along the Petitcodiac and Memramcook Rivers, off the Shepody Bay, the river frontages that emptied into the Cumberland Basin, and the River Philip farther to the east (Map 4). Several families went even farther afield, settling in Annapolis and Minas townships in the southwest of the province.[24]

Most new arrivals were shocked by the scale of the wilderness that greeted them. As their ship neared Halifax Harbour, John Robertson and Thomas Rispin thought the coastline "appeared very discouraging and disagreeable — nothing but barren rocks and hills presented themselves.... This unfavourable appearance greatly dampened the spirits of most of the passengers and several of them began to wish themselves in Old England before they had set foot in Nova Scotia." And, on the way from Halifax to Sackville, "we passed through nothing but dreary wastes or forests of rocks and wood."[25] Robertson and Rispin blamed this "unfavourable appearance" on the place being "populated so thinly" and the failure of its New Englander settlers to adopt good farming practices.

However, the immense potential of the land soon became apparent and the two men concluded that their economic future and that of the others lay in improving it. It was theirs for the taking: "A man may have as much land as he pleases; the first year he pays nothing; for the next five years a penny an acre; the next five years, three pence; for five years after that six pence; and then one shilling an acre forever to him and his heirs."[26] John Robinson immediately returned home to Yorkshire to bring his family back with him: "A large sum of money would not induce me to stay any longer" in England.[27] A new world with no masters and servants had opened up and the province now had the prospect of increasing its population with hard-working and self-reliant Yorkshire families.

Methodism played its part in helping settlers like Charles Dixon find a moral dimension to their new life. They had wanted to escape from what they saw as England's corruption and over-worldliness and sought

Courtesy Library and Archives Canada, e010764804.

The Reverend William Black was known affectionately as Bishop Black. He was often referred to, long before his death in 1834, as the father of Methodism in Nova Scotia and New Brunswick.

a refuge for themselves and their families in a British-held wilderness. Their Methodist religion provided a vital support mechanism by drawing people together regularly for worship and it was also an important link with their English past. Methodist fervour was sustained by a great many of the immigrants, but by far the most outstanding example was William Black, who arrived in the *Jenny* in 1775 as a boy of fourteen with the rest of his family. Thirteen years later he had become the spiritual leader of the entire Nova Scotia Methodist community and thereafter became one of the most important Methodist leaders in North America.[28]

Oddly enough, Britain's defeat in the American War of Independence, which began in 1775 and ended in 1783, worked to Nova Scotia's advantage. Ongoing defence concerns caused the British government to relocate large numbers of Loyalists to what would become western Nova Scotia and southern New Brunswick.[29] Although they were largely American-born, later census data would reveal that most had been of English descent. When the war ended, around forty thousand Americans who had taken the British side in the war came to British-held territory seeking sanctuary and land. Receiving land grants and financial help under the British Loyalist Assistance program, about thirty-five thousand refugees moved to Nova Scotia, while the remaining five thousand went to the old province of Quebec. Most of the Nova Scotia Loyalists had originated from New York and New Jersey.[30] Around fifteen thousand went to the future New Brunswick, which became a separate colony after it was divided from the peninsula in 1784, and nineteen thousand went to what is now Nova Scotia (Map 5).[31] Fearing more loss of territory to the United States, the British government encouraged most of them to settle along both sides of the militarily important Bay of Fundy.[32] Taken together, Loyalists doubled the population of peninsular Nova Scotia and swelled the population count to the north of the Bay of Fundy fivefold.[33]

Loyalists became dispersed widely in Nova Scotia.[34] About three thousand settled in the Annapolis Valley and around the fertile Minas Basin at the head of the Bay of Fundy, where they would have joined already-established Planter communities.[35] By 1785, Halifax had acquired about 1,200 Loyalists; Digby had around 1,300, while Shelburne (formerly Port Roseway) suddenly gained ten thousand Loyalists, making it the fourth largest town in North America, after Philadelphia, New York, and Boston. Meanwhile, the New Brunswick Loyalists were mainly to be found along the St. John River Valley and its tributaries and in Charlotte County (Map 5).[36]

However, Loyalists were far from satisfied with what they found. There was seething discontent felt over the government's failure to administer land grants satisfactorily.[37] The problem was compounded by the fact that some of the best agricultural land had already been granted to the Planters. Another problem was the shortage of women. A substantial number of Loyalists were young, single men who had served in the disbanded Loyalist regiments or as regulars in the British Army. If they were to settle and raise families, they needed to find wives.[38] And, unlike the Planters, who had arrived previously and simply took over Acadian farms, Loyalists often had the backbreaking task of clearing vast wildernesses. These factors, plus an ongoing desire for a better situation, stimulated a constant movement of Loyalists within and from the Maritime provinces. In fact, the most remarkable feature of the Loyalist influx was

Map 5: Locations of Loyalists in the Maritimes, c.1785

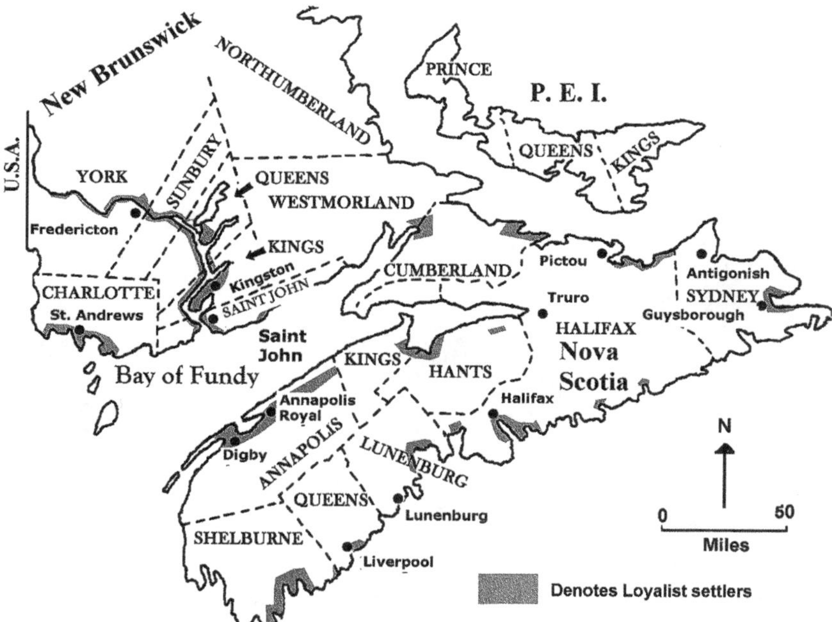

the speed and extent of the exodus that followed.[39] Within a year of their arrival, nearly two thousand Loyalists are believed to have left Nova Scotia, almost half of the departures coming from Shelburne.[40]

Despite early disappointments and setbacks, many Loyalists remained and benefited from the region's improving economic growth. The ongoing wars between Britain and France that started in the 1790s created obvious disincentives to any immigration directly from Britain; but with the end of the Napoleonic Wars in 1815, it steadily increased again. The greater availability of transatlantic crossings, made possible by the timber trade and bleak economic conditions in England just after the wars ended, brought a sudden influx of Yorkshire settlers to the region in 1817. With most of the best land in Nova Scotia having already been taken up by this time, they focused their attention on Prince Edward Island and New Brunswick. A group of 159 people sailed for Saint John in the *Trafalgar*,[41] while another 196 came in the *Valiant*[42] to Charlottetown. Those in the *Trafalgar* were lucky to have escaped with

Courtesy Library and Archives Canada, C-000370.

Timber booms on the St. John River, New Brunswick. *Illustrated London News,* 1866. Without Atlantic Canada's timber trade with England, the influx of English settlers could not have happened.

their lives when the ship became grounded at Brier Island on its approach through the Bay of Fundy.[43] It hit rocks in a thick fog, but thanks to Captain Welburn's navigational skills, the passengers and crew were saved, even though the ship was not.[44]

Benjamin Chappell, one of the New London settlers to have arrived in 1775, observed that the 1817 Yorkshire arrivals "appear very cautious; they don't settle as yet but a Mr. Fishpond is here from Bedeque [Prince Edward Island] endeavouring to get them to go there."[45] Mr. Fishpond would have received little encouragement. The Yorkshire settlers had already done their homework. One of the *Valiant*'s passengers, Vincent Bell, had previously visited the island and "found a country suited to North of England folk with agricultural leanings."[46] The shortage of freehold land on the island did not deter them.[47] Choosing to settle in the middle of the island, they founded their Little York (Lot 34) settlement and joined already-established communities at Crapaud (Lot 29), where they rented land from Lady Westmorland (Map 6).[48] According to John McGregor, who visited Little York nine years later, their land was "under excellent cultivation … the neatness and cleanliness of everything about them reminded me of England."[49] Much later, A.B. Warburton would refer with good reason to the "industrious and careful settlers from Yorkshire."[50]

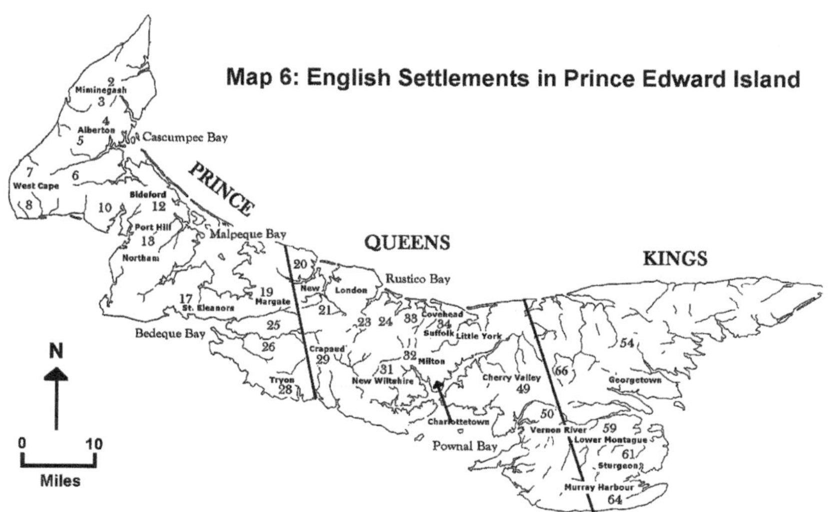

Map 6: English Settlements in Prince Edward Island

While most of the *Valiant*'s passengers had settled on the island, a few, like John Towse, opted for the Sackville area on the opposite side of the Northumberland Strait:

> John Towse with his three brothers entered the colony [New Brunswick] in 1817. They cleared land, constructed homes, planted gardens, and built an "up and down saw-mill" on a swift flowing stream. Sending for their families they gathered at the shore to meet them and as the ship approached one exclaimed "Here be our bairns!"[51]

Quickly grasping the tenor of pioneer life, the Towse brothers had created their farms and built the necessary infrastructure to support them before their families arrived. They were joined by William Lund and David Cook and their families, who also arrived in 1817.[52] Cookville, Lund Road, and Towse Road, all a stone's throw from each other, would eventually bear witness to the close-knit Yorkshire community that had once lived north of Sackville.

By the mid 1820s, most English immigrants destined for Canada were setting their sights on Upper Canada, preferring it to the Maritime provinces. New inland roads and waterways were gradually opening it up to settlers who were attracted by its fertile land, relatively good climate, and job opportunities. However, while this development halted the Yorkshire

Courtesy Public Archives and Record Office, Prince Edward Island, Acc 4981.

Meacham's Atlas, 1880, 45a: Abraham Gill's farm residence at Little York, Prince Edward Island (Lot 34). One of the original Little York settlers, Abraham originated from Devon.

influx, it had the opposite effect on people from Devon, who remained loyal to Prince Edward Island. A slow trickle that began in 1818 became a major emigrant stream during the 1830s and 1840s, a period when economic conditions in Devon were particularly grim.[53] A factor in the island's appeal was its shipbuilding industry, which had been receiving considerable financial backing from West Country merchants.[54] John Cambridge, one of the early shipbuilders, had told his sons that "the most effectual way of getting my debts remitted" was by "building a ship annually and loading her with timber," and selling both in Britain.[55] This is precisely what he and the other merchants did. They reaped the combined profit of the timber and shipbuilding trades and in so doing helped to stimulate the steady flow of people from Devon to the island.

West Country merchants were regularly sending shipwrights, carpenters, and skilled workmen from Bristol and Bideford to their island shipyards. The availability of periodic ship crossings gave people from Devon and Cornwall affordable access to an island with good agricultural land and a thriving shipbuilding industry. Of all the shipbuilders, Thomas Burnard, Bideford's leading merchant and shipowner, was to have the most profound impact. His decision to recruit a small group from North Devon to establish a shipyard at what would become New Bideford (Lot 12), on the west side of the island, sparked the large-scale exodus from Devon and, to a lesser extent, Cornwall. Between 1830 and 1844, when conditions in Devon were particularly dire, around 1,500 people sailed to the island from West Country ports, with the majority leaving from Bideford.[56] This large influx spilled over into the adjoining Lot 13, whose Devon inhabitants are commemorated in the Port Hill and Northam place names (Map 6). Having founded these communities on the west side, Devon and Cornwall people later went on to colonize large parts of Queens County in the middle of the island.[57] It is estimated that the island acquired up to 2,000 West Country people by 1845, making them the island's dominant English group.[58]

Devon and Cornwall settlers became widely dispersed as Francis Metherall, the island's first Bible Christian missionary, discovered.[59] Established in 1815, mostly in Devon and Cornwall as a separatist Methodist group, the Bible Christian mission was bound to have widespread appeal. Metherall, a native of North Devon who arrived in 1832, was soon joined by Philip James, a native of Cornwall. Between them, the two missionaries presided over thirty-six preaching places that extended from Sturgeon and Murray Harbour in the east to West Cape and Cascumpec Bay in the west (Map 6). Predictably, the Bible Christian movement did particularly well in areas that had experienced a sizable intake from Devon and Cornwall, but it was less successful in Northam and Port Hill, on the west side of the island, where Wesleyan Methodism and Anglicanism had many followers.[60] Metherall was replaced in 1856 by Cephas Barker, who came from Chatham in Kent. Promoting "aggressive evangelism" for nine years, he achieved a dramatic increase in Bible Christian membership and won respect for being "a friend of the oppressed and a stern and indefatigable advocate of the rights of the working classes."[61] Despite his stalwart efforts, the Bible Christian movement made little impact when compared with other religions.[62] An obscure and little-known sect, it could not compete with the dominant Roman Catholic and Presbyterian faiths.

The Reverend Cephas Barker presided over the building of several Bible Christian churches, including one in Charlottetown. Engraving by D.J. Pound, n.d..

Courtesy University of Manchester, John Rylands Library, MAW Ms94.7.

In addition to dominating the English influx to Prince Edward Island, the West Country was also the principal supplier of English people to Newfoundland, although the manner of their coming was totally different. The movement began in the seventeenth century when some fishermen, employed by West Country merchants, decided to remain in Newfoundland once their contracts had expired.[63] However, this was not the result of some long-deliberated emigration decision; it was more of an afterthought. Anglican clergymen often stressed the severe challenges that went with living there. People did not move to Newfoundland for a better life, but came for work-related reasons, which prompted them to remain. This was certainly how the Bishop of Newfoundland viewed it:

> I am still more in want of men than of friends and if you know any good man who would rather be useful in his generation than comfortable and be a blessing to others, rather than be himself preferred, let him come to Newfoundland.[64]

The fishermen who went to Newfoundland were given little encouragement to settle since the merchants who employed them ran the fishery as an off-shore extension of England. The fishery's labour and provisions were supplied entirely from England.[65] It lined the pockets of the merchants and provided jobs for West Country workers, not just for fishermen and mariners, but also for the hundreds of craftsmen and tradesmen who grew or made every commodity that would be needed:

> Fortified by religion at home and rum in Newfoundland, generations of men sailed off to the fishery. To the poor it provided a living and for the lucky, a chance to rise; the spirited country boy found a chance of adventure and the ne'er-do-well found a refuge. Though weavers, cobblers, farmers or blacksmiths might never set foot on a ship, the fishery gave them their employment; but those who gained most, upon whom all the rest depended — were the West Country fishing merchants.[66]

In the late eighteenth and early nineteenth centuries, many a man and boy sought temporary employment in the Newfoundland fishery. Judging from the numerous requests made for poor relief upon their return to England, some lived in a constant state of near or actual poverty. Thomas Taylor from Kingsteignton (Devon) and Thomas Leaman from Combeinteignhead (Devon) commuted as children yearly between Newfoundland and Devon in the summer. They picked up what labouring jobs they could in the winter, but in later life were dependent on parish assistance.[67] The Somerset-born John Deverill had obtained "his meat, drink and clothes" from a local tradesman from the age of nine, and when aged twelve worked his summers in Newfoundland and as a servant in Stoke-in-Teignhead (Devon) in the winters, but he ended his days as a near-destitute farm labourer in Combeinteignhead.[68] It wasn't much of a life, but at least the fishery jobs provided extra cash in the summer months.

It was claimed that, from as early as 1774, Devon and Dorset supplied "lads from the plough, men from the threshing floor and persons of all sizes, trades and ages from manufactories [who] flock annually in the Spring … in the hope of returning with £6 or £10 from the land of the fish."[69] George Penney of Wimborne Minster (Dorset), who worked for two Fogo planters, was one of them.[70] Back in his native Dorset he would likely find work as an agricultural labourer, but given the low wages and high unemployment that prevailed, he would remain at the bottom of the social scale for the rest of his life. Faced with this bleak alternative, Newfoundland was an escape from poverty for those who had a sense of adventure and an ability to learn new skills.

The American Revolutionary War, beginning in 1775, marked a major turning point in Newfoundland's development, since it broke the merchant's monopoly. Because the war destabilized their participation in the fishing trade, people in Newfoundland had greater access to fishery jobs, thus boosting the local economy. The war also created a sudden demand for other forms of labour beyond fishing. A large variety of trades became established, leading to a rapid growth in the island's year-round resident population. But progress was slow. In 1787, when William Dyott had sought refuge at Cape Broyle Harbour during a bad storm, he observed "very few inhabitants who remain here all the year." Those who lived there permanently were "principally Irish of the lowest class …. The country is quite a desert — nothing but rocks, spruce and fir. I did not see an animal of any sort."[71] By the end of the eighteenth century, when the fur trade and seal hunting had been established as winter pursuits, the island could offer greater incentives for year-round habitation.

Map 7: English Settlements along the "Old English Shore," Newfoundland, 1675–77

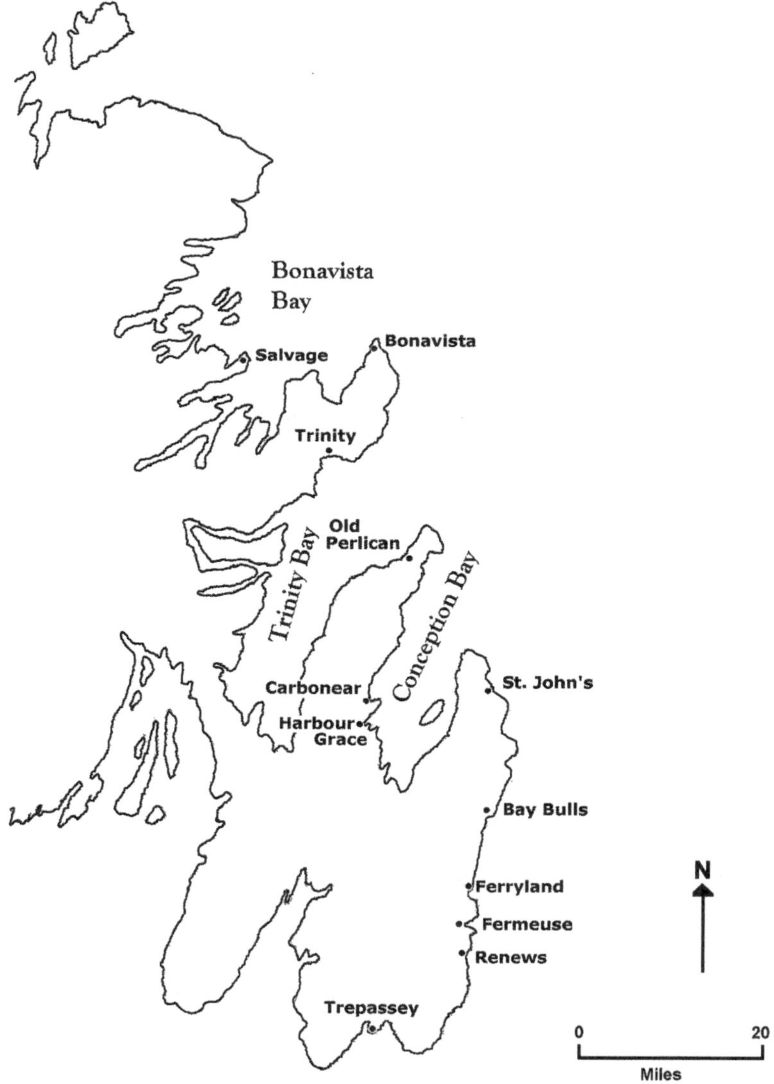

Apart from the teachers, clergymen, and clerks who came from many parts of England, mainly to work in St. John's, most of Newfoundland's English settlers owed their presence to the fishery. Originating from Devon, Dorset, Somerset, and Hampshire, they had made the decision to remain once their contracts expired. Unlike the great surge in Irish immigration that had occurred between 1811 and 1815, the English influx was gradual. A family would often clear land, build a house, and run a fishing station, but retire to the West Country, leasing property to a new arrival who might decide to remain. A combination of temporary and permanent settlement, together with the natural increase in the already-settled population, caused the best fishing harbours in the "Old English Shore" gradually to fill up with settlers (Map 7).[72]

Hard times came to the island with the economic recession that followed the end of the Napoleonic Wars in 1815. Fire swept through St. John's the following year, burning more than 130 homes and merchants' premises, and this added to their misery. An Anglican minister noted how "families, which at 10 o'clock were in affluent and respectable circumstances, were reduced to poverty and many of them to absolute beggary" later that same day.[73] The town was near collapse:

> The streets are now filled with beggars of the lower order by day and those of the Middle Class of society by night who are yet ashamed to acknowledge themselves reduced to a state of mendacity while it be light — poverty and disease are now constantly in view and the number of paupers having lately doubled the funds of the Public Charitable Institutions are almost exhausted. This town now relieves upwards of 1,800 persons daily and chiefly by voluntary contributions ...[74]

The accelerating slide into crisis produced a lawless gang "consisting in public of about 100 men," and an "Armed Association" was formed to deal with the threat it posed to people and property: "The inhabitants ... keep up a regular patrol and about 35 persons parade the streets all night to check depredations which otherwise would be constantly committed and to prevent unlawful assemblages."[75]

To offset this gloom were the benefits being gained by the increasing use of local labour in the fishery.[76] West Country fishermen stopped coming to the island in 1820, since by then the labour demands of the fishery were being met by local residents.[77] Those who remained had added significantly to the English population while the trading links of the merchants who had employed them determined where they settled.[78] For instance, Bristol merchants generally confined their trade to the St. John's region, while their counterparts in the south Devon ports of Teignmouth and Dartmouth usually sent their men to the St. John's region and Conception Bay. On the other hand, the Poole merchants of Dorset operated on a more expansive scale, recruiting their workers from Dorset, South Somerset, and West Hampshire, and sending them alternatively to Conception Bay, Trinity Bay, Bonavista Bay, Notre Dame Bay, Placentia Bay, or Fortune Bay (Map 8). This explains why the St. John's region acquired a high proportion of Devon residents and why Conception Bay had a mixture of Devon and Dorset settlers. Trading links account for the later presence of Dorset, Somerset, and Hampshire residents in Trinity Bay as well as in Bonavista Bay, and also explain the substantial number of Dorset settlers along the south coast.[79]

Courtesy Library and Archives Canada, PA-124337.

Summer fishing station at St. John's, Newfoundland. Photograph by G.F. Briggs, n.d.

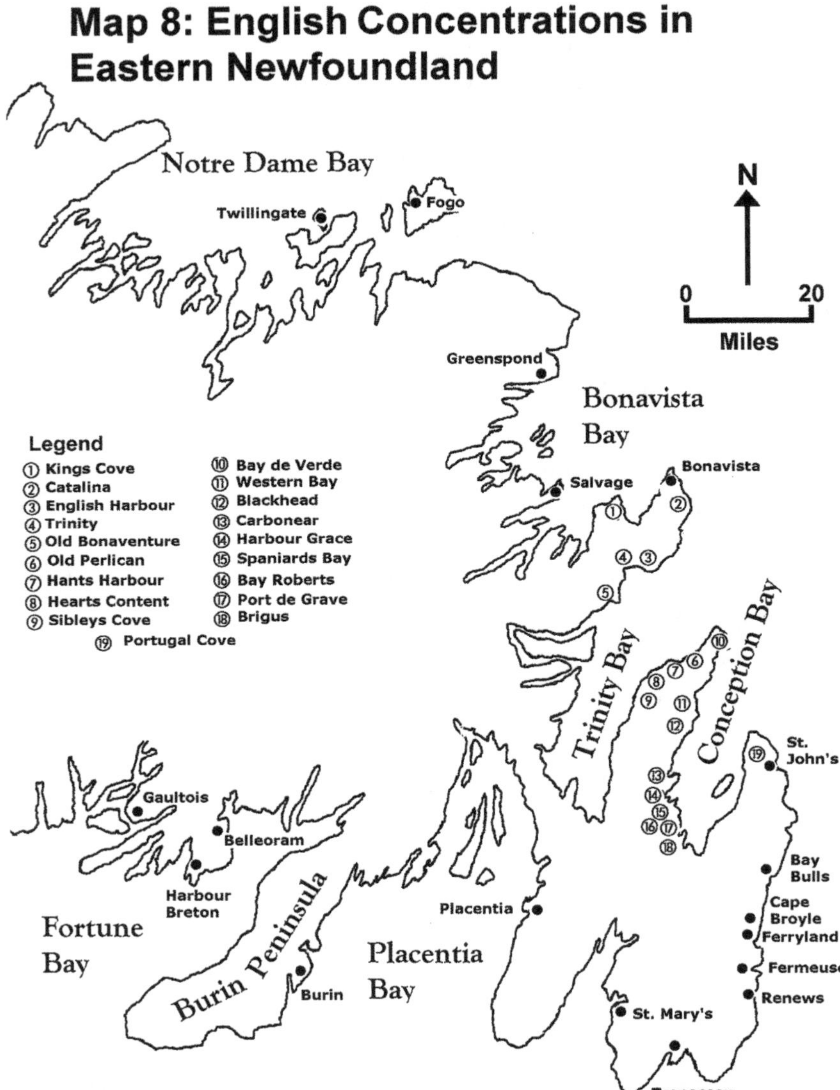

Map 8: English Concentrations in Eastern Newfoundland

Meanwhile, a few years after Newfoundland's supply of English settlers had dwindled, Prince Edward Island began to acquire immigrants from East Anglia. Although most of the people who came during the short-lived influx from 1829 to 1834 were self-financed, the arrivals included poor farm labourers who had been assisted to emigrate by their parishes. Greater mechanization in threshing corn and in land drainage had destroyed countless labouring jobs. The soaring unemployment that followed gave labourers a miserable existence and poor relief payments became an increasing burden for parishes. Legislation passed in 1834 enabled English parishes struggling with this predicament to raise funds to give their poor a chance of a better life while reducing the poor rates of their residents.[80] For instance, the families of John Birt, John Cook, William Smith, Charles Gibbs, and Samuel Mayhew, all from Benhall Parish in Suffolk, received £19 10s. for clothing, £35 10s. as spending money, £17.2.7 for provisions, and £54 for their passages to Charlottetown.[81] The total bill of £126 8s represented an average cost of £25 per family, which approximated to the annual cost of maintaining a family in a workhouse.[82] The Cook, Birt, and Smith families even managed to obtain an allowance of one gallon of gin per family for the crossing.

In all, Prince Edward Island acquired over five hundred settlers, mainly from Suffolk and some from Norfolk, many arriving with sufficient capital to buy farms.[83] First to come in 1829 were twelve people who included William Butcher and family. Clearly pleased with what he found, Butcher returned home a year later to collect his grandparents and bring them back to Charlottetown, where they all settled.[84] Possibly he had acted as a scout on behalf of this wider community, since many more followed. Arriving in 1832, William Peacock visited various Suffolk people living on the island who had purchased between two hundred

Courtesy of Dorset County Museum.

Painting of Benjamin Lester's premises and fishing station at Trinity Harbour, circa 1800, by Michael Corne. Born in Poole in 1724, Lester became the wealthiest and most influential businessman in Newfoundland. In Trinity Harbour alone, he had five fishing establishments, twenty-three houses, a large farm, and a shipyard.

and three hundred acres of land, thinking he would do the same. But he apparently changed his mind and instead settled near York (later Toronto) in Upper Canada.[85]

William Cattermole, a Canada Company agent, welcomed Peacock's change of heart, since he had been running a strident newspaper campaign disparaging the island's climate, land, and job opportunities. With Cattermole's persistent hard-sell of Upper Canada and the British American Land Company's effectiveness in extolling the benefits of its land in the Eastern Townships in Lower Canada, the East Anglian influx to the island ended in 1834.

Although they were widely scattered, Suffolk people became concentrated in the Charlottetown area (Lot 33). The Suffolk place name in the adjacent Lot 34 is a lasting testimony to their presence (Map 6). Wiltshire also lost a small number of people to the island during the 1830s. Having been recruited by a compatriot, the Devizes-born William Douse who had arrived a decade earlier, they founded New Wiltshire (Lot 31).[86] But, yet again, there were few followers. Tombstone inscriptions reveal that a scattering of people also came from Somerset, Gloucestershire, Lincolnshire, Lancashire, and Cumberland.[87] By the mid nineteenth century very few immigrants were arriving on the island from anywhere in Britain. Nova Scotia fared slightly better. Although it had little good farmland to offer, most of it having been acquired by earlier settlers, it did have a coal-mining industry that attracted English miners over many decades.

After its formation in 1826–27, the English-owned and managed General Mining Association invested considerable funds in its coal mining operations near New Glasgow (Pictou County) and at Sydney (Cape Breton).[88] Initially, many of its skilled workers were recruited from the North of England, although most of the later workforce was locally based. One hundred and twenty-five miners duly arrived from Liverpool in1827 with "all the necessary engines and machinery to work the mines at this place," while others followed over the next twenty years.[89] According to Reverend Alfred Brown, an Anglican missionary who had been sent to Glace Bay, Cape Breton, by the Society for the Propagation of the Gospel, even more English miners arrived in the 1860s. After 1858, when the General Mining Association's coal monopoly had been broken, production was "thrown open to public enterprise."[90] New towns and villages sprouted and the population rose, bringing in people from "the coal mining districts of England." Following them were Cornish miners who arrived during the 1860s and 1870s to work in the province's gold and lead mines.[91] Cheap imports from Australia had decimated the Cornish tin industry, leaving "many able-bodied miners seeking in vain for employment."[92] Attracted by the prospect of well-paid mining jobs in Nova Scotia, some had obtained government assistance to emigrate. But despite this flurry of activity, English industrial workers and their families represented only a small fraction of the total immigrant population in the province.

Meanwhile, New Brunswick, which still had huge expanses of wilderness land to offer prospective farmers, continued to attract English immigrants, especially those wishing to settle together in groups. One hundred and ten people who came mainly from Berwick-upon-Tweed in

Map 9: English Concentrations in Southern New Brunswick

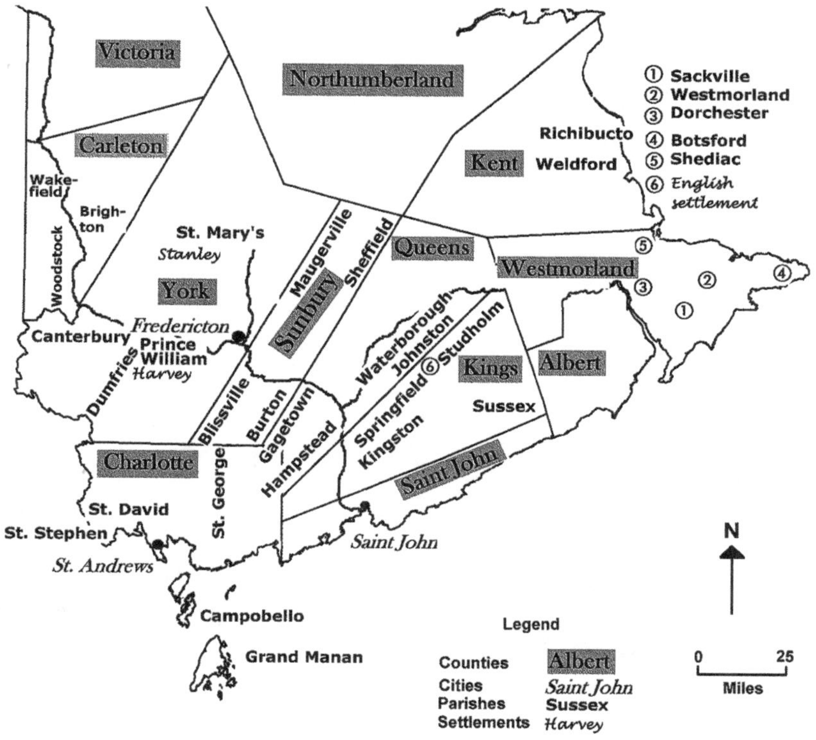

Northumberland, and some from the Scottish Borders, arrived in 1836–37 to found the future Stanley and Harvey settlements in York County on land that was being marketed by the New Brunswick and Nova Scotia Land Company (Map 9).[93] A Saint John reporter was moved to whimsical prose when he met them: "These people are regular practical farmers of good character and highly respectable appearance … and [they] bring along with them the unsophisticated and gentle manners of 'Merry England' with the beautiful associations of Border ballad and Border chivalry."[94] However, they were actually poor agricultural labourers who came with little or no capital, their passage money having been advanced to them by the company. Problems quickly surfaced. After being promised "considerable advantages" by the company, they "found that there were neither houses nor crops ready for our reception as promised." And to make matters worse, the company had reneged on its commitment to provide them with employment.[95] Being "in danger of starving for want of food" in 1838, eighteen family heads petitioned the British House of Commons for help.[96] The company had little choice but to offer the Stanley immigrants more generous settlement terms and paid employment to tide them over until their crops were ready.[97]

The Harvey settlement, founded a year later, also attracted more families from Northumberland and some from the Scottish Borders. In all, 137 people (twenty-three families and several single men) sailed in 1837 from Berwick to Saint John.[98] The men were mostly labourers, though

Courtesy Library and Archives Canada, C-000017.

Clearing town plots at Stanley. The New Brunswick and Nova Scotia Land Company established the town of Stanley on the Nashwaak River in 1834.

some were tradesmen; there were no farmers in the group.[99] Intending to obtain company land, they rejected the site offered and instead opted to settle along the road, then being constructed, between Fredericton and St. Andrews. As was the case with Stanley, problems arose initially, although this time the provincial government, and not the land company, had to pick up the pieces. But quick progress was made. By 1838, officials took "much pleasure reporting most favourably of their conduct and deem them a most valuable acquisition to the country and especially to the road on which they are located."[100] Five years later, 292 acres had been planted with crops.[101] So the superlatives continued. Officials appointed to oversee the scheme thought that "for industry, sobriety and perseverance no men can surpass them, while they only want an opportunity to introduce the most approved systems of agriculture as now pursued in England."[102] Despite the success of the Harvey settlement, there were few followers, since, as ever, people in England were much more attracted by the richer opportunities to be had farther west.[103]

It is impossible to determine precisely how many British immigrants settled in New Brunswick.[104] The available evidence indicates that the influx before 1817 was dominated by Scots and after this by the Irish, who far

Map 10: Predominant Ethnic Groups in Nova Scotia and Cape Breton, 1871.

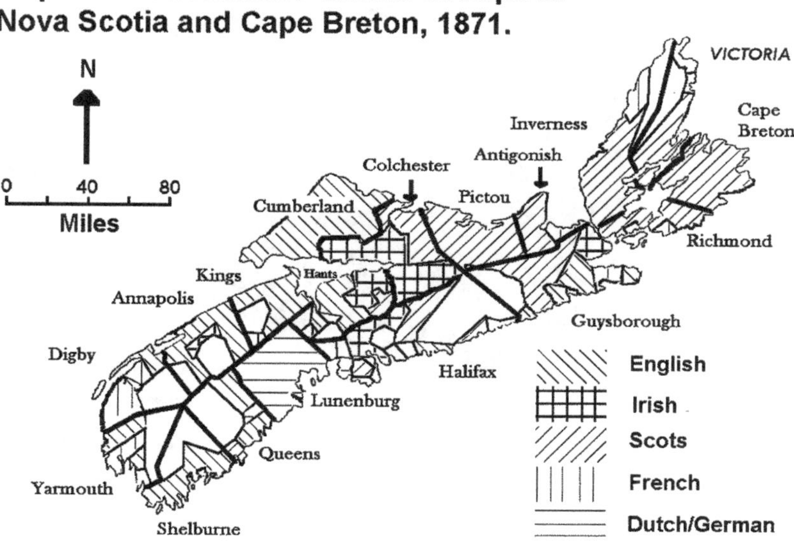

outnumbered all other immigrant groups.[105] The influx averaged around six to eight thousand immigrants a year between 1834 and 1847, although most were in transit to the United States.[106] By 1851, the Irish-born accounted for a staggering 71 percent of the total immigration, with the Scottish-born representing 12 percent and the English-born 10 percent.[107] However, if ancestry rather than country of birth is considered, the picture changes dramatically. When the descendents of the numerous English Loyalists, who arrived from the United States during the late eighteenth century, are taken into account, the English component of the population rises significantly. According to the 1871 Census, the first to record their number along with immigrants directly from England, the English represented 29 percent of the population — only six percentage points behind the Irish.[108]

Map 11: Percentage of People in New Brunswick of English Origin, 1871.

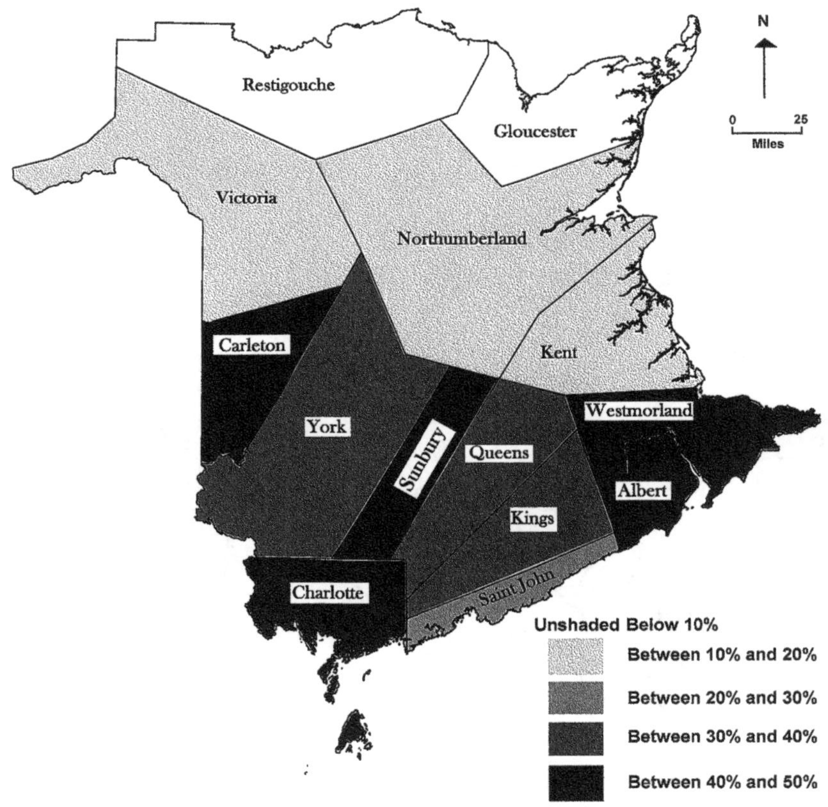

Like New Brunswick, Nova Scotia attracted relatively few immigrants directly from England, and yet the 1871 Census reveals that 29 percent of the population at that time claimed English ancestry. The sizable Yorkshire influx, beginning in the late eighteenth century, had made Cumberland County in Nova Scotia and Westmorland and Albert Counties in New Brunswick English strongholds, but this alone does not explain how they became the dominant ethnic group in large areas of western Nova Scotia and parts of southern New Brunswick (Maps 10 and 11). Once again, the explanation lies in the early intake of Americans who came first as Planters and then as Loyalists. When later generations were asked by census-takers to state the ethnicity of their European ancestors, they categorized themselves as English, even though their links were very distant.[109] By including ancestry in this way, the census added significantly to the English concentrations in both provinces, although the majority were Americans of English descent.

While Prince Edward Island was far more successful than Nova Scotia and New Brunswick in attracting English immigrants, their numbers were relatively small. Murray Harbour (Lot 64) was the only area where they predominated, and even here a sizable proportion of those claiming English ancestry were probably the descendents of Channel Islanders

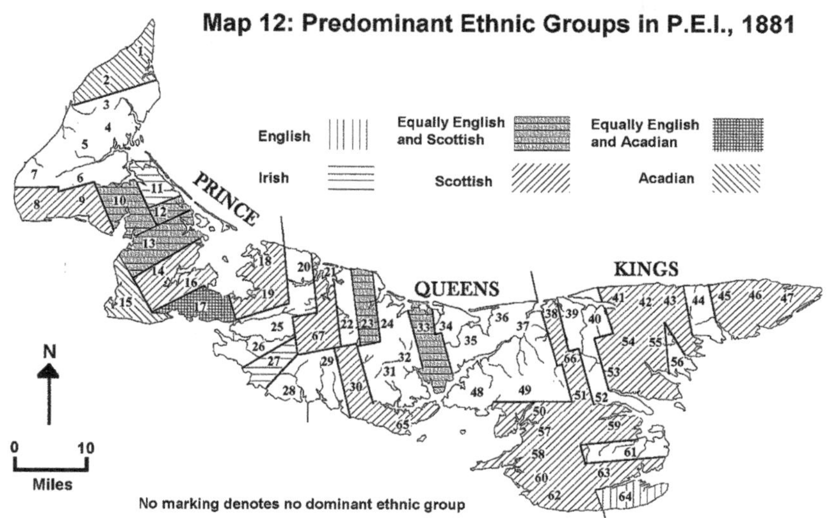

(Map 12).[110] The island had no Planters and very few Loyalists. So its English came directly from England. And the 1881 Census reveals that they only accounted for around 20 percent of the population. However, the English represented a higher proportion of the population later on. With the arrival of steamships, the island's shipbuilding industry collapsed and, while this caused the Scots and Irish to leave in droves, most of the English remained.[111] This meant that by the mid twentieth century the English and Scottish elements of the population were equal at around 30 percent, with the Irish and Acadians making up the difference.[112]

Oddly enough, Newfoundland, which relied almost entirely on West Country fishermen to bolster its early immigrant population, ended up as Canada's most English province. The 1991 Census records that a staggering 82 percent of the population claimed to have some English ancestry, although most of the influx occurred long before Newfoundland had officially recorded immigration statistics.[113]

People from England and Americans of English descent came to Atlantic Canada in substantial numbers from the mid eighteenth to mid nineteenth centuries. A few were the wealthy and elite, but the majority were ordinary people. They settled in large numbers in the cities and towns and excelled as pioneer farmers, with the Yorkshire arrivals being the outstanding example. When Lord Dalhousie, the lieutenant governor of Nova Scotia, viewed their farms, he marvelled at "the large fields, extensive crops and gardens about their houses," which far outshone those of their neighbours.[114] These settlers would do the same in Lower and Upper Canada, as would many more people from all parts of England.

CHAPTER 3

Growing Numbers Who Headed for Quebec and Ontario

The town is inhabited by people from different nations, such as English, Irish, Scotch and Dutch, with a few Canadians and Yankees, but the English have the pre-eminence, and are the most dominant. We have people from all parts of England, with a great many from Yorkshire. The place resembles England the most of any place I have seen.[1]

Francis Jackson, a Yorkshire tailor, had found a home away from home in York, the future Toronto. He had the companionship of many Yorkshire people and had access to shops on King Street that "are well-stocked with all kinds of goods — same as in Hull." By 1831, when Jackson wrote home, Canada had Yorkshire blood flowing through its veins. Having colonized vast swathes of the Maritime region from 1772, Yorkshire people had turned their attention to Upper and Lower Canada soon after the Napoleonic Wars ended in 1815. In doing so, Yorkshire lost more people to these areas over the following two decades than any other English county. Meanwhile, in the intervening years, a large American influx had taken place.

With Britain's defeat in the American War of Independence in 1784 around forty thousand Loyalists — Americans who had supported the British in the war — were relocated to British-held territory in North America. A relatively small group of five thousand Loyalists were sent to the old province of Quebec, while the overwhelming majority were resettled in the Maritime region.[2] Initially, the Quebec group was concentrated in the military camps and garrisons being established at Sorel and Machiche (now Yamachiche) near Trois Rivières, and along the strategically important Richelieu River, notably at Chambly, St. Jean, Noyan, Foucault, and St. Armand (Map 13).[3] However, when the war ended, most Loyalists left the area, having been granted land along the Upper St. Lawrence River, just to the west of the French seigneuries. Following the division of the old province of Quebec into Upper and Lower Canada in 1791, they would find themselves living in Upper Canada.

Most of the Upper Canada Loyalists settled in townships along the north shore of Lake Ontario[4]; a smaller number went either to the Bay of Quinte region to the west of Kingston,[5] the west shore of the

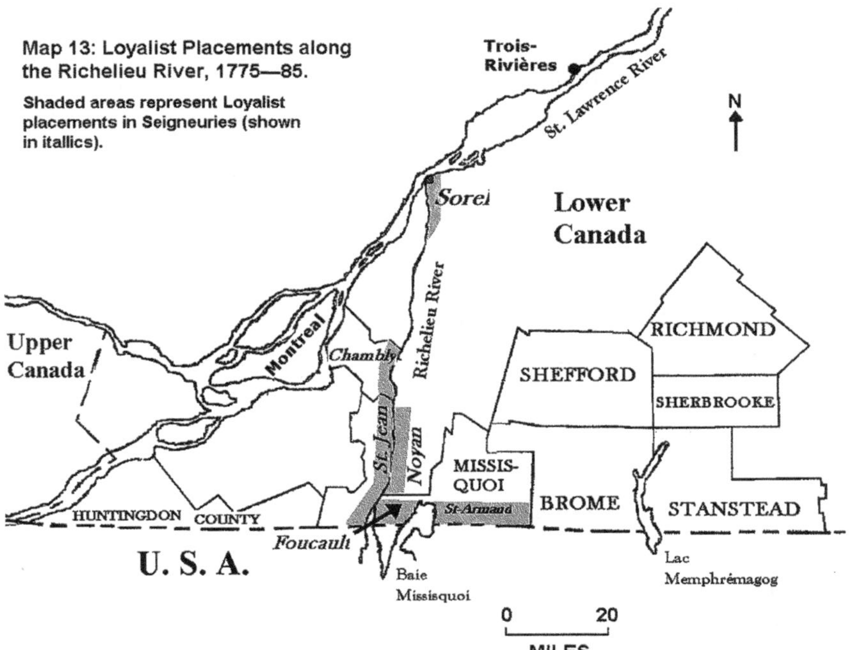

Niagara River, or the southwestern tip of the province in Essex County, in the latter case finding homes among the earlier French-speaking settlers (Map 14).[6] Delays in administering land grants and an ongoing desire for a better situation caused many to move west. Before long, Loyalists had extended their territory along Lake Ontario from the Bay of Quinte region to York (later Toronto) and from Niagara to the Long Point area in Norfolk County. All the while, they were being joined by followers from the United States, who were being lured more by the prospect of free land grants than by any loyalty they might have felt to Britain.

By as early as 1799, American colonizers had penetrated large swathes of southwestern Upper Canada, being concentrated especially in York, Wentworth, Lincoln, Welland, Norfolk, and Kent Counties.[7] This development was welcomed by the British government, which, at the time, was loath to lose its own people to the North American colonies. In any case, the war between Britain and France from 1793 to 1801 and the later Napoleonic Wars, which began in 1803 and ended in 1815, made transatlantic travel extremely hazardous and uninviting. As a consequence, much of Upper Canada's population growth before 1815 can be attributed to American immigration. Judging from the fact that the population reached seventy-one thousand in 1806, the influx must have been considerable, involving several thousands of people.[8]

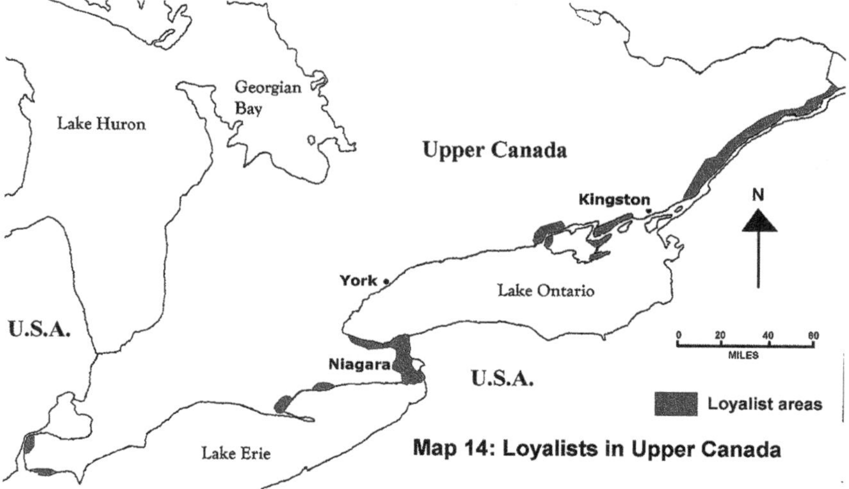

Map 14: Loyalists in Upper Canada

Having taken up land in important boundary locations considered vulnerable to attack from the United States, Loyalists had strengthened Upper Canada defensively and provided its first immigrant communities. However, Lower Canada was handled quite differently.[9] Sir Frederick Haldimand, the governor of Quebec, was adamant that good relations with the long-established French-Canadian population could only be maintained by keeping English-speaking colonizers out of their territory.[10] So, he sought to preserve the status quo; but he could not stop the inevitable. Having become aware of the rich farmland to the east of the Richelieu River, some Loyalists wished to settle in the area between Baie Missisquoi and Lac Memphrémagog (Map 13).[11] Despite Haldimand's misgivings, a compromise was reached. Loyalists were allowed to settle as tenants in three seigneuries in the region — Foucault,[12] Noyan, and St. Armand (later in Missisquoi County). With the creation of the Lower Canada Assembly in 1791, new townships appeared around the existing seigneuries, thus providing freehold tenure to Loyalists and the many New Englanders who soon flocked across the border to join them.[13]

Lieutenant-Colonel John Graves Simcoe, the first lieutenant governor, actively encouraged Americans to move to Upper Canada during the 1790s, believing that they could be persuaded ultimately to show allegiance to Britain; but this was a vain hope. Americans certainly did not wish to have the feudal constraints of the Old World imposed upon them. A pioneer society, wedded to egalitarian ideals, had little time for the elitist and class-based ways of the mother country. The real test came when Britain went to war in 1812 with the United States. Defended by only a few regular soldiers, and having mainly American residents, whose loyalty to Britain in some cases was doubtful, Upper Canada must have seemed a particularly easy target. There was no hope of more troops being sent by Britain while the conflict with Napoleon continued, and so it was a plum ripe for the picking. Yet the American invasion was successfully repulsed in 1814, primarily because of Britain's superior naval power. The War of 1812–1814 left the people of the Canadas with a clearer sense of their own identity. It also made them more wary of the continuing threat they faced from their republican neighbours and more aware of the need to hold fast to the British tie for protection. However, more than anything, the war highlighted the folly of relying on American immigration to grow the population.

There was an obvious need to encourage immigration from Britain. Most eighteenth-century emigration had been directed to the Maritime region, which was closer to reach and cheaper. But, as it became more widely known that much better land and climate were to be found in the Canadas, those British immigrants who could afford the longer journey switched their allegiance. Harsh economic conditions in Britain stimulated the exodus, and with the greater availability of transatlantic shipping made possible by the growing timber trade, it gathered pace from 1817. However, the English only left in appreciable numbers after 1830, when the economy once again nose-dived.[14] Before then, despite the considerable poverty being experienced in parts of England, emigration seemed too risky. The benefits had yet to be proven. Even when the government took the previously unthinkable step of funding emigration schemes in 1815 and the early 1820s, few English came forward, leaving the Scots and Irish to take up the offers of subsidies to get to Upper Canada.[15]

The English exodus began initially from the north. There were some, like the five hundred unemployed colliers from Bitton near Bristol, who sought government assistance to emigrate in 1817, but they were very much the exception.[16] Overall, 75 percent of the eighteen thousand or so English people who are known to have sailed for Quebec between 1817 and 1830 left from northern ports; of these, around a third had sailed from Hull in the East Riding of Yorkshire.[17] Thus, while the zeal to emigrate was particularly strong in the North of England, it was especially pronounced in Yorkshire. In 1819 alone, some nine hundred people sailed from Hull to Quebec. For northerners, accustomed to living in remote and sparsely populated areas, the prospect of starting a new life in an isolated wilderness was less daunting than it would have been for their more comfortably off southern cousins.

Yorkshire immigrants were the first to grasp the opportunities to be had from the Richelieu Valley's timber trade in Lower Canada. The catalyst was an English seigneur's family links with Yorkshire. The seigneur in question was Gabriel Christie, who, after having served in the Seven Years' War as a general in the British Army, had purchased an estate that included six timber-rich seigneuries straddling both sides of the Richelieu River.[18] At the southernmost end, on the west side, was Lacolle, a seigneury that would eventually attract a steady stream of settlers from Yorkshire.[19] The Yorkshire involvement began around 1784, when Christie's son Napier married Mary Burton, the daughter of a wealthy landowner. In addition to being the lord of various manors in the East Riding of Yorkshire, Mary's father, Ralph Burton, was also governor of Montreal. Her father's exalted station in life probably explains why Napier adopted the Burton surname from the day of his marriage. Following Gabriel Christie's death in 1799, Napier inherited his father's Lower Canada estate.[20]

Map 15: English settlers in the Lacolle area, Lower Canada.

① Bogton
② Hallerton
③ Roxham
④ Odelltown
⑤ Beaver Meadows
⑥ Îsle aux Noix
⑦ Lacolle
⑧ Burtonville
⑨ Henrysburg
⑩ Ormstown
⑪ Russeltown
⑫ Edwardstown

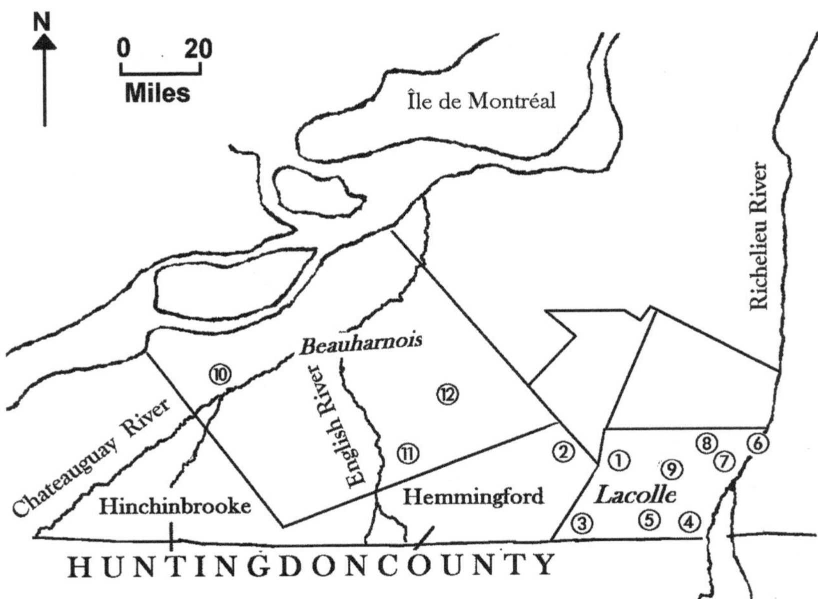

Some eighteen years later, when it was once again safe to cross the Atlantic, farmers and tradesmen began arriving in Lacolle, mainly from the East Riding of Yorkshire — from those areas where Napier's father-in-law had extensive land interests.[21] The actual number who came is uncertain, but a minimum of eighty-one families have been identified through genealogical research.[22] The Lancashire-born Robert Hoyle was pivotal in developing the region's important timber trade.[23] Arriving during the American War of 1812–1814,[24] he became a major timber merchant and prominent politician.[25] The timber trade flourished under Hoyle thanks to Lacolle's location near the American border, which enabled it to access both the English and American markets. For the English trade, timber was sent on floating rafts via the Richelieu and St. Lawrence Rivers to Quebec and from there transported across the Atlantic in timber ships. The large increases in tariffs that had been levied on Baltic timber during the Napoleonic Wars made this a highly profitable trade.[26] For the American market, timber was sent to the southern end of Lake Champlain and from there along the Hudson River to New York City.[27]

Yorkshire communities soon sprouted close to the American border in Odelltown,[28] Beaver Meadows, and Roxham, and at Henrysburg and Burtonville on the northern side of the seigneury (Map 15). In time, Yorkshire settlers moved into Bogton and Hallerton in Hemmingford Township and later acquired holdings in Ormstown, Russeltown, and Edwardstown in Beauharnois seigneury. This was a major influx. The village of Lacolle was established in 1823 and within ten years it had a post office; a year or so later, Odelltown's first Methodist church was being built. However, as the fertile lands in the western peninsula of Upper Canada became more accessible, Lacolle's appeal waned, and by 1830 few Yorkshire people were drawn to it. This pattern of immigrants heading west to obtain better land opportunities would repeat itself over and over.

Cumberland was another northern county to lose people to Lower Canada, and here again local intelligence fuelled the initial interest. Having arrived in St. Andrew's (Saint-André-Est) in the Argenteuil seigneury in 1818 to take up his duties as an Anglican missionary, the Cumberland-born Reverend Joseph Abbott was required to visit outlying areas. This led to his discovery of the good farming prospects in Vaudreuil seigneury, just west of Montreal. A keen supporter of emigration, Abbott conveyed his favourable assessment of the area to people back home in the Penrith area.[29] The economic depression after the Napoleonic Wars and the loss of traditional weaving jobs brought on by the introduction of power looms had created havoc in this textile-processing area. So, the Reverend Abbott was knocking on an open door and many emigrated.[30]

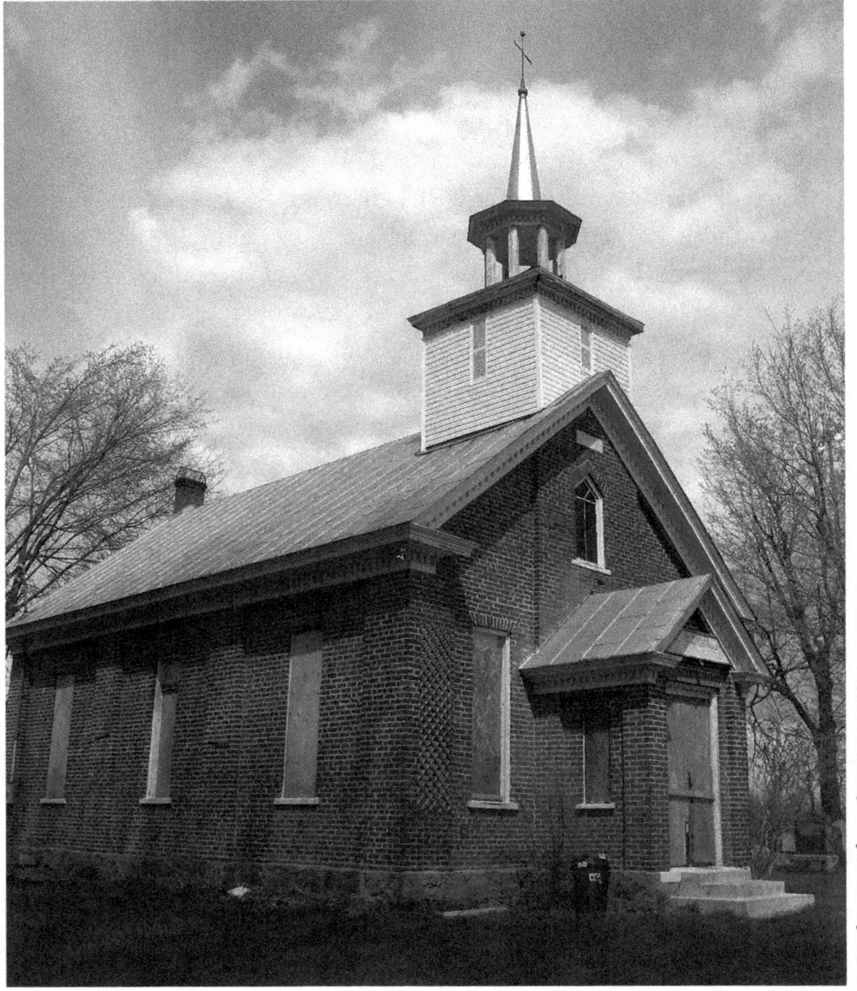

Methodist (Wesleyan) Church built in Henrysburg, Lower Canada, in 1861. Methodism was brought to the Lacolle area by the Yorkshire-born James Booth who arrived in 1823. He had been sent by the British-based Methodist Missionary Society.

People from Cumberland's Eden Valley began arriving in Vaudreuil a year later. In some cases three generations of the same family came, and, according to the Reverend Abbott, many were "excessively poor."[31] By 1837, Vaudreuil had acquired at least sixty Cumberland families.[32] Significantly, nearly all originated from places within a ten-mile radius of Penrith.[33] They had a choice of two locations in Vaudreuil. The poorest went to Côte St. Charles, which offered cheaper rents, while the more affluent families settled along the Ottawa River in Cavagnal (now Hudson), where they joined American farmers and former employees of the Hudson's Bay Company who had been there since 1801.[34] However, even they had to accept leaseholds and live under the supervisory wing of a seigneur. Their obvious success led the Reverend Abbott to comment in 1825 that although Cumberland people had been "comparatively poor as new settlers ... yet, strange as it may appear to a dweller in the old country, they are well-off in the [new] world."[35] They had little money with which to buy goods, but they had more than acquired the essentials of life.

Meanwhile, the ongoing economic depression in 1817 drew English northerners like James and Ann (Gardiner) Emerson from Weardale in County Durham to Upper Canada, despite the difficulties in travelling this far west. Setting sail for Quebec with their extended family, they had to endure two shipwrecks and, upon reaching the Gulf of St. Lawrence, had to purchase their own bateau and navigate themselves to Quebec. After living in Kingston for two years, they settled in Cavan Township (Durham County), where they experienced the gruelling demands of pioneer life: "The people did not clear their land very fast, about four to five acres each year. As soon as there was any grain to dispose of they had to take it to Port Hope; they drew it with oxen and were two days getting away a small load."[36] Given that just over 1,300 people are recorded as having sailed to Quebec from Sunderland between 1817 and 1820, the Emersons were clearly one of many County Durham families to leave at this time.[37] William Peacock's ships frequently carried such families from Sunderland to Quebec, and, when they did, he wrote on their behalf to the Colonial Office requesting land grants in Upper Canada, together with "the accustomed aid," although the latter was never forthcoming.[38]

A substantial group from Alston, in Cumberland County, an important lead-mining district, also left for Upper Canada in 1817. Taking advantage of the government's £10 emigration scheme[39] introduced that year to encourage group colonization, they established themselves in Smith Township in Peterborough County. They were followed by a second group who came in 1832 (Map 16).[40] John Langton, an English gentleman farmer who lived near Sturgeon Lake in Victoria County, visited the area in 1835 and confirmed the presence of a "Cumberland settlement in Smithtown, near Peterborough." He also noted a second group "of Cumberland miners who settled along [the] road from Mud Lake to Peterborough and one of the most thriving settlements in the district; it is of their children that the settlement is forming on Balsam Lake; there are also several Yorkshire and other English in the township and another batch of Peter Robinson's Irish settlers in the northern part."[41]

In addition, eleven families from Newark in Nottinghamshire had been attracted by the government's £10 emigration scheme and came to Peterborough County at around the same time as the Cumberland group.[42] Led by Captain Francis Spilsbury, they chose a site in Otonabee Township. Following them, between 1819 and 1824, were people from Carlton on

Map 16: English concentrations in Northumberland, Peterborough, Durham Victoria, Ontario, York, Simcoe, Peel and Halton Counties (based on 1881 census).

Trent, near Newark, who were assisted to emigrate by their parish.[43] At around this time yet another northern group, this time from near Hexham in Northumberland, founded the "English settlement" in London Township (Middlesex County). Having emigrated to New York State five years earlier, they had moved north to Upper Canada and soon after were joined by more of their compatriots who came directly from Northumberland.[44]

The English influx to Upper and Lower Canada grew steadily during the 1820s, mostly emanating from the northern counties. In 1827, the *Montreal Gazette* reported that "emigration is almost daily taking place from the West Riding of Yorkshire," and calculated that "1,300 emigrants must have quitted the shores of their native country at Liverpool during the last month."[45] The *Quebec Gazette* observed that about three hundred immigrants had already arrived in the spring of 1828, "chiefly farmers from Yorkshire." Several had been assisted to emigrate by their parishes, and soon after their arrival most found employment near Quebec "at from £2 to £3.10 a month"; but it noted that the majority would be heading for Upper Canada.[46] A factor in emigration's increasing appeal was the economic havoc being experienced in industrial regions of Britain owing to increasing mechanization. Especially hard hit were the many hand-loom weavers in Yorkshire, Cumberland, and Lancashire who were losing their jobs to power looms. Faced with redundancy or very low wage rates in a factory job, many opted for emigration. The Colonial Office was bombarded with requests for aid, which were always refused, but such was the sense of hardship and frustration that the government had to look again at the question of assisted emigration.

A parliamentary select committee, appointed in 1826–27, recommended that aid be given to destitute people wishing to emigrate, but the advice was rejected because of the high costs involved.[47] Innumerable petitions were sent by destitute weavers, clothiers, tradesmen, and labourers, all seeking help.[48] Twenty-six labourers from Liverpool, suffering from "the depression of trade"[49]; twelve petitioners from Winwick Parish in Lancashire, complaining of low wages and "depressed trade"[50]; and eleven heads of families, "distressed weavers" from Manchester, each pleaded their case for government funding.[51] The Blackburn Society of Emigrants' petition referred to the "awful distress in manufacturing districts in this County [Lancashire]" and asked for "kind and liberal aid" to go either to "the northern parts of Nova Scotia" or Upper Canada, while five miners' families from Evesham in Worcestershire, suffering "from the badness of trade and employment," asked for assistance to emigrate. In the end, however, all petitions of this nature were rejected.[52]

By the early 1830s, English immigration ceased to be dominated by the north, with arrivals coming in more or less equal numbers from both the north and south.[53] One factor that helped to drive the growing exodus from the south was the use of poor rates by parish councils to finance the emigration expenses of their paupers.[54] The introduction of threshing machines and other forms of machinery had caused hundreds of agricultural workers in the south to lose their jobs. A crisis point was reached when farm labourers, led by the fictitious Captain Swing, rioted over high unemployment rates and severe poverty, with Kent, Wiltshire, Sussex, and Norfolk being in the forefront of the disturbances. A debate raged over how public funds might be used to alleviate the suffering of the poor. This led to the passing of the Poor Law Amendment Act of 1834, one of the most significant pieces of social legislation ever enacted. It allowed English parishes to finance the emigration costs of their poor by borrowing money from their affluent parishioners. By making a one-off payment, parishes helped their paupers to a better life, their ratepayers were spared the burden of continuing poor relief costs, and Canada acquired more people.

Parish-funded schemes brought thousands of paupers to Upper Canada, especially from the English counties of Norfolk, Suffolk, Sussex, Kent, Wiltshire, Somerset, and, to a lesser extent, Surrey. While most headed for Upper Canada, a significant number, mainly from Norfolk and Suffolk, went to the British American Land Company acreages in the Eastern Townships in Lower Canada.[55] Formed in 1834 and modelled after the Canada Company founded eight years earlier, the company promoted the colonization of 850,000 acres of Crown land stretching across the Eastern Townships.[56] One section (596,000 acres) lay in the St. Francis Tract[57] between Lake Megantic and the St. Francis River, while the second section (251,000 acres) was scattered throughout Shefford, Stanstead, and Sherbrooke Counties.[58] Its fertile land and access to trade outlets in Quebec City made the region a prime candidate for large-scale colonization, but that was easier said than done. As the Quebec immigration agent made clear to the 1826 Emigration Select Committee, many British people "dislike Lower Canada, on account of the French language and laws; the peasantry all speak French, and the emigrant is quite lost among them."[59]

Norfolk and Suffolk people clearly had no qualms about settling in the Eastern Townships. Three thousand eight hundred and fifty-five of them were assisted to emigrate to the Canadas in 1835–36,[60] and of these some 1,200 were expected to go to Lower Canada.[61] This can be corroborated by the *Quebec Gazette*'s report in 1836 that around 1,400 immigrants had reached Sherbrooke in the Eastern Townships, principally from Norfolk and Suffolk.[62] However, their actual numbers in any one location cannot be calculated, since many of the early arrivals became disheartened and left the area.[63] Some acquired company land in Sherbrooke County, but a more substantial number made their way north to Bury, one of the recently opened townships in the St. Francis Tract (Map 17).

Map 17: English concentrations in the Eastern Townships, Lower Canada (based on the 1881 census of Lower Canada).

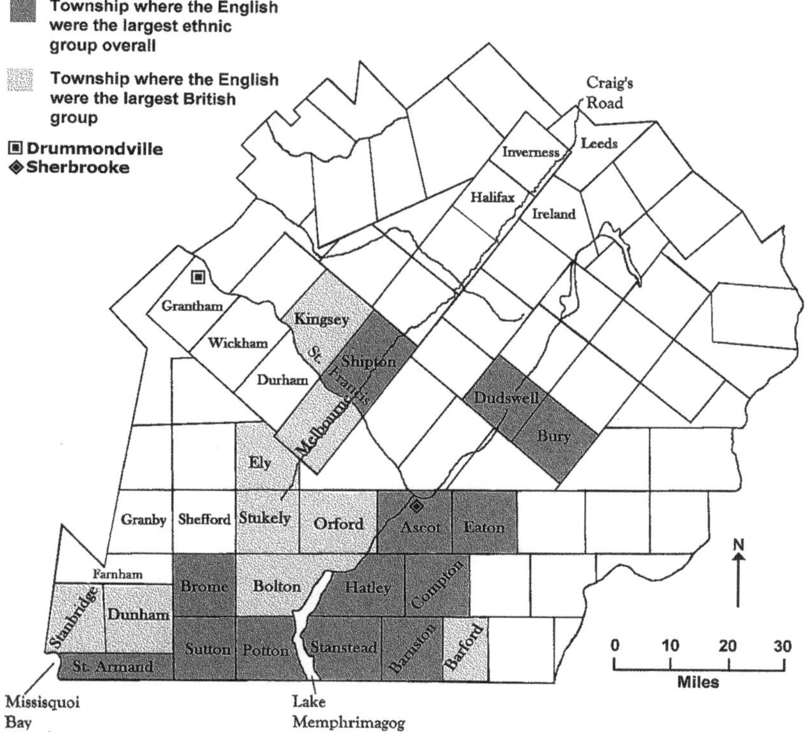

When he arrived in Brookbury (Bury Township) from Suffolk in 1853, Josiah Clarke commented on the good progress that had been made by Norfolk and Suffolk settlers: "Here is them that left England seventeen years back and have got cows, oxen and land of their own and a horse to ride on and when in England had not enough to eat and many might be better off than they are if they would work but they are too idle to. A man that will work can live here but a lazy man cannot, as here is no parish [relief] to go to."[64] Other favourable accounts confirm this rosy picture,[65] but Bury's Anglican minister, the Reverend John Kemp, thought otherwise. His congregation of "mostly English pauper emigrants" were still "comparatively poor."[66] Few were able to meet the interest payments on their land or settle the debts they owed to the local storekeepers and "most had difficulty in providing for their families.

Judging from comments made by contemporary observers, such as the Quebec immigration agent and Anglican and Methodist missionaries, relatively few English immigrants came to the Eastern Townships. Of those who did, many left, relocating to either Upper Canada or the United States.[67] And yet, the 1881 Census reveals that the English were the dominant ethnic group in eight of the seventeen townships nearest the American border, and in another four townships outnumbered both the Scots and Irish (Map 17).[68]

The English dominance in Bury was undoubtedly due to the large influx from East Anglia during the 1830s, but even in the adjoining township of Dudswell the English population consisted mainly of Americans having English ancestry. In 1854–55, their Anglican minister, the Reverend Thomas Shaw Chapman, referred to "the Americans by whom Dudswell was colonized 50 years ago."[69] In other words, English ethic origins, as shown in the 1881 Census, do not necessarily reflect substantial immigration from England. Where there is a strong English presence it is more likely to be due to the arrival in the late eighteenth century of American-born Loyalists and their followers, who came mainly from New England.[70] Later generations were categorized as English in the 1881 Census because their ancestors' Old World family links were with England.

While English parishes were grappling with the social problems caused by high unemployment, Sir John Colborne, the lieutenant governor of Upper Canada, was fretting over the province's inability to attract British immigrants. He had become alarmed over the continuing influx of Americans to Upper Canada, doubting their loyalty to British interests. He believed that Upper Canada's prosperity and welfare depended on the acquisition of large numbers of British immigrants.[71] Thus, he

Saint John Anglican Church, Bury Township (Compton County), Lower Canada, built 1842–45.

viewed the arrival of English paupers as beneficial. The five thousand or so who came in 1831–32 accounted for 30 percent of the total arrivals from England, and they were a similar proportion in 1835–36.[72] The province needed to bolster its British population while England desperately wanted to get rid of its surplus farm labourers. This was a win/win solution — although it was not without its critics.

William Cobbett, the radical journalist and social reformer, travelled around the South of England raging against the practice of assisting the poor to emigrate. He claimed that able-bodied workers were being lost to the colonies, while "the idlers, pensioners, and dead-weights" were being left behind. Like many others, he argued that labourers, no matter how poor, were the life-blood of the country and that under no circumstances should they be assisted to leave. However, harking back to a golden age that had never existed, he was somewhat removed from reality. In addition to the continuing demise of traditional agricultural labouring jobs caused by the invention of threshing machines, the growing use of mechanization in most sectors was destroying jobs, especially in cloth-making. There were hordes of destitute people who needed help, and emigration at least offered them the hope of a new start and a better life.

Nevertheless, Cobbett and other anti-emigration campaigners did their best to thwart the exodus by writing letters to newspapers, highlighting the miseries of sea crossings and the perils awaiting people in North America. This meant English parishes could not simply coerce their poor to emigrate. They had to be convinced, and this only happened when people they trusted gave positive accounts of life in Canada. Sensibly, a small number usually went out first to see for themselves what life was like, as happened in 1830 when a group from Corsley in West Wiltshire, the first to opt for assisted emigration, sent favourable letters home. This letter, written by William Singer, a former bricklayer, is a typical example:

> If any of my old acquaintances is got tired of being slaves and drudges tell them to come to Upper Canada to William Singer and he will take them by the hand and

> lead them to hard work and good wages and the best of living. Any of them would do well here.... We have eight English families within about two miles, all from Westbury or Corsley [Wiltshire].[73]

Similarly, Philip Annett was also very upbeat:

> I think you was better sell your house and ... come to Canada whilst you have a chance. If you don't come soon it is likely you will starve and if you don't your children will.... I was agreeably surprised when I came here to see what a fine country it was. It being excellent land bearing crops of wheat and other corn for 20 or 30 years without any dung. You have no rent to pay, no poor-rates and scarcely any taxes. No gamekeepers or Lords over you.... I think no Englishman can do better than come as soon as possible, if it cost them every farthing they have, for I would rather be so here than in England with £100 in my pocket.[74]

Their buoyant aspirations can be contrasted with Maude Davies's unsympathetic views, expressed in her history of Corsley nearly eighty years later. However, far from being useless degenerates, the Corsley immigrants grabbed the employment opportunities that were now available to them, thus sparking off a more or less immediate outflow of people from the neighbouring parishes of Frome in Somerset and Horningsham and Westbury in Wiltshire.

Between 1830 and 1832, the Corsley/Frome area lost around eight hundred poor people, mainly to Upper Canada, all of whom were assisted by their parishes.[76] Most of the Wiltshire and Somerset paupers headed west to Southwold Township in Elgin County[77] (Map 18), while a smaller number settled in newly surveyed areas of Dummer Township in Peterborough County (Map 16). Samuel Strickland, a gentleman farmer who had settled at nearby Otonabee Township three years earlier, judged them to be doing well despite being granted less assistance by the government than had been the case for Peter Robinson's Irish settlers who had been sent to Douro Township: "The Dummer people had no shanties built for them, no cows, and were given much worse land; and yet they have done much more in a shorter time."[78]

And people like Levi Payne did astonishingly well. Having immigrated to Dummer with his wife and extended family, including his brothers from Frome, Levi acquired a gristmill, sawmills, a general store, and a farm by 1839.[79] James Treasure, a shoemaker, and W. Clements, a labourer, both from Corsley, wrote approvingly of farming conditions in Elgin County. According to Treasure, "The people here wonder that more do not come.... We are a great deal better and comfortabler [*sic*] than we expected to be in so short a time," and Clements wrote even more persuasively: "If I had stayed in Corsley I never would have had nothing. I like the country very much.... If the labouring men did but know the value of their strength they would never abide contented in the old country.... No poor-rate, no taxes, no overseers, no beggars."[80]

At this time a great many Wiltshire and Somerset paupers were also being sent to equally remote situations in Simcoe County, where they settled alongside people from Yorkshire. In all, a total of three thousand people (430 families) were reported to have been relocated to Oro, Dummer, and Douro townships during 1831–32.[81] Mary Sophia (Gapper) O'Brien, from Charlinch in Somerset, viewed their communities in Oro when she visited in the 1830s:

> Now for the first time I saw quite a new settlement. We passed on for two miles through a road just cut out on each side of which at short intervals were log houses of a very respectable class. Some were finished externally but almost all stood completely in the forest. In some places there was perhaps an acre or two chopped, but generally hardly so many trees seemed to have fallen as were necessary to construct the buildings.... In five or six years every house will be surrounded by a productive farm. Most of these settlers are farmers from England.[82]

While assisted English paupers were flooding into Upper Canada at this time, many labourers, farmers, and tradesmen of very modest means also came without any public subsidies at all. There were even some like William Rooke, son of Major General Sir Henry Willoughby Rooke, owner of a large Gloucestershire estate, who had plenty of capital, but first needed to learn how to cope with pioneering conditions. Wasting a great deal of time "living at the Inn, doing nothing" when he first arrived at Rama Township (Ontario County) in 1835, William eventually acquired land and found a man who "works with me, to whom I pay $10 per month, and he and I work from light 'till dark; it is really a very pleasant way of employing one's time, indeed one has to here."[83]

Meanwhile, the disastrous economic conditions that had afflicted the Corsley area in West Wiltshire were also being experienced in Downton Parish on the southeast side of the county. Poor harvests between 1828 and 1830 added to the gloom, as did the growing use of threshing machines. Once again, parish-assisted emigration was offered. As before, an advance party of twenty-five Downton people went out to Upper Canada in 1835 to assess its prospects. Their journey began with a five-night stay at the Quebec Hotel in Portsmouth Harbour while they waited for their ship to sail. Judging from the food and drink they consumed, no expense was spared.[84] Breakfasts with lobster, mackerel, or steak were followed in the evening by meals of salmon, steak, lamb cutlets, and lamb chops, all washed down with copious quantities of ale, port, and other alcoholic beverages.

Map 18: English concentrations in Middlesex, Elgin, Oxford and Brant counties (based on 1881 census).

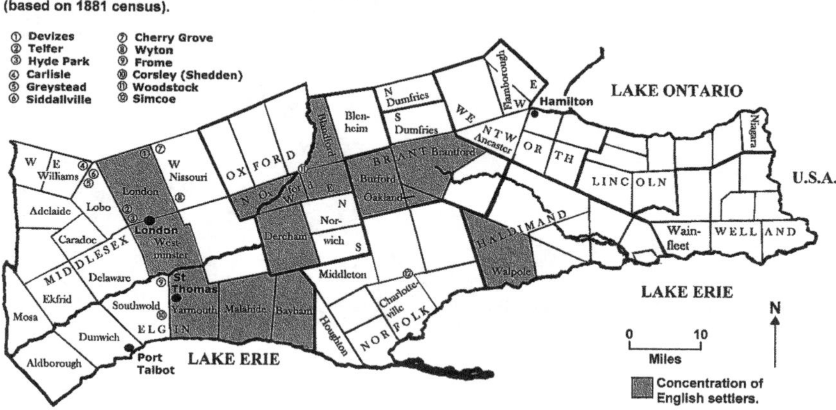

The inescapable conclusion is that fine food and drink were being offered to very apprehensive people to get them off to the best possible start. And it would seem that the strategy worked. After a non-eventful crossing, their early reports were highly favourable, and in the following year 220 more people from Downton and fifty-nine from Whiteparish sailed from London. Most settled in Elgin County, probably in Yarmouth, Malahide, and Bayham townships (Map 18).[85] Twenty-six years later, while visiting the area, Mr. W. Heurk would report that "Yarmouth, London Westminster, Southwold and Malahide [Townships] is principally settled with English and Irish emigrants, most of them ... are in comfortable circumstance and many of them independent."[86] No doubt he was describing some of the Wiltshire paupers.

Eight families from Stockbury Parish in Kent, who were assisted to relocate to Whitby Township (Ontario County) in 1837, also seemed somewhat reluctant to leave and only did so when they had heard from already-established Stockbury people living in "New Whitby" (Map 16). According to the Reverend Twopenny, who organized their departure,

Courtesy Library and Archives Canada, C-000544.

Settler's house in the forest on the Thames River, near London, Ontario, 1842. Painting by Henry Francis Ainslie (1803–79).

"Now they really desire to [go] ... and more would go next year. Some are respectable and some we shall be glad to be rid of."[87]

Perhaps they sensed the element of truth in his final comment. Certainly, the parish had been very generous, providing expenses of about £250 — roughly £30 per family — to cover the cost of passages and clothing.[88]

Three years earlier, Stockbury paupers had placed conditions on emigrating. Jesse Stunden said he would leave with his wife and eight children "on condition that the parish will pay the expenses of the passage and £50 on his landing in America; the parish agreed to offer £30 and he is to consider"; James Burn said he "would emigrate with his wife and four children if the passage was paid and he was given £30 on landing;" he declined the £18 that was offered, but later changed his mind; George Kitney, a single man, wanted his passage plus £5, but the parish only offered £3, which he declined.[89] In other words, they would only leave if sufficient money was offered. Five years later, the Quebec immigration agent noted the arrival at Quebec of around 240 paupers, mainly from Kent, many of whom planned to settle with friends who were already ensconced on the northwest side of Lake Ontario or to the west of Hamilton.[90]

While there are helpful clues to indicate where Kent paupers settled in Upper Canada, the locations of the two thousand or so Norfolk paupers who arrived in 1835–36 remain a mystery, since only a tiny amount of documentation survives. The available evidence suggests that between 1831 and 1836 two Norfolk parishes — Briston and Edgefield — sent their paupers to Oxford and Waterloo counties.[91] At one stage Briston and Edgefield immigrants were reported to be living side by side in Blenheim Township (Oxford County). Perhaps the many Norfolk paupers who left from the neighbouring parishes of Holt and Saxthorpe and the nearby parish of Fulmodeston also made their way to Oxford County.[92] Similarly, the destinations of the five hundred or so Suffolk paupers who were assisted by their respective parishes to emigrate in 1835–36 are unclear. Fifty-two people from Kettleburgh Parish went to Etobicoke Township near Toronto in 1836, where they joined another Kettleburgh group of fifty-two people who had emigrated five years earlier.[93] But apart from this group, most Suffolk immigrants vanished without a trace.

The largest group to come as assisted immigrants were the 1,800 men, women, and children from the West Sussex estate of George O'Brien Wyndham, the third Earl of Egremont. They came to Upper Canada between 1832 and 1838 from over one hundred parishes. Although most originated from West Sussex, especially the Petworth area, the group included seventy-seven people from Dorking in the neighbouring county of Surrey, as well as people from East Sussex, the Isle of Wight, Cambridgeshire, and a scattering of parishes across Southern England.[94] Once established, the Petworth immigrants wrote a total of 144 letters from Upper Canada, emphasizing its work opportunities and other benefits. Their letters home reveal that they primarily settled along the north and west side of Lake Ontario, especially in York, Halton, and Wentworth Counties, and in Middlesex, Oxford, Brant, and Waterloo Counties in the southwest of Upper Canada (Map 19).

The Petworth immigrants seemed to have been particularly well organized and showed every sign of taking the first opportunity that presented itself, whatever it might have been. Those who went to the long-established townships on the western side of Lake Ontario were

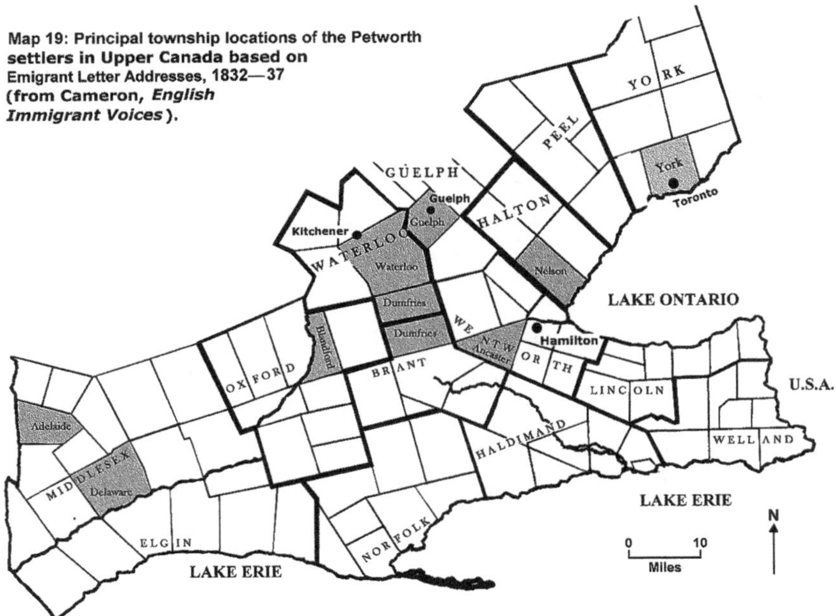

Map 19: Principal township locations of the Petworth settlers in Upper Canada based on Emigrant Letter Addresses, 1832—37 (from Cameron, *English Immigrant Voices*).

able to find farming work very easily, most having wide-ranging agricultural skills. They could thus obtain useful work experience and use the money they earned to buy land and eventually become farmers in their own right. This more enlightened approach replaced Colborne's earlier policy of encouraging assisted immigrants to become instant farmers by locating them on wilderness land and supervising the beginnings of their settlements. This well-intentioned but impractical paternalistic approach failed to recognize that newly arrived immigrants needed time to adjust to their new environment; only then could they fully realize what might be achieved and what their actual options were.

William Wright from Dorking found that: "after coming to York (Toronto) I was only three days idle, when I found work about 20 miles from York, where I worked 13 days on the road at the rate of 2 s. per day and board." Three days later he was approached by William Dornorman, a farmer from Nelson Township (Halton County), who hired him for a year at an annual wage of £22.[95] William Spencer from Linchmere in Sussex also had a smooth entry into Nelson: "I have hired with Mr. Truller by the year and I am getting good wages; and if you feels any ways inclined to come I think it would be better for you, for I think you will get a better living here than you ever will in England."[96] Obadiah Wilson, one of a small group from Bassingbourn Parish in Cambridgeshire who travelled with the Petworth Emigration Committee in 1832, went on to acquire a home farm in Whitby Township and numerous other land holdings in Scott and Reach Townships together with a hotel and even more property in the village of Udora, farther to the north. Obadiah, a remarkable example of a poor man who made good, ended his days with an estate valued at $24,000.[97]

Meanwhile, a group of Petworth immigrants from Walburton in West Sussex effectively created a New Walburton for themselves at Thornhill in Vaughan Township (York County). Already having local contacts, new arrivals could all the more easily find work. When Frank Mellish arrived in 1835, "Thomas Messenger came on board the steamer and gave directions where to find George Wells and the two Birchs and I have been at work for George Wells ever since. [William] Cole is working just by and Charles Leggatt is working about three miles from here.... Mr. Birch, Mrs. Norris, G. Wells and all the Walburton live close together."[98]

A year later, John Ayling provided a progress report on the growing Walburton community:

> George Leggatt is at work about one mile from Thornhill, he has $8 a month and his meat; John Norris and George Booker is about 10 miles from George Lintot; George has $10 and John $8 a month. George Cole is with George Wells. Charles Richards is about 12 miles from George. John Millyard is 11 miles from here; he has gone apprenticed to a carpenter. Thomas Norris has got a place and has hired for a month. Richard Cooper is at work for Mark Messenger and Cornelius Cook is at work at Toronto as a butcher's boy; he has not been up to Thornhill at all. Ruth Leggatt is with Edmund Birch and I have hired up at Newmarket for $11. I have got a very good place about 18 miles from George Lintot.... I don't work hard but lives very well, that is £2 15s a month and my board and lodgings, that is better than working in England.... Never be afraid to come to America, don't be afraid to come, you will do better here.[99]

For Ann (Downer) Mann, who emigrated in 1836, Adelaide Township in Middlesex County was a dream come true, despite its rough and ready state and having to cope with the death of her husband in Montreal. In Adelaide she could, at long last, escape from the poverty that had haunted her all her life. She arrived with four of her youngest sons as well as her oldest son, together with his wife and children. Despite the loss of her husband, she gave her adult sons back home in West Sussex a glowing account of her new situation. She was elated by the fact that all of her children had found jobs as domestic servants in the nearby towns and that she would never have to face life in the dreaded workhouse ever again:

> I don't want for nothing; my children are all out at service; I could get them places if I had twenty more ... if any of your children wish to come to America do not

> hinder them; for I shall say this is a good country to come to; I wish I had come when my first son came[100]; but thank God I am here. What would have become of my children if they had been in England and I had been put into some poorhouse; but now if I go out of the [front] door I do see great comfort.... Let my letter be copied off and be stuck up at the Onslow Arms [Inn] to let everyone see that I lives in Adelaide; don't leave no one thing out that I say ...[101]

Assisted emigrants from West Sussex also colonized Delaware Township, to the southeast of Adelaide, adding to the English component of Middlesex County. George Carver was struck by the different social structure that he encountered and how it gave poor labourers like him an advantage over "your spirited farmers and their wives," who had made his life a misery back in England:

> They would not like *to sit down at table after their servants have done* meals and eat what is left, for here they would be obliged to beg and pray to get a man for a few days to help them instead of blustering and swearing as they do over you in England. Here if a man wants any common labour to be done he must do it himself or let it go undone, but if he wants to raise a house or a barn or any such thing as that his neighbours readily come and assist him and he does the same in return.[102]

While the Petworth settlers showed every sign of being very well organized, the three thousand or so Chelsea Pensioners[103] who arrived in Upper Canada between 1830 and 1839 soon floundered.[104] As wounded British Army war veterans, they had been granted pensions. Foolishly, many agreed, under encouragement from the British government, to have their pensions commuted to a lump sum to fund their relocation to the New World.[105] A cynical and contemptible policy, which enabled the War Office to reduce its pensions bills, the result was misery and chaos for the hapless thousands who were persuaded to leave England. Most were between forty and fifty years of age, and little care was taken in selecting suitable recruits.[106] Mrs. Anna Jameson, who travelled from London to Port Talbot in 1837, was horrified to learn from the Upper Canada emigration agent that half of the Chelsea Pensioners were afflicted in some way: "some with one arm, some with one leg, bent with old age or rheumatism, lame halt and even, will it be believed, blind!"[107] Inevitably, many ended their days in great distress.

Most of the war veterans were sent to Middlesex, Simcoe, Victoria, and Peterborough Counties where they endured countless setbacks.[108] The Chelsea Pensioners should never have been encouraged to emigrate. Many thought that they were giving up their pensions for four years only and would receive them again, but that was not the case. In 1833, Sir John Colborne ordered the cessation of the scheme and decreed that the saddest cases be moved to Penetanguishene, where they were put under the protective wing of an army officer. But when Lord Durham[109] received Edward Shuel's petition in 1838, it soon became clear that more had to be done. This was a man with a wife and six children who was incapable of work, because he was paralyzed on one side of his body from a wound received in twenty-three years' service in the army. Lord Durham demanded that his and other army pensions be restored immediately. Although this did not happen, at least a system of poor relief was established. When aid was first distributed in 1840 there were 654 Chelsea Pensioners still resident in Upper Canada, representing only a quarter of the original group, the rest having already died.[110]

However, despite the high visibility of the poor during the 1830s, the exodus from England continued to be dominated by self-funded emigrants who unfortunately left little or no documentation behind. When unemployed lead miners from Cumberland and Durham Counties headed for Upper Canada in 1832, they paid their own way and became dispersed in Upper Canada and the United States. A chance letter, written in 1854 by John Graham, brother of one of the immigrants, reveals the progress being made by ex-miners from Weardale (County Durham) who had settled west of Hamilton:

> [John] Fleamen and [Joseph] Wearmouth has bought 100 acres of land about the same place and speak highly of the place, they say there is plenty of work to get of all sorts … and good wages too, it is grandest and flourishing counties they ever saw; We had a man the name of John Featherston who went from this country 20 years ago [to Upper Canada] who is a relation to many a one in Weardale, who is very rich in property now, and when they went first they were a great family of them; they had not a penny left when they landed, and I think that is encouragement, and all the names that I have mentioned over has gone into Upper Canada and a great deal more not mentioned, for their was over a 100 of men, women and children left this Spring, all for America, and John Featherston, who went to America about a year ago, writes that they will very soon have a little Weardale there.[111]

The directional flow of emigrants from England changed once again in the 1840s. Some 57 percent of all departures began in Liverpool, with ports in Yorkshire, Northumberland, Durham, and Cumberland playing little part in the embarkation of emigrants during this and later decades.[112] By this time Liverpool had become England's most popular emigrant port, drawing people from across the entire country. And an increasing number were coming from the industrial areas of England. As an example, twenty-three people from Burslem Parish in the Staffordshire potteries region were assisted to emigrate by their parish in 1849.[113]

As machines threatened to replace people in the pottery processes, those who feared they would be cast aside, as in this case, opted for emigration. This was also a period when emigration from southwest England surged ahead, accounting for 23 percent of all departures. Most of the emigrants from the southwest originated from Devon and Cornwall, with many Cornish settling along Lake Ontario between Port Hope and Toronto (Map 16), while many Devon people headed for the Huron Tract, a vast area within southwestern Upper Canada (Map 20).

Map 20: English concentrations in Wellington, Waterloo, Perth, Huron, Bruce and Grey counties (based on 1881 census).

A deepening economic depression during the 1840s in Cornwall, both in agriculture and mining,[114] made people particularly responsive to the glowing reports being sent by family and friends already living in Upper Canada. Emigration soared during this decade.[115] In 1840, the Quebec immigration agent noted the 146 "very respectable people" who had arrived from the Cornish port of Padstow: "They are all going to settle in the township of Whitby (Ontario County) and near Port Hope (Durham County) in Upper Canada."[116] And later that same year he noted fifty-eight more Cornish people, "chiefly mechanics and farmers," who had sailed from Padstow, and were mainly heading for the townships of Asphodel (Peterborough County) and Darlington (Durham County).[117]

In the following year, arrivals from Padstow tripled to six hundred.[118] However, as Jacob Jenkings, a Cornish plasterer, discovered, it was not just the English who were flocking to the Lake Ontario region. Having landed a job in Kingston, he was trying to find his place in a multi-ethnic immigrant society: "Everyone had his own fashion of working; we have English, Irish, Scotch, Welsh, Dutch and Canadian and Yankees," with the latter being "a sort of independent people."[119]

Meanwhile, Yorkshire continued to furnish the Lake Ontario region with a steady supply of its people, many having outstanding farming credentials. Two Yorkshire farmers caught the eye of the Quebec immigration agent in 1839 when they stepped off their ship from Hull. They were not recent immigrants, but were in fact "returning to their families in the neighbourhood of Toronto, where they have settled for many years; they have brought out a number of their friends with them who intend to purchase lands and settle in their neighbourhood."[120] A year later he commented on the Yorkshire families living in Markham Township (York County) who had sailed back to England to collect their families and "some very fine sheep and a young Yorkshire colt." Many who sailed with these families from Hull were very affluent, bringing out between £1,200 and £1,500 collectively; but they also included some young men who had lost their jobs in the Yorkshire woollen mills and were "going to Boston for employment in the factories there."[121]

Isaac Bravender was yet another Yorkshireman made good. Originating from Malton in the North Riding, he had adapted easily to pioneer life, and by 1846 he was singing the praises of Brock Township (Ontario County) to his children still in Yorkshire:

> The sons and daughter that came over with us has bought a place about a mile and a half and they had about 200 bushels of apples and plums in abundance, we have a cow and a heifer that we are raising and I bought two ewes this Spring…, we have two fat pigs…. I am doing very

> well better than I expected for I have very good friends around me; we had eight ploughs, ploughing some sod for me belonging to the neighbours in one day. I intend to have a yoke of oxen in another year if all is well ...[122]

Isaac's son wrote home soon after from Vaughan Township (York County) with an even more upbeat message: "We thank God that we are in a fine part of the country amongst old neighbours of the Old Country." He now had a larger farm "and a much more healthy situation with better land ... and more like the Old Country all together," with his neighbours including Robert Hall, James Craven, Thomas Fletcher, and James Monkman — all Yorkshire people. "If any friends should be wishing to come to Canada my advice to them is not to go back to the 'Wild Bush' but to come to the Gore of Toronto or Vaughan where they will be sure to find some farms to rent or buy."[123]

R. Kay, a West Riding farmer, offered similar advice following his extensive tour in 1845 of the townships along the northwest side of Lake Ontario. He concluded that Nelson and Trafalgar Townships (Halton County) offered the best land. An added bonus was their "nearness to a good town and market." And, having been "settled principally by English" they had "a home like appearance...." He continued: "I did not hear one single dissatisfaction [*sic*] expressed by any of the steady, attentive farmers upon their change of country, but on the contrary, all were satisfied that their prospects were greatly superior to what they could have been in England."[124]

Six years later the *Yorkshire Gazette* reported that "every village in the neighbourhood of Driffield" in the East Riding was losing people to Canada, while "in a village near Bridlington, which contains a population of about 300 souls, nearly 200 out of this number are also preparing for America."[125] By 1858, the *Beverley Guardian* saw fit to warn its readers that "it would be worse than foolish for any class of persons to come out here [Canada] as the country has no manufactures, being purely agricultural and as a colony is greatly overstocked with tradesmen, clerks, shopmen [*sic*] and mechanics of all kinds."[126] Presumably, its anti-emigration stance reflected local concerns over the steady depletion of the East Riding population.

As was the case with Yorkshire people, most immigrants from Devon and Cornwall paid their own way, although there were some exceptions. In 1842, the Cornish parishes of St. Agnes, Perranzabuloe, St. Blazey, St. Columb Major, Cuby, St. Eval, Mawgan, and St. Merryn, taken together, assisted a total of forty-five people to reach Upper Canada, while in the following year sixty-three people from St. Columb Major, St. Issey, and South Petherwin also received help.[127] More poor Cornish people "of the labouring class" arrived at Quebec in 1846 with the intention of settling on the northwest side of Lake Ontario, where, according to the Quebec immigration agent, "they have friends."[128] The Cornish Women's Institute survey of people who had immigrated to the colonies certainly reveals the Cornish preference for this one region. Of those who arrived during the 1840s and 1850s, most settled between Cobourg and Whitby (Map 16).[129]

The strong Cornish and Yorkshire presence along the northwest side of Lake Ontario helped to make this an English-dominated area. By 1881, people with English ancestry were the largest ethnic group in Durham, Ontario, and York Counties and were especially well-represented in Darlington (69 percent English) and Whitby Townships (57 percent English).[130] While some of the English presence can be attributed to the early influx of Loyalists to the area, immigration directly from England was clearly a major factor. Not surprisingly, the Bible Christian movement, a Methodist sect that had been developed in Cornwall from 1815, made great strides in this area. By 1861, Durham County had the largest Bible Christian population in Upper Canada, while the town of Bowmanville became a major Methodist centre.[131] Much of the movement's success can be attributed to the Kent-born Cephas Barker, who, upon his arrival in 1865, served in Bowmanville until his death in 1881. His funeral service, held in the Bowmanville Bible Christian church, "was packed to the doors. The audience was composed of many from the country, some being present from Enfield, Hampton, Orono, Port Hope [in Durham County] and a large number from Ebenezer, Salem and other surrounding districts."[132]

The Methodist New Connexion, another splinter group imported from England, was introduced to Upper Canada in 1841. Since it gave ordinary lay members a greater role in running services in their places of

Courtesy Archives of Ontario, Acc. No 2588 S 152.

Bible Christian Church members photographed in 1865 at Bowmanville, along Lake Ontario. The Bible Christian Movement became established in Upper Canada in the 1830s.

worship, it might have been expected to resonate well with Canadian-born residents, but its appeal was greater among first-generation immigrants.[133] Having first visited Lower Canada in 1837, the English New Connexion missionary John Addyman went on to establish Methodist preaching circuits in Upper and Lower Canada three years later. Preachers were in place at Montreal and Henrysburg (Lacolle seigneury), a city and town with substantial English populations,[134] but his placements at Goulbourn and Lansdowne Townships in eastern Upper Canada are more difficult to explain since their immigrants were mainly Irish. Similarly, the preachers he based at Cobourg (Hamilton Township) and Cavan Township, midway across Lake Ontario, would have found many Americans and first-generation Irish, but few English. No doubt, competition from the Bible Christian and Wesleyan Methodists was too strong in this well-settled region for the New Connexion to make much of an impact on English immigrants. But in western Upper Canada, which was just being opened up, the Reverend Addyman was knocking on an open door. Preachers were sent to Caledon Township (Peel County), Nelson and Trafalgar Townships (Halton County), and the towns of Hamilton, Ancaster, Welland, Waterford, London, and St. Thomas, all being areas that acquired a growing number of English people as the spread of colonization had moved west.[135]

By the 1840s English colonizers were pouring into the Huron Tract — a vast area of 1.1 million acres, fronting on Lake Huron, which constituted nearly half of the holdings of the Canada Company.[136] Having been established in 1826, the company provided land and jobs to settlers and also supported the building of roads, schools, and churches.[137] Nonetheless, the Canada Company was regularly accused of exaggerating the state of development of its lands and of selling land at inflated prices and, overall, earned little credit for its colonizing efforts. Its shareholders expected quick profits that were never realized, while many farmers who settled on its lands felt dissatisfied with their treatment.[138] But plenty of ordinary settlers were pleased with the reasonable terms on offer and those seeking to settle in groups were drawn to the huge expanses of the Huron Tract. The English, many of whom were from Devon, went principally to Huron and Perth Counties.

Devon settlers created a sprawling settlement that encompassed four townships in two counties. Their communities developed in a north/south direction along both sides of the London Road through Usborne, Stephen, and Biddulph[139] Townships in Huron County and eastward along the Thames Road through Fullarton Township in Perth County (Map 20). The trailblazer had been John Balkwill, who, having acquired land in Usborne and Stephen Townships by 1831, returned home to Devon to drum up support for his new undertaking.[140] William May, his brother-in-law, arrived a year later, and shortly after that came several brothers, who took up land in Usborne, Stephen, and Hay Townships.[141] Other Devon people followed during the 1830s, some joining Balkwill and others colonizing the future Centralia in the northern tip of Biddulph Township.[142] Two of Balkwill's friends, George and John Snell, also settled in the area.[143] John Balkwill went on to found the future Devon at the junction of the London and Crediton Roads, while John Snell settled a short distance up the London Road at the future Exeter. John Mitchell, another of the early pioneers, acquired land to the west of Devon at the future Crediton.[144] These were all Devon place names, chosen to commemorate the geographical origins of the first wave of settlers.

Exeter (Usborne Township) received an added boost to its economy during the 1840s when Isaac Carling,[145] a businessman, storekeeper, and politician who had been born in nearby London Township (Middlesex County), came to live there. Forming a business partnership with his brother John, they operated a tannery in Exeter, which brought much-needed employment to the area. Isaac may have acquired some of his workforce in Devon, England, since this was when he was apparently instrumental in encouraging Devon immigrants to settle in the Exeter area.[146]

While Carling's family roots were in Yorkshire, his wife's were in Devon. She was Ann Balkwill, the daughter of John Balkwill, the first Devon man to settle in the area. Her and her father's continuing contacts with family and friends would have enabled Isaac to attract Devon immigrants to Exeter. Sixty years later, John Hurdon remarked in a letter that Exeter had become a thriving village with about 1,900 inhabitants, one quarter being of Devon descent: "Seven miles away is the village of Crediton and to the north twenty miles away is Clinton, all Devonshire names."[147]

The sudden appearance of substantial Methodist congregations in Huron County in the 1840s testified to the strong English presence in the region. The first preaching circuit extended north along the London Road, passing through Biddulph, McGillivray, Stephen, Usborne, Hay, and Tuckersmith Townships in Huron County (Map 20). Stephen Township had its so-called "Devonshire Chapel" by 1845, and twelve years later a Wesleyan Methodist chapel appeared at Francistown in Hibbert Township (Perth County). Four Bible Christian circuits were also established by 1846, covering much of the Huron Tract. One was based at Clinton (Hullett Township), a second at Exeter (Usborne Township), a third at Mitchell (Logan Township), while a fourth one was in London Township in Middlesex County. All were positioned on major colonization roads.

Stephen Township had its first Bible Christian church in 1855 and in the following year so had Exeter.[148] The Exeter circuit would acquire the Cornish-born Stephen Henry Rice sometime after 1871, thus keeping alive the long-standing West Country links that had developed in this region.[149]

Meanwhile, immigrants from Devon and Cornwall had also moved to Fullarton Township (Perth County) at the eastern end of the Huron Tract during the 1840s.[150] This placed them alongside the already-established "New Devon" communities in south Huron County, providing a continuous settlement chain between Usborne, Stephen, and Fullarton Townships.

While the English were particularly well-represented in south Huron County, they also established major enclaves farther north in Colborne and Hullett Townships, becoming the dominant ethnic group by 1881 (Map 20). The magnet had been the Canada Company town of Goderich, located in Colborne Township. The town attracted a good many English labourers and tradesmen because of the well-paid and plentiful jobs that it had to offer. A typical example was the Suffolk-born John Freeman, who, having arrived in Goderich around 1831, found work as a carpenter more or less immediately, and shortly after this acquired 163 acres of land. "If I clear ten acres every year I shall soon have a good large farm.... When I work for the Canada Company I take half cash and the other half I set off towards paying for my land." By November 1832, he hoped to "give up my carpentering trade ... and work wholly on my farm."[151] This was a well-trodden path for people who came with insufficient cash to set up as farmers immediately.

There were also people like Mary Young and her family who arrived at Wawanosh Township[152] in the 1850s with plenty of capital, having sold their farm at Port Credit in Toronto Township (Peel County).[153] After having emigrated twenty years earlier with her husband, Samuel, from Aughton Parish in the East Riding of Yorkshire, Mary was probably seeking a fresh start after becoming widowed, while her family probably wanted to take advantage of the new farming opportunities that were becoming available in this region.[154]

William Cattermole, the Canada Company's East Anglia agent, was instrumental in attracting hundreds of people in his area to the western peninsula. His sales pitch was directed at both the poor and affluent alike, but he especially targeted men with capital and farming experience. In 1831, Cattermole supervised the crossings for 1,200 mostly poor Suffolk, Norfolk, and Essex farm labourers and their families, but in the following year he hit the jackpot when he persuaded a moneyed group from Suffolk and Kent to emigrate. Many settled on the Canada Company lands in and near Guelph. In all, Cattermole organized the departure of around 750 South of England immigrants in the spring of 1832.[155] On June 26, the *Montreal Gazette* reported the safe arrival of 460 of them — forty of whom left at Kingston, ninety at Cobourg, 156 at York [Toronto], and 174 who "were heading for Hamilton." Many of the latter "were highly respectable families who came out in the *Caroline* with Mr. Cattermole and proceeded to Guelph and Goderich."

The steady influx of English people to the town of Guelph and the surrounding area made them a major presence in the southeastern part of Wellington County. By 1881, the English were the largest ethnic group in Guelph Township, and in Eramosa and Pilkington, its neighbouring townships (Map 20). Most had come entirely unaided.

The even more remote areas between Lake Huron and Georgian Bay were the last areas in the western peninsula to be colonized. To encourage settlers to come to the region, the government had offered fifty-acre lots as free grants on either side of the new colonization roads, which extended through Bruce and Grey Counties. Both the Garafraxa Road, linking Guelph with Owen Sound (formerly Sydenham), and the Durham Road, linking Durham with Kincardine, helped to facilitate a growing influx of people (Map 20). The strategy worked, and by as early as 1843 the government had to announce that "lots on the Garafraxa and Owen Sound road" were "no longer open for settlement on the principle of free grants" because most had been occupied. However, the government would make grants available "on the same conditions in the immediate vicinity of the roads, which will afford the means of advantageous settlement."[156]

The availability of free land in a newly opened region was a major lure to already-established settlers as well as to immigrants from Britain. The enterprising Joseph Bacon from Essex ventured into Bruce County shortly after the construction of the Garafraxa Road, having first settled in Arthur Township (Wellington County) in 1840. A labourer from Debden Parish, he and his wife, Susannah Franklin, had arrived in 1835 and almost certainly received assistance to emigrate.[157] When free grants became available along the Durham Road, the Bacon family moved immediately to Brant Township in Bruce County. By 1850 the family were living "in a shanty and clearing." Joseph's "brave wife" was remembered as "the first woman to become a permanent settler in the township."[158] Initially, Joseph and six of his seven sons owned land near Walkerton and his four daughters also lived in the area. However, by 1881 only two of his eleven children still remained, with the rest having gone to Manitoba or the United States.[159]

Thomas Parkin and Robert Legge, both farm workers from Beeford Parish in the East Riding of Yorkshire, also had a tough beginning. Emigrating with their wives in 1857, they rented land initially in Scott Township in Ontario County, a region that had strong appeal to Yorkshire settlers. By 1881, they had saved sufficient funds to purchase wilderness land in Manitoulin Island in northern Ontario.[160] Having plenty of sons to carry out the backbreaking work of felling trees and planting crops, they established a farm. But life was a constant struggle, and in 1910 their surviving children moved to Saskatchewan and the Kootenay region of British Columbia.[161]

By contrast, Ella Tanner's great-great-grandfather had a far easier time. A chemist (pharmacist) from Somerset, he came to the Niagara District around 1836 with plenty of capital: "I am told that he had considerable money when he came to Canada as he bought farms and had a general store in the village of Smithville, and his income from other properties in the larger centres enabled him and his family to live comfortably and later to loan money to his children to start them in business."[162]

The family went from strength to strength when Ella's grandfather William Tanner established a lumbering business in the area. Selling it in 1872, he then repeated the process at "a place on Georgian Bay" in Tay Township (Simcoe County) that he called Tannerville [near Waubaushene] where, with his sons' help, "he built lumber mills and houses for their employees."[163] And later generations of Tanners would go on to acquire large farms near Regina, Saskatchewan."[164] This pattern of colonizers establishing themselves in well-settled areas, then selling up and moving on to buy land on favourable terms in remote stretches of Upper Canada or the Prairies, would be repeated over and over again.

The free grant lands, available in some remote areas of central and northern Ontario, were a great enticement, although the rewards required Herculean effort and stamina. A Canadian government communiqué in 1870 stressed that immigrants who took up free grant lands without first having provided a financial cushion for themselves were likely to fail. They needed to earn sufficient money to subsist until they could obtain their first crop. This should not have been a difficult hurdle, given the stated vacancies for thirty to forty thousand agricultural labourers at the time.[165]

Nevertheless, some people threw themselves into farming without the necessary experience, in some cases having been enticed by unscrupulous agents who glossed over the difficulties they would face. For instance, Henry Verrall was discouraged from running lectures in Ontario promoting free grant lands by no less a figure than the Ontario Commissioner of Immigration. The commissioner could not support any agent who failed to mention that "a probationary period is required for most immigrants, in the more unsettled parts of the country, in order that they may obtain sufficient experience to make these free grants lands a satisfactory home from which they can earn a livelihood."[166]

By 1870, the Ontario government was running promotional campaigns to attract colonizers to the Algoma District in northern Ontario. One-hundred-acre free grants were offered to settlers on condition that a stipulated area was cleared and cultivated within a stated period and a house was built.[167] A farmer from Norfolk, who had been living near Sault Ste. Marie for twelve years, thought that the district's big advantage was the availability of mining and lumbering jobs in the winter. "The kind of farmers to come here and the men who would make themselves well-off in a very short time are tenant farmers and others with a little capital and a good practical knowledge of farming ..."[168]

He may well have been speaking of the Cornish miners and their families who settled at Bruce Mines starting in the mid 1850s.[169] The Cornish miners provided the managers of the Bruce copper mines and were the key component of its workforce, thus bringing a steady flow of Cornish people to the area.[170] But when the mines closed in 1876, they moved out, dispersing to other mining centres, especially those in the United States.[171] Nevertheless, in 1881 the English were still the dominant ethnic group in Bruce Mines, accounting for 52 percent of the population, while in Sault Ste. Marie they represented 39 percent of the population (Map 21).

Map 21: Reference Map of Northern Ontario

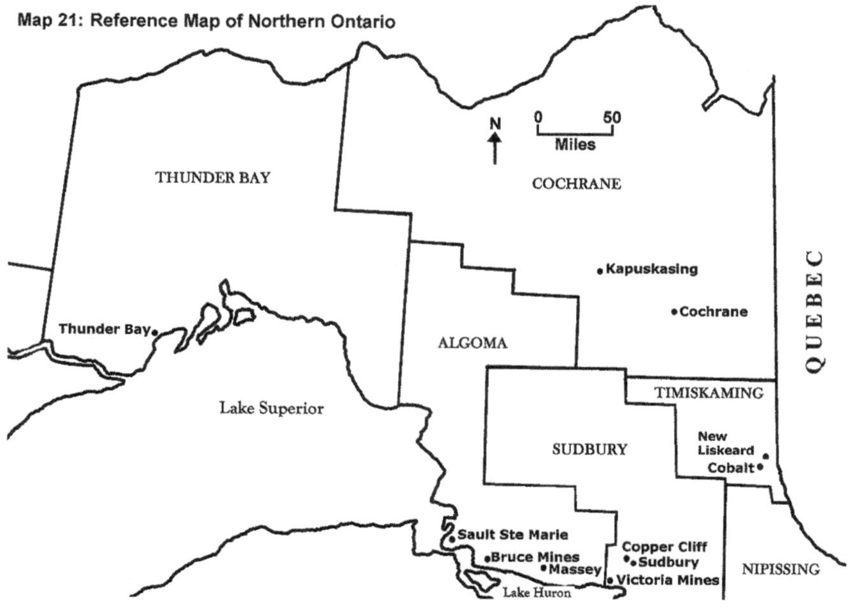

Courtesy Library and Archives Canada, C-028460.

Mr. and Mrs. Sotheran, photographed near New Liskeard (Timiskaming District), Ontario, in 1928. Named after Liskeard in Cornwall, it was established in the late 1890s. With the discovery of silver deposits at nearby Cobalt in 1903, mines were opened soon after.

The free grant lands being offered in the Muskoka and Parry Sound Districts to the east of Georgian Bay were a factor in the growing influx of English immigrants to the area, so much so that the Society for the Propagation of the Gospel in Foreign Parts had an Anglican missionary in the region by 1882. In his report written from Aspdin in the Muskoka District, the Reverend William Compton noted that at least two thirds of his congregations originated "from country places in England."[172]

In his congregation at Burk's Falls in the Parry Sound District was the widow of a Shropshire rector, two sons of different English rectors, and the sons of two English squires. "This fact alone will show what a serious mistake is made by many who have got the notion into their minds that the settlers on the Free Grant Lands are generally of a low and ignorant class."[173] One or two of the wealthier church members may have been upper-class "remittance men," since the remote stretches of central Ontario were well-known boltholes for such people.[174]

Flushed with the successful completion of Saints Church at Burk's Falls, his sixteenth "place of worship in the Backwoods," Reverend Compton marvelled that four years earlier there had not even been a road "through the Bush to where now stands the nucleus of a considerable village."[175] The choir at the opening ceremony, which attracted "upwards of one hundred and seventy people — nearly all from England," included a bass singer from London, a Winchester [Cathedral] chorister, a tenor who had been "a Lancashire collier," and "a young lady from Bedfordshire."[176] Four years later, the Society for the Propagation of the Gospel received a report stressing the need for an Anglican missionary to be sent to the Rabbit Mountain area in the Thunder Bay District, where a silver mine had just been opened, and to the region just east of Bruce Mines in the Algoma District.[177]

Location preferences changed as new areas were being opened up for settlers. The Maritimes had lost out to Upper and Lower Canada by 1830, but later in the century it was their turn to lose out to the Golden West. The arrival of steamships and a coast-to-coast trans-Canada railway had made mass migration feasible. The English dominated this influx, having been attracted by the manufacturing jobs being created in the expanding industrial areas of Ontario and Quebec and by the good agricultural opportunities on offer in the Prairie provinces and British Columbia. A new chapter in the colonization of Canada had begun.

CHAPTER 4

Westward to Manitoba and Saskatchewan

> *Part of the charm of the west, and of the people there, was that you could walk into a shack on the prairie and find three copies of Punch and Tatler[magazines] on the table, see an old family portrait or a piece of antique silver.*[1]

May Newnham had first-hand knowledge of the Prairie West's appeal to the much-maligned affluent, middle-class Englishmen who, having fallen on hard times, had sought a new life in Western Canada.[2] Her husband, Noel Jackman, son of a wealthy stockbroker from Kent, "wanted something more exciting than working in an office" — his fate when his father's business was facing disaster. So, he and his brother, aged eighteen and seventeen respectively, headed west in 1904, taking up homesteads in Shellbrook near the city of Prince Albert in Saskatchewan. Then, following the stock market crash of 1913, their parents joined them, they too leaving "a comfortable life in England" for "a log cabin on the prairie."[3]

Despite their privileged start in life and inexperience of farming, the brothers prospered. When Noel married the Canadian-born May Newnham, daughter of Saskatchewan's Anglican bishop, in 1922, "the rigorous homesteading days were over and the farm was all established; but conditions were still pretty primitive by modern standards.... In the very cold weather everything froze up at night as tight as a drum, the water in the pails ... the kettle on the cook-stove and even occasionally the bread in the cupboard. There was hoarfrost on the blankets and on our eyelashes when we wakened in the morning."[4]

Of course, the English middle classes were just one small component of the great stream of people who came to the Prairies. Ontario supplied many of the earliest waves of migrants during the 1870s and 1880s, although substantial numbers also came from the Eastern Townships and the Maritime provinces. As news spread "of the new frontier, with its prairie land, which held neither stone nor stump to check the plough," hundreds of people sought the better life that beckoned.[5]

The 1870 arrivals travelled along the newly opened Dawson route, linking the Great Lakes with Red River (Winnipeg), and the trails that connected the various fur-trade forts.[6] As the Bishop of Saskatchewan reported in 1881, "in the district of Prince Albert, on the northern branch of the Saskatchewan River, the population has risen within the last two years from about eight hundred to between four and five thousand. Settlers have travelled from three hundred to eight hundred miles without the aid of a railway so as to obtain the advantages of the first choice of land in the new settlements."[7] However, a decade later journeys were being transformed by the building of the Canadian Pacific Railway lines. They snaked their way across vast prairie landscapes, revolutionizing communications for both people and goods. And for the towns and villages that lay in their path, the railways brought a new era of economic growth and prosperity.

Farmers of English descent who had settled previously in the western peninsula of Upper Canada were particularly well-represented in this influx of people. By 1926, Saskatchewan had more Ontario-born residents than Manitoba and Alberta combined, the majority having English origins.[8] People who came directly from England did not arrive in appreciable numbers until the 1890s, but by the early 1900s their population was soaring. They, too, favoured Saskatchewan. Nearly 50 percent of all English-born farmers and farm workers who had settled in the three Prairie provinces by 1926 were to be found in Saskatchewan. By this time, English settlers had become concentrated in southwest Manitoba and across great swathes of southern Saskatchewan.[9]

Before colonization could begin, the Hudson's Bay Company had first to relinquish control over its vast fur-trading territory. This had been achieved through the passing of the Rupert's Land Act in 1868. But this transfer of territory to the new Dominion of Canada did not please everyone. The French Métis population,[10] who were understandably outraged at not being consulted, felt that their status, land rights, and way of life were being placed under threat. So, feeling threatened, they mounted a campaign of resistance led by Louis Riel.[11] However, both the Red River Resistance of 1869–70 and subsequent Northwest Rebellion of 1885 were put down swiftly.[12] Having secured its jurisdiction over Western Canada, the government then regulated agricultural settlement by passing the Dominion Lands Act of 1872, which provided basic rules for homesteading. Under this legislation a settler could obtain 160 acres of free land for a $10 registration fee.[13] Full legal title was given after three years occupancy if the settler cultivated forty acres and built a house.

While Manitoba acquired large groups of Mennonites from southern Russia and large contingents from Iceland in the mid 1870s, the influx from Britain was slow to materialize.[14] Nevertheless, with the completion of the Canadian Pacific Railway in 1895, the adoption of faster-maturing wheat that suited the shorter growing season, and the growing scarcity of good farmland in the United States, more and more British immigrants set their sights on Western Canada. Strenuous promotional campaigns run by the federal government and the Canadian Pacific Railway Company helped British immigration levels to soar. These reached a crescendo by the early 1900s, when Clifford Sifton became minister of the interior in the Canadian government. Believing that the future prosperity of Canada depended on large-scale immigration, he convinced the federal government to invest heavily in promotional campaigns that would bring experienced agriculturalists from a variety of countries to Western Canada.[15] The people who responded hoped to benefit from the better prospects that they believed the Canadian West had to offer. However, as many would discover, the reality of what they found sometimes fell short of their expectations.

With its extensive land holdings of 25 million acres, lying between Winnipeg and the Rocky Mountains, the Canadian Pacific Railway Company also became a major player in the colonization of the Prairies and was particularly anxious to promote settlements, since its revenues depended on both land sales and the growth in railway traffic that would come from an expanding population. Adopting promotional tactics similar to those used by the federal government, the company employed agents to tour Britain, giving lectures and handing out leaflets, and also flooded eastern Canada with newspaper advertisements and posters.[16] But, as stated previously, the influx of settlers began long before the railways were constructed. Being already acclimatized to

Map 22: English Concentrations in South Western Manitoba, 1911.

SOURIS Census districts where English were the largest ethnic group and at least 35% of the population.

◆ City
● Town/village

pioneering life, the first settlers from eastern Canada were better placed than foreigners to cope with the arduous conditions. They arrived both as individuals and in groups.

The Ontario-born John Ralston, a woollen manufacturer from Huntingdon (Quebec), was the first of three leaders to bring settlers to Rapid City,[17] north of Brandon, Manitoba (Map 22). Arriving in Winnipeg in 1873 with over three hundred people recruited from eastern Canada, Ralston hoped to launch communities in the four planned townships along the Little Saskatchewan River that he had obtained from the government; but things did not go according to plan. When grasshopper-infested fields near Winnipeg came into view, his group panicked. While Ralston went on to Rapid City and built a number of the town's early residences and became one of its leading businessmen, the group dispersed, some heading east, while others settled in Winnipeg.[18] Three years later the shipping agent Creasey J. Whellans, who originated from Huntingdonshire, brought two hundred mainly English settlers to six townships along the Little Saskatchewan River, which he had obtained from the government.[19] Then, in 1878, the Quebec-born Reverend Louis Olivier Armstrong, an Anglican minister, encouraged fifty families in the Montreal area to settle in Rapid City. Acting as their leader, his brother-in-law, George Lindsay, became a prominent Rapid City merchant.[20] Undoubtedly, Rapid City owed its strong English presence, as revealed later in the 1911 Census, to this early influx from eastern Canada.[21]

Crystal City, located southwest of Winnipeg near the American border, had a Cornish founder — Thomas Greenway. Having immigrated to the Devon and Cornwall stronghold of Centralia in Huron County (Upper Canada) as a child and later becoming a prominent merchant and politician, Greenway purchased an eight-hundred-acre farm in Manitoba in 1878. He then returned to Centralia to gather together family, friends, neighbours, and other followers who formed his group. To ensure land transactions ran smoothly, he established the Rock Lake Colonization Company. He brought out more settlers over the next three years, many of whom probably shared his West Country roots, and then set to work building a store, church, and school as well as homes for the rapidly growing community.[22]

Predictably, the Bible Christian movement, a Methodist sect that had originated in Cornwall, appealed to Greenway's Centralia recruits. By 1882, Bible Christian circuits had been established in Crystal City and nearby Darlingford and Thornhill: Thomas's brother, the Reverend John Greenway, "preached in Crystal City in the morning and Alexandria (near Thornhill) at night."[23] However, the sect had only a short existence, becoming absorbed by the wider Methodist movement two years later.[24]

Meanwhile, the prospect of homesteading in the West was beginning to find favour in Cornwall itself. Mr. Cole, an immigration agent based in Cobourg, Ontario, informed the immigration department in Britain in 1876 that he knew of people from twenty-five to thirty Cornish parishes who wanted to emigrate to Canada, some wishing to go west.[25] The likelihood is that news of the Crystal City success story had reached Cornwall. The concentrations of Bible Christians in and near Neepawa and Portage la Prairie in 1891 suggest that these areas may have also attracted people from Devon and Cornwall (Map 22).[26] "A considerable settlement of English people" had been established in Glendale around 1879, and shortly before this some English settlers had gone to live in the area between Neepawa and Eden. Some had actually moved into the area from the longer-settled districts of Red River and Portage la Prairie.[27]

In addition to these managed groups, plenty of English people came to Manitoba on their own. Roger Bell is a typical example. Having arrived from London Township in Ontario with his wife in 1871, he worked initially as a farmhand before acquiring farmland northeast of Portage la Prairie. Another example is R.D. Byers. Having previously resided from boyhood in Argenteuil, Quebec, and later Hawkesbury, Ontario, he came to the Portage la Prairie area soon after, as did the Yorkshire-born Thomas Swales, who made a similar detour with his life via Ontario.[28] Swales bought land three miles (4.8 kilometres) north of the city and built the region's first frame house. By 1881, Portage la Prairie was said to be "a thriving town of about two thousand inhabitants and it is just like Winnipeg, only smaller. It is thronged with Englishmen of very good families, who seem very nice fellows, only a little too fond of billiards and sporting of one kind or another."[29]

John Angus transformed himself from being a policeman in Whitby, Ontario, to being the owner of Elkhorn's first butcher shop (Map 22). Establishing a farm near the Saskatchewan border, he, his wife, and their ten children added to the growing English population in the Brandon District.[30] Then there was John Lund, descended from one of the many Yorkshire families who had settled near Sackville, New Brunswick, in the 1770s. He arrived at Lipentott near Elkhorn in 1882.[31] Yet another Yorkshireman, David Harrison, formerly from London, Ontario, arrived in the area in 1882. Becoming a rancher, he was elected within months of his arrival to represent Minnedosa West in the Legislative Assembly of Manitoba.[32] And when the Devon-born William Hey Palmer began farming at Greenridge, south of Winnipeg, in 1890, he proclaimed that "Manitoba is a great country for the poor man; our land is good, equal to the best loam land of Sandford or Crediton[in Devon]."[33] Presumably he was doing well.

Shortly after Thomas Greenway felt inspired to found Crystal City, the Ontario-born William Sowden made a similar move. Together with his recruits, he founded Souris to the southwest of the city of Brandon. He assembled a colonization syndicate composed of businessmen from his home village of Millbrook in Cavan Township (Durham County) and obtained two and a half townships along the banks of the Souris River. In 1881, his Millbrook colonists, together with their cattle, boarded a train and travelled to St. Boniface (Winnipeg) "with supreme optimism, tense eagerness and suppressed excitement," taking two and a half days just to reach Portage la Prairie.[34] When James Hoskin, son of English immigrants, arrived at the town of Souris from Peterborough in 1882 to serve as its Bible Christian preacher, he no doubt found plenty of people wishing to uphold their old world religious traditions.[35] Later on came John Atkinson from Penrith (Cumberland), who took up work as a farm labourer in Boissevain to the south of Souris.[36]

Five years later the local Anglican missionary, Reverend Corroe Coggs, commented that some of Souris's English residents had more money than sense: "In my visiting I come across numerous instances of well-educated young men from our English public schools and universities" who were frittering their time away. He tried "to reach them through the channels of their sports" — especially through cricket — without much success, and concluded that "drink" was to blame. "It is a plague amongst us and the frequent remittances [regular payments] from parents tend to encourage it among the thriftless."[37] Rich or poor, people of English origin accounted for 42 percent of Souris's population by 1911 and they were also dominant in most of the nearby towns and villages in the Brandon District (Map 22).

There was certainly a huge contrast between the English dandies in Souris, who so annoyed the Reverend Coggs, and Ernest Smith, a labourer from Weston-Super-Mare (Somerset). With the railway line having reached Brandon by 1881, it must have seemed a good place to settle. Arriving in Brandon two years later with plenty of determination but little money, Ernest's first abode was the immigrant shed.[38] "Here it does not cost me anything for lodging and I can board myself for about $2 a week, whereas the cheapest boarding house in the town is $5 a week."[39] As it was June, he hoped to find employment on a local farm. But that was not to be, and so he travelled to Alberta to take up a job on the railways. Passing through Calgary, "a very pretty place on the Bow River consisting at present mostly of tents and a few log houses," he headed for a railway camp, where his sleeping accommodation would be the underside of a wagon.[40] Unfortunately, Ernest succumbed to the "tiresome journey" he undertook with his fellow workers. The rough roads and extreme cold were unbearable. His friend Octavius "kept warm stones to his feet" and later carried him "as he could hardly stand," but he died soon after from typhoid fever. The friend's final act of kindness was to write to Ernest's family offering his condolences.[41]

The rosy picture painted of Manitoba by Thomas Moore, an English commentator and emigration promoter, made no mention of the world that Ernest Smith had experienced. Moore visited Birtle, to the north of Brandon, in 1883, to gather material for a booklet he was writing, highlighting the area's high desirability as an overseas destination. Coming from Staffordshire in the Midlands, he slanted his comments to find favour with English northerners who might have fancied living in a genteel and pleasant version of Surrey:

> We are nearing Birtle. This is Surrey surely — hill and dale, wood and river, farm houses peeping out from their resting places, wheat and oats growing luxuriously…

> Picture to yourself a Malvern [Hills] doubled — hills on each side.... The neighbourhood of Birtle is exceedingly fertile; there is quite a large agricultural community there and most of them English. I was told that at the last ball given in the winter there were more than seventy ladies present, so you see it cannot be uncivilized.[42]

Whether anyone in England was actually taken in by this silly hype is open to question!

In the meantime, the Red River colony,[43] founded in 1812 during the heady days of the fur trade, had become the city of Winnipeg, and with the coming of the railways its commerce and industry were expanding rapidly by 1897. This in turn brought a rapid rise in population, among whom the English were well represented. Of course, the fur trade had brought a substantial British presence to the area long before

St. James Anglican Church, Winnipeg, built 1853. A new church was built in 1935 to replace the original church, which was restored in 1967, and is now a provincial heritage site.

this. Ever anxious to establish Church of England congregations in the New World, the Society for the Propagation of the Gospel had sent the Reverend William Henry Taylor to Rupert's Land in 1850 to serve as its first Anglican missionary. He presided over the building of St. James Anglican Church, which was completed three years later; but due to ill health, the reverend returned to his native Worcestershire in 1867.[44]

Initially, Reverend Taylor's congregation consisted of forty families (two hundred people), who were mainly English and Scottish. He had regularly to navigate himself through dangerous terrain and needed great reserves of stamina and resilience, even when making the relatively short journey to a local school:

> As the Spring advanced the travelling was not good … and the journey obliged me to be on horseback. The soil naturally soft and sticky — let the horse in so deep and adhered so fast to the legs and hoofs of the poor animal, that it was the greatest work of all getting along at all. Then, the creeks were all swollen with the melting of the snow and were in places so wide and deep to be crossed [only] with great trouble and difficulty.… When I came to the great creek … I ventured [across] and the ice broke, letting both myself and horse into the stream that was running underneath — the more the horse plunged the greater the hole and I found that in order to get out I must dismount.… I was struggling with the great pieces of ice while the horse, landing on the other side, was going briskly for the school room. A neighbour … seeing the horse without a rider, expected what had happened and catching the horse brought it back to me.[45]

When she visited Winnipeg from Manchester forty-three years later, Margaret Ashton noticed that it had "Chinese laundries with the smiling Chinese at work ironing in a window — there were hotels that had only a billiard room and a bar visible from the entrance, eating houses of all sorts and hotels without numbers.… It is the first growing western city we have seen and has wild-west streets, with the railway through one and a very new look about it, as if it all had been begun yesterday."[46] When Richard Goodridge from Devon, a retired army officer who settled at Headingley near Winnipeg, first came to the area, he noticed the self-satisfied English exhibitionists who paraded along its streets:

> There is a class who come out here simply to live, and to take things easily. Such people seem entirely out of place in a progressive country like this; if they do not go forward with the advancing tide, they must inevitably fall behind. One sees numbers of young, smartly dressed fellows, ornate with gold chains, rings and solitaires, with finely starched linen — fresh arrivals from England — lounging about the streets of Winnipeg; and we wonder whether they have all realized what farming in Manitoba means![47]

Goodridge had purchased a farm for his three sons, not intending to settle at Headingley himself, but he remained for eight years. Initially he had been highly critical of the area: "Speaking for my wife and myself, we should indeed be very sorry were we compelled to live here always. It is a pioneer country — everything rough, and by contrast with previous experience of other countries, terribly uncivilized."[48] However, by 1889, Goodridge's assessment had changed: "The pioneer character of the entire country is rapidly disappearing; and so far as the neighbourhood of Winnipeg itself, in the city may be obtained every luxury that money can procure, as in any city of the Old World."[49] It also gave James Simpkin his break in life. Born in Blackburn (Lancashire), James had been employed in a cotton factory since the age of ten. Transforming himself into a Winnipeg carpenter in the early 1900s, he was later elected to the Winnipeg city council.[50]

While slow to begin, the influx from Britain grew steadily from the late nineteenth century. The severe economic depression that gripped the old country, the greater use of mechanization in both farming and industry, and rising imports of cheap food from abroad contributed to the miserable plight of labourers, who found themselves surplus to requirements.

They hoped to find work in the cities and towns but instead merely swelled the ranks of the unemployed. Foreign competition and the demise of traditional forms of employment were making a miserable situation worse for many people. Not surprisingly, against this background emigration beckoned. However, as far as the Canadian government was concerned, the wrong sorts of people were heading west. The Prairies were crying out for men with agricultural skills to operate ploughs and plant crops, but instead England was sending out hordes of its destitute urban workers. Some might have agreed to be retrained, but many had little or no interest in farming. Thus there was a fundamental mismatch between the English preference for urban living and the provinces' need to fill agricultural job vacancies. As often happens in such situations, both sides skirted around the problem. The English re-established themselves in prairie urban centres, while agents employed by the government conveniently mislabelled them as farm workers to protect their bonuses.

Federal and provincial agents promoted Canada's farming opportunities, but the actual task of transporting immigrants went to the booking agents of the steamship and railway companies who were stationed across the cities and towns of Britain.[51] For their part, the booking agents received a bonus of £1 for each so-called desirable immigrant (farmers, farm workers, and domestic servants) who purchased a steamship ticket; but many agents abused the system by falsely describing urban workers as potential farmhands.[52] As a result, an increasing number of Englishmen were seeking work in the Canadian towns and cities. Fearing that they would take jobs away from Canadian workers, leaders of the Labour movement were highly critical of this development. Also, they were genuinely moved by the plight of the men who were unable to find work:

> Nine tenths of the destitution of Canada today [1908] is caused by the heartless misrepresentation of unprincipled and unscrupulous immigration agents, bonused by the government at so much per head for every immigrant they could induce to come to Canada.... It is nothing less than a crime for the government to stand by and allow this injustice to continue.[53]

The antics of A.J. McMillan, an agent with a Warwickshire address but based in Brandon, help to explain the extent of the deception. In December 1896, the federal and Manitoba governments each agreed to pay him $900 for the recruitment of 250 English farmers and farm workers whose travel arrangements he was to organize.[54] McMillan immediately produced glossy posters advertising his "personally conduced party to Canada," in the hope of attracting the people he was contracted to locate. The group would sail in the *Numidian* from Liverpool in April 1897 and "a competent government agent, would be available on the crossing to give advice and assistance to settlers."[55] However, instead of obtaining his own recruits, McMillan simply took the names of people who appeared on booking agents' lists and sent them to officials in Canada. His defence, when challenged, was to blame the agents — "a little clique … who, from motives of jealousy and fear [of his] changed methods in conducting immigration work are determined … to discredit me if possible in official quarters in Canada."[56]

Naturally, when McMillan's group reached Winnipeg, immigration officials were already on their guard. His cryptic telegram spoke of "about 40 British [people] for the immigration hall," who included several families; others would go to a hotel. In addition, there were three married couples who wanted farm employment while "about sixty young men, a lot of them practically agriculturalists, require work, some at homesteads." But he did not provide names. After checking the passenger list, it was obvious that McMillan's group amounted to forty-four at most. And far from being the agriculturalists, as claimed by McMillan, they were, in fact, town dwellers:

> They were mostly undersized town-bred men, and without means, and of whom four are still in this town [Winnipeg] helpless and useless.… it is wrong to send such domestic failures, who are more fitted to be cared for in a Salvation Army barracks than to live in a Manitoba homestead.
>
> The whole system of bonussed emigrants is pernicious, for it necessitates the employment of agents, in itself an

> error, for to earn the bonus the agent will ship anybody, and among the crowd are sure to be some who are utterly unfit for the position of life they have chosen.[57]

Officials concluded that McMillan had recruited "not more than half a dozen bona fide settlers, that is, men with means who were prepared to engage in farming on their own account." He certainly would not have received his $1,800, nor did Manitoba get its much sought-after agriculturalists.

Surviving agents' lists would suggest that McMillan's attempted hoax was not that unusual. The Lancashire-born T. Bernard Willans, employed as an immigration agent by the federal government between 1902 and 1907, had a convincing line of chat, but he too bent the rules. Having moved to Neepawa, to the northwest of Portage la Prairie, Willans made annual visits to England to find his recruits. He ran lecture tours promoting Western Canada in the counties of Lancashire, Yorkshire, Middlesex, Surrey, and Norfolk, "where he is well known." In 1905, his advertisement in the *Daily Telegraph* extolling Manitoba's merits had apparently attracted replies from over two hundred people, and afterward he had an average of "thirty to forty people calling to see me."[58] But the list of ninety people he submitted to the immigration department in 1906 made a complete mockery of his job description. He had only recruited two farmers, and they were returning Canadians. The rest were urban workers, some coming with their wives. No doubt, the painters, plumbers, carpenters, bricklayers, clerks, butchers, bakers, blacksmiths, general labourers, engineers, warehousemen, drapers, boilermaker, miners, tailors, and bartenders in Willan's list found work in the town of Neepawa and the surrounding area, but that had not been the object of the exercise.

Be that as it may, English immigrants made the transition to prairie life on their terms. Having been educated in a private school and working as a clerk in London, England, the Cumberland-born Frederick Wicks emigrated to Manitoba in the 1890s in the hope of improving his wages. He worked first as a farmhand and later as a bookkeeper and carpenter in the village of Hamiota to the west of Minnedosa. Then, in 1903, he moved to Shoal Lake where he launched an agricultural implements and livestock business and worked as a manager for Mr. J.H. McLean.[59] Ernest Baxter, who originated from Devon, was homesteading at the time at Hun's Valley,[60] which was also near Minnedosa. The photographs he sent to his mother, of his neighbours and their houses, reveal a man who was well-integrated into his local community. His principal complaint was that the roads were a sea of mud. "Because we ran out of oats I drove over to a man about one mile from here and borrowed a bag to go on with it."[61] It would be several days before he could get to the nearest town and get adequate supplies.

Life was tough for everyone, even for the anonymous wealthy Englishman who railed against the conditions he found in Manitoba. To let off steam he wrote a book "not for the purpose of running down America, but for the purpose of letting anyone who is thinking of emigrating to America know what they may have to go through."[62] He had come to Manitoba in 1891 with the intention of establishing a farm but claimed that he had been hoodwinked by "the many books, pamphlets, etc. (mostly untrue) that have been written about the charms and

Courtesy Glenbow Archives, NA-3080-1.

Log dwelling in Hun's Valley, near Minnedosa, Manitoba, photographed in 1889 by Ernest Baxter, who originated from Devon.

beautiful climate of the North West of Canada."[63] Being a remittance man, and thus having a regular income sent to him by his parents, he had no financial worries. Having been promised plenty "of society, hockey, football, cricket, tennis etc …, I was never so disgusted in my life when I saw the shack that was to be my home for some time."[64] This man could not even begin to understand the intricacies of the world around him, but there were some wise people like Mrs. Cecil Hall who did.

When Mrs. Hall visited her brother's farm in Manitoba in 1882, she discarded her "lady's ways" and threw herself into jobs that she would never have dreamt of doing back home. She helped with hay-making, painted the barn roof, and drove posts into the ground for new fencing "with a fearfully heavy mallet which I can hardly lift." She also drove the wagons regularly. Of course, her brother did the same. In England he could have had any number of labourers and paid them a pittance; but in Manitoba, where wages were high, he "he had to sink the gentleman."

> It is very certain that no gentlemen ought to come out to this country, or, when here, can expect to prosper, unless he has some capital, heaps of energy and brains, or is quite prepared to … work as a common labourer. The latter command the most wonderful wages; there is such a demand for them that one can hardly pick and choose.… It is surprising to me that the whole of the poorer classes in England and Ireland, hearing of these wages, do not emigrate, particularly when now-a-days the steerage in the passenger ships seems to be so comfortable, and that for about six pounds they can be landed on this side of the Atlantic.[65]

In 1921, the English were the largest ethnic group in Manitoba, where they accounted for 28 percent of the population. While there were large concentrations of English in the city of Winnipeg (especially the St. James district) and in Stonewall, just north of Winnipeg, the majority were to be found in the southwest of the province.[66] They were mainly concentrated in a large block extending west from the lower part of Lake

Manitoba to the Saskatchewan border on the north, and along the American border to the south (Map 23). Their numeric presence was strongest in the towns and cities throughout, as would be expected given that a large proportion of the early-twentieth-century arrivals from England had been urban dwellers.

Victorian England was changing, too. Inspired by their Queen, large families of ten and twelve children were common — too many for a business, be it farming or manufacturing, to support; and so the idea of one or two members of a family seeking "their fortunes" overseas was encouraged. As for Saskatchewan, it first acquired British immigrants in

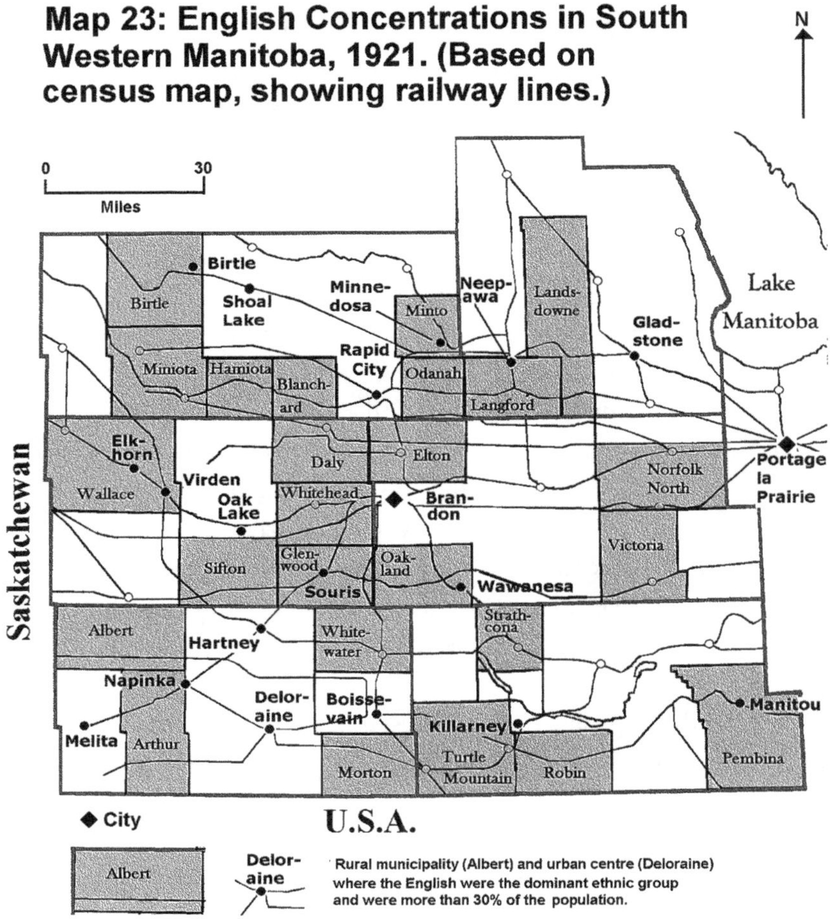

substantial numbers in the early 1880s. Men with capital spotted their chance to turn its vast acreages of open prairie into productive farmland.

Having fallen on hard times, Captain Edward Mitchell Pierce, a Somerset wine merchant and landowner, founded an English colony south of Moosomin, in southeastern Saskatchewan, in the hope that it would restore his fortune (Map 24). Naming it Cannington Manor[67] after

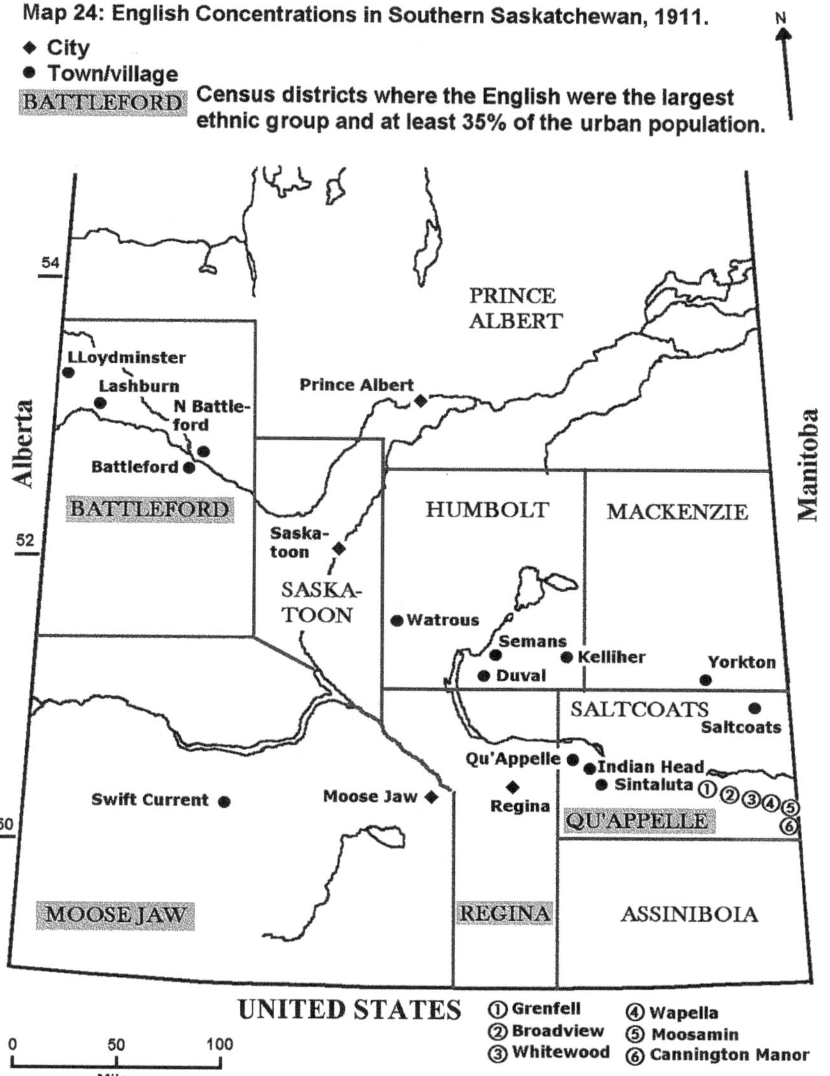

his native Somerset Parish, he arrived with his wife and nine children in 1882 to begin building his English community. His announcements in English newspapers targeted genteel English families whose younger sons might be interested in a western adventure and good farming opportunities.[68] The future Cannington Manor settlement would be a place where gentlemen could "lead and enjoy an old English squire's existence of a century ago."[69] This touch of nostalgia worked and Pierce soon had his first recruits, whom he vetted personally.

Pierce laid out the townsite himself and talent-spotted a Canadian carpenter by the name of Charles Pryce to help him build All Saints Anglican Church, which was completed in 1884. Pierce and his relations raised most of the funds and it was the first Anglican Church in the Qu'Appelle Diocese, to be consecrated: "The cross on the bell tower, porch, front

Captain Edward Mitchell Pierce, founder of the Cannington Manor English settlement in the Qu'Appelle region of Saskatchewan.

Courtesy Library and Archives Canada, MG31-H13.

doors, and pews were all hand-carved. Pryce proved that his talents as a carpenter went beyond driving pegs into the ground by handcrafting the choir stalls, bishop's chair, and faldstool [bishop's backless folding chair] out of birch wood brought down from the Moose Mountain."[70]

Realizing that he needed a regular income stream, Pierce established an Agricultural College. For £100 a year he offered parents with young sons the prospect of having them transformed into gentlemen farmers. The approach proved successful, and between 1884 and 1888 a steady stream of young Englishmen with capital, totalling sixty in all, began arriving at Cannington Manor. Pierce's advertisements also attracted families, some of whom came with servants and lavish possessions to begin their new life. By this time Pierce had built a general store, post office, and gristmill, and soon after that the Mitre Hotel was erected.[71] Henry Brockman, an Anglican clergyman's son who arrived with his brother in 1885, remembered "annual rifle shoots at Winnipeg, Brandon, Virden and Regina and regular games of tennis and cricket in and around Cannington."[72] Everything seemed to be going so well; but Pierce's health was deteriorating and he soon lost interest in trying to educate his pupils.

Later commentators were dismissive of his colonization venture, claiming that Pierce was simply cashing in on gullible parents by taking exorbitant fees for non-existent training. Moreover, it was alleged that many of his "pups," as they became known, were totally unsuited to farming, preferring to waste their time in leisurely pursuits. As their "trunks stuffed with tennis rackets, cricket bats and stumps, gun cases, books, paint-boxes, easels, musical instruments, evening dress and riding habits" were unloaded from the railway carriages, Pierce's pupils certainly gave every impression that they intended to cling on to their gentlemanly old world lifestyle.[73] Yet, as Jessie Beckton, Pierce's daughter, wrote later, this emphasis on frivolous pursuits fails to address the fact that Cannington Manor had been founded with the best of intentions:

> My father's original plan … was to found a settlement in which Englishmen with small capital or incomes could create homes, enjoy a simple life, farming or otherwise and provide an outlet for their sons. Much has been

> said and some ridicule attached to the farming of the "English dudes" usually by those who accord first place to the spade or plough, forgetting that, wonderfully useful as it is, it is not the only implement necessary for the development of the Empire.[74]

A grandson, H.V.S. Page, reiterated this sentiment, claiming that younger generations of the family wanted Jessie Beckton to set the record straight by providing a less biased account of the settlement:

> For many years, sensational and highly coloured accounts of Cannington Manor have appeared in many newspapers and magazines in western Canada, written from hearsay evidence and superficially researched; and giving the impression of a settlement built on racing, steeple-chasing, fox-hunting, hunt ball, tennis parties, etc., which have given a totally incorrect picture of the settlement. References to "remittance men" were common but.... There was not one remittance man in the true settlement.[75]

Although some of Pierce's recruits attracted considerable criticism for their seeming disregard of farming and preference for sporting activities, the settlement did flourish. By 1888, the year of Pierce's death, it was a mixed community of homesteaders, tradesmen, upper-class families, and young bachelors, having between 150 and 200 settlers. Four years later, an anonymous writer referred to the "several hundred people who have devoted themselves successfully not only to farming but to the raising of cattle" living south of Moosomin. "They have postal facilities, stores, mills for grinding flour and sawing lumber, and form the nucleus of what will quickly develop into a populous and wealthy district."[76] Arthur Hewlett, son of a wealthy Lancashire businessman, was clearly one of Pierce's prodigies. He began farming in his own right in 1897, helped by a loan from his father, and despite initial setbacks he developed a successful farm on which he was able to employ "numerous young fellows from England."[77]

And there were other former pupils like William and Ernest Beckton, both well-educated boys from Manchester, who went on to establish a famous horse-breeding ranch at Cannington in 1888, using money they inherited after the death of a grandfather. They lavished funds on Disbury Ranch, named after their hometown near Manchester. It was claimed that "the horse stable was finer than most of the Canadian settlers' homes, or those of the Becktons' British neighbours for that matter."[78] Unfortunately they lacked the necessary business acumen to succeed, and with mounting debts the brothers returned to England in 1895, while other English families sold their property and moved out soon after. The final blow came in 1902 when the new Canadian Pacific Railway branch line bypassed Cannington by ten miles (sixteen kilometres). This misfortune brought the town's twenty years of existence to a sudden and conclusive end.

Just as Cannington Manor was being founded in 1882, another group of mainly English settlers from York County, Ontario, were making their way to the future Yorkton in southeastern Saskatchewan, near the Manitoba border (Map 24). They were joined by a smaller number of people from other parts of Ontario, Quebec, the Maritimes, Manitoba, Britain, and the United States. All had been recruited by the York Farmers' Colonization Company. Two years later, Yorkton had around 164 settlers, and with the arrival of the Manitoba and North Western Railway line in 1890, many more followed. Its future was now secured, although the townsite had to be moved closer to the railway station.

Also in 1882 came Ontario people who travelled under the auspices of the Temperance Colonization Society, run by Methodists in Toronto. Their Temperance Colony of around one hundred settlers inadvertently laid the foundations of the future city of Saskatoon. Located along the South Saskatchewan River, the settlement grew slowly at first. Lack of experience with prairie conditions, its isolated location, and the impracticality of trying to maintain a teetotal society in a newly forming pioneer community hindered its development. Later, with the completion in 1890 of a rail line from Qu'Appelle to Prince Albert, which crossed the river at Saskatoon, the colony's future was guaranteed. The increasing trade in commodities spurred its economic life and settlement growth increasingly became concentrated around the railway station.[79] By 1905, when the trickle of immigrants into Saskatchewan became a flood, Saskatoon's population reached 3,011.[80]

Then there was the London Artisan Colonists Society, formed by Lady Burdett-Coutts, Lady Hobart, and others, in 1884 to help unemployed tradesmen in London's East End find jobs in northwest Canada. Twenty families from Bethnal Green were assisted to relocate to an agricultural site near Moosomin, but by 1891 only five families remained on the land.[81] This outcome is hardly surprising, given that few would have had any farming experience. This mistake was repeated three years later when the Church of England Colonization Land Society organized the relocation of English urban workers to a settlement near Saltcoats, to the northwest of Moosomin. Despite finding houses ready for occupancy and some land already under cultivation, the colonists floundered and the site had to be abandoned. Once again, well-meaning organizers failed to recognize that England's urban dwellers did not necessarily want to transform themselves into farmhands and farmers.

However, the deaf men and boys from English cities who were assisted by Jane Elizabeth Groom, herself a deaf missionary, had greater success when they relocated to Wolseley, just south of Indian Head, in 1884 (Map 24). While some found jobs with local farmers, most became cabinet makers, shoemakers, bricklayers, and saddle and harness makers in nearby towns. While the *Manitoba Daily Free Press* in Winnipeg was critical of Groom, bemoaning the fact that "a consignment of deaf mutes has been brought to that city [Winnipeg] from England and dumped into the Immigrant Sheds," other newspapers were far more sympathetic.[82] Groom returned soon after with twenty-four deaf settlers and their families, who included Francis Jefferson, whose letter to a Manchester newspaper indicated that he and his fellow colonists had found work. As an added bonus "many of the [hearing] farmers can converse well with fingers, and they speak highly of the mutes' intelligence, honesty and quickness in learning agricultural work."[83]

In contrast to Groom's modest scheme was Major William Robert Bell's large-scale agricultural venture, which he launched near Indian Head. After founding the Qu'Appelle Valley Farming Company in 1882 and obtaining a staggering 53,000 acres of land from the Canadian government and the Canadian Pacific Railway Company, he embarked on a major development program that included the construction of one hundred buildings. Coming from Brockville, Ontario, he no doubt hoped to attract Ontario people to what would become known as the Bell model farm. Individual plots of 213 acres were offered to farmers, but with mounting debts and poor harvests, Bell's business began to fail. Three years later he had to sell some of his land to appease his creditors.[84] A strenuous attempt was made in 1886 to restore the Bell farm's viability by attracting English farmers with capital. A booklet seeking land sales made it seem like a prosperous, elegant, and sociable haven: "Music

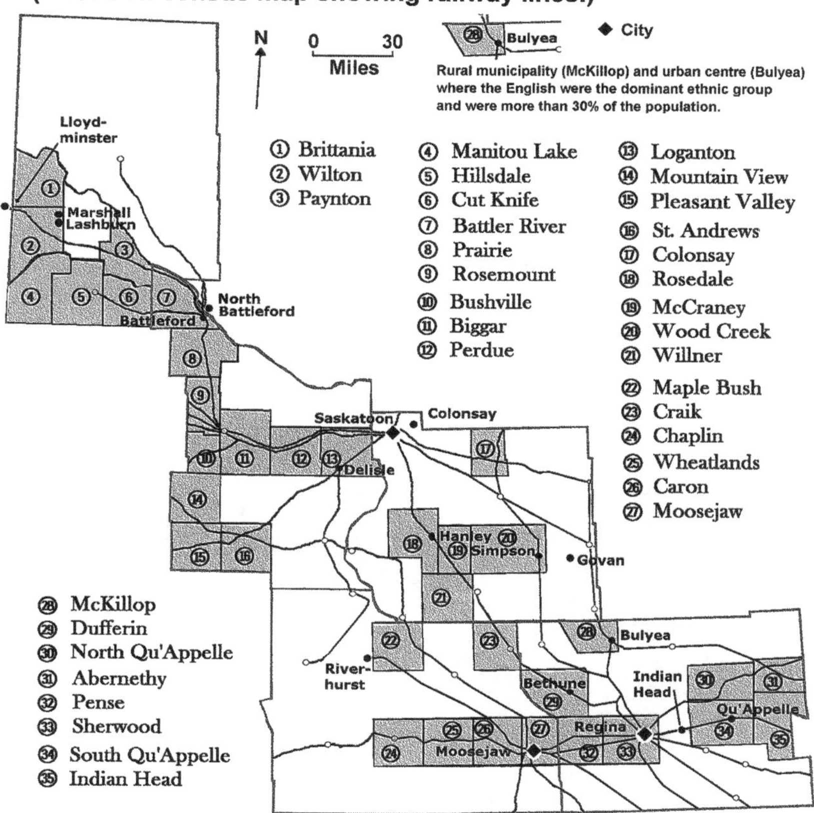

never fails, whilst whist and crib maintain their full sway.... In the winter livestock can be safely entrusted to the farm servants, with the occasional oversight of a neighbour, should the proprietor decide to pay a visit to the Carnival scenes in Montreal or a trip across [the Atlantic] to spend his Christmas in the old country."[85] Alas, this approach had little success and eventually Bell lost everything to his creditors.

Meanwhile, as the desire to emigrate spread across England's industrial heartland in the early twentieth century, an Anglican clergyman had the vision of founding a farming paradise in the Canadian West. The Barr Colony, established in 1903 on the Saskatchewan-Alberta border, was the brainchild of the Reverend Isaac Montgomery Barr, a naïve and inept man who attracted considerable controversy from the very beginning. Nevertheless, despite his shortcomings and the setbacks suffered, his two thousand colonists laid the foundations of an extensive English enclave north of Battleford that complimented the settlements that were also forming west of Saskatoon and overflowing across the border into Alberta (Map 25).

Although the Reverend Barr was convincing in his promotion of Canada's merits, he lacked common sense and organizational ability. He had a misty-eyed, imperialistic notion of founding an all-British agricultural colony, yet recruited most of his colonists from urban England,

Courtesy Library and Archives Canada, a038667.

A photograph, taken in 1903, of the tents near the Immigration Hall at Saskatoon, which provided the initial accommodation for the Barr colonists.

seemingly unaware of their unsuitability as prospective farmers. He sent two thousand people off in late March 1903 in the SS *Lake Manitoba* — a vessel designed to take 700 passengers — and subjected them to numerous delays and discomforts. Having travelled to Saskatoon in filthy immigrant trains, they were cooped up in tents near the immigration hall until preparations were made for the final stage of their journey — a two-hundred-mile trek by wagon to Battleford.[86] With tempers flaring, the group ousted the Reverend Barr as their leader and elected the Reverend George Lloyd (the colony's chaplain) as his replacement.

A settler recalled the bitter recriminations at the time:

> The feeling of dissatisfaction and mistrust culminated shortly after reaching the permanent camp. Mr. Barr had betrayed the trust we had placed in him and the colonists were so enraged he had to literally flee for his life. Fortunately for the future of the settlement the Reverend Lloyd, a man of principle and foresight, took charge. Everyone felt so grateful to Mr. Lloyd that it was decided to call the settlement Lloydminster.[87]

Incredibly, only about 20 percent of the people recruited by the Reverend Barr knew the first thing about farming.[88] However, given that the Canadian Northern Railway reached the area by 1905, the market in tradesmen's jobs grew rapidly. Perhaps some of the colonists who came with an industrial background — such as E. Blackburn, a railway employee, J.J. Blythe, a furnace man, C.H. Bulmer, an iron founder, John Costello, a brakeman, Elijah Fisher, a railway guard, H.Y. Palmer, a switch-maker, A.A. Parsons, an electroplater, and A.J. Gillett, an engine driver — were snapped up by the railway company.[89] Alfred Causley certainly found work as a pump-man, remaining in his job for eleven years, after which time he retired to Saskatoon with his wife and family.[90] Yet people must have questioned whether W.H. Holland, a cigar importer, J.W. Turner, a vagrant master, and the various gamekeepers, boot makers, decorators, tailors, and weavers in the group were up to the job! And yet, these people coped and somehow managed to establish themselves as prairie homesteaders in an isolated section of the Northwest Territories. The town of Lloydminster and the nearby communities of Marshall and Lashburn prospered, as did their farms.

It takes a special sort of person to cope with the perils and hardships of pioneering. The achievements of the Barr colonists are remarkable since few had the relevant skills. In the end, boldness, determination, and an unshakable desire to succeed saw them through their ordeals. Joe Hurrell, a former Cornish tin miner who relocated in 1906 to North Battleford, south of Lloydminster, had these qualities in abundance. Even as a young boy, he writes, "I had a childish resentment about that part of the catechism which said I had to be content in the state in which God had called me," and, when he turned twelve, "I felt my independence and went to the Wesleyan chapel."[91] By this time Hurrell was earning his living as a buddleboy[92] at a tin mine, earning sixpence a day. Later, he became a Methodist preacher and "that gave me access to all kinds of farms and cottage homes throughout a few parishes in and around North Hill and Linkinhorne."[93] This background gave him an understanding of country life, which he put to good use. Having worked for a year in Manitoba before coming to North Battleford, he had saved enough money to begin farming his first sixteen acres:

> All that I had to start with was my year's wages; but I got a team of oxen and a plough built a sod shack and went to work, and a lot of other people moved in that Spring, some with full equipment; but for the first year my nearest neighbours were nearly two miles away. Most of the early settlers had oxen. I was fortunate in being able to go [to] North Battleford and back in one day. There were others [who had to go] all the way up to 40 and 50 miles — several days journey to town and home again. That first summer I cut the wild hay for the winter with a scythe and got it together with a pitchfork and that winter went to North Battleford with 25 loads of wood (dry poles and trees) on sleighs at $5 a load. Then I bought another steer and seed oats and eventually worked four oxen for ten years.[94]

Joe's determination to succeed was understandable. His father, a tin miner like him, had died at the age of forty-one, as did most miners at that time.[95] He was building a new life for himself that his father could barely have imagined, let alone achieved. Nor was he alone: "Jack Geake farms about 20 miles east of me. He came from Stoke Climsland Parish [in Cornwall]; he was a butcher's apprentice, near Launceston then worked at a butcher's shop in Plymouth before emigrating." He also knew Arthur Bater from Truro who had emigrated in 1903 with his parents, having previously worked as a miner in Caradon.[96]

Of course, like-minded people sometimes formed small groups, without the backing of a sponsoring organization. In 1910, Philip Minifie, a hay and feed dealer from Shropshire, joined a group of Ontario farmers in establishing a homestead near Swift Current, west of the city of Moose Jaw (Map 24). And, he put his own stamp on it by naming it Malvern Link, after the town in Worcestershire with that name.[97] Around this time, another group came to this same area directly from England. Richard Pearce and his large extended family, who originated from Cheltenham in Gloucestershire, appear to have planned their venture particularly well. The photograph taken of them at their house at Sandford Dene in May 1912 reveals a confident, well-attired group who made the transition to prairie life very quickly and easily. Apparently, "there were other Gloucester and Cheltenham people living nearby, who could not get away to be photographed."[98] They named their place Pittville (now Hazlet) after the village to the north of the city of Cheltenham from which they originated.[99] A second Cheltenham group followed three months later, and included a postman, a dairyman, and a pony-carriage driver, together with their families.[100] There were other ventures as well, such as the Coal Creek Colony, formed by thirty-eight English families in 1930, but it floundered.[101]

However, the majority of English people actually came on their own or in small family groups. As ever, they generally left few records behind. The available evidence indicates that they came from all backgrounds, with many having little or no experience of farming.[102] Generally they knew brothers, uncles, cousins, workmates, friends, or neighbours from home who had preceded them to their destinations; so they had a sense of what to expect and had a place to stay when they first arrived.

J.R. Appleby, a coal miner from Newcastle-upon-Tyne, made the leap from industrial worker to homesteader in one bound. Arriving at Winnipeg in 1903, he, his son, and a friend spent their first night sleeping "on a big table" in the Immigration Hall. The following day they were met by a friend, who "drove us five miles to his place at Esteven where he and his good wife sheltered and cared for us with great kindness until we got fixed up with our own place." However, Appleby still needed help. "Not one of us could put the harness on a horse nor even take it off when it was put on for us."[103] Yet again his friend came to the rescue and enabled him to become a successful homesteader, being joined later by his eldest son, who acquired the land next to his.

Paul Grove's father, a shoe manufacturer from Kettering (Northamptonshire) encountered many difficulties before he could even raise the money to finance his new life. The demise of his business and the series of dead-end jobs that followed convinced him that he should follow his brother-in-law's example and move to Regina, where "employment was obtainable." Arriving in Regina in 1907, he soon found a job in a "pioneer furniture store," and a year later his family joined him. In addition, he worked as a part-time caretaker at a Methodist church and made shoes at a shoe store. Then he became a night-watchman at the Regina Trading Company, "where he put in a 13 or 14 hour shift each night for seven days a week." Finally, by 1913, he had sufficient resources to start farming. His son remembers leaving Regina for Paswegin, to the west of Saskatoon, "with a carload of settlers' effects, which included two oxen and a cow and a heifer. At first living in a tent, we later purchased a gable-roofed shack from a homesteader who was abandoning his homestead and going back to Minnesota."[104]

W.H. Gomme, a homesteader already living in Paswegin, hoped that his parents and brother in England might join him. To expedite matters, he wrote to the Canadian government requesting financial aid for his brother, who was an experienced flax grower, believing that "there may be room for some development of this industry in Canada." But his request was rejected.[105]

In 1916, Charles Best was doing his best to attract people from the village of Framilode in Gloucestershire to Swift Current. Boasting of having landed a good job managing a furniture store on Central Avenue, he wrote to friends in his native village — men like Frank Cookley the coal merchant — advising them "to come out to me. I am certain that if you can adapt yourself to new circumstances you can do better."[106] Certainly, Swift Current was attracting many English workers, as was noted by the Reverend Charles Wright, the local Anglican minister.[107] Many English immigrants were like Charles Best in seeking out urban centres. By 1921, the largest English concentrations were to be found in and near the cities of Regina, Moose Jaw, Saskatoon, and North Battleford, and the town of Lloydminster. Overall, the English were the largest ethnic group in Saskatchewan, accounting for around 27 percent of the population (Map 25).[108]

This story of dogged determination to succeed and mixed fortunes was repeated yet again as immigrants from England headed to the far west in search of better opportunities. The gentlemen farmers from England, who invested in ranching in Alberta and large-scale fruit farming in British Columbia, have attracted much interest while little attention has been paid to the unassuming individuals who arrived with little or no capital. In fact, they represented the majority. The expectation of greater prosperity fuelled a good part of the influx but success was far from guaranteed.

CHAPTER 5

Even Farther West to Alberta and British Columbia

> *In the winter of 1901–1902, there appeared in English newspapers, advertisements of 'Homestead Farms and Ranches in Western Canada', with some fine pictures. I procured some of these pamphlets ... and by January, 1902 my older brother Percy and I decided to try Western Canada.... We and the other newly-arrived settlers were met in Calgary by the Dominion Immigration Agent, and were given free lodging until we could get jobs or arrange to take up land.*[1]

Richmond Bird and his brother had been inspired by the information given in English newspapers of southern Alberta's farming opportunities. A particularly enthusiastic publicity campaign mounted by both the federal government and the Canadian Pacific Railway Company ensured that cities, towns, and even remote rural areas across England were swamped with promotional literature extolling the farming advantages of Western Canada. People came in droves despite the thousands of miles that had to be travelled.

Arriving in Calgary in 1902, the Bird brothers were greeted by a seemingly well-oiled reception process that offered practical help. As the sons of an Essex dairy farmer they had some knowledge of cattle rearing and were thus well placed to land jobs as ranch hands. However, their ultimate aim was to establish their own homesteads. Despite what they may have read in the glossy brochures, pioneering was labour-intensive and slow to produce results. They had first to earn the requisite funds to buy stock and equipment. In Richmond Bird's case, this took several years to achieve.

Courtesy Glenbow Archives, PA-3855-10.

St. Thomas Anglican Church, Dinton, Alberta, built in 1906. It stands as a reminder of the community, now disappeared, which once flourished here.

By 1905, Richmond had applied for homestead land and immediately set to work building his first shack; but he still needed the wages accruing from his job on a ranch near Calgary to fund his farming ambitions. Five years later he could change gears. He built an extension to his shack and "a good stable," and married Violet Wood, a local girl. After their wedding ceremony they returned to the homestead, where "our furniture, which was purchased from Eaton's Mail Order catalogue … was hauled home. With Pat Perry's help it was put together and arranged in our little house. Some kind neighbours gave us some hens and a nice Berkshire sow; we bought more chickens and some milk cows. And so began the building of our home."[2] The Birds' farm was located in the growing community of Dinton, north of High River, and several years later Richmond became a local councillor and served on the Dinton School Board. This progression from paid employment to land purchase gave Richmond financial independence and respectability — the two biggest and most sought-after rewards of the aspiring immigrant. For those with capital to invest, ranching was another option.

The colonization of the Alberta ranch lands, spreading east from the foothills of the Rocky Mountains, represents one of the most iconic periods of Canada's pioneering history. Ranchers, wild-west cowboys, and fortunes won and lost excite the imagination, but, in truth, the tale must be told in more mundane terms. As in most things, ranching success was determined by hard work, good luck, and an iron will to succeed. Wealthy Englishmen were quick to spot the commercial opportunities to be had in investing large amounts of capital in ranching, and in so doing greatly expanded Alberta's cattle industry. Ranching was initially centred in the Fort Macleod district, but with the arrival of the Canadian Pacific Railway in 1883 it became increasingly concentrated farther north around Calgary (Map 26).

One of the most successful of the early ranch owners was the Staffordshire-born Alexander Staveley Hill, a member of the British House of Commons and a major landowner. Having visited Alberta and assessed the best locations to establish a cattle ranch, he bought two vast tracts of land to the north of Fort MacLeod at present-day Champion and Staveley, the latter place taking his name. There, in 1882, with other English investors, he founded the famous Oxley Ranch, which he named after his country estate, Oxley Manor.[3] The ranch flourished, and with the arrival of the extension of the Calgary and Edmonton Railway from Calgary to Fort Macleod in 1892, its long-term future was secured.

Map 26: English Concentrations in Southern Alberta, 1911.

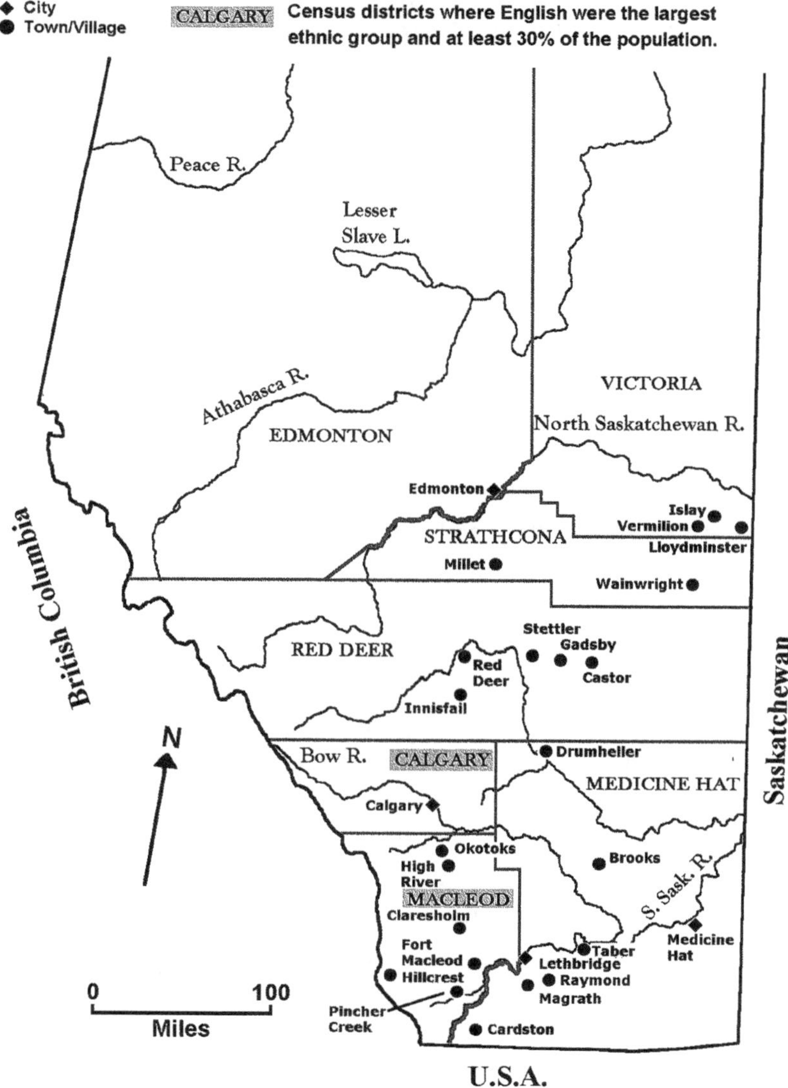

The Quorn Ranch, located near Okotoks to the south of Calgary, was another major farm established by wealthy English investors. Originating from Leicestershire, they named their ranch after the Quorn Hunt Club, located in their home county. Launched in 1885–86, during the height of the cattle boom, the ranch initially sought to breed thoroughbred horses for an English market, only later expanding into cattle rearing. However, the combined problems of extravagance in its operations and its failure to develop markets led to the Quorn Ranch's demise in 1906.[4]

As the Bird brothers had realized, working on a ranch was a useful stepping stone. Not surprisingly, a number of young men from Leicestershire made a beeline for the Quorn Ranch. Charles Linzee Douglass brought seven stallions from Market Harborough to Quorn in 1885, while Edmond Cuffling and his nephew Jonathon came out with even more English stallions the following year.[5] The Devon-born Edmund Hardwick began working at the Quorn Ranch in 1889 as a boy of sixteen, and later acquired his own ranch in the Snake Valley to the southeast of Calgary. Edward Hills, also born in Devon, followed an even more circuitous route. Before working as a cowboy on ranches near Calgary for a number of years, he had joined a Dominion land survey party. He thus obtained first-hand knowledge of some of the areas being opened up in Saskatchewan in the early 1880s, but despite this he chose to settle in Alberta, acquiring a ranch near High River. Returning to England several years later, he and his wife then moved to Kenya to run a coffee plantation and in later life they retired to England.[6] It would seem that, in their case, adventure rather than fortune-hunting had been the driving force.

Meanwhile, men like the Lancashire-born Joseph Laycock brought prized skills and knowledge with them to the Canadian West. Becoming highly respected as a pioneer stockman in Alberta by 1887, he became a member of the Dominion Board of the Holstein-Fresian Breeders Association and member of the council of the Alberta Association.[7] William Roper Hull and his brother, the sons of a wealthy cattle farmer in Dorset, used similar skills to make huge profits from selling meat. They were the first to integrate cattle-raising, meat-packing, and retailing into an amalgamated process. Having moved to their uncle's ranch near Kamloops, British Columbia, in 1873, they had learned the basics of ranching, and by 1880 they were ranching near Calgary. Shortly after this they set up a butchering and livestock-trading business and became large-scale meat-packers, the first to be established in Alberta. The partnership was dissolved in 1892, with John taking the Kamloops holdings and William the Alberta interests.[8]

Lieutenant Colonel Alfred Wyndham, a younger son of a wealthy Wiltshire family, arrived in Alberta in 1886 with a much more limited objective — to set up a ranch for himself and his family. Born in Dinton, Wiltshire, Wyndham had immigrated with his wife Caroline Stuart to London, Ontario, during the 1850s and later came west to command the 12th Battalion of the York Rangers in the North West Rebellion of 1885. Having become convinced of Alberta's farming merits, he acquired a prime site on the Bow River and sent for his wife and family, who joined him two years later.[9] Thus did he establish Dinton Ranch, located near Carseland to the southeast of Calgary, which he named after his ancestral home in Wiltshire. The completion of the railway line from Calgary to High River in 1892 made the area attractive to homesteaders, who acquired land south of the Bow River, thus ensuring Dinton's future as a farming community. However, judging from what was said about Alfred

Courtesy Glenbow Archives, NA-84-11.

A painting by Alfred Wyndham of his Dinton Ranch, which he established in 1887 near Carseland, Alberta. The Dinton Post Office was built later on Wyndham's land.

Wyndham by one of Caroline's cousins, it appears that he frittered away much of his capital, although his ranch remained in the possession of the Wyndham family until modern times[10]:

> A young Englishman who came out to Canada with a good deal of money; an honest true-hearted Christian gentleman, but one of many of that type who seem to be born with a genius for muddling away wealth; but if he lost money, he won respect and affection; and there is many a man up here today who has cause to bless the name of "the dear old Colonel" as he was always called.[11]

Claude Gardiner was another son of a wealthy Englishman, although he had a tougher introduction to ranching than did Alfred Wyndham. Arriving in 1894 at the age of twenty-three, he worked as a ranch hand at James Bell's ranch near Fort Macleod, earning £2 per month plus room and board. "This was a generous allowance for a green Englishman, particularly during the winter months, when many men were glad to exchange their labours for nothing more than an assurance of food and lodgings."[12] However, he hated the landscape and must have doubted whether he would remain: "You can drive anywhere on the prairies; there is not a hedge or bush or a tree and hardly a hill between here and Macleod. Anything more monotonous you never saw."[13] Yet his adventurous side won out and in the following year Claude learned that his grandfather would be giving him £1,000 to establish his own ranch. He celebrated by renting accommodation in the town of Macleod: "I have taken a room in town while looking about. I can live very cheaply in town in a nice clean place, a Temperance Hotel they call it. You bet I slept last night. I have not slept in such a bed for a long time. I was glad to leave Bell's house in town; it is small and full of children and I had to sleep on the kitchen floor."[14] A new life beckoned and soon Claude was employing his own workforce and was able to buy a mowing machine, horse rake, and a threshing machine. And by October 1895, he had "ninety-four head of cattle with my brand on."[15]

Calgary had made the rapid transition from a fort to a town to a major city in less than fifty years. The North West Mounted Police had established Fort Calgary in 1875 at the confluence of the Bow and Elbow Rivers, making it the precursor of the town that was laid out by the Canadian Pacific Railway Company in 1884. Seven years later its population amounted to just under four thousand. However, when Mr. A. Ancell, a tradesman from Manchester, visited it in 1906 he found that it had "a population of about 20,000 people of all nations … the houses or shacks are all built of wood and they have cooking stoves in them; they don't have fire places — same as [at] home."[16]

In 1911, an Anglican missionary by the name of Martin Holdom saw a "booming" Calgary:

> There were huge buildings going up all the time, I should think that the trade of the town would equal Leicester [England] pretty well. And then the town is far more up to date, than any English town; the streets are very wide, they are all lighted with electric lights. Although the stores close at 6.00 p.m. the windows are all kept lighted up until midnight. Another very good law is that no woman is allowed unattended on the streets after 8.00 p.m.[17]

By 1921 Calgary's population would reach just over 63,000. As a major economic hub, Calgary naturally attracted many English workmen. George Machon, a harness maker by profession, was remarkably adaptable. Having settled for a while in Simcoe County (Upper Canada), he and his family moved to Winnipeg in 1876 where he worked as a harness maker with a Dominion land survey party that ventured up to Battle River. He subsequently settled in Calgary, where, once again, he pursued his craft.[18]

Then there was the Devon-born Thomas Emworthy, who, having gone initially to Muskoka, moved to Calgary in 1883, where he ran a sandstone quarry and supplied much of the stone used in Calgary's early buildings. Later, he set himself up as a market gardener, selling his fruit and vegetables in Calgary. And with the profits realized from these ventures he purchased a homestead on the Elbow River.[19]

Mr. Ancell from Manchester had a much more difficult time: "I do believe that a man can get on here, but he must work and he must tackle anything. The first job I got was fixing Dobby horses up. The next was concreting and the next was making cement bricks, and the next was a plasterer's labourer. I am doing this until I can get in a regular job."[20]

Judging from surviving genealogical records,[21] the English often arrived in southern Alberta in their twenties, some newly married, and a substantial proportion came from Ontario, rather than directly from England. By 1911, Calgary and the towns of Okotoks and High River to the south were manifestly English. Henry Crick, born in Suffolk, and his wife, Lizzie Walker, born in Perth, Ontario, arrived in Calgary in 1885 when Henry was aged twenty.[22]

Bertram Alford from Tavistock, Ontario, arrived three years later, aged only seventeen, first settling at Jumping Pound (on the Elbow River) then moving to Morley, west of Calgary, where he married Annie Sibbal, who had come to the area from Barrie, Ontario, as a four-year-old.[23] The Derbyshire-born Walter Moss arrived in 1889, aged twenty-eight, with his wife Mary Lipton, who had been born in Grassington, North Yorkshire, and they settled at Shepard near Calgary.[24]

The Kent-born Edward Shelley came to Calgary a year later, aged thirteen, having previously lived in Hamilton, Ontario, while his future wife, Mary Gardiner, born in Toronto, arrived that same year as a fourteen-year-old.[25] The common thread throughout was that young people were heading for the Calgary district and preferentially choosing urban locations. Thus, while settlement in Western Canada is usually associated with farms and agriculture, much of the English population expansion actually occurred in the villages, towns, and cities.

Having previously emigrated to South Africa and Australia, Joseph Tyas followed a different learning curve. He discovered the hard way that successful homesteading required specialist skills and a good location. In 1902, after his wife, Minnie, "sewed fifty golden sovereigns into a money belt and waved him good-bye," he left his comfortable home in Australia for a prairie homestead, located near Balzac, north of

Calgary. Minnie claimed "it was the biggest shock of her life to land in what she described as the bald-headed prairie, miles of parched grass and not a tree in sight. She had pictured a rambling farm house like the ones in Australia ... what a rude awakening! When father showed her the rough wood shack she thought it must be the chicken-house."[26] Given that "water had to be carried in pailfuls from a spring a quarter of a mile away," conditions were indeed very spartan. Minnie contributed to the family's finances in the early days by working as a nurse in Calgary, but later the homestead flourished and eventually Joseph could dabble in local politics and become a justice of the peace. As their son Philip acknowledged later, the Herculean efforts of the early settlers should never be forgotten:

> Hundreds of early settlers struggled through difficult times but they were built of hardy stock and persevered. It is these pioneers we honour today for braving the hardships of pioneer life in the new land and opening up the West.[27]

The Macleod district, south of Calgary, also had a predominance of English settlers by 1911. They included men like Arthur Cox from London, England, who had worked on the construction crew of the Canadian Pacific Railway at Medicine Hat in 1882 and later joined a Dominion land survey party. He and his wife, Mary Willock, established a ranch at Pincher Creek, where he opened the town's first school.[28] The Devon-born Arthur Raper and Charles Leeds, born in Richmond, Surrey, both came to the area when only nineteen years old, while the Lancashire-born James Lambert arrived as a twenty-three-year-old, having previously joined the North West Mounted Police at Winnipeg. He later "followed his trade as a building contractor" at Fort Macleod.[29]

By the 1890s the tide of immigration was fully underway. Between 1901 and 1905, forty thousand homesteads were granted in Alberta. And while the English were well-represented in this farming bonanza, they were even more dominant in the cities, towns, and villages that were sprouting across the south of the province (Map 26).

Cumberland-born Robert Nimmons spotted the rewards to be made in running a stone quarry in Lethbridge, while countless men from the North and Midlands of England found work in the coal mines that were being opened up during the 1880s.[30] Harry Fleetwood, an English miner who arrived in 1889 with his wife, turned his attention to founding schools in later life, becoming known as the "father" of the Lethbridge schools.[31] The Lancashire-born Nathan Wallwork, who came to Lethbridge in 1884 with his Lancashire wife Rachael Kirkman, was almost certainly a coal miner.[32] In fact, many of Alberta's English coal miners originated from Lancashire. The Reverend Martin Holdom, whose Anglican congregation was based at Castor to the east of Red Deer, met some of them at the Drumheller coal mines, northeast of Calgary. He was surprised to learn that they were poorly paid, but had little sympathy for them, believing that they were living in the past and failing to grasp new opportunities:

> There is quite a settlement of Lancashire miners here — they are nice people but they do not care for it much out here. I found some of them hard up; like all English miners they are improvident; it was the first time since coming to this country that I have been asked for old clothes, it seemed so funny to be asked for anything that I was quite delighted; it seemed just like old Leicester days, they probably remember that the clergyman at home is looked upon more or less as a relief officer....
>
> The Lancashire miner seems to be of little use outside of a mine. Except for poaching they have no idea of adapting themselves to anything else. They seem to be the most pessimistic of men, with a natural hatred of capital and love of strikes. They seem utterly at sea in the country of individual opportunity.[33]

Like the Lancashire coal miners who brought their expertise to Alberta, Mormons from Utah beat a path to Cardston, south of Lethbridge, knowing that their legendary irrigation skills would be put to good use. Many had English ancestry. Having been recruited by the Alberta Railway and Irrigation Company in the late 1880s to assist with the cultivation of this arid district, they introduced an irrigation system and founded Cardston, the first of a number of Mormon settlements in the area.[34]

Magrath, to the east, was established in 1899 by Utah and Idaho settlers sent by the Church of Jesus Christ of Latter-day Saints.[35] Included in the group was the Lincolnshire-born John Booth Merrill who had immigrated to Utah in 1892. Becoming a Mormon a year later, he had married Elizabeth Gibb, also a Mormon, and moved to Lethbridge, where he established a nursery business and "supplied trees for the streets of Lethbridge." Eleven years later he repeated the process in Hill Spring to the northwest of Cardston.[36] Also arriving in 1889 from Utah was Yorkshireman Richard Pilling, who settled in Aetna, near Cardston, having come with "100 head of extra good short-haired Durham young cows and about 50 head of good horses."[37] William Payne, who had been born in Northamptonshire, also settled in the Cardston area, having married Carrie Davidson, a Mormon from Utah.[38]

And so it went on. The 1911 Census would reveal that people who claimed English ethnicity accounted for 82 percent of the population of Magrath, 60 percent of Cardston, and 55 percent of nearby Raymond. This definitive English dominance was no doubt greatly enhanced by the Utah influx.

Cardston even attracted a remittance man by the name of Richard "Dicky" Bright, who managed to dupe his father into thinking that he owned a ranch in the area: "Bright would write his father in England telling him how great things were going, a band of horses and countless cattle; but could he spare a few quid of short money to tide him over 'till the long money from the cattle came in." But, when Dicky's father arrived suddenly in Cardston in the 1890s demanding to see his son's ranch for himself, he straight away hired "a fancy driving team and buggy" and paid "some Mormon boys" to round up a good-sized herd that he claimed were his. They "ran his brand" on the one calf he happened to own in front of his father and let his father think that the assembled herd had the same brand. Apparently, "the old doctor went back to England well satisfied with Dicky's business ability."[39]

Arid conditions created problems for the early farmers near Stettler (Map 26). When the Nottinghamshire-born Richard Mackley Syson[40] visited in 1905, as a member of a Dominion land survey party, he noticed the very sandy soil, which could only support "long spear grass that grows at the seashore, no trees ... water was very scarce. We often had to go without drink at dinner, no wood to make a fire, the wood for the camp had to be hauled a long distance."[41] He was told how most of the early settlers living near Ponoka, north of Red Deer, had originated from Idaho: "These first settlers had a rough time," having to purchase their household goods in Lacombe, the nearest town on the Calgary and Edmonton Railway line, some fifty miles (eighty kilometres) distant.[42] They were happy to work together — "helping to build the shacks, and log houses, loaning machinery, anything that you had that could be loaned. Bachelor parties were very much in evidence; there were very few married couples." Once they had created their homesteads, most of the Idaho settlers sold their land "for as much as they could get, which was not much," and left the area.[43]

However, there was plenty of rich, loamy soil between Calgary and Red Deer, and once it was opened to homesteaders, a substantial number of English settlers appeared on the scene. By 1921 their colonization activities stretched over many districts (Map 27). Some Northamptonshire settlers, including Ebenezer Green and his wife, Mary William, and Emmanuel Reeves and his wife, Ann Williams, probably came as a group, all having originated from, or having connections with, the agricultural village of Tiffield. Arriving in the mid-1880s, they chose locations in and near Innisfail and Penhold, south of Red Deer.[44] And to the east of Penhold was "an old English settlement" at Pine Lake, founded in 1893. According to the Reverend Christopher Greaves, its Anglican minister, Pine Lake's population in 1906 was 70 percent English. The community had an Anglican church by this time, which had cost £1,250 — half of the money having being raised "from England by the Misses Alford of Taunton, Somerset."[45] No doubt, the present-day Taunton place name near Pine Lake records the geographical origins of its Somerset settlers, most of whom had become ranchers by 1906.

**Map 27: English Concentrations in Southern Alberta, 1921.
(Based on census map showing railway lines)**

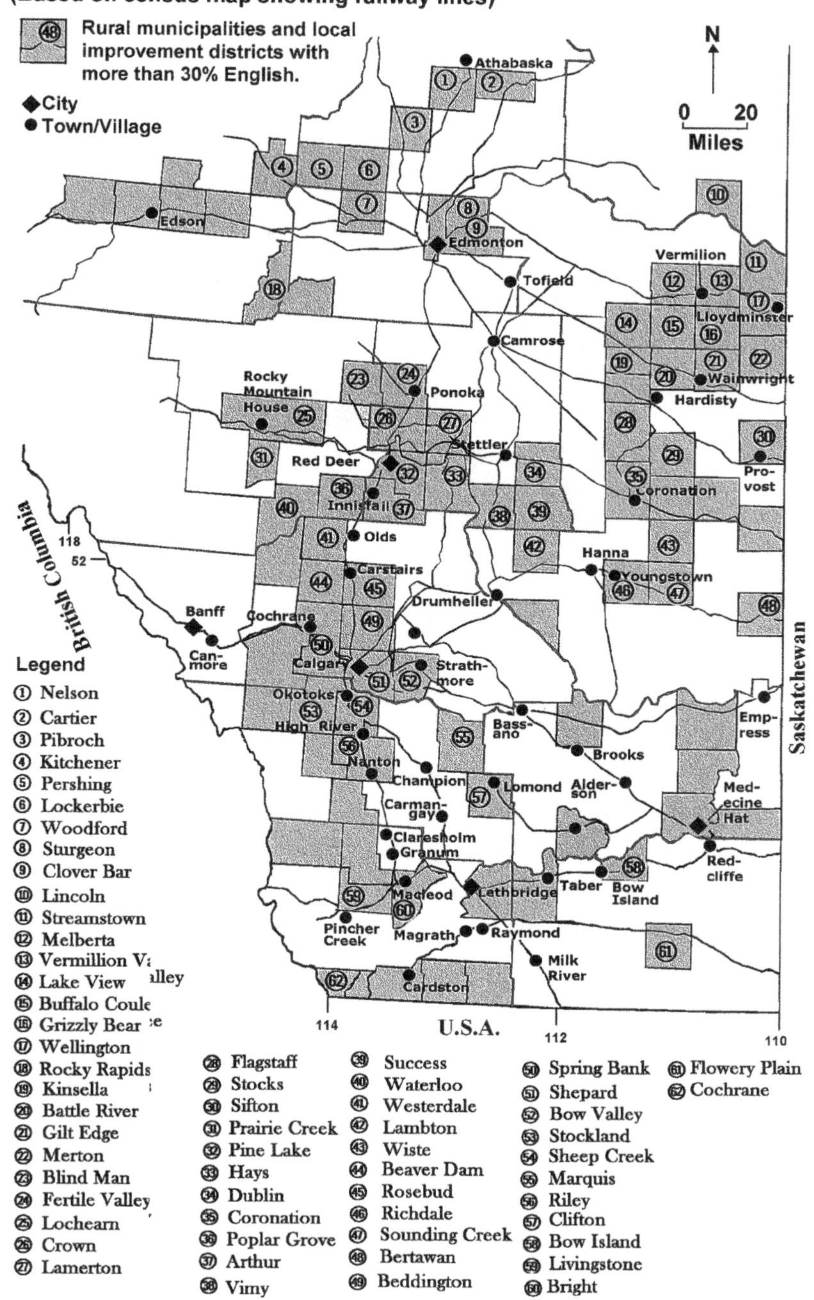

Courtesy Library and Archives Canada, PA-021035.

Canadian Pacific Railway Company station and grain elevators at Wetaskiwin, south of Edmonton, 1913. The grain elevators were an iconic visual symbol of the amazing productivity of western Canada's wheat farms.

Cornishman Horace Meeres had several jobs, including working on the construction of the Calgary and Edmonton Railway line, before establishing his homestead southeast of Red Deer.[46] A keen witness to the rapid building expansion taking place in the area was the Reverend Martin Holdom.[47] In 1912, on a visit to Coronation, a town east of Castor, he stayed at "a hotel of 60 rooms and every latest convenience; six months ago I could ride across this town-site and see nothing — perhaps but a couple of homesteaders' shacks and the Nose Hills in the north. Today we have a flourishing town of some 600 people, three or four general stores, numbers of other places of business, a Norwegian Lutheran Church and a fine railway station with waiting rooms etc."[48] The Reverend Holdom also had forthright views about who made the best settlers:

> After careful observation I have come to this conclusion: that the emigrants drawn from the upper artisan class and the aristocrats are the people from home [England]

> who best adapt themselves to conditions out here. The former are often well educated and refined ... the latter class may have lived in luxury, but they can adapt themselves. They have breed and pluck.... They can if necessary live on a bean a week quite happily.[49]

As for well-bred men with pluckiness, he might have been referring to John and Charles Morgan, brothers who had been born on a sugar plantation in British Guiana (now Guyana) of English parents. Having moved to England with their parents, and after living there for a few years, they immigrated to British Columbia in 1898. They found work straight away as road builders — "not much of a job, but it pays well.... We only work ten hours a day but it is pretty heavy work." However, before long, John "wishes himself back in the bank," no doubt a reference to his cushier job back in England.[50] Yet, despite some initial misgivings, the brothers remained in Canada. In March of the following year, Charles told his mother:

> I have the gold mining craze badly and think I shall drift into mining as soon as I can. You see it is absolutely certain that a man would never make anything working for wages on a ranch and of course he might not in mining and prospecting but there is at least a chance there. This country is on the eve of a very great mining development.... I believe that in two years time Canada will lead the world in gold producing for, besides the Klondike and Atlin goldfields, the whole of the southern part of British Columbia is one large gold field.[51]

Be that as it may, two months later Charles and John Morgan were negotiating with government land agents in Alberta in the hope of obtaining a good site for their future ranch.[52] Acquiring land at Harmattan, located roughly halfway between Calgary and Red Deer, John built his first cabin later that same year and four years later had sixty acres under cultivation.[53]

Photograph, circa 1910, of John Morgan, who established a ranch at Harmattan, Alberta, in the first decade of the twentieth century. He married the Cheshire-born Elsie Grange in 1909 in Wimbledon, Surrey. After the wedding, the couple lived in a log cabin for a year before moving to their new house, where they lived for the rest of their lives.

Courtesy Glenbow Archives, PA-3744-1.

Crucial to their rapid progress was their mother's generous funding. In November 1901, Charles thanked her for the £120 already received and requested an additional £200: "I shall need fully that for more horses, implements, wages, seed, wire and cattle; I want to put not less than $600 into cattle alone."[54] That same year John reported that "the rush of settlers had somewhat slackened but there are some coming in all the time." A Mrs. Thompson served them dinner — peas and Yorkshire pudding. Charles described her as "English and quite a nice old lady," and informed his mother that "she is making my bread for me while I am haying and washing my clothes."[55] Another high point in his life was a visit that year to the Queen's Hotel in Calgary "to get some teeth seen to and to see the Duke and Duchess of Cornwall, who passed through on Saturday while I was staying here."[56] However, two years later he complained that the area had become too "settled up" and he was contemplating looking for more land in the interior.[57] Life was never going to be perfect, but John Morgan had made the transition from English gentleman to Alberta rancher by dint of hard work — and a good cash flow from his mother.

Like Calgary, the city of Edmonton had its beginnings long before the province was formed.[58] It commenced as Fort Edmonton — a fur-trade centre. When the Reverend William Newton arrived in 1875 to establish an Anglican congregation, it was at the threshold of its transition from a trading post to a city and a provincial capital: "I had been sent as a missionary to settlers; but where are they? I could not find such persons as we usually designate as settlers. Beyond the mission stations even a potato patch was seldom seen, and a farm never."[59] Substantial population growth had to await the arrival of the Canadian Northern Railway, which only reached Edmonton in 1905. Before then, permanent settlers, who were mainly employees of the Hudson's Bay Company, were few and far between.

Nicknamed "the little doctor" because he had a Ph.D. and was only just over five feet tall, Dr. Newton travelled great distances to reach his scattered congregation, which in 1882 consisted of only twenty-five families.[60] He certainly had many problems and minor irritations to deal with. In cold spells he had to "place ink on a stove to thaw when he wished to write and even then it would sometimes freeze on his pen before he touched the paper."[61] But far more serious was his inability to empathize with his congregation who, having endured his eccentricities, ineptness, and arrogant demeanour for as long as possible, petitioned for his removal in 1887. He was replaced three years later. Nevertheless, the Reverend Newton did establish Edmonton's first Anglican Church and congregation.

There was certainly a huge contrast between the embattled Reverend Newton and the Reverend John Gough Brick, another Anglican missionary whose success and popularity soared after he arrived in the Peace River district in 1882. Settling in what is now the Shaftesbury settlement, he became an acclaimed agriculturalist, winning a prize for his "Red Fife" wheat at the World's Columbia Exposition, held in 1893 in Chicago.[62]

Another outstanding Englishman at this time was Richard Philip Ottewell, who came to the Edmonton area in 1881 from Huron County, Ontario.[63] Settling at Clover Bar, now on the east side of the city of

Edmonton, he amassed a fortune from farming, coal mining, and his flour and lumber mills, building himself a seventeen-room brick mansion in 1910.[64]

Ottewell's discovery of the rich agricultural land to be found in the Clover Bar area attracted a large group of followers from Parry Sound, Ontario, in 1892. Having struggled with stony and swampy soil, they seized the opportunity of relocating to a much better area. A total of 298 souls came in a single group with eighty-six horses and 170 head of cattle. Their rapid success attracted even more Parry Sounders, with their total number reaching 630 by 1894. These well-prepared and well-organized pioneers settled east of Edmonton in Clover Bar as well as in other areas to the north, extending their reach to Fort Saskatchewan and Lamont.[65] The strong English presence in Clover Bar and in urban centres such as Beverley by the time of the 1921 Census suggests that a substantial proportion of the migrants had English ancestry.[66] By this time a separate and much larger English enclave had become established to the east

The Reverend John Gough Brick, an Anglican missionary, photographed in the late 1890s by Siegel Cooper. In 1906 he became the first member of the provincial parliament for Peace River.

Courtesy Glenbow Archives, NA-3858-1.

of Edmonton. Representing the remarkable overspill of the Barr Colony, founded in 1903 on the boundary between Alberta and Saskatchewan, it encompassed several rural municipalities and major urban centres, including Lloydminster, Wainwright, and Vermillion, each being places where people of English origin dominated (Map 27).

Two years after the First World War began in 1914, city workers like Mrs. Eva Martin (née Tibbitts), living in Edmonton, were unable to find work. In desperation she pleaded with her mother in Gloucestershire to send her some money:

> It is impossible to get work, everywhere is closing down. Every third store out here is closed and, those that are open are nearly all Chinese labour, as it is so cheap. The only thing I could do is work for my board and room in a private house where I would have to do all the washing and go to a farm and do the dairy work and baking and this I am not strong enough to do.[67]

Failing to extract help from her mother with this hard-luck tale, Eva admitted in a subsequent letter to having married an Englishman and that they were planning to move to the United States so that he could escape conscription.[68]As many others would discover, emigration to the Canadian West did not always have a happy ending.

The completion of the Canadian Pacific Railway line in the mid-1880s was a crucial final stage in Canada's development. Linking British Columbia with the rest of the country, the transcontinental railway allowed for the creation of the Dominion and greatly facilitated emigration to the province. The federal government's campaigning efforts in the 1890s, promoting British Columbia's many advantages, stimulated a steady influx of British people, of whom the English were the dominant group. Over the following decades, English people mainly gravitated to the towns and cities in the southwest of the province, while the remainder became dispersed along the north-south valleys in the south, where they farmed, or along the railway lines in the industrial regions (Map 28).[69]

However, British Columbia's immigration story began much earlier. In fact, the province grew out of two quite separate British colonies. The Vancouver Island colony, founded in 1849, was followed by the mainland colony, established in 1858. The latter colony came into being in the same year that gold was discovered on the banks of the Thompson River at Fraser Canyon. A second gold rush in the early 1860s, triggered by the discovery of the gold belt in the Cariboo region, led to a major expansion of the roads and the laying down of mining towns, but the cost of providing this basic infrastructure greatly exceeded the mainland colony's resources. This indebtedness forced a union with the Vancouver Island colony in 1866, thus creating the province of British Columbia with Victoria as its capital city. Chosen as the principal railway terminal, Vancouver's population surged ahead, soon eclipsing Victoria as the main commercial centre.

Initially the Hudson's Bay Company, rather than the British government, acted as the custodian of Vancouver Island. Building Fort Victoria in 1849 as a trading post, the company was meant to act as its colonizing

Map 28: English Concentrations in British Columbia, 1921. (Based on census map, showing railway lines.)

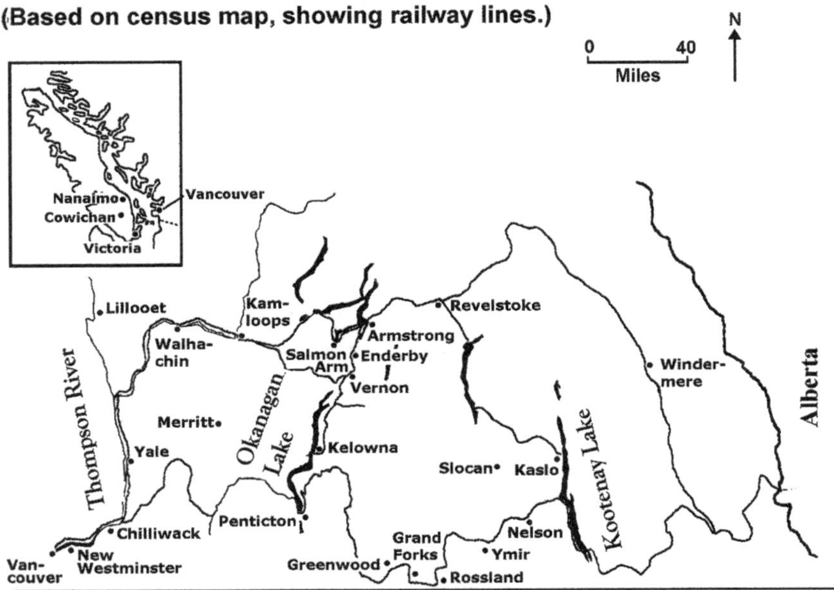

agent, but it failed to attract settlers. The company lived in an Old World time bubble, seeking only to attract "British landholders, who hold high the social and ethical standards of mid-Victorian England, and who could be counted on to despise the crasser values of 'the irregular squatters,' who flocked to new lands in search of material benefit."[70] In other words, aspiring tradesmen, farm workers, and farmers — the stalwarts of any pioneering community — were not welcome! Thus, few colonizers came to the province initially. But with the gold rush of 1858, they came in their thousands. Hordes of prospectors made a beeline for Victoria, boosting its economy almost overnight, despite the fact that most of them only stayed long enough to obtain their provisions and equipment.

Although the gold rush had been a major catalyst for population growth, coal was actually mined first. The Hudson's Bay Company began mining operations at Nanaimo on Vancouver Island in 1852, employing a small English and Scottish workforce. A much greater effort was made two years later when twenty-three miners and their families from the Brierley Hill colliery in Staffordshire responded to the company's advertisement in London newspapers.[71] Their long route in the *Princess Royal* around Cape Horn to the Pacific coast meant that the families, consisting of eighty-three people, were at sea for an incredible 179 days, during which time they endured extremely cramped and unpleasant conditions.[72]

Having agreed indenture contracts, the men were required to work for five years as Hudson's Bay Company servants, in return for which they received free passages to Nanaimo.[73] Moving into the modest houses built by the company, they soon adjusted to their new life. The daughter of one of the miner's families recalled how "they seldom allowed the central fireplace to go out, banking it with coal each night. There was usually a pot boiling over the fire. Water was carried in powder cans up the steep banks of the gully for her father's bath when he came home at night from the mine. The spring at the ravine became a popular place for the young people to meet, and several romances began when a boy offered to carry the girl's pail up the bank."[74]

Joining the Staffordshire miners were self-funded Cornishmen, who preferred to mine coal in Nanaimo rather than follow the lure of gold into the harsher regions of the Interior."[75] In 1854 the fledgling mining community, then named Colvile, had a population of just over 150.[76] Nine years later there were reported to be: "nearly two hundred Cornish [people] on Vancouver Island — a fact which took many old residents by surprise."[77] Presumably, many were connected with the Nanaimo mines. While the number of Cornish miners who worked at Nanaimo cannot be quantified, a Cornish boatman's observation in 1897 that "Cornish miners rather abound at the mines in this neighbourhood [Vancouver Island]" suggests that they were present in considerable numbers.[78] The English mining connection with the island involved other counties as well. English miners from Cumberland (England) were recruited in 1871 by Robert Dunsmuir to dig for coal in newly opened mines west of Comox. Their mining community, named Cumberland after the founding group, grew in size rapidly, although followers came from many corners of the world. Thomas Hope, a County Durham miner, was being employed at the coal mines in 1901, while twelve years later Charles Page, a baker from Gloucester, was anticipating his new job at the Nanaimo provincial jail.[79]

Photograph taken in 1854 of George Baker, a former Staffordshire miner, who owned the Dew Drop Inn in Nanaimo, British Columbia.

Courtesy Nanaimo Museum Collection, Image I1-6.

The gold rushes of 1858 and 1861–64 greatly stimulated the province's economy and generated substantial population growth. Although thousands of men headed for the Fraser Canyon in 1858, this gold bonanza was short-lived and dominated by Californian miners, who in many cases left as quickly as they had arrived. The Devon-born Edgar Dewdney, educated as a civil engineer, sought his fortune but instant wealth eluded him. Instead, he settled for surveying work and building trails to the mining camps.[80]As for the Cariboo Gold Rush of 1861–64, it too attracted a great influx of prospectors, mainly from Britain and other parts of Canada. The declining state of Cornwall's copper industry had led its miners to seek new opportunities in both of the gold rushes. Among the fortunate who struck it rich at Cariboo was Martin Raby, a Cornish veteran of the Californian and Australian gold rushes.[81] But he was very much the exception. John Teague, another Cornishman, made a brief appearance in the Cariboo gold fields before devoting himself to more orthodox employment, working as a general contractor erecting buildings for mining companies. Soon after this, he found work in Victoria as a carpenter and later became a highly successful architect.[82] Billy Barker, a former seaman who was also said to be Cornish, made and lost a fortune in the Cariboo, but had the distinction of having the town of Barkerville named after him.[83] Gold fever took many victims.

The gold rush communities of the mainland were short-lived and some, like Barkerville, became ghost towns, while others like Yale diversified into logging or road and railway building. Another problem at the time was the lack of women. A ball held in the Cariboo region to raise money for road-building attracted 120 miners, but just nine women.[84] In 1862, Victoria was said to be overflowing with down-and-out miners. In earlier times many had been professional men, army officers, and merchants. Gold fever had been their downfall. New Westminster, the mainland city that had been launched by the Cariboo Gold Rush, now received the disappointed men who were returning empty-handed. According to Arthur Birch, the colonial secretary at New Westminster, the city was "over-run" with well-connected young Englishmen, many of whom were working at jobs that "under normal circumstances they would have shunned." The son of a Somerset clergyman "is chopping wood" while "half the stokers on the river steamers are decayed Gentlemen."[85]

As gold mining reached the Kootenay region in the 1860s, yet more mining communities formed with some, such as Nelson and Rossland, later attracting miners from Cornwall (Map 28).[86] A prospectus produced by the Kootenay Company in 1887 quoted the Marquis of Lorne,[87] who, having explored the land to be mined on the banks of the Kootenay River, claimed that it had "gold in all the creeks." Recognizing the need to attract men with capital, the prospectus stressed that "the Kootenay Valleys possess ... many features that render them particularly attractive to English gentlemen emigrants and retired officers, a few of whom have already settled there."[88] Yet, it was the British Columbian countryside, not gold, which attracted the greatest response from the English middle and upper classes. Their ultimate aim was to become country squires in areas of British Columbia selected for their natural beauty and fruit-growing potential.

Courtesy Glenbow Archives, NA-3047-9.

Hewitt Bostock, cattle rancher, fruit grower, newspaper proprietor, and politician with his family, circa 1895, at Monte Creek, British Columbia. Born in Surrey in England, he founded the *Province*, a weekly Victoria newspaper, and served as the member of Parliament for Yale-Cariboo from 1896 to 1904. He was appointed to the Senate in 1904.

A wealthy Englishman by the name of Charles Busk was just such a person. During the 1880s he launched a fruit-farming venture near Nelson, in the Kootenay region. He had not anticipated the sandy soil and arid conditions, however.[89] Regardless, he acquired a large tract of land, built a mansion, and founded a town, which he named after Lord Balfour in England. But with the demise of his fruit farm, he ran through his capital paying for his opulent lifestyle and died a disillusioned and insolvent man. Other "gentlemen emigrants," as they came to be known, were attracted by the beautiful Cowichan Valley on Vancouver Island, whose inhabitants in 1903 were said to be primarily English and included "naval and military men, pensioned India civil servants and gentlemen's younger sons."[90] However, the favoured destination of this special breed of Englishman was the Okanagan Valley, to the west of Kootenay region (Map 28). The catalyst in creating its great fruit-farming potential had been Lord Aberdeen's investment in irrigation systems.[91]

After purchasing his land in the 1890s and irrigating it, Lord Aberdeen sold it in lots to selected British settlers "of a very good class."[92] A man who had the capital to purchase ten acres of land and irrigate it, build a house, establish an apple orchard, and keep it for five to ten years to allow the trees to mature had the makings of a profitable enterprise. With its comfortable time frame, fruit-growing was judged to be an ideal occupation for a gentleman; thus began the large influx of wealthy English people to the Okanagan Valley. Most of the arrivals were the families of retired professionals, businessmen, and ex-army and navy officers, who came, not only to make their fortune, but to enjoy what they perceived would be an elegant and socially exclusive lifestyle. The climate was mild and there were limitless opportunities to enjoy hunting, shooting, and fishing in a congenial environment.

Unlike the Prairie provinces, which attracted large numbers of settlers from the United States and Europe, British Columbia's main influx during the late nineteenth and early twentieth centuries came from Britain, with the English accounting for 60 percent of the total British arrivals. By 1911, people with English ancestry accounted for one third of the entire population, and ten years later they represented 42 percent of it.[93] By then, around 50 percent of the population of Kelowna, Vernon,

Armstrong, and Salmon Arm in the Okanagan Valley could claim English ancestry (Map 28).[94] This strong presence owes more to the mainstream influx of tradesmen, small farmers, labourers, miners, and clerks from across England than to the arrival of a few elite families, although the latter were the ones who most fascinated contemporary and later commentators. Thus, while the majority were overlooked, the experiences and lifestyle of the middle and upper classes were well recorded.

In 1909, the town of Kelowna, in the centre of the valley, was described as having "an air of English neatness and prosperity, the well-built houses standing back in large gardens, and the streets being wide, while behind the town was a large expanse of farm land, intersected by fenced roads."[95] Public and preparatory schools, modelled on their English counterparts, appeared across the valley,[96] while "cricket, tennis, croquet, even polo were all played as a matter of course … in virtually identical fashion to that of home."[97]

Meanwhile, an Anglican missionary based at Okanagan Lake in 1911 revelled in the knowledge that his "whole parish [had] scores of University and Public School men."[98] Two years later, another Anglican, the Reverend Ernest Grice-Hutchinson, whose ministry was based near Salmon Arm at the northern end of the valley, was conversing with local remittance men. According to Grice-Hutchinson, Biddulph, "a typical aristocractic degenerate" and great-grandson of Lord Biddulph, had been "shipped out here to be out of the way.… He is remarkably well-read and we had some interesting talk."[99] Thynne, another remittance man, had gone to Charterhouse public school in Surrey, England.[100]

In fact, the Reverend Grice-Hutchinson's life was an almost constant round of socializing. On one typical day he and his wife, Maude, had "lunch at the Kinghorn's and in the afternoon Mrs. St. George, Mrs. Kinghorn's mother, Stewart H. George, Mrs. Kinghorn's brother, who lives with them, and I rowed up the lake as far as another brother's place, some little way off — quite a nice place with a large orchard, most of which is bearing [fruit]."[101] On another occasion he had "an excellent tea" with the Barnards and saw their "big orchard, which is beautiful" and later met "a pleasant Englishman on the Okanagan at dinner" who told him that, after eight years, his fruit farm had failed to produce any profits.[102] Undoubtedly, his world of high teas, lunches, picnics, and tennis matches was far removed from the stoic existence of missionaries farther east, who endured gruelling travel conditions and long distances to preach and minister to their scattered communities.[103]

While most ordinary people were happy to be assimilated into the general population, the genteel classes constructed social barriers in order to set themselves apart. Not surprisingly, some Canadians objected to their snobbery. A resident in Vernon, to the north of Kelowna, complained that as "English people from the so-called upper classes began to come in with their families, many of them seemed unable or unwilling to shed their prejudices; they formed a distinct social set among themselves, people who for some obscure reason thought they were superior to mere colonials."[104] There was no doubt that an elite inner circle had taken root. As late as 1926, a British visitor to the Okanagan Valley met "English people who cannot remember that they are not still in England, who never fail to apologize for the climate, the silver and the lack of servants, and end by asking you to tea next Thursday."[105]

The enormous popularity of Okanagan fruit farming led developers to seek out other regions in the province with favourable locations. An elite but inexperienced group of Englishmen, including the Marquis of Anglesey, hoped to make substantial profits from farmland at Walhachin, west of Kamloops, but they failed to appreciate the site's climatic and soil deficiencies (Map 28). Even though the first families who arrived in 1907 had the necessary capital and determination to work hard, their irrigation skills were inadequate to cope with Walhachin's dry climate. In 1910 the community had about fifty-six English settlers and three years later the numbers had risen to around three hundred. However, the site was ineptly managed and the settlers were ill-prepared for pioneering conditions. The final blow came in 1914 with the outbreak of the First World War, when most of the Walhachin men joined the armed services and headed for Europe. That same year it became a deserted site, providing a lasting reminder of the harsh realities faced by early settlers.[106]

Another fruit-growing area that attracted investors was to the east at Windermere, in the Kootenay Valley (Map 28). Jack and Daisy Philips, a middle-class couple from the South of England, came to the area in 1912 but experienced difficulties.[107] Their immediate reaction was to blame the land company, from whom they had purchased their site, accusing it of supplying misleading information about what could be accomplished. According to Daisy, "the company are too greedy and trying to build and do much more than they can possibly finish."[108] But Jack's inexperience of farming and the prejudices instilled by their elitist background would have also held them back. Despite their setbacks, Daisy and Jack were very happy with their life in Windermere.[109] They established a small farm, although it was never commercially viable, and would have remained in the area but for the outbreak of the First World War. In 1912 they travelled to England to enable Jack to rejoin his old regiment and neither of them returned.[110]

Meanwhile, the Vancouver Island gentry had overseen Victoria's transformation from a gold rush town to a sedate provincial capital city. By 1911, people with English ancestry accounted for 50 percent of Victoria's population and, through their numbers and influence, created an aura of Englishness that pervaded the general society. A British traveller of 1890, who met an English family residing in Victoria at a dinner party, had remarked that they were "English in every way, and yet I think it might be nigh thirty years since any of them had seen Great Britain."[111] The predominance of English people prompted a visiting *London Times* journalist to declare that "Victoria is the most English of all the towns of Canada. The society of the place largely consists of Englishmen and Englishwomen of the better classes, and the English element is conspicuous in the clubs."[112] The tradesmen, industrial workers, and clerks had a more circuitous route to acceptance. Oddly enough, Victoria became home to most Cornish immigrants despite the appeal of the gold-mining communities in the Fraser Valley and coal-mining centres in and around Nanaimo.[113] Inevitably, Victoria's high-status people attracted all the attention, but it should be remembered that there were many large groups like the Cornish who simply faded into the background.

While the genteel English created an exclusive social environment in a substitute England, most others assimilated themselves into the various strands of British Columbia's pioneer society. As ever, many in the latter category found solace in commemorating their Old World links.

Having emigrated to Vancouver, artisans from the town of Wellington in Somerset[114] formed "the Wellingtonians" — a support group that held regular meetings in a Vancouver hotel.[115] In 1910, they had forty-nine members and, "just as a for instance, you might possibly like to hear that when one or two of our members got married all the mechanics got together in their spare time and assisted in erecting their home without asking for any pay, which goes to show for the feeling that exists among Wellingtonians out here [in Vancouver]."[116] They also agreed at one of their meetings that "the unanimous wish of all present was to "give every assistance to anyone desirous of coming to the far West,"[117] and later considered in more detail what practical help would be offered to Wellington people who were moving to Vancouver.[118] The relocation of a stone, taken from Tintagel Castle in Cornwall, the legendary birthplace of King Arthur, to the community named after it in British Columbia, is yet another example. People living in Tintagel, located west of Prince George, marked the anniversary of Confederation in 1967 with great solemnity by commemorating their links with Cornwall.[119]

The colonization saga that reached Canada's Pacific coast in the late nineteenth century had its beginnings over two centuries earlier in Atlantic Canada. A host of farmers, agricultural labourers, craftsmen, tradesmen, industrial workers, fishermen, miners, clerks, business and professional people, and even the landed gentry, joined the English influx to Canada that peaked during the early twentieth century. With Canada's improving economic prospects, well-advertised promotional campaigns, and a rise in imperialist sentiments, the English switched their earlier preference for the United States and arrived in droves. In 1903, around 47,000 English people had immigrated to Canada, but that the number spiralled to 243,000 in 1912. However, despite the attention that has been focused on the colonization that took place in the Prairies, the major influx of English immigrants experienced by Ontario at the time received little comment. In fact, Ontario's industrial expansion proved to be more of a draw than the Golden West's farming opportunities.

CHAPTER 6

The Great Twentieth-Century Exodus from England to Canada

I had to take the first job I could get. That job is farming 120 miles from Toronto. I have to work like a slave ... for 10 dollars a month (Sundays as well) and my food.[1]

Having moved to Ontario in 1907, an unemployed Bristol man with the initials F.D. wrote home complaining that he had been required to accept a farm labouring job. As a recipient of public funds from Bristol City Council, needed to finance his emigration costs, he was expected to help relieve Canada's chronic shortage of agricultural labour, but, coming from a city, he naturally preferred urban employment. Thus, while British policy-makers hoped that loyal and industrious people from the crowded English cities would serve Canada's needs by working on farms, many refused and made a beeline for the urban centres. This trend was compounded by the fact that four-fifths of Britain's population at the time was urban. Thus, the English, who were the largest component of the major British influx to Canada that occurred during the first three decades of the twentieth century, were not going to be the saviours of Canadian agriculture. An English bartender, lamplighter, draper, bookkeeper, or clerk could not easily be persuaded to adopt the back-breaking life of an agricultural labourer in the newly opened Prairies. That was a reality of life that had to be accepted.

During the peak emigration period of the early twentieth century, English immigrants arrived as individuals or, less frequently, in family groups, some to establish farms, homesteads, and ranches, but more commonly to seek employment in the towns and cities. The reluctance shown by many to take up the recommended occupation of farming was a sore point, but it was perfectly understandable. Some had experience of the new machinery being used in industry; others had wide-ranging practical and marketable skills. A large number could easily find employment in relatively unskilled service occupations, such as domestic servants, general and agricultural labourers, waiters, janitors, night watchmen, or department store workers. The increasing concentration of English workers in Canadian urban centres caused the labour unions to complain that they were swamping the jobs market and depressing local wages. Be that as it may, the town- or city-bred English were attracted far more by the prospect of factory, machine-shop, or other urban employment than by the possibilities of agricultural settlement.

A century earlier the situation had been very different. Then, farming was the main attraction. A steady stream of self-financed English settlers established themselves in rural areas across eastern and mid-Canada, although their numbers were modest when compared with the Scots and Irish. Upper and Lower Canada suddenly acquired a sizable number of English agricultural workers during the 1830s who, having been made redundant by the arrival of threshing machines, had their emigration costs financed by their parish councils. Whether financially assisted or independently funded, many more followed, often writing letters home extolling the merits of Canadian farming; but by the end of the nineteenth century the situation was very different. With the escalating use of mechanization across Britain, people had been moving in great numbers from the country to the city. As a consequence, an increasing proportion of the English immigrants who arrived in Canada at this time were urban workers.

As machines reduced the requirement for intensive manual labour in the country and by the same token opened up new manufacturing and

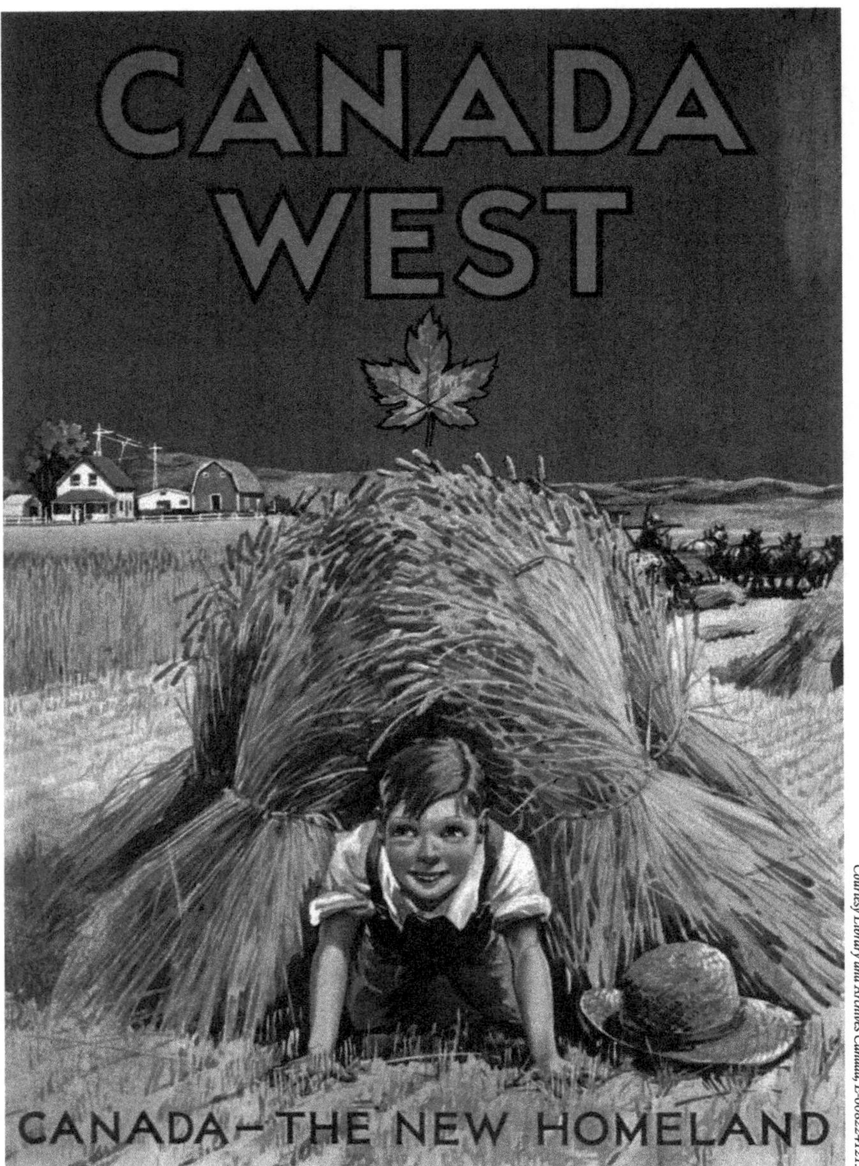

Courtesy Library and Archives Canada, E-008224121.

Front cover of the 1927 edition of *Canada West*. The magazine promoted the Prairie provinces in the hope of attracting British and American immigrants.

construction opportunities in the cities and towns, it was inevitable that such a population shift would occur in Britain. However, it was unsustainable. Jobs could not keep pace with the demand, leading to exceedingly high unemployment and, for those who could find work, often pitifully low wages. Emigration was again seized upon as the solution; but many of those seeking help to emigrate were now the urban poor, even though some were recent arrivals from the country.

This mismatch between Britain's surplus urban labour and Canada's almost insatiable requirement for farm workers happened just as the British influx to Canada was reaching its peak. While before Confederation the English were a relatively small proportion of the British immigrants coming to Canada, they formed an overwhelming majority of the much larger group who poured into Canada in the late nineteenth and early twentieth centuries (Table 1).[2] Those with a farming background probably sought work in the country, but otherwise most chose to benefit from the employment opportunities being created in the towns and cities as agricultural settlement progressed.

The explosive growth in English immigration at the turn of the century reflected Canada's improving economic prospects, the intensive promotional efforts of agents acting for the provincial and federal governments — who drew special attention to the new opportunities available in the Prairies and British Columbia — and the rising preference for Empire destinations. In the 1880s and 1890s, fewer than 20 percent of the English who emigrated chose Canada, with most heading for the United States; but starting in the 1900s that trend began to reverse. By 1903, Canada started to acquire almost as many English as the United States, and by 1910 it had become far more popular. In 1910 alone, just over 108,000 English immigrants arrived in Canada, representing 72 percent of the total intake from Britain (Table 2).[3] In fact, the English were the largest immigrant group in Canada in every decade from Confederation (1867) until the 1960s.

Understandably, the provincial and federal governments did what they could to attract English farm labourers, running promotional campaigns and employing battalions of agents in southern and central England, where much of the country's best arable land was concentrated.

A welcome development was the formation of the English agricultural trade union movement in 1871, which more or less immediately advocated emigration, with Canada being the principal beneficiary. Canada's labour unions initially welcomed the arrival of the English farm workers, recognizing the need for their labour, but after it became clear that urban workers, masquerading as farm labourers, were taking advantage of the cheaper fares on offer, they opposed immigration. However, bona fide English farm workers were much in demand and well-managed recruitment schemes, run during the 1870s, brought a steady stream of them to Canada.

As he toured Wiltshire, Dorset, and the Midlands in the mid 1870s, George T. Denison, the Ontario Immigration Commissioner, found plenty of enthusiastic gatherings but also met resistance from some Dorset farmers who feared that emigration would bring a demand for higher wages for those who remained.[4] Many "are beginning to be afraid of the agitation in favour of emigration and often the clergymen, who have control of the venues, refuse to hire them or let them be used for emigration lectures." Sometimes he had to "speak in the open air to the poor labourers [either] in the street or village green." While "in some places the leading people are very kind and very willing to assist me … the farmers are very much opposed to our movement." Nevertheless, in one week, in mid-March, he managed to canvass North Dorset comprehensively, giving lectures every night for a week (except Sunday) at Weymouth, Bridport, Dorchester, Milton Abbas, Poole, and Wimborne [Minster].[5]

Moving on to Oxfordshire, he drew a large audience at Wootton, a village to the north of Oxford, where he learned some would emigrate but "want of money alone prevents many more from leaving."[6] He spoke to large gatherings at Wellesbourne, close to Leamington Spa, and at Fenny Compton. Upon learning that people in Herefordshire were leaving for Virginia or Minnesota, in the United States, he headed for Ledbury and Ludlow. Ending his tour at Leintwardine in Herefordshire, a short distance from Ludlow, Denison pronounced that, through his exertions, the people of Herefordshire, Wiltshire, Dorset, Oxfordshire, and Warwickshire "were now talking of going to Ontario … as I have been almost alone in working up Ontario in Canada among them."[7]

A year after Denison's tour, emigration was given a stimulus in the eastern counties, particularly in Suffolk and Cambridgeshire, when around six thousand agricultural trade unionists were locked out by farmers in an attempt to destroy their union. Many "were in fact escorted by union officials to Ontario, where they were apparently soon able to obtain employment."[8] Another group of 588 farm workers and their families, who mainly came from Lincolnshire, left the following year for Ontario. However, by this time trade union involvement in emigration was beginning to wane, and by 1881 it came to an abrupt end. Trade union leaders could see little sense in encouraging the emigration of what were usually their most able members and doubted the value it had in increasing the bargaining position of those who remained behind, since the numbers leaving at any time were relatively small. So, while the emigration of farm labourers continued after 1881, it did so without any support from the agricultural trade unions. It relied instead on funds provided by parishes, land owners, and the increasing number of philanthropic bodies that were being formed to assist poor people to emigrate.

As a much sought-after group, farm labourers were offered reduced sea-crossing fares but, as opposition to assisted emigration increased, the Canadian government was forced to withdraw its subsidies in 1888, after which time it instead offered bonus payments to the booking agents who recruited them.[9] But in 1872, agricultural trade unionists and their families paid only £2 5s. per adult for a crossing to Quebec, with men planning to settle in Ontario paying even less at £1 0s. 4d., the Ontario government making up the difference.[10] Ten years later the rate for passages from Liverpool to Quebec rose to £3 per adult for agricultural labourers and their families, female domestic servants paying the same, while mechanics, navvies, general labourers, and their families had to pay £4 per adult.[11]

Farm workers usually went off in groups, a typical example being James Miller's Yorkshire contingent who left for Quebec in 1882.[12] Acting as agent for the Dominion Steamship Company, Miller recruited thirty-nine people from the East Riding and accompanied them to Driffield railway station to begin their long journey to Canada. They were said to be "of the agricultural class, all bound for Canada and the North West."[13] Such offers were being taken up across the country and, with the farmer delegations being sent from England, Canada's agricultural opportunities became even more widely known.

Of course, English farmers with capital were particularly in demand. The Lincolnshire-born Colonel Francis Fane, one of four wealthy English farmers to visit Canada in 1890, by invitation of the federal government, pronounced that the country had a good deal to offer farmers and farm labourers. An immigrant could buy "a nice farm with a good house and cleared land at about $30 (£6) an acre in the Eastern Townships — in doing this he would avoid the hardships of Manitoba and the North West and would be in the midst of comparative comforts and society and within easy reach of markets, schools, etc."[14]

Henry Simmons, from Wokingham (Surrey), another member of the group, noted that productive farms could be bought in Ontario at from £10 to £20 an acre "with good houses, buildings and fences, and land all under cultivation, and where every comfort of life can be obtained and enjoyed just as easily as and more economically than in England." Simmons also believed that Ontario farmers made excellent prairie settlers, "making openings" in many parts of Ontario for newly arrived immigrants with capital. He travelled to the London area, where he met the Lincolnshire-born J. Gibson who had a farm in Delaware Township. In driving there he noticed "the original log huts … standing at the rear of the new, substantial well-built brick residences. All the houses had gardens and trees planted around, giving them a homelike and English appearance."[15] However, the really intensive promotional activity was directed at potential farm labourer recruits.

Having emigrated as a young man and taken up homesteading in Saskatchewan, the Kent-born John Hawkes could speak with unrivalled authority about Canada's farming potential.[16] The federal government employed men like him to return to places in England where they had contacts, to persuade farm workers of Canada's merits. Speaking with first-hand knowledge and experience of Canadian farming methods and conditions, Hawkes would have exercised considerable influence. Well-pleased with Hawkes's results, W.D. Scott, the superintendent of immigration for the federal government, reported to the minister of the interior in 1905 that he "is thoroughly well posted on our western

Courtesy Library and Archives Canada, C-063260.

The Canadian Coronation Arch, erected in Whitehall, London, in 1902 to commemorate the coronation of King Edward VII. The temporary arch had emblazoned on its front: "Canada — Britain's Granary. God Save our King and Queen." And on the reverse: "Canada: Free Homes for Millions: God Bless the Royal Family."

country," having led "a personally-conducted party." Judging from his lecture itinerary the following year, when Hawkes toured his home county of Kent as well as Essex, Middlesex, and Sussex, his canvassing work was concentrated in the southeast of England.[17]

Similarly, Berkshire-born Rice Sheppard, who farmed near Edmonton and helped to found the Alberta Farmers Association, visited England as a farmer delegate in 1906–09, concentrating his efforts in Berkshire, Hampshire, the Isle of Wight, Oxfordshire, and the Channel Islands.[18] The great demand for agricultural labourers and domestic servants was always stressed while government newspaper advertisements proclaimed that in going to Canada immigrants would "get a piece of the earth in the Empire." They would be "under the Flag, in Britain's nearest overseas dominion."[19]

Edward Brewster, the son of an affluent farmer from near Myddle in Shropshire, who had prospered in Compton in the Eastern Townships, was seen as another ideal ambassador. Having emigrated around 1877 when in his early twenties, Brewster was snapped up in 1906 to work alongside Henry Mitchell, the Canadian emigration agent for the West Midlands, who was based in Birmingham.[20] His tour covered the major towns and cities to the north and west of Birmingham, including Wolverhampton, Tamworth, Walsall, Belper, Dudley, Kidderminster, and Stourbridge.[21] He was particularly well received in Shropshire, visiting Shrewsbury, Market Drayton, and Oswestry, where he organized many meetings and held hundreds of interviews. At Rushbury he attracted about one hundred "of the very best class — young men, farmers' sons and farm labourers, also some domestics." At Chetwynd there were "about 80 present, chiefly of the agricultural class, a large number being young men, just the class wanted … at Weston Rhyn: about 100 present, principally young people of the agricultural class [who] showed great interest." Also at Pontesbury, there was "a splendid audience composed mostly of agriculturalists. Many in the audience had friends and relatives in Canada."[22]

Meanwhile, Henry Goodridge, yet another farmer delegate and federal government agent who was based in Edmonton, toured the southwest of England in 1906, lecturing in Bristol, Bath, Cheltenham, Gloucester, Hereford, Stroud, Swindon, Salisbury, Taunton, Bridgwater,

Street, Cheddar, and Tiverton.[23] Given that another Canadian immigration agent, H.M. Murray, was based at Exeter in Devon at the time, it would seem that this was yet another hotspot for recruiting farm labourers.[24] Yet Albert J. Wilkinson, from Bishop Auckland in County Durham, had little success in drumming up interest in Canada's farming opportunities, attracting instead the wives of painters, bricklayers, fitters, and carpenters who had already emigrated and for whom no bonus payment could be claimed.[25]

With the rapid growth in Canada's population since the late twentieth century, the demand for domestic servants became extreme. Women were needed in great numbers for household work, child rearing, and, in the case of farms, to help with outdoor chores and the dairy.[26] Most female domestics who went to Canada were British, with the English forming the majority. Apart from their practical usefulness, they were much-valued for the beneficial effect they had on the gender imbalances between the two countries. By emigrating they helped to reduce the female surplus in Britain, while supplementing the female population in male-dominated regions of Canada, whose imbalances were particularly severe in Saskatchewan, Alberta, and British Columbia.[27] The federal government immigration agent, John Hawkes, who was based in Saskatchewan, made a particularly heartfelt plea to British women to come to the Prairies. In an article entitled "Where a Woman Has a Chance," published in *The Woman's Magazine*, he outlined the benefits of being "objects of distinction" in a country where women were relatively scarce. "Any domestic servant who can get to the Canadian west will only need glance at the *Manitoba Free Press* to see opportunities galore in the advertising columns of this influential newspaper." British women would "get a better return for their labour in Canada," and men would find wives:

> She is needed because there are lonely and distant men whose lives are incomplete. Any good woman can make a home or find a home in Canada; but, after all, the answer to the problem lies in the fact that there are more men than women in Canada. The question is coldly statistical, but it is also full of sentiment.[28]

While many working-class women responded to the challenge of employment in Canada as domestics, middle- and upper-class women generally needed more persuasion. The problem was that in seeking to become domestic servants in Canada, they were accepting work they would have shunned in Britain.[29] However, those who were trapped in low-paid jobs and had not yet found a husband could see how Canada might be a stepping stone to better economic prospects and even marriage. Nevertheless, a drop in social standing was seen as inevitable and even feared. To lessen such concerns, opinion-formers in Britain suggested, rather disingenuously, that domestics would be treated as social equals. In reality, though, high-status Canadians were unlikely to want to associate socially with the woman who washed their floors. Pride in Empire was also invoked. As John Hawkes stressed in his article, women were needed, not just to fill job vacancies, but ultimately to become the wives of British settlers and mothers of the next generation of Canadians.[30] However, negative feedback from middle-class women about their treatment in Canada prompted the Colonial Intelligence League for Educated Women to employ Ella Sykes as an undercover reporter to investigate conditions for herself.[31]

Pretending to be an impoverished English gentlewoman, the upper-class and wealthy Ella concluded that "Canada is certainly the paradise of the labouring classes; but the girl who goes by the name 'lady' in the British Isles will find that her culture is little if at all appreciated by her employers."[32] Canadian employers simply wanted a well-trained, well-presented, and industrious servant:

> But whatever she undertakes, a girl must not think of coming out to the Dominion without a knowledge of cooking, washing and so on, this being absolutely necessary in a country where only five percent of the women have servants. She must also be smart in appearance, as that will tell greatly in her favour when seeking work. An English lady, living in a big Canadian town, told me that she always knew her own country-women by their ill-hung skirts, their badly-cut blouses, with a gap between skirt and waistband, and their general slovenly

> appearance, in strong contrast to the Canadian working woman, in her well-starched "waist" or neat cotton dress. British girls make a great mistake when they think that "anything will do" for an office.[33]

Because they were in such demand, British domestic servants were initially offered subsidized fares for their sea crossings and later booking agents could claim bonuses for selling them places on steamships.[34] Many women's emigration societies had formed to help them with their travel arrangements and secure employment, the most prominent being the British Women's Emigration Association.[35]

As ever, government immigration agents and steamship booking agents also played a significant role in promoting job opportunities. Henry Martin, a booking agent who was based in Beswick, near Manchester, clearly felt that the announcement that been placed in a local newspaper by the Society for the Organisation and Protection of Female Immigrants would attract greater numbers if promotional leaflets were made available. Writing to

Courtesy Library and Archives Canada, C-009652.

British females on their way to Canada to take up employment as domestic servants. Photograph taken in Quebec by William James Topley, circa 1911.

a Canadian government minister in 1881, he offered to produce a small handbill "stating concisely the benefits to be derived and the advantages to be gained from emigration to the Dominion" and giving "the names of ladies to whom servants can be referred on arrival in Canada." Since his Post Office was also a Registry Office for domestic servants, Martin expected that his efforts would encourage many local women to move to Montreal.[36]

The British Women's Emigration Association was the prime advocate for middle- and upper-class women who sought employment overseas, with or without the goal of eventual marriage. In the early 1900s, it sent a number of high-ranking ladies to Empire destinations to assess job opportunities for women, primarily looking at openings for domestic servants and factory workers.[37] It sent Miss A.L. Vernon to Canada in 1904 to "inquire into the conditions of women's work in factories, the demand for them in various towns, and especially to ascertain what could be done to provide suitable board and lodging for them."[38] Touring Quebec, Montreal, Ottawa, Toronto, Hamilton, London, Paris, and Winnipeg, Miss Vernon soon discovered that there was a demand for machine operators, particularly in the clothing industry, and that jobs were well-paid:

> The position of all working people in Canada is better than with us. They live better, are more independent, and have a far greater chance of owning their own homes than they ever would here. In my opinion it is therefore to the advantage of the better class of women factory workers to emigrate to Canada, provided always that definite employment is assured, and that reasonable board and lodging can be secured, which must not be reckoned at less than $3 a week.[39]

However, when she spoke to employers in the various cities and town that she visited, it was made clear to her that, although they sought women to fill factory jobs, "there was a much more crying and general demand for [female domestic] servants." Nevertheless, she persevered with her visits to clothing factories, meeting the owner of the Allen Manufacturing Company in Toronto, which employed five hundred girls. While he could make use of more female workers, "as many of his machines are idle for lack of workers," he pointed out that they had "very little respect for 'loafers' no matter what their previous social position may have been."[40]

On a visit to another Toronto factory, Miss Vernon met Miss Bell, who told her that she disapproved of immigration: "There are already more women than they can look after, and English immigrants have imported many of the vices," including going into a public house.[41] A Mr. Bear, who ran a garment factory in Toronto, "feared we could not send out any girls of so good a class from home, as he employed," while the owner of the Toronto Carpet Manufacturing Company said he "did not think that there was much demand for women workers at this moment."[42] In the end, Miss Vernon had to agree. There were not the employment opportunities in Canadian factories that she had anticipated. A few females found jobs in factories, but no actual scheme was ever implemented. The main conclusion reached was that British females were only likely to land a factory job if they were prepared to fall back on domestic work during periods when business was slack.

Miss Vernon had more success as one of the leading lights of the Leaton Colonial Training Home, established in Shropshire in 1890 by the British Women's Emigration Association. It set out to prepare high-born women for domestic service overseas, offering lessons in housework, milking, bee keeping, laundry, and needlework. The Leaton pupils were generally women "who have had little or no training in domestic duties and who, being obliged to work for their living, prefer to try their fortunes abroad rather than to seek employment in England where almost every branch of women's work is overcrowded."[43] As "home helps," middle-class English women would earn far higher wages and, since it was argued that they would go to places in Canada where no one knew or cared about their social status, they could more easily reinvent themselves as servants.[44] Their ultimate aim was to find husbands, but if that did not happen they could move on to a better-paid and higher-status job later on.[45] And it seems the college was very successful. In 1907, Miss Vernon wrote proudly that "it may fairly be claimed that, in Canada at any rate, they have made such a name for their Training Home that over and over again applications come from mistresses who only wish for a girl trained at Leaton."[46]

It would seem that a good many of the high-status home helps ended up in British Columbia, a province having an abundance of middle- and upper-class English families, able to pay for their services.[47] Between 1911 and 1921 it experienced a substantial growth in its female population, nearly halving its male surplus.[48] And in 1921, women of English origin accounted for just under half of the total female population of the province (Table 3). The inescapable conclusion is that British Columbia had attracted more English domestics of all classes, high-born or not, than did the three Prairie provinces. Meanwhile, English females were less represented in Alberta, Saskatchewan, and Manitoba, where they accounted for only around 30 percent of the total female population. Although a disproportionate number of English females had clearly gone to British Columbia overall, the majority would have found employment in Toronto or Montreal, either as domestics or factory workers.

Having acquired their settlers from the late eighteenth century, Ontario and Quebec both had long-established communities, whose populations by the early twentieth century had a more or less equal balance between males and females.[49] While Toronto and Montreal continued to attract the largest English populations, Toronto's appeal grew far more dramatically. By 1921, Toronto's English, at nearly 261,000, accounted for half of the city's total population, while Montreal's 88,000 English represented a paltry 14 percent. Meanwhile, the English accounted for at least 70 percent of the population growth that had occurred in Vancouver, Victoria, London, and Halifax between 1911 and 1921.[50] Overall, people of English ancestry were strongly represented in London, Victoria, Halifax, Toronto, and Hamilton, where they represented at least 50 percent of the total, and Saint John, Calgary, Vancouver, and Regina, where they represented at least 40 percent of the total (Table 4).[51] Towns and cities suited them.

The Census of 1921 reveals the strong preference of the English-born for urban areas (Table 5).[52] Ninety-one percent of Quebec's English lived in towns and cities, while 72 percent of Ontario's and just under 70 percent of Nova Scotia's English did the same. They were also to be found mainly in the urban centres of Manitoba and Alberta, although by a narrower margin when compared with country locations. While they were more or less equally divided between town and country in British

Columbia and New Brunswick, they displayed a marked preference for country in Prince Edward Island, but less so in Saskatchewan. The overwhelming conclusion is that English immigrants were essentially urban dwellers who continued as such in Canada.

The rapid growth of population in the western provinces created a large new market for manufactured goods, which in turn stimulated a great expansion of industry in central Canada between 1900 and 1914. With its rich natural resources and central location, its population grew by around 35 percent during the first two decades of the twentieth century, while during this same period the population of the less-favoured Maritime region rose by only 12 percent.[53] Across Canada, the industrial, construction, agricultural, and service sectors provided jobs for miners, dockworkers, railway construction workers, tradesmen, clerks, domestic servants, general labourers, factory workers, carters, shopkeepers, warehouse workers, shoemakers, tanners, iron and steel workers, blacksmiths,

Courtesy Library and Archives Canada, a024627.

The Northern Electric Company factory in Montreal, circa 1916. The growth of manufacturing and a service sector created job opportunities for semi-skilled workers, often women.

boilermakers, and many others.[54] Britain had been the home of new technology, and those who came with sought-after skills would have received a ready welcome. People in higher-status professional jobs, such as bankers, economists, lawyers, and teachers added to the concentration of the English in urban centres. The available data suggests that during the last quarter of the nineteenth century, middle/upper-class males accounted for 27 percent of all British emigrants, making them second in number to general labourers.[55] This unprecedented rise in the number of young and educated single men entering Canada was a further indication of its growing appeal over the United States

A desire to continue working in a particular trade could help to determine settlement choices. After marrying, Eliza Jane Anakin and Richard Ernest Cape, from Bridlington, in Yorkshire, moved to Chatham, Ontario, around 1880, with Richard hoping to find work as a cooper and Eliza hoping to carry on with her bonnet making. They had clearly chosen Chatham since she had an uncle living there who was a bonnet manufacturer and she duly became one of his apprentices.[56] However, for unskilled workers, finding employment could be problematic. A Bristol

Courtesy Glenbow Archives, NA-1328-64401.

Men at work at the Great Northern Tannery Ltd. in Edmonton, Alberta, circa 1910.

bricklayer who had been assisted to emigrate by Bristol City Council in 1907 claimed that "in Toronto there is no work. There are hundreds of men walking the streets.... I answered an advertisement this afternoon for a labourer's job and when I got there 100 [men] were there before me." Another man complained that the hours of work were onerous and a former boot finisher found that there was plenty of work available "but you have to search about until you find the right job."[57]

In 1903, female machinists in London's East End were being encouraged by the British Women's Emigration Association to seek work in the Montreal clothing factories; but they were warned that they might become temporarily unemployed and may have to fall back on domestic work.[58] English female hosiery workers, who came mainly from the East Midlands, were able to benefit from the new jobs being created in Canada with the expansion of its knitwear industry. Between 1907 and 1928, around seven hundred women were advanced money by the Penman Company to enable them to relocate to Paris, Ontario. Representatives of the knitwear company not only recruited the skilled female workforce, who came mainly from Nottinghamshire and Leicestershire, but also visited the East Midlands in order to purchase knitting and looping machines from local suppliers. Being attracted by the better pay and conditions, most of the East Midlands women worked at the Penman factories in Paris for many years, despite marrying and raising families.[59]

While there had been unprecedented growth between 1903 and 1906, and again from 1909 to 1911, Canada's economy was in decline between 1913 and 1915, thus increasing unemployment in the major urban centres. The Yorkshire-born Tom Morfitt worked at the newly constructed Toronto General Hospital at this time, "polishing marble and waxing floors for the opening day," at a pay rate of $2 per day. But once the hospital opened he became one of twenty-five to lose his job. He then attempted to "get on to the [Toronto] Exhibition staff," which would guarantee him work "for 3 months at $2 per day," but this failed to materialize.[60] He blamed his being out of work for eight weeks on "slack times; the [First World] War has made things bad in Canada and the United States.... Toronto is full of soldiers from all parts of the provinces."[61] Meanwhile, someone he knew called Tommy was still working in the shoe factory, and, having joined the union, "he gets a rise of $1 per week, more with promise of another rise later on — there was talk of a strike but it is settled now."[62]

Understandably, Canada's labour leaders were concerned about the unsettled state of the jobs market, voicing disapproval over the increasing flood of English immigrant workers, who, in their view, were exacerbating the problem. Trade unionists had actually been running campaigns in England to discourage emigration, arguing that English immigrants would either take jobs away from Canadians or, in the case of the work-shy ones, become vagrants who would place heavy burdens on taxpayers and local charitable institutions.[63] Some trade unionists claimed that unscrupulous employers were using immigration as a means of obtaining cheap labour. In 1906, it was alleged that agents acting for a firm in Toronto deceived tradesmen from Staffordshire into thinking they would be given jobs in Winnipeg when in fact they were redirected to Toronto to act as strike breakers.[64] Labour leaders also complained about the considerable number of Britons who had falsely claimed to be agricultural labourers. According to them, "the *Daily News* seemed to capture the argument well when it called farm labour the sieve through which thousands of destitute urban dwellers had passed."[65] In their view, the proclaimed need for farm workers was merely a device for bringing more urban labour to Canada, causing intolerable pressure on the jobs market.

Owing to the immense increase in agricultural production that had taken place in the United States, Canada, and Argentina, British agriculture was in a severe crisis by the early twentieth century. Poor labourers, unable to find work in the countryside, had gone to the industrial cities, only to find that conditions there were even worse. The movement of labour from country to city effectively concentrated the nation's surplus labour in the city slums, where unemployment levels were soaring.

Emigration offered a way out, but the government only agreed to provide the necessary funding when the situation became desperate. Having resisted calls in the past from social reformers to provide public funds to assist paupers to emigrate, it changed tack when faced with what was rapidly becoming a major humanitarian disaster.[66] In 1905, it passed the Unemployed Workmen Act, which spawned a nationwide network of distress committees to channel funds raised by city councils to the unemployed.[67] Predictably, their arrival in Canada provoked a furious outcry from trade union leaders who were deeply upset by Britain's continuing use of Canada as a receptacle for its surplus urban workers.

Among the first to arrive under the scheme were six families and two single men, nearly all in their twenties, who were assisted in 1905 by Leeds City Council.[68] A second group from Leeds that followed two years later dispersed widely, with nine out of the fourteen heads of households stating they were heading for eastern Ontario, while the others went to Bowmanville, the Lake Erie region, Toronto, and Montreal.[69]

Lying in the heart of an agricultural area, Norwich had suffered badly during the agricultural depression, leaving a great surplus of unwanted labour. Thus it, too, had a distress committee by 1905. Once again, emigration was encouraged and the first group of eighteen men, two wives, and three children left the following year. They were met at the Toronto train station by an emigration agent "and, miracle of miracles, we all had work offered to us by 9 a.m."[70] With this promising beginning, a second group consisting of eighteen families followed, but they were said to be drunk and unruly. However, despite this setback, many more Norwich people were assisted to emigrate. Between 1905 and the outbreak of the First World War in 1914, a total of 1,501 Norwich people were helped by the city council to emigrate to Canada.[71] Similarly, the Birkenhead Distress Committee assisted some of its poorest families to emigrate to Canada between 1906 and 1915.[72]

The majority of those assisted under the scheme came from London. A group of 7,550 people from Greater London were assisted to emigrate to Canada between 1905 and 1917, with some settling in British Columbia.[73] The Central Unemployed Body for London (CUB) coordinated the work of each of the distress committees set up for each London borough and raised additional funds.[74] In 1908, it organized funding for some 825 London families (4,268 people) and, despite having raised £22,000 together with the West Ham Distress Committee, the amount was insufficient to fund their emigration costs.[75] In the end, the Charity Organisation Society had to find the necessary donations to meet the remaining costs.

Meanwhile, the Bristol Distress Committee assisted sixty-one families (307 people) in March–June 1906, at a cost of nearly £2,000. Their departures, clothing needs, and spending money were organized by the Bristol Emigration Society, which also assisted the men to find work. Although they were mainly labourers, the group also included painters, boot makers, bricklayers, and carpenters. Those with some farming experience were snapped up quickly as were the general labourers, who were "able to do rough work of a varied nature, chiefly on the farms." Most of the others found work in Toronto, with some voicing surprise at the wide choices available:

> I came out to this country having been practically out of work for six months in England and no more likely to get a situation than when I was first out. What strikes me about this place [Toronto] is the very thing I have been looking for — work: It is very plentiful. I know if I set out this morning I could get another place before night and fair wages.[76]

An added problem at the time was the stagnating state of Britain's textile industries. That, too, had its principal cause in foreign competition. A prime trouble spot was the mill town of Bolton, to the northwest of Manchester, which had been a major centre of cotton production. Following the loss of trade, Bolton cotton workers were laid off in great numbers. Emigration was seen as their only hope. Between 1912 and 1926, the Bolton and District Card and Ring Room Operatives' Provincial Association[77] organized the departure of around five hundred of its members to various destinations, including Canada. Since the First World War put an effective stop to emigration between 1915 and 1918, most departures occurred between 1912 and 1914 and 1919 and 1926.[78]

Throughout the early twentieth century Canada's labour movement viewed all forms of assisted emigration with alarm, singling out voluntary societies such as the Salvation Army for particular criticism. While the Army did help paupers to emigrate, most of its organizational work was done on behalf of the British working classes, who were usually able to fund their own relocation costs.[79] The people it helped were generally domestic servants, farm labourers, and urban workers, who mainly came from England. By 1922, the Salvation Army claimed to be the world's largest emigration agency, priding itself in having a rigorous policy for selecting suitable candidates and finding them appropriate job placements. Most of those it helped relocated to Canada.[80] The Army received grants from the Canadian government to help it to fund its supervised sea crossings, hostels for newly arrived immigrants, and its organizational and promotional activities.[81] Nevertheless, some trade unionists spent more time vilifying the Salvation Army than complaining about the paupers they were sending to Canada. They claimed that the Army was taking advantage of the most impoverished and vulnerable simply to obtain the $5 per immigrant bonus, which it could claim from the Canadian government. According to *The Industrial Banner*, an Ontario trade unionist newspaper, the "poor unfortunates," on whose behalf the Army received its bonuses, were to be seen "wandering the streets at night with no shelter provided, hungry, destitute and friendless."[82]

With the outbreak of the First World War in 1914, immigration to Canada from Britain reduced sharply. But as the war came to an end in 1918, it resumed again, only to dwindle to a trickle as the Great Depression hit world markets at the end of the 1920s. These were difficult times for Canadians, as John Muir of Pictou indicated in his letter to the *Manchester Guardian* in 1924. Concerned that the British government's efforts to resume immigration would add to Canada's escalating unemployment problems, he questioned how an influx of settlers "will make for prosperity as long as thousands of people are walking the streets looking for work."[83]

While Henry Jenkin from Cornwall found work in Niagara Falls at "a big electric company" backed by the government,[84] the Worcestershire-born Olwin Payne reported in 1928 that "we have a terrible lot of unemployed in the city of Calgary," although "I am pretty lucky to be working these days."[85] By this time, state-aided emigration from Britain was being promoted with a vengeance, thus reversing the government's previous non-interventionist approach. The Empire had taken centre stage.

Courtesy Library and Archives Canada, PA-031666.

The grandeur of the Canadian Pacific Railway Station in Vancouver, built in the early twentieth century, is a reminder of the prosperity that flowed from the arrival of the railways.

Enthusiasts of Empire longed to see an increase in the British population of the white dominions. There was a widespread belief that subsidized emigration would deal with Britain's unemployment problems, while providing the dominions with the good British "stock" they needed to help farm their lands and develop their economies. The outcome was the Empire Settlement Act of 1922, which committed the British government to providing £3 million per annum to fund loans and grants for emigration schemes over a fifteen-year period.[86] The imperialist propaganda in favour of emigration, which underpinned the legislation, even found expression in a magistrate's court in Birmingham. Objecting to a decision taken by the Canadian minister of immigration to bar "a man named Petit," who had been charged with drunkenness and attempted murder, from entering Canada, a Birmingham magistrate provided this assessment of Canada's needs:

> Canada requires more population … if he [the magistrate] could induce three hundred such persons [a convicted criminal] to take up residence in Canada, the Dominion in his view would greatly benefit by them.[87]

Understandably, Canada was a reluctant partner to Empire settlement.[88] Having grown weary of being used as a dumping ground for British outcasts, the Canadian government only provided limited assistance to three specified groups — domestic servants, agricultural workers, and children aged between eight and fourteen years of age sponsored by a voluntary society. However, far from promoting harmony, most of the collaborative ventures carried out under the terms of the Empire Settlement Act were plagued by bad planning, high costs, and a failure to repay loans. [89] Thus, they proved to be contentious and disappointing, none more so than the Harvesters' Scheme of 1928, which brought 8,500 British miners to the Prairies to help with the harvest. The majority of these workers were English.[90] It was hoped that after the harvest was collected they would settle permanently; but the miners had no wish to do so. In fact, the scheme was a total disaster — hardly surprising, given that most of those recruited were unsuited to farming and any who might have been suited were not given any relevant training.

The miners had been promised wages of £3 to £5 per week and free board, but on arrival were offered considerably less than this.[91] Some, having no intention of working on farms, headed for the urban centres or the United States, while others, fortunate in having family or friends owning farms, found a congenial slot for themselves. However, the majority sizzled with rage over what they viewed as worker exploitation. Being told that as mere novices they would have to accept reduced wages, they stood their ground and demanded the experienced man's pay that they had been promised. If their terms were not going to be met, they demanded to be sent home immediately.

Waging a clever campaign, they alleged that they were being exploited by greedy employers in Canada and an uncaring British government that was seeking to ship its social problems abroad. The miners were convinced that they had been wronged and were determined to agitate until they got their way. Attracting the support of both the Communist Party of Great Britain and the Communist Party of Canada, they caused a considerable stir. Predictably, their belligerent methods made them thoroughly unpopular in Canada, this in turn attracting vitriolic press comments in Britain about Canada's callous employers and uncaring officials. Faced with this calamitous situation, the Canadian authorities ordered a special train to take the "misfits, malingerers and malcontents" to Quebec so that they could board ships to Britain. In the end, 6,368 of the 8,500 original recruits accepted the offer of free transport home.[92] Quite clearly, this attempt to secure cheap farm labour through assisted immigration had backfired.

The demise of the Harvester's Scheme occurred at a time of severe economic depression. After 1930, emigration from Britain effectively ended, assisted or otherwise. As the Manchester-born Edith Baker, living in Eburne, near Vancouver, reported in her letter home to her uncle, times were extremely difficult. Growing disenchantment with the general economic situation had caused Edith and her family to join Canada's Socialist Party: "The capitalist system has failed miserably and people are being ruined under it."[93] Edith's aunt, Mrs. Speakman, came out alone "in her eightieth year" to visit her, bringing news of her grandchildren. "who have gone out pioneering in the still wild regions of Alberta. One of them has a family of five children and they are living in a log house only partly roofed as yet."[94]

They were some of the few to come from Britain at this time and settle in the Prairies. While the British-born population in Ontario and Quebec increased by eighty-three thousand between 1921 and 1931, it only increased by three thousand in the Prairies.[95] Thus, despite the money that had been poured into subsidized emigration schemes to further land settlement, only around 20 percent of the British-born population were employed in agriculture in 1931.[96]

Although the Empire settlement schemes had been a great disappointment, the self-funded Anglican missionary by the name of Eva Hasell made an exceptional contribution to the cause of Empire through her preaching in far-flung locations across Western Canada.[97]

An indomitable upper-class woman from Cumbria, Eva launched a Caravan Mission in the 1920s to bring Sunday school classes to children in isolated communities. In her eyes, encouraging pride in Empire came second only to promoting the teachings of the Anglican faith.[98] Realizing that motorized vans could be used to visit the isolated homesteads in the Prairies, she ordered one to be built in Winnipeg — "much like a tradesman's van in appearance. It was painted black, with 'Sunday School Mission, Anglican Church' lettered in red and gold on one side."[99] By 1928, Eva owned nine vans, whose costs she funded herself.

Eva continued her work into her eighty-fourth year. Her presence each year at various places across Western Canada would have brought ethnic and spiritual comfort to countless English settlers. And the more orthodox work of the Church of England clergy and the Society for the Propagation of the Gospel in Foreign Parts also helped to cement links between the two countries by invoking the Church's special responsibilities in regard to the British Empire.[100]

While the heavily subsidized immigration of the 1920s failed to realize its objectives, the largely self-funded influx that occurred between 1901 and 1921 achieved a spectacular growth in Canada's English-born population (Table 6).[101] Their overall numbers trebled, while the English presence increased fivefold in British Columbia and sixfold in the Prairie provinces.[102] However, despite this dramatic population growth in the West, the English-born maintained a more or less equal balance in their numbers when compared with Ontario and Quebec. In 1921, around 369,000 lived in Ontario and Quebec compared with around 300,000 who lived in the Prairies and British Columbia. Thus, the factories and other forms of urban employment in the middle regions of Canada had been a great attraction, although their take-up by the English went almost unnoticed by commentators.

What is also evident is that the major English presence in the Prairies stems not from the English-born but from the people having English ancestry who relocated there from eastern and mid Canada as well as from the United States. In fact, as early as 1911, half of the population of the four Western provinces was Canadian-born. Between 1901 and

1921 the English-born population in the Prairies and British Columbia grew by around 163,000, but when North American–born people having English ancestry are take into account, the English presence swelled to around 627,000 (Table 7).[103]

Thus, the offspring of the English immigrants who had settled earlier in other parts of North America played a much more important role in the opening up of the West than did the settlers who arrived directly from England. People in England, who were accustomed to an urban way of life, generally found the prospect of a factory job in mid Canada more appealing than homesteading in the Prairies. On the other hand, people of English ancestry, having experienced farming in the Maritimes, Ontario, Quebec, or the United States, grabbed the West's new farming opportunities with both hands. While the vigorous advertising, lecturing campaigns, bonuses, and offers of assisted passages clearly had only a limited impact in England, the grapevine and favourable feedback had brought a flood of North American migrants who carried their English origins with them to the Western provinces. Nevertheless, put into perspective, their overall presence was far greater in Ontario. A long-settled English population, some of whose ancestors can be traced back to the Loyalist influx of the late eighteenth century, was supplemented by successive waves of English people who came first to benefit from its rich agricultural land and later its great industrial growth. By 1921, Ontario had acquired nearly half of Canada's English population (Table 8).[104]

In addition to the various government-inspired schemes, a great many Victorian charities also sprang up in Britain to come to the aid of people who it was thought would benefit from emigration. Thousands of destitute girls and boys from the slums of Liverpool, London, Birmingham, and Manchester ended up in Canada, not by choice, but because they were sent there by well-meaning philanthropists and agencies. However, allegations of cruelty and exploitation led to serious doubts as to the eventual fate of these exported children.

Table 1

Passenger Arrivals in Canada from England and Wales, Scotland, and Ireland, 1900–30

[Carrier & Jeffrey, *External Migration*, 96]

Year	England and Wales	Scotland	Ireland	Great Britain and Ireland
1900	15,748	1,733	962	18,443
1901	12,176	2,235	1,346	15,757
1902	20,985	3,811	1,497	26,293
1903	46,760	10,296	2,596	59,652
1904	54,051	12,715	2,915	69,681
1905	64,876	14,214	3,347	82,437
1906	88,099	22,278	4,482	114,859
1907	110,329	33,393	7,494	151,216
1908	57,798	16,705	4,088	78,591
1909	60,241	18,423	4,106	82,770
1910	108,268	35,570	6,367	150,205
1911	129,241	41,218	6,807	177,266
1912	131,353	36,835	7,442	175,630
1913	142,616	39,866	8,372	190,854
1914	59,415	15,446	3,709	78,570
1915	13,031	2,887	854	16,772
1916	9,540	3,093	911	13,544
1917	1,918	407	161	2,486
1918	1,448	217	44	1,709
1919	70,060	7,919	1,130	79,109
1920	93,467	22,084	3,346	118,837
1921	49,080	15,453	3,394	87,907
1922	30,328	12,278	3,212	45,818
1923	52,500	29,070	7,323	88,893
1924	38,850	19,136	10,278	68,284
1925	24,280	11,040	5,203	40,523
1926	28,550	14,735	8,336	51,621

1927	31,316	15,473	7,941	54,730
1928	33,264	15,434	7,609	56,307
1929	38,154	20,090	9,080	67,324
1930	18,822	8,878	4,421	32,121

TABLE 2

Passenger Arrivals in North America from England and Wales, 1909–13

[Carter & Jeffrey, *External Migration*, 96]

	Canada		**U.S.A.**	
Year	**English**	**British**	**English**	**British**
1903	46,760	59,652	68,791	123,663
1904	54,051	69,681	76,546	146,445
1905	64,676	82,437	58,229	122,370
1906	88,099	114,859	78,179	144,817
1907	110,329	151,216	91,593	170,264
1908	57,798	78,591	49,841	96.079
1909	60,241	82,770	50,787	108,884
1910	108,268	150,205	62,127	131,064
1911	129,241	177,266	60,054	120,108
1912	242,574	324,052	97,937	190,110
1913	142,616	190,854	46,435	94,691

TABLE 3

Growth in the English Female Population*in the Prairies and British Columbia, 1911–21
[1911 Census of Canada, Vol. I, Table XII, 368–69; 1921 Census of Canada, Vol. I, Table 25, 358–59]

	Manitoba	**Saskatchewan**	**Alberta**	**B.C.**
1911				
All females	205,558	200,702	150,674	140,861
English females*	53,033	47,653	38,859	54,587
English as a % of females	25.8	23.7	25.8	38.75
1921				
All females	289,551	343,810	261,246	231,173
English females*	80,930	93,881	83,191	105,989
English as a % of females	27.95	27.3	31.8	45.8

**females of English origin*

TABLE 4

English* Populations in Canadian Cities in 1911 and 1921 Expressed as a Percentage of the Total Population
[1911 Census of Canada, Vol. II, Table XIV, 372–73; 1921 Census of Canada, Vol. I, Table 28, 542–43]

	1911 (%)	**1921 (%)**
Calgary	38.1	43.3
Edmonton	31.9	38.6
Halifax	47.9	52.9
Hamilton	45.2	49.9
London	52.0	56.4

Montreal	13.4	14.2
Ottawa	23.2	23.8
Quebec	4.5	3.8
Regina	39.4	41.5
Saint John	42.5	48.9
Toronto	48.15	50.9
Vancouver	36.4	42.6
Victoria	50.1	55.4
Windsor	33.1	37.0
Winnipeg	31.2	34.3

**people of English origin*

TABLE 5

Distribution of English-Born Populations Between Rural and Urban Residences in 1921

[1921 Census of Canada, Vol. II, Table 51, 303–10.]

English-born across Canada	**Rural** (%)	**Urban** (%)
Total immigrant-born	43.6	56.4
Total English-born	35.8	64.2

English-born by province	**Rural** (%)	**Urban** (%)
Alberta	44.9	55.1
British Columbia	49.1	50.9
Manitoba	42.5	57.5
New Brunswick	48.5	51.5
Nova Scotia	32.2	67.8
Ontario	27.6	72.4
Prince Edward Island	62.2	37.8
Quebec	8.7	91.3
Saskatchewan	56.3	43.7

Table 6

English-Born Populations by Province in 1901, 1911 and 1921
[1901 Census of Canada, Vol. I, Table XVI, 450–51;
1921 Census of Canada, Vol. II, Table 36, 240–41]

	1901	1911	1921
Alberta	(10,752)*	42,606	62,664
British Columbia	19,385	69,036	100,792
Manitoba	20,036	56,659	68,080
New Brunswick	3,257	4,701	6,425
Nova Scotia	4,745	10,009	11,133
Ontario	120,600	230,244	313,514
Prince Edward Island	717	418	371
Quebec	20,589	43,418	55,393
Saskatchewan	(10,752)*	52,987	67,616
Total English born	199,901	510,674	686,663

*Northwest Territories, later Alberta and Saskatchewan.

Table 7

English-Origin Populations by Province in 1901, 1911, and 1921
[1921 Census of Canada, Vol. I, Table 23, 354–55]

	1901	1911	1921	Percentage English origin in 1921
Alberta	16,490	97,922	180,478	31.0
British Columbia	52,863	133,186	221,145	42.0
Manitoba	64,542	122,875	170,286	28.0
New Brunswick	104,683	106,017	131,664	34.0
Nova Scotia	159,753	177,701	202,106	38.5
Ontario	701,413	884,479	1,211,660	41.0
P.E.I.	24,043	22,176	23,313	26.0

Quebec	114,710	153,368	196,982	0.08
Saskatchewan	17,543	124,091	206,472	27.0
Total English origin in Canada	1,260,899	1,823,150	2,545,496	29.0

TABLE 8

Distribution of the English-Origin Population by Province in 1921

[1921 Census of Canada, Vol. I, Table 23, 354–55]

	Percentage English-origin
Alberta	7.1
British Columbia	8.7
Manitoba	6.7
New Brunswick	5.2
Nova Scotia	7.9
Ontario	47.6
Prince Edward Island	0.9
Quebec	7.7
Saskatchewan	8.2

CHAPTER 7

Child Immigration

> *The Committee quite recognised the importance of keeping healthy and honest children at home and preparing them for work in our own country. But there were boys and girls who need to be rescued every year from degrading and dangerous surroundings, and it was only this class that they emigrated.*[1]

The Lord Mayor of Manchester's "official farewell to a party of fifty-two boys, who are being sent to Canada," was warmly welcomed by Thomas Ackroyd, secretary of the boys' and girls' refuges in Manchester and Salford. However, in his speech, delivered at the Town Hall in April 1910, Ackroyd let slip the uncomfortable truth that the best hope for needy children under their care was to send them to good homes in Canada. "After thirty-seven years experience, the [Poor Law] Committee were convinced that it was definitely better to send this particular class of children to a country like Canada than to keep them at home," where they would suffer from "degrading and dangerous surroundings." And it was also cheaper since the annual cost of their upkeep in a charitable institution was between £15 and £30, while the one-off cost of shipping them off to Canada was a mere £12.[2]

Although Manchester ratepayers must have welcomed their departure, the lack of adequate inspection procedures in Canada meant that child removal schemes were far from perfect. Nevertheless, the various agencies generally tried their utmost to protect children in their care, and although there were well-documented instances of exploitation and abuse, most children benefited from their fresh start in Canada.[3]

Canada's intake of child immigrants was breathtaking in its scale. As ever, Britain's need to rid itself of its excess urban poor and Canada's insatiable requirement for manual labour were the principal driving forces, although "child saving" and the cementing of the ties of Empire also helped to justify this extraordinary movement of children.[4] Between 1868 and 1925, around eighty thousand orphaned, abused, or abandoned children — the so-called "home children" — were sent to Canada, many

Courtesy Manchester Archives, M189/7/6/1.

Photograph of fifty-two boys being sent to Canada from refuges and workhouses in Manchester and Salford, April 15, 1910. The boys are standing on the steps of the Manchester Town Hall alongside local dignitaries, with the Lord Mayor appearing in the centre toward the back. Each boy was presented with a new sixpence by the Lady Mayoress.

being under the care of parish guardians, charitable institutions, or individual philanthropists like Thomas Barnardo.[5]

Desperate economic hardship in the city slums of Britain had worsened the plight of many children, and parents who were no longer able to provide for their children increasingly placed them in charitable homes. The escalating costs of caring for these children in institutions soon led to calls for large-scale assisted emigration schemes, and a host of philanthropic people emerged to organize these departures and placements. The children came to Canada as indentured farm labourers (boys) or domestic servants (girls). After serving their indentures, some of the boys took up farming, although most opted for the well-paid factory and service jobs to be found in towns and cities.

Despite grave concerns on both sides of the Atlantic that children were being neglected, overworked, and in some cases abused, the emigration schemes grew rapidly in scale. About five hundred home children were sent to Canada annually during the late 1870s, and this number more than trebled between 1879 and 1883.[6] More than eleven thousand children arrived in Canada between 1870 and 1914, and this number mushroomed to eighty thousand by 1925. The first two removals were launched in 1869–70 by Maria Rye and Annie Macpherson, both deeply religious women, who had been troubled by the suffering they had witnessed in the slums of London and Liverpool. Miss Rye's children came from workhouses and industrial schools, while Miss Macpherson's youngsters were mainly street waifs gathered from London's East End.[7]

In both cases the children were sent to Ontario and Quebec.[8] However, Rye and Macpherson, lacking the necessary management skills, made unsuitable placements and provided inadequate supervision, failings that were criticized severely by Andrew Doyle, a senior inspector for the Local Government Board in Britain.[9]

As the founder of the Liverpool Sheltering Home, Mrs. Louisa Birt, Annie Macpherson's sister, organized the relocation of around 347 English children to Nova Scotia between 1873 and 1876.[10] She was assisted by Colonel John Laurie, an influential farmer who persuaded the provincial government to pay part of the total emigration and placement costs.[11] Guaranteeing the rest of the funding himself, Laurie also accepted responsibility for finding suitable locations for the children. His ledger reveals that most were sent to the province's industrial heartland in Pictou and Cumberland Counties.[12] The rapid expansion in mining and other industries since the 1850s had created a sudden demand for labour, and this had drawn farm workers away from agricultural employment. Hard-pressed farmers in these industrial areas probably agitated the loudest for Mrs. Birt's children. Judging from their later addresses, it would seem that some even ended up in industrial premises: Henry Brown was sent to the "Gold Mines Office, Halifax," Thomas Gallagher and Stephen Baniman to the "Nelson & May Office at New Annan" in Colchester County, George Duffin to the "Loading Ground, South Pictou," and Jimmy Francis to the "Acadian Mines, Londonderry," in Colchester County. [13] In 1877, Louisa Birt closed down her Nova Scotia operations and opened a new home at Knowlton in the Eastern Townships of Quebec.[14]

By this time, Dr. John Middlemore, a medical doctor and son of a wealthy businessman, had founded his Children's Emigration Homes in Birmingham. But unlike Mrs. Birt, he retained complete control over the placement of his children. The extensive files kept for each child reveal the care taken to monitor progress and to respond to the regular reports of the Canadian inspectors who visited the various children at their new homes.[15]

Middlemore sent his first group to Ontario in 1873, having established a receiving home for them in London. Twelve years later, he expanded his operations, building another receiving home in Halifax, after which time he began placing more of his children in the Maritime provinces.[16] Between 1894 and 1932, Middlemore brought a total of 3,331 children to the Maritimes, with 57 percent being relocated to New Brunswick, 38 percent to Nova Scotia, and 5 percent to Prince Edward Island.[17]

With the growing humanitarian crisis during the late nineteenth century in cities such as London, parish guardians of the various boroughs were increasingly using their powers and funds to send poor children under their care to Canada.[18] They employed philanthropists and charitable institutions, already experienced in managing child emigration schemes, to make the necessary arrangements for transporting their children and finding them suitable placements in Canada.[19] Between the

1890s and 1930s, hundreds of children were sent by the Board of Guardians of the London boroughs of Hampstead, Fulham, Westminster, Islington, Holburn, and Poplar on the north side of the Thames and from Lambeth, Camberwell, and Greenwich on the south side.[20] Other boards of guardians took similar action.

During the 1880s and 1890s, the Leeds Board of Guardians used Maria Rye and Louisa Birt to manage the relocation of 2,455 of their children to Canada.[21] While Ontario received most of them, some went to New Brunswick, such as William Lyne and John Borus, who settled in Sussex Parish and the Chambers settlement respectively, both in Kings County.[22] While the Leeds Guardians' thorough investigation of the receiving homes in Canada was laudable, they appeared to have a naïve faith in the goodness of the employers who would eventually house their children.[23] Effusive phrases from letters written by their boys — which peppered the Leeds Guardians' annual reports — painted an idyllic picture: William Lyne said that he "liked the people [he was] living with; they are very kind to me," while John Borus said "this is a splendid country. I wish you would show this letter to the boys who did not want to go to Canada."[24] However, since placement checks were usually cursory and

Courtesy Library and Archives Canada, PA-117283.

English boys and young men with their chaperone photographed with their trunks stamped "Liverpool to Hamilton."

ineffective, the Leeds Guardians, like other sponsors, were shielded from the possible perils facing children who ended up in isolated locations.

The Manchester and Salford Boys and Girls Refuges adopted a similar approach to the Leeds Guardians, sending 2,129 of their children to Canada between 1872 and 1921. They relied heavily on the services of Ellen Bilborough, an associate of Annie Macpherson, who in 1870 had opened the Marchmont Home in Belleville, Ontario. The Manchester and Salford children were sent initially to this home, which, from 1877, was under Miss Bilborough's management, and thirteen years later under the control of her husband, Robert Wallace.[25]

Although the Manchester and Salford Boys and Girls Refuges dominated the outflow from the area, a register compiled by the Chorlton Poor Law Union reveals that some of the child immigrants had been in the care of the Chorlton Union workhouse, the Liverpool Catholic Protection and Rescue Society, the Canadian Catholic Emigration Association, the Catholic Emigration Society, Liverpool, and the Central Refuge at Strangeways, Manchester.[26] While the Catholic children went to Quebec Province, mainly to areas near Montreal, the Protestants, who represented the majority, were relocated to Ontario, with an appreciable number being placed in the general vicinity of the Marchmont Home in Belleville.[27]

All but a few were placed on farms with people they had never met. An exception was eight-year-old Elsie Haydock, a former resident of the Chorley workhouse who had been sent out to board with a Mrs. Hardacre. Travelling with her to Sydney Mines, Cape Breton, Elsie would continue to live with Mrs. Hardacre at her son's house in Cape Breton. But for most of the Manchester and Salford children it was a leap into the unknown. Some moved several times. Having gone to Glengarry in 1905, Cornelius Higgins was living in Sudbury six years later, working at the King George's restaurant. Thomas Green, aged twelve, went to Nipissing, but by 1912 he, too, had landed a job at the same Sudbury restaurant. The boys, sent by the Catholic Emigration Society, were clearly friends who managed to stick together. Twelve-year-old Ellen Williams, from the Salford Refuge, began her new life in Peterborough, but moved to Muskoka three years later and, after a brief stay in the Gravenhurst Sanatorium, got married and moved to Toronto. And William Leighfield, aged ten, moved from his initial residence in Cavan to Peterborough to take up employment with a firm of pork-packers. Each of these children had opted for the better-paid jobs to be found in urban locations.[28]

Having first been employed in Foxboro, seven-year-old Thomas Houghton moved to Saskatchewan, sixteen-year-old Thomas Clarke ended up at the Pendre Boot Factory in Detroit, having first lived in Corbyville, and nineteen-year-old Frank Jennings in Winnipeg, having initially lived in Lonsdale.[29] What they all had in common was an initial residence, close to the Marchmont Home, presumably assigned to them so that they would be more accessible to visiting inspectors. However, claims made in 1910 that "in the interests of cheap labour," children from the Manchester and Salford refuges were being overworked in Canada and, "in consequence, are not receiving an efficient education," caused grave concern.[30] These allegations surfaced just six years after Thomas Ackroyd, the secretary of the refuges, had given a glowing report of what he had personally witnessed in Ontario.

When he visited the Marchmont Home, Ackroyd found the Manchester boys and girls to be "perfectly happy … as I saw them living in a good home with an abundant supply of food and clothing, cared for and loved by those who have taken them." When he reflected on "their conditions when rescued I realise, as never before, the great value of our emigration work.… May I dispel the idea, if it should now exist in the minds of some people as it did in the early days of the movement, that the children are badly treated." From his inquiries to farmers, public officials, and the children themselves, he concluded, "they received every care and kindness."[31] He went on:

> Perhaps the most important feature so favourable to the comfort and happiness of the boy or girl is the ease and natural way in which they take their place in the family circle. The idea of servant is very quickly lost.… All sit at the same table and share the comforts as well as the work. The farms themselves are often roomy comfortable houses, with a fine orchard and outlying pasture lands or cultivated fields. There is ample space and the

> fine clear air of these Canadian uplands is very bracing and a wonderful contrast to the crowded conditions of our towns from which our children come. It is remarkable how contented the children become and how attached [they are] to their new surroundings: they almost invariably express a preference for the new land and deprecate the idea of returning to England — a good proof surely of their contentment.[32]

And Miss Olga Hertz of the Chorlton Board of Guardians reported that she received dozens of letters from children every year — "not a single one has ever complained of hardship."[33] Nevertheless, the Guardians were sufficiently troubled by these later allegations that they stopped sending their school-age children to Canada in 1910.[34]

In contrast to the large refuges and orphanages that had been established in English cities, the Worcester Board of Guardians cared for their boys and girls in Cottage Homes designed to cater to relatively small

Courtesy Library and Archives Canada, PA-041785.

Children from Barnardo's Homes at a landing stage at Saint John, New Brunswick. Undated photograph by Isaac Erb.

groups in a homely rather than institutional setting.[35] The dozen or so Worcester children who emigrated to Canada most years between 1905 and 1913 had their arrangements overseen by John Middlemore's Children's Emigration Homes in Birmingham. In keeping with his preference for the Maritime provinces by this time, predictably their placements were either in either Nova Scotia or New Brunswick. The clustering of their locations in eastern Nova Scotia and southeastern New Brunswick was probably done to simplify inspection procedures, something that Middlemore's agency took very seriously.

Of course, the greatest of the advocates for relieving child poverty and distress through emigration was Thomas Barnardo.[36] Director of the homes that sent more British children to Canada than any other, he combined great philanthropic zeal with a practical eye for detail. He stumbled upon his mission in life quite by accident. Having enrolled at the London Medical School in 1866, he was called into service as a volunteer medic when a cholera epidemic broke out in London's East End — an area that was then synonymous with poverty, overcrowding, disease, and criminality. This experience of caring for the sick and dying opened his eyes to a miserable underworld that he never knew existed. Overwhelmed by the sight of so many homeless children huddled together in London's back alleys, he resolved to dedicate his life to their rescue. Night after night he walked the back streets gathering up waifs and strays and taking them to Stepney Causeway, a large building he had purchased in 1870 and converted to a children's home. Later on, children were brought to him in great numbers by parents or relatives unable to care for them.[37]

His motto, "no destitute child ever refused," brought needy children to Barnardo in their thousands. Within ten years of operation he had several homes caring for more children than any other agency in England. It was just a question of time before increasing costs and decreasing employment opportunities for children drove Barnardo into launching emigration schemes. Between 1882 and 1939 he would bring over thirty thousand children to Canada.[38] Having selected virtuous and healthy children, he gave them a rudimentary education, their departure date, new clothing, and a trunk containing the Bible, a Hymn Book, a copy of John Bunyan's *Pilgrim's Progress*, and a *Traveller's Guide*. By 1901, he had established a home in Toronto (for boys), another in Peterborough (for girls), a third in Winnipeg, and a farm at Russell, Manitoba.[39]

Barnardo's eagerness to save children from what he considered to be their corrupting home influences meant that he occasionally sent them to Canada illegally, without their parents' consent. In such cases he was accused of tearing up family links in a mindless quest for moral correctness.[40] Although it sometimes caused unease to children and parents, Barnardo's "philanthropic abduction" was allowed to continue, despite several hard-fought court cases and a lively public debate.[41]

The correspondence relating to twelve-year-old Mary Ann Warren, from Wellington Parish in Somerset, reveals how the parish guardians and Barnardo conspired together in 1913 to have her released from the grip of a father "who has been convicted and imprisoned for cruelty to children."[42] When her father had first entered the workhouse, the guardians became "particularly desirous of emigrating her [Mary] as they wished her removed from the undesirable influence of her friends and relatives."[43] Although her father had coerced her into "refusing her consent" to emigrate, the guardians arranged for Mary's transfer to the Barnardo Home in Stepney Causeway, London. From there she was sent to the Margaret Cox Home for Girls in Peterborough, and soon after was found a placement in Strathroy, Ontario. Eight months later she was reported to be "well and doing nicely."[44] But after being diagnosed with tuberculosis she was transferred back to England so that she could be treated at a sanatorium in the Girls' Village Home in Essex, run by Barnardo. By June 1915, when "her chest was gradually getting worse," her prospects were grim.[45] Messy compromises had to be made and success was by no mean guaranteed.

Meanwhile, children discharged from reformatory schools began entering Canada from 1858, although emigration from such institutions did not become an established practice until the mid 1880s. A typical example was the Wiltshire Reformatory for Boys, which sent Charles Tanner to Canada in 1870, Joseph Kimber and James Frost in 1871, and Martin and Eli English in the following year, all on the basis that they would receive a grant to help with their emigration costs. In Eli English's case, funds would only be provided "if he could get £5 from the Police Court which sent him to the school."

Courtesy Library and Archives Canada, PA-117285.

Boy ploughing at Barnardo's industrial farm, Russell, Manitoba, circa 1900. The farm, which offered training to those over seventeen years old, was shut down in 1908.

A deciding factor in encouraging the boys to emigrate was the belief that "it is manifestly most undesirable that they should return to their homes."[46] But, it would seem that the three boys who were brought before the committee in August 1875 were not entirely convinced about the benefits of emigration. It was made clear that "in consequence of the kindness shown and the expense incurred by the Committee, they were not to think of returning to England until they had been at least four years in Canada and had honestly tried to make their own way there." Numbers increased from the mid 1880s, at which time stringent regulations were introduced to admit reformatory children on probation.

There were understandable concerns in Canada about receiving boys convicted of crimes before they had completed their sentences; but they were also seen as helpful additions to the labour force. And in Britain there was the obvious advantage of saving the cost of their maintenance at a school.[47] But after some debate, reformatory children were admitted on probation at the discretion of the Canadian Emigration Commissioner in London. Good management and supervision procedures ensured a steady increase in their numbers.[48] Through the use of local agents, the behaviour and welfare of each child was carefully monitored, with detailed reports being sent both to the school and parents on a regular basis. One such agent was Mr. Gold, based in Melbourne (Richmond County), in Quebec, who took charge of the many reformatory boys being sent to the Eastern Townships during the 1880s. Children from the Hertfordshire Reformatory School for Boys normally spent their first year or so under his beady eye in Melbourne.[49]

After working for a milkman in Melbourne, William Forrester moved to Sherbrooke, where, according to his father, "he seems to have quite settled down and is evidently pleased with the country."[50] After working in Melbourne, Anthony Crabb moved to Kingsey, to the north of Melbourne, where he "thinks of marrying his master's daughter" and has changed his name to Smart "in order to conceal his identity."[51] William Martin was unhappy with Melbourne and wanted to go back to England but, according to Gold, his mother "does not encourage the thought of his return."[52] After finding him a printing job in Sherbrooke, Gold reported that Martin's mood had improved. James Hoyle and Henry Putt both worked at Windsor Mills, to the east of Melbourne, before landing well-paid jobs in the United States.[53] Having been joined by his father, mother, and sister, Putt was said to be "comfortably situated."[54] After cutting ice in Melbourne, Robert Smitham found lucrative employment in Toronto.[55] And, after their time in Melbourne, William Binder joined the Salvation Army in Montreal while Thomas Ridding joined the army, serving at the Citadel in Quebec.[56]

The early 1900s saw the arrival of more Hertfordshire reformatory boys in the mining areas of northern Ontario.[57] One example was Thomas Wells, who landed his first job as a cook at the Prospect Hotel in

Cobalt (Timiskaming District), and later found employment at Copper Cliff (Sudbury District) as a watchman at a silver refinery. By 1906 he was reported to be "in a good position and doing well," having nearly paid off his debt to his brother and sending money to his sister back in England. A year later he reported from the Larose Mine in Cobalt that he had "plenty of work to do in the silver mines."[58] John Carrier Eacher found employment initially with a lumbering company in Massey (Algoma District) "at 30s. per week with board." However, lumbering work did not suit him, nor did working as a cook on a steamer based in Toronto, from which job he was sacked, presumably because of misconduct. His last known address was North Bay (Nipissing District). John Ernest Sutton, discharged from the same school in 1909, was recruited by the New Idea Suit Hanger Company in Toronto, being paid $10 a week. His aunt, who lived in Toronto, had apparently "got him" the job, but he hated it; so he moved north where he found work as a chainman in the Canadian Northern Railway survey party. By 1913 he had moved to Winnipeg and was expecting "to go even further west."

The generously funded emigration schemes, made possible by the passing of the Empire Settlement Act in 1922, brought a steady stream of English children to Canada, most of them aged between fourteen and seventeen — in other words, of school-leaving age.[59] One of the first groups to arrive were the so-called "boy farmer" recruits, who were given training at the Vimy Ridge Farm near Guelph as a preliminary to their placement with local farmers.[60] After working on a farm for three years, for which they were to earn wages and receive food and lodgings, it was expected that they would become self-sufficient and be able to pursue their own farming career.[61] Newspaper announcements in 1926 calling for three hundred recruits meant that this was a substantial scheme. However, Richard Robertson remembered how he and the others were regarded disparagingly as "the lost men and boys from England's teeming cities, [who] were turned out to work on Canadian farms, many not having the slightest comprehension of rural life or association with farms or farm animals."[62] Certainly, trade union leaders voiced strenuous objections to the importing of labour at a time of rising unemployment. Their view that it was time to close the gates was very understandable![63]

Nottingham, like other rapidly expanding English cities, turned to emigration to relieve the plight of its young paupers. Prominent businessmen launched the Dakeyne Farm, near Falmouth, Nova Scotia, modelling their ideas on Mrs. Ellinor Close's concept of a training farm, which she founded in New Brunswick.[64] With the help of government funding, Captain Oliver Hind, a local solicitor and magistrate, purchased the farm where the Nottingham boys would receive training before being placed with individual farmers in the province.[65] When Mr. G.B. Smart, supervisor of Juvenile Immigration, visited in 1924, there were 126 boys who were apparently happy and well cared for.[66] He observed "the large commodious dormitory, in which all the boys sleep — there are thirteen beds, for the thirteen boys continuously in residence at the farm — small, single beds, with plenty of clean bedding and pillows. Next to the dormitory is a large room used as a wardrobe by the boys; the walls of this room are dotted with pegs and each boy has his own peg on which his Sunday suit of clothes was neatly hanging." He noticed "a fine esprit de corps amongst all hands" and general satisfaction "with their home life and treatment generally."[67]

The United Church of Canada's scheme, funded under the Empire Settlement Act, to bring five hundred English boys between the ages of fourteen and eighteen to their farm near Guelph in 1932 provoked an angry response from the International Association of Machinists, based in Montreal.[68] The organization did not believe that the boys would necessarily remain on the farms. There was understandable concern that once they got their bearings, the boys would head for a town or city, where rates of pay would be higher. It was claimed that "the action of the Government is absolutely unjust to the boys themselves, and totally unwarranted as a far as the Dominion of Canada is concerned, when we look throughout the Dominion and find the deplorable conditions now existing due mainly to unemployment."[69]

The oft-repeated lament that child immigrants were either unsuitable for the tasks given to them or that they interfered with Canada's labour market ensured that they had a largely unfavourable press. Their arrival was viewed with actual alarm in some quarters. Some well-meaning people in England believed that they had acquired an "indescribable workhouse brand" that needed to be removed from them, ideally before emigrating.[70] Some Canadian doctors believed that immigrant children imported diseases, such as syphilis, and were imbued with anti-social tendencies from birth. The notion was spread that they would have criminal tendencies and be morally degenerate.[71] Their unfamiliarity with farming also provoked criticism. But, despite these misgivings and criticisms, tens of thousands of English children were successfully relocated to Canada. They deserve to be recognized for their bravery and resilience and thanked for the enrichment they brought to their adopted country.

Canada's population increased dramatically in the first decade of the twentieth century, primarily because of an explosive rise in immigration from Britain. The arrival of steamships and the construction of a coast-to-coast trans-Canada railway had made mass migration feasible. And with a widespread preference being shown for Canada over the United States, the British-born population here soared. The English dominated this influx, having been attracted by the manufacturing jobs being created in the expanding industrial areas of Ontario and Quebec and the good prospects of agricultural settlement in the Prairies and British Columbia. However, some of the English attracted considerable controversy and criticism.

CHAPTER 8

How the English Were Regarded in Canada

> *The crowning insult to me is the cool way in which they say "but we do not look on you as a Canadian!" and they mistake this for a compliment! It makes my Canadian blood boil. I answer that, though I have married an Englishman, I have not lost my identity and I am purely Canadian and proud of it. They simply do not understand that I really mean it.*[1]

The Ontario-born Mary Inderwick, wife of an English immigrant turned successful Alberta rancher, detested the smugness of her upper-class English visitors. Arriving in the 1880s, in the heyday of Empire, they believed themselves to be a superior race, distrustful and sometimes even scornful of foreigners. Hence her visitors thought they were being kind in telling Mary that they did not regard her as foreign. Bringing their condescending ways with them when they came as immigrants to Canada, many added insult to injury by grumbling about what they regarded as Canada's deficiencies. Inevitably, Canadians treated such people with contempt.

At the other end of the social spectrum were the many thousands of English paupers who were being assisted financially to come to Canada.

Courtesy Toronto Reference Library, B12-33A (T10729).

Photograph of St. James Cathedral, Toronto, in 1874. Built in the Gothic Revival style in 1853, it symbolizes the grandeur of Victorian architecture and the glory days of the British Empire.

They, too, were vilified for being a drain on the public purse and taking jobs away from Canadians. Thus, while the Scots, Irish, and Welsh were viewed as welcome additions to Canada's population, many of the English were treated with derision and disdain. Newspaper editors on both sides of the Atlantic had a field day stirring up controversy, but to little effect. Despite their apparent unpopularity, the English came in ever greater numbers, dominating the British influx throughout the late nineteenth and early twentieth centuries.

Many English arrived in Canada with the naive expectation that Canadian society would differ little from theirs, having been misled into this way of thinking by the promotional literature being produced by the Canadian government and Canadian Pacific Railway Company. They assumed wrongly that, having been born in what was then termed the Mother Country, Canadians would look up to them; instead, they were treated as equals. Richard Goodridge, a retired army officer who farmed near Winnipeg in the 1880s, was troubled by what he regarded as the "insufferable roughness" of Canadians. Their desire to treat one another on equal terms and their "familiarity" shocked him, having become "accustomed to the more reserved proprieties of European society." Needless to say, Goodridge's adjustment to pioneer life was slow and painful![2]

Prospective immigrants were assured by immigration authorities that they would be "welcomed on the other side and that Canada [wanted] British workers," but the reality proved somewhat different.[3] The English would soon learn the hard way that they were not easily understood by Canadians, nor were they readily accepted. A young man from London's East End, who came to Toronto after the Second World War, was deeply offended by what he regarded as his hostile reception: "It was a real shocker those first few times, as if I was in a foreign country, and here I was thinking Canada being part of the British Empire and all that, that I would be received as a wonderful person."[4]

Originating from the most powerful nation on earth and belonging to an Empire that dominated the world, the English were endowed with a strong sense of self-assurance. This applied to everyone, including the labouring classes. While having pride in one's country was understandable, many upper-class English carried this farther by flaunting their perceived superiority. These "Don'ts for Englishmen," published in a guide for new settlers, were intended to enlighten such people:

> Don't when you arrive in Canada try to impress people how much better they do things in England. It is a mistake that is frequently made by newcomers.
>
> Don't talk about your station in life, especially if you have any titled relations. The Canadian does not care a rap for your pedigree.
>
> Above all, don't brag about being an Englishman; be proud of it by all means, but do not thrust the fact down your neighbour's throat. More Englishmen have made themselves disliked for this reason than for any other perhaps.[5]

However, many were beyond redemption. The Reverend Martin Holdom, in charge of the Anglican Church at Castor near Red Deer, Alberta, was scathing in his criticism of the English families in his area. In his view they clung to outmoded English ways while deriding the culture of the country they had come to join. A typical example was Percy Jaques and his family, who, he wrote, "refuse to adapt themselves to the country and in consequence people do not like them.... They talk of their life out here as exile and penal servitude which just makes me tired. Mrs. Jaques would like to be walking down Bond Street and Percy hunting and playing polo; they still talk of servants, autumn, lunch and dinner."[6]

Holdom was equally disapproving of a Bristol family who lived nearby:

> The women folk are absolutely lost, they have thirty two boxes of crocks [dishes] coming — where they are going to put it all in their little three room shack is a mystery to them as well as to me; they seem to have thought that they would find conditions very much the same as at home. One of them actually said that Canadians ought to come round to English ways.... [It] is thoughtless

> words like these that make English people so utterly detested wherever they go.[7]

For reasons that were blatantly obvious when they arrived, many upper-class English were totally unsuited to pioneer life. Those who came with the peculiar belief that belonging to a "good family, being a good rider, a first-class shot and being fond of country pursuits" were somehow going to be essential qualifications for success in the colonies rightly won the scorn of author John Rowan.[8] Laziness and a substantial bank balance led some English gentlemen to pursue a life of leisure, much to the annoyance of Canadians, although they were not necessarily the norm. Not all were as incompetent or misguided as contemporary commentators would have us believe, although criticisms of them did occasionally appear in immigrant letters. Eighteen-year-old Edward Folkes, farming in Manitoba, told his mother that "there is a great prejudice against English gentlemen [here] — they are generally lazy and do little work"[9]; while Claude Gardiner, an Alberta rancher, found himself in the company of the "usual English sort who does nothing but play polo and drinks and plays the fool generally.... Nearly all Englishmen out here [Alberta] go on in the same way ... and are the laughing stock of all the Americans."[10]

Martin Holdom observed: "We only want the best Englishmen out here [Alberta]; the people with their heads full of dress, theatres, cheap art, and useless women had better stay at home, we don't want them; we only want people who are willing to work and work hard."[11]

Courtesy Toronto Reference Library, J. Ross Robertson Collection, 6691.

Photograph of the Toronto Hunt Club in full regalia in autumn, 1877.

Predictably, Holdom was forthright in his condemnation of remittance men — the ultimate English hate figure:

> Remittance men, who lived on allowances sent from home, were ill-equipped by their expensive education in the classics and athletics to do anything of practical value. Instead of applying themselves, British gentlemen wasted their time sleeping, hunting and sipping tea, all the while complaining about life in the colonies; and displaying a naivety of local conditions that readily made them the butt of jokes and pranks.[12]

However, it seems that the chief concern was not so much that Englishmen were upper-class or lazy, but that they complained a lot:

> The efficient Englishman who has learned the lesson of the great public schools "to keep his pores open and his mouth shut" is not likely to come to grief. But the complaining, superior idle creature, whether to be a loafer from the slums or a remittance man of aristocratic birth

Courtesy Toronto Reference Library, 984-3-3(Repro: T30997).

Photograph of the Toronto Cricket Club, taken at a match in Hamilton, 1886.

> is sure to find us a hard and unsympathetic people, averse to picking up carrying a grown-up man who ought to be able to support himself.[13]

While much of the criticism of the English was focused on the upper classes, the working classes were also found wanting. Martin Holdom thought "there must be something wrong with the training of the working classes at home, for most of them seem utterly useless out here [Alberta]. Instead of working they spend their time grumbling, I am more ashamed of my countrymen everyday."[14]

A similar view was expressed by A. Ancell, a tradesman who originated from Manchester. He claimed that "a lot of young Englishmen that is here [Calgary] are not fit to be here — they are a disgrace to our land and of course they put every Englishman down alike."[15] The *Canadian Courier* commented on those English immigrants who, as they put it,

> … proceed in the most irritating fashion to compare all Canadian customs and practices with those of home, very much to the disadvantage of their new habitation. This brand of immigrant has been met so frequently in the last five years that Canadians have become supersensitive on the subject of English criticism and are likely to be on the defensive at the very moment of introduction.[16]

The Ottawa *Morning Citizen* claimed "that a certain class of English, usually from London, are among the least satisfactory that come to this country. They are lazy and indifferent and, when they do condescend to accept work, preserve a superior and contemptuous air towards the country and their employers.… The same trouble does not arise with the Scotch or Irish immigrants, or, in fact, almost any other class."[17] An editorial written that same year in the *Southport Visitor*, a Lancashire newspaper, also blamed their unpopularity on "the grumbling spirit among the English.… He expects to find a reproduction of England, where men of British blood will be welcomed in the most friendly manner. He soon discovers, however, that he is one of a minority, and he at once is made to understand that Canada is not England."[18] Such was the strength of feeling that some employers went as far as inserting "no English need apply" notices in their job advertisements.

When he visited Canada, the British writer Basil Stewart certainly found plenty of evidence that the English were disliked. In his book *No English Need Apply*, published in 1909, he noted that he had "never met a man, never spoken with a man, who did not admit there was a solid foundation of truth in the charge that the Englishman as an ordinary immigrant is less considered than a member of any other nationality."[19] Despite this damning criticism, Stewart believed that the English were being unjustly vilified. Their constant grumbling, which in his view was the cause of their unpopularity, was, he claimed, a justifiable reaction to their extreme disappointment at being misled by the wild claims of unscrupulous agents who had oversold Canada's benefits:

> There are so many people in Canada today who would return to England if they had the means to do so, because of having formed an entirely wrong impression of the country from the glowing accounts which interested persons gave them, they have when too late been sadly disillusioned.[20]

Yet all immigrants must have experienced some disillusionment. Stewart does not explain why it was only English complainers who were out of favour. The British Labour M.P., Kier Hardie, who also visited Toronto at this time, concluded that English immigrants were disliked principally because of their inability to adapt:

> I was not long in the country [Canada] before I ran up against a fact which surprised and startled me. *The English immigrant is not popular in Canada.* This remark applies in a special degree to the Londoner. Professor Mavor has an advertisement cut from a local paper asking for workmen, and which states that no English need apply. Scotsmen, Welshmen, Irishmen and Scandinavians

> are the favourites, pretty much in the order given. The reason, so far as I can make out for this strange fact, is the Englishman's inveterate habit of grumbling and his unwillingness to adapt himself to new conditions. He reaches Canada with the notion that being from the Mother Country he knows all there needs to be learned. He wants the kind of house that he had in Seven Dials [London], and, where the method of work or the arrangement of the workshop differs from what he has been used to, he sets that down to the ignorance of the colonist, whom he has come to instruct. For him there is only one standard of perfection to which he is always referring and the consequence is that by workmates and employers alike he is generally voted a nuisance.[21]

Unflattering reports of the English in Canada were reported widely in the British press, heightening fears in Britain that the English would stop emigrating, thus denying Canada their skills, some of which were believed to be essential to its developing economy.[22]

Claiming that he had been the victim of job discrimination, a disgruntled Englishman wrote to *Reynolds Weekly Newspaper*, a U.K. publication having socialist leanings, enclosing three job advertisements, all appearing on July 6, 1909. The *Toronto Globe* advertised for "an honest reliable man; able to do all kinds of farm work, No Englishman need apply," while the *Toronto Evening Telegram* displayed notices for a "Caretaker of a public building, married man with no encumbrance. No Englishman" and a "handy young fellow with tools for concrete work. No English."[23]

In 1914, the *Toronto Telegram,* the *Ottawa Citizen*, and the *Hamilton Spectator* published similar job advertisements stating "Englishmen not wanted."[24] There were countless other examples, many attracting the attention of the British press, which published them with great indignation.[25]

However, when emigration officials in both in Britain and Canada investigated the employers named in the advertisements they found no evidence that the claims were genuine. The fact that a prosecution resulted in the award of $200 in damages against "the harm done to the public interest" confirmed that at least one anti-English claim had been fabricated. From then on newspaper proprietors refused to cooperate, fearing legal action.[26] It soon became clear that the people named in the newspapers were fictitious and that a campaign was afoot to provoke hostility

Courtesy Glenbow Archives, NA-3683-10.

An Englishman in Canada, 1901. Canadian cartoonists played their part in lampooning the English upper classes, this being a typical example.

toward the English immigrants.[27] The whingeing of the newly arrived elitist English had provided useful ammunition, but the real target were the growing numbers of tradesmen, craftsmen, and labourers who were flooding into the country. Canada's labour movement was strongly opposed to their arrival, fearing they would take jobs away from Canadian workers.

When the immigration agent in Toronto reported to his equivalent in London that, in his view, the "no English need apply" notices were fictitious, he added the caveat that "the great difficulty of keeping English immigrants out of cities" lay at the heart of the problem.[28] He was, in fact, referring to the controversy being caused by the influx of English paupers — especially the many people who had been assisted to emigrate by their city councils following the passing of the Unemployed Workmen Act in 1905. Most of them originated from London. Instead of taking up jobs in rural areas of Ontario and the Prairies, which were crying out for farm labour, they had slipped away to the towns and cities, where jobs were far scarcer. This outcome alarmed Canada's labour leaders, who feared that they would exacerbate unemployment, cause wages to fall, and become a burden on local taxpayers. This latter concern no doubt prompted D.C. McIntyre of Brockville, Ontario, to write to the Immigration Department complaining about the English malingerers in his town:

> The unemployed from London has not turned out satisfactory in many cases: farm life is not what they expected and some of them drift back to town where some of them pursue their original calling of regular out-of-workers.[29]

Still the complaints continued. When "a trainload of forty British immigrants, homeless, friendless, penniless and discontented," were deposited in Chatham, Ontario, in 1907, the *Free Press* of London (Ontario) claimed, "the farmers do not care a great deal about hiring them, because they know from experience that these immigrants from the large English cities are practically useless on the farm."[30] And, presiding over a criminal case in 1912, the Chief Magistrate of Hamilton was quoted as saying that "the majority of Englishmen get sick at the sight of a little work."

An indignant local businessman, having read the magistrate's comments in the *Hamilton Spectator*, asked the Immigration Department to take retaliatory action: "He has done more in five minutes to keep [English] emigrants out of Ontario than will take a year to counteract.... Emigrants won't come out to Ontario if they feel that this [antipathy] exists."[31]

And so it went on until 1914, when, with the outbreak of the First World War, immigration reduced sharply.

Some commentators did occasionally rally to the support of the English. When Hertfordshire-born Mrs. Lloyd-Jones, wife of a successful Ontario farmer, wrote an article in the *National Review* in 1910 describing the middle-class Englishman as "a namby-pamby creature at best,"[32] an anonymous "English Canadian" asked, "Why is it that English migration into Ontario has increased so rapidly of late years...? One has heard too of the Sons of England, several hundred members of which organization visited England from Ontario this summer." What is more, "the talk of middle-class Englishmen not being tough enough or capable enough for farm life ... is poppycock and mischievous at that."[33] Undoubtedly, most English immigrants, whatever their background, had made the necessary cultural transitions, but in some cases that was easier said than done.

Leaving a long-cultivated farm in a beautifully landscaped part of England, run with the help of servants, to homestead on the Prairies must have been a daunting experience. Martin Holdom observed members of a family, travelling by train to Castor (Alberta) in 1910 to join two sons who had made such a transformation:

> There was the father, mother, a grown up daughter, and son, son-in-law and grand-children. It was funny to hear them talk, absolutely no idea of the country at all, most of the people in the train were smiling at them, they were dressed in the latest English fashions; one could not help wondering what they would do in a shack...it made one sad to consider the hundreds of people like them at home that would be absolutely helpless without servants.[34]

Having attracted his eye on the train, Holdom noted their discomfort when they reached the railway station. Their sons were there to greet them, but the father was surprised at having to carry his own luggage:

> Two bronzed, well-set-up Englishmen were at the station to meet them; it was a great meeting, evidently a reunion after many years of separation. And then of course Father must go and see about the luggage, probably very surprised to find no porters, and being actually obliged to get his own box out of the van and then the hundreds of little bags, rolls of shawls etc., etc. … which looked so absolutely out of place here. It was indeed a bunch of well-to-do English people who had never known what it was to do without servants, porters, and the general tip-seeking parasite, stranded on a Canadian platform with none of these accessories, utterly lost, utterly useless.… As I walked home I could not help smiling to myself as I thought of the father driving out to the homestead perhaps 60 or 100 miles in a wagon over a bad trail.[35]

Holdom's appraisal of this family was unduly harsh and unsympathetic. It would take time to adjust to the crudely constructed buildings and what seemed to them to be the unduly flat and uninviting landscape of the prairies. They had come from the wealthiest and most industrialized country on earth, having a highly developed society and economy, which offered the most advanced way of life on the planet. The travel writer John Foster Fraser recognized that such people needed to be able to see into the future:

> If your soul's eye can see beyond the shanties, the miry roads, the railway tracks in chaos, the lumped elevators, the snorting and evil-odoured engines, all indeed, that is revolting to aesthetic taste, to what these really mean — the mastery of the West, where these giant plains, slumbering through the ages, are being roused to give bread to man.[36]

The English had been attracted to the Canadian West to better themselves financially, and in time most would come to love its natural beauty, help to shape its society, benefit from its rapidly expanding towns and cities, and, like Mary Inderwick, take pride in being Canadians.

While English immigrants of the early twentieth century were subjected to anti-English rhetoric, its significance was probably minimal. The elitist types, who brought such derision upon themselves, together with the many destitute, urban workers, some of whom were probably unemployable, provided Canada's labour movement with perfect anti-English targets. Newspaper allegations that animosity and job discrimination awaited anyone from England foolish enough to emigrate were intended to halt the influx, but instead it actually raced ahead. Having played second fiddle to the United States throughout the nineteenth century, Canada increasingly became the favoured destination of most English. Labour leaders were simply unable to stop this trend.

One of the most gruelling experiences that had to be endured was the sea crossing. The majority of English immigrants arrived in the early twentieth century, at a time when steamships were available. They provided shorter and safer crossings than was the case with the earlier sailing ships. Sea transport was very basic in the late eighteenth century, when the first of the English came; but conditions improved with the growth of the North American timber trade, which transformed the scale and cost of transatlantic shipping.

CHAPTER 9

Getting There: Sea Crossings and Journeys Beyond

> *We sailed from Liverpool, May 3rd 1904 on the ship* Lake Erie, *often called the "Lake Weary." It was a very rough passage.... We had several accidents on board including two deaths. My stepmother was almost washed overboard by a big wave, but a male passenger caught her as she was being swept through the rail.*[1]

As Clara Williams and her parents discovered, travelling in a steamship carried an element of risk. Despite having been designed with passengers' needs in mind, steamships were a far cry from modern-day ocean liners. Computer-controlled ship stabilizers, air-conditioning, and oil-fired turbine engines had still to be invented. In the early twentieth century, people crossed the Atlantic in steam-propelled ships fuelled by coal. They were unsteady, poorly ventilated and very noisy. Nevertheless, they were an immense improvement over sailing ships, in that they offered much more spacious accommodation, faster and predictable voyage times, and better safety.

Accommodation below deck in a sailing ship was basic, to say the least. However, for those who could not afford the greater privacy and comfort of a cabin, the steerage was the only affordable means of travel. Timber cut from Canadian forests filled a ship's hold on its eastward voyage to Britain, while passengers were accommodated in the same hold on its westward crossing to Canada. Wooden planking was simply hammered over cross beams, while temporary sleeping berths were constructed along each side. George Roberts, travelling to Quebec in the *Sir Henry Pottinger* from Bristol in 1854, described how "there was no division between the berths, so we put up sheets round to enclose us.... The places to lay in were fixed alongside the ship about three feet wide and six feet long, one over the other."[2] The only means of ventilation was through the hatches, and in stormy seas they could be kept battened down for days. William Fulford, who sailed in 1848 from Bideford to Charlottetown, Prince Edward Island, in the *Civility*, recorded how they were "so closely situated in our berths" and breathe "much impure air; and [with] the nauseousness [*sic*] of our chamber slops 'tis almost enough to create the plague."[3]

Courtesy Library and Archives Canada, C-002671.

King's Wharf at Quebec. Trade was booming by the 1820s. Over the years, all exports such as timber, potash, and wheat passed through this harbour, as did thousands of immigrants. Watercolour by Amelia Bayfield (1814–91).

The fact that there were any ships at all was due entirely to the explosive growth of the timber trade. The higher tariffs imposed on European timber in 1811 effectively priced it out of the British market, deliberately making Canadian timber the cheaper alternative. Ever-increasing numbers of vessels plied between British and Canadian ports to collect timber, and, as they did, some carried emigrants on their westward journeys. However, although emigrants were a much-valued source of extra revenue, little attention was paid to their creature comforts. It would not be until the steamship era, beginning in the 1850s, that custom-built accommodation would become available for passengers. Until then, passenger needs had a low priority. Vessels were selected primarily for their timber-carrying capabilities and robustness in withstanding North Atlantic gales. Passengers had to endure cramped and crudely built accommodation, foul-tasting water, inadequate cooking facilities, primitive sanitary arrangements, and, on occasion, harrowing storms that put their lives in real danger.

With the continuing growth of the timber trade, the number of English immigrants who were recorded as having arrived at Quebec rose year by year, although these figures do not signify settler numbers, since some were merely in transit to the United States.[4] To complicate matters, Canadian-bound immigrants occasionally did the reverse, sailing via New York in faster, more comfortable ships, despite having to pay higher fares. An example of the latter is Frederick Grigg, who, having sailed to New York in 1821, travelled by steamer via the Hudson River and Lake Champlain to St-Jean-sur-Richelieu. From there he went a short distance by land to La Prairie, where he boarded a steamer for Montreal and Quebec.[5] Similarly, having sailed from a Cornish port to New York, Sophy Caldwell "landed at St. Johns [St-Jean-sur-Richelieu]," breakfasted there and then progressed in rail cars to La Prairie, "where a boat awaits to convey you to Montreal — right glad were we to bid adieu to American Ground, and again tread English soil as Canada's may truly be termed."[6]

When crossing the Atlantic by sailing ship, passengers suffered dreadfully from seasickness. It was no picnic being cooped up in a ship's hold for four to six weeks, particularly during long, stormy periods. Elizabeth Peters managed to keep food down during her crossing to Quebec aboard the *Friends*, which sailed from Plymouth in 1830, but could not bear the stench and taste of the drinking water: "I am now so well accustomed to the ship that if we could get fresh water, I should not at any time dislike a sea voyage."[7] Because it was stored in crude wooden casks, the water soon became contaminated. Vinegar was often added to alleviate the offensive odour and taste, but it was still obnoxious unless it was boiled. William Fulford had no grumbles about his food while sailing to Quebec in the *Civility* in 1848, but the water, he said, "stinked aloud!" To make it more palatable, peppermint had been added as flavouring.[8]

The hold had to be fumigated from time to time, as well. This required passengers to huddle together on the deck while the captain and crew used the fumes from a bucket of hot tar to kill fleas, lice, and cockroaches and deal with the stench in the hold. Francis Coleman and his family observed this fumigation process for themselves during their crossing in the *Priam* from Plymouth to Quebec in 1834:

> He [the captain] began by putting a red hot iron in a tub of tar which made such a shudder that soon drove all [passengers] on deck. But this was such a muddle and confusion as I scarcely ever witnessed and immediately undertook to get on deck, many exclaiming on the unmannerly behaviour of the throng. Elizabeth [his wife] and I just escaped in time. A female came on deck with just a cloak thrown over her shoulders. They continued their fumes between decks until mid-day. It certainly improved the smell below.[9]

Standards of service were particularly grim in the early stages of passenger travel. Legislation had been in place since 1803, stipulating minimum space and food requirements for passengers, but it was largely unenforceable. As passenger numbers increased, shipowners began running regular services, doing so by the mid 1820s, with their desire for repeat business being the main factor that maintained standards at a reasonable level. Food provisioning on sea crossings was better-organized by the 1830s, and transatlantic fares were costing less. During the 1820s, fares had averaged £3 10s. for steerage passengers who supplied their own food, but in the following two decades they fell to between £2 and £3.[10] As ever, space was at a premium.

Shipowners, wishing to attract immigrants, often offered a more generous floor-to-ceiling space ("between-decks") for passengers than was required legally. Before 1842, the only stipulation was that "ships are not allowed to carry passengers to the Colonies unless they be of the height of five and a half feet between decks."[11] However, in reality, many of the ships carrying immigrants during the 1820s and 1830s offered six feet between decks.[12] With the passing of the 1842 Passenger Act, shipowners had to provide passengers with a minimum height between decks of six feet, and this minimum figure rose to seven feet in 1855.[13] As before, some vessels, such as the *Clio* of Padstow, which offered seven feet between decks in the 1840s, were ahead of their time in meeting passenger needs.[14]

While immigrants sought the most comfortable accommodation they could afford, they also had to cope with ferocious storms. At sea, everything depended on the navigational skills of the captain and crew. There were no technical aids. This was a time when captains shouted out their latitude and longitude to each other to help them get their bearings when their ships passed at sea. Cornishman Francis Coleman, travelling in the *Priam* to Quebec in April 1834, watched as the captain and crew looked up in the sky "to observe the sun and ascertain their latitude correctly. They found they were too much to the south, so soon after tacked about and sailed in a more northerly direction."[15] Three days later, as high winds and rain swept over the vessel, the captain and crew were once again put to the test: "In a short time the wind hastily rose and our ship began to roll very much so as to tumble the things about in all directions … kettles falling over the fire, cups and dishes rolling over the table and the sea breaking over us, coming in between decks. Sometimes they [the waves] would strike the ship with great force and noise." At such times, the crew had the dangerous task of shortening the top sails, which they completed "in 5 ½ minutes."[16] Of more consequence was the thunderous noise made by the *Priam* when passing through "a large quantity of floating ice" near Cape Breton; "it certainly shook us in our berths."[17] Once again the captain and crew rose to the challenge.

There were even worse hazards. When Francis Thomas, travelling in 1833 from London to Quebec in the *Hebe*, reached the southwest coast of Newfoundland, he was "nearly dead with terror." His ship was being driven onto rocks and the passengers were in imminent danger[18]:

> The shock was like that of an earthquake and threw many of the passengers down and bruised several more. There was general screaming from the women and children and a rush made to get upon the deck.... After a little time a rope was thrown ashore and two sailors got to land, who were soon followed by several of the passengers and we all now began to hope that our lives would be saved. I now removed Mrs. Thomas and my family to that part of the ship nearest the land, but in doing it, we were greatly rolled about from the violent motion of the ship — after a little time I got the children up the side of the ship near the shrouds and standing on the outside myself took them down and threw them ashore and they were all safely caught by the sailors and then safely landed, Mrs. Thomas following after.[19]

However, when it came to endurance, few could match what the twenty-three Staffordshire coal miners and their families experienced when they sailed in 1854 from London via Cape Horn to Esquimalt Harbour near Victoria, British Columbia, in the *Princess Royal*, a Hudson's Bay Company ship.[20] They had to tolerate an arduous voyage of almost six months (179 days), during which ten of the 110 passengers died.[21] Their ship was navigated safely around the notorious Cape Horn despite "a terrific storm" in which they encountered strong winds, large waves, dangerous currents, and icebergs. Nevertheless, the crew squabbled and swore at one another, the steward was regularly drunk, and some of the crew deserted when the ship reached Honolulu. After setting off again from Honolulu, Sarah Incher's baby died and "the body was thrown overboard and no more notice taken of it than as if it had been a dead cat"; although, when another child died soon after, she was buried at sea with "the usual ceremony" performed by Captain David Wishart.[22]

Disease was always a major concern. Dr. Thomas, the *Princess Royal*'s ship's surgeon, dealt with all passenger illnesses by prescribing "brandy, rum, gin, or wine as medicine."[23] No doubt, his cynicism and incompetence contributed to the high death toll. However, care of the sick was taken more seriously on most crossings at this time, with the captain and crew normally following a strict daily routine for ensuring basic cleanliness and controlling the spread of contagious diseases.

The port of Quebec first experienced the arrival of poor immigrants in need of medical care in 1819, and to meet the demand, rudimentary facilities managed by the Quebec Emigrant Society were put in place. Together with charitable donations of "clothing, firewood and provisions," funds were raised from the general public to cover the running costs of a hospital, which treated around 500 sick immigrants in its first year.[24] Having sent back some of the "deluded and helpless beings" who arrived in 1819, the Society wrote to the Colonial Office stating that it should warn British immigrants of the perils of abandoning their homes "in a vague expectation of relief" when they reached Quebec.[25] However, little notice was taken of their warnings and Quebec continued to be inundated with penniless immigrants, many of whom were Irish.

Halifax had specially built quarantine facilities in place by the mid 1830s. They were constructed with money raised from the five-shilling head tax, payable by immigrants, which had been introduced in 1832.[26] Although New Brunswick also levied the same head tax on immigrants, the province did not construct a quarantine centre until 1846–47, when a great humanitarian crisis galvanized it into action.[27] Having suddenly to cope with twenty-six thousand starving and disease-ridden immigrants, who were mainly Irish, the authorities built a quarantine station at Partridge Island, a short distance from Saint John.[28] Before then, health checks were fairly rudimentary. When the 137 Berwick-upon-Tweed emigrants who sailed in the *D'Arcy* of Sunderland in 1836 reached Partridge Island, they were "visited by Dr. Hardy about eight o'clock and he ordered us to wash all our dirty clothes, which we did." The doctor returned at twelve o'clock to see if they had done so, and pronounced that 'he had never examined cleaner people."[29] Having been cleared by the doctor, the group travelled in a steamer to Fredericton and then overland to their final destination at Stanley.

A severe outbreak of cholera in Europe in 1832 was the catalyst for building a quarantine station at Grosse Île, near the port of Quebec, which, like the others, was funded by an immigrant tax of five shillings.[30] The introduction of the new tax, which was understandably opposed by shipowners, no doubt contributed to the sharp fall in immigrant arrivals in 1833, as had been feared. The Upper and Lower Canada Rebellions of 1837–38 acted as a further deterrent, but by the early 1840s the British influx began to rise steadily again.[31] Meanwhile, although the new quarantine facilities at Quebec were well-intentioned, they were initially poorly managed. Vessels having fifteen or more steerage passengers were given only rudimentary inspections, while cabin passengers were usually exempted from the process. These haphazard measures meant that many immigrants unwittingly carried their illnesses with them, thus infecting the wider population. In 1832 alone, there were 2,723 cholera-related deaths in Quebec City, 2,547 deaths in Montreal, and countless more people died elsewhere in the nearby countryside.[32]

Some of the Petworth immigrants from West Sussex who had arrived that same year in Easthope Township (Perth County) in western Upper Canada had first to carry out the sorry task of burying their loved ones. John Capling buried his wife and four of his eleven children within days of arriving. He had to "wrap them up in the rinds [bark] of trees and dig holes and put them in [him]self."[33] Apparently the Petworth group had been "dumped on the Huron Road" in nearby Wilmot Township (Waterloo County).[34] Of the thirty-two immigrants who travelled with John, twelve succumbed to cholera and died. No doubt the authorities had been anxious to disperse them as quickly as possible once they arrived, fearing that they would have caught the disease onboard ship and might still be carrying it. Writing home the following year from Wilmot, William and Elizabeth Daniels advised their family that "if any of you think fit to come … it will be much better for you than it was for us; you will have a place to come to, as we only had the woods to shelter us."[35]

Despite the imposition of quarantine regulations and the best efforts of the medical authorities at Grosse Île, a second cholera outbreak ran its course in 1834 followed by further outbreaks in later years. When Francis Coleman and the other passengers on the *Priam* reached Grosse Île in May

1834, having been transported with their belongings from the ship in small boats, they were told by the captain that "everything was to be landed and examined by the commissioner and all dirty clothes to be washed." Francis added, "This was much against our wishes but we were forced to comply."

He says they had to drag their baggage "about 200 yards from the water" to the quarantine station, where an official, after inspection, "ordered many things to be washed, chiefly bed clothes and bedding.... It was a very fatiguing day and showed us what poor emigrants had to go through after they have left their native land."[36]

These were instructions that could not be challenged. Conditions improved in the 1840s, but prior to that time immigrants endured an unwelcome and often troublesome delay in their journey, at a time when they were tired and anxious to reach their final destinations.[37]

When the *George Marsden*, sailing from Rye in West Sussex, arrived at Quebec in July 1841, the captain reported that there had been fourteen deaths on the crossing and one person had been placed in quarantine. However, such instances of English deaths were overshadowed by the greater number of fatalities among the large Irish contingents who arrived from Liverpool during the 1840s.[38] Many thousands of mostly Irish immigrants perished in the dreadful typhus and dysentery epidemic that gripped Grosse Île and Quebec City in 1847. The port had been exceptionally busy that year, with the 1847 arrival numbers being three times greater than normal. Around 17,500 Irish emigrants died either on board ship, or shortly after landing. Never before, or since, had such large-scale misery and suffering been experienced by immigrants on their way to Canada.[39] By this time, the Irish accounted for some 60 percent of the total arrivals at Quebec.[40]

Of course, for the people on their way to Upper Canada, reaching the port of Quebec and continuing on to Montreal was simply the first phase of a long and gruelling journey. They had a choice of two routes. They could travel on barges, towed by a succession of steamboats along the Ottawa River via Bytown (Ottawa), and then along the Rideau Canal to Kingston, where they could board a steamer taking them across Lake Ontario to Toronto or Hamilton. This was the most comfortable route, although the long series of locks that had to be navigated meant that it was slow and tedious.[41] After boarding a steamer in 1834, Francis Coleman observed "nine contiguous locks" at the entrance of the Rideau Canal: "Our boat took hours passing them ... on each side rise immense hills between which this canal is constructed."[42] Francis Thomas, travelling through the canal that same year, counted a total of forty-eight locks between the entrance and Kingston.[43] Alternatively, immigrants could travel via the St. Lawrence River, but, because of the rapids just beyond Montreal, they needed to transfer to large Durham boats, which had to be dragged upriver to Prescott. It was a laborious and very slow means of conveyance.[44] "The boats measuring nearly 100 feet long were powered by sail, pushed by pole, or drawn by horses or oxen part of the way." Sometimes, as George Jackson discovered, "the passengers themselves got out and pulled."[45] Assuming all went well, they would reach Hamilton in about two weeks.

At Prescott, people went by steamer up the St. Lawrence to Lake Ontario, disembarking at either Toronto or Hamilton.[46] The final destination was then usually reached by wagon. This, too, had its perils. Henry Rastall, from Farndon Parish (Nottinghamshire), complained: "The sea voyage was nothing to the journey by land, although I got some very bad gales ... your Boughton back roads are nothing to it; it is very bad indeed, up and down sometimes your head against the top — it broke my hat to pieces, my hat being thick, I suppose, I did not get bruised."[47] A trip to the western limit of the province, a distance of eight hundred miles (1,287 kilometres), was exhausting and could cost as much as £14 to £15, without provisions or accommodation.[48]

With the coming of steamships in the 1850s, sea transport entered a completely new phase. Steamship crossings were shorter and, because they were no longer dependent on the vagaries of the weather and wind direction, ships could depart at a predetermined time. Crossing times were greatly reduced, and death rates fell rapidly. Dramatic changes were much in evidence by the late 1850s and early 1860s, when Allan Line steamships began to dominate transatlantic passenger services.[49] With their greater size and ability to make up to five crossings per year, popular ships such as the *Anglo Saxon*, *Bohemian*, *Hibernian*, and *Nova Scotian* carried more passengers in a single year than their sailing ship predecessors had achieved over many decades.[50] More and more emigrants opted for their greater speed, safety, reliability, and creature comforts, and by 1870 steam had entirely replaced sail.

With their great size and sophistication, steamships could only operate from major British ports, the main ones being Liverpool, Glasgow, and Southampton. This increasing centralization heralded the introduction of stricter controls and better enforceability of passenger-travel regulations. And with the extension of railway networks in Britain, and the new railways that were constructed in Canada, immigrants really did have a more streamlined service by the end of the nineteenth century. They no longer had to endure a four- to six-week sea crossing in a cramped, smelly hold and follow that with an arduous journey by small boat or wagon to their final destination. Now there were timetables, booking procedures, enforceable controls, interconnecting shipping and rail services, and few delays.

When Henry Welch, together with his wife and children, arrived at Quebec from Liverpool in 1881, they had to push their way through throngs of people at the quay who, like themselves, were trying to locate their luggage and clear customs. Their tumultuous arrival could not have been more different from their departure from "dear old Camelford [Cornwall] in a baker's van," which brought them to Plymouth, where they boarded a train to Liverpool — "a long and tiresome journey."[51] When the Welch family reached Quebec they encountered the "bustle and noise in getting onshore, and then the trouble of getting all our boxes together among the thousands that are hurried onto the quay." To their amazement, Mr. and Mrs. Welch found that their daughters were being approached by prospective employers looking for domestic servants:

> Several ladies and gentlemen [were] on the lookout for servant girls.... Annie, Kate and Bessie might have had a situation there and then; a lady so much wanted them she promised to serve them as if they were her own children, but as Quebec was so far from where we were going we did not like to leave them so far away among strangers.[52]

Cornishman John Adams, one of the 120 cabin passengers who travelled first-class to Quebec in the Allan Line's *Circassian*, had an enjoyable crossing, making friends with some of the Canadian cabin passengers, "who are extremely pleasant people and are most kind in offering us their hospitality."[53] Others were less satisfied. About his 1906 crossing, Major H.R. Davies complained about "the horrible musty smell one only gets on board ship. One of the worst smells in the ship is just outside my cabin."[54] Elizabeth Strong, sailing from Liverpool to Quebec three years later, was also troubled by the "peculiar smell in all the cabins." The pitching of the ship as it was buffeted by powerful waves added to her discomfort:

> The waves were continuously washing over them, then the boat rolled a good bit and pitched; it seemed to me to go up and down and roundabout; then we could feel the thump, thump of the engines and the throbbing of the screw [propeller], and when we got further out into the Atlantic, the sea was very rough and sometimes the propeller was right out of the water, then the ship would shiver violently all over, there was no rest anywhere as I felt the motion much worse in the berth, it quite shook me from side to side[55].... If ever I have another trip like that I will not be on the main deck but on the upper; there we can have the port holes open unless the weather is very bad and I think would not feel the throbbing quite so badly.[56]

By the early 1900s the Canadian Pacific Line had become one of the major steamship operators of its day, having introduced its first fleet of ships to transatlantic passengers in 1903 and later acquiring the Allan Line's ships.[57] However, despite the much larger and more luxuriously appointed ships it could offer, passengers still had to endure seasickness and rough seas. Martin Holdom, travelling in the *Empress of Ireland*[58] in 1909, complained that "the boat pitches terribly owing to her great height out of the water," and, when in a storm, "very often the propellers were right out of the water. A huge sea came over the brow and we were drenched."[59]

For people paying the cheapest fares and travelling third class in the steerage, conditions were even worse. Someone named Dick, who originated from Hull in Yorkshire, and his travelling companion Harry, complained about the poor ventilation in the *Alsatian* during their crossing from Liverpool to Halifax. One of 850 passengers, they were accompanied by 450 people in second-class accommodation and about ninety travelling first class: "There are about 350 men and boys employed on this ship. So, what with them and the passengers there is close upon 1,500 souls aboard." Dick's main concern was that he had to travel with "foreigners of all descriptions — a proper mob, Scandinavians, Russians, Frenchmen, Italians.... The bulk of the English are quartered forward. Harry and I have struck it rather unlucky being placed aft among the foreigners, although there are several more English chaps." Referring frequently to them in his diary as "the dagos," Dick was well on his way to making himself very unpopular with Canada's immigrant population!

Beverley Emigrants on the Landing stage, Liverpool,
previous to departure for Canada. 10/4/06.

Courtesy Beverley Archives, DDX 1321/5/8.

A postcard showing fifty agricultural labourers from Beverley, in the East Riding of Yorkshire, leaving from Liverpool for Quebec in 1906. Having been assisted to emigrate through funds raised locally and by the Church Army, an Anglican organization, they were heading for farms in Ontario. The well-dressed man standing on the extreme right in the first row was probably a representative of the Church Army, while the woman standing next to him was probably his wife.

Courtesy Library and Archives Canada, C-009660.

Immigrants skipping on the deck of the SS *Empress of Britain*, which sailed from Liverpool to Quebec circa 1910.

Dick found that his Hull accent attracted unwanted attention from the stewards seeking "the dollars" as tips: "They think that they can see you coming, so I am altering my vocabulary a bit to suit the folk." He also complained about the paucity of females, "apart from foreigners." He hated the "liver and potatoes" served most days, but enjoyed having access to the ship's recreational facilities: "I spent this afternoon in the lounge room and whilst I sat there I felt a little better. I played a fellow a couple of games of draughts [checkers] and Harry played another chap a game and won.... Things aboard this ship are not like the things they point [out] in their handbooks. There is no gym and no baths [in] third class. No games in the card room....We had an impromptu concert this afternoon. You know the sort, anybody singing. After tea there was dancing on the deck but there is very limited room for that sort of thing."[60]

By the late nineteenth century, health check procedures, customs controls, and baggage collection arrangements at arrival ports had become much more streamlined. When Jack Cameron, from London, England, arrived at the Louise Basin pier at Quebec in 1905, on his way to Saskatchewan, he entered a large purpose-built hall where the necessary immigration procedures were carried out under one roof:

> After breakfast about five o'clock we went on land and were marshalled along to a point where those going to the States were separated. Those for Canada were herded into an immigration hall where after waiting for an hour or two were marched one by one past two doctors who stamped our railway tickets. Then we passed to two immigration officers who were fortified with information which he had had to fill up onboard ship — information as to nationality, county of birth, profession, age.... Here our tickets were again stamped and we passed on and had them exchanged at the railway office. Next part of the proceedings was the claiming of baggage and getting it past the customs and having it checked. This I duly did declaring that everything was wearing apparel ... except the beds.... I

> had to pay a dollar for them and they will be at Lipton [Saskatchewan] in another week now.[61]

Prior to his arrival at Quebec, Cameron would have experienced the new disinfection facilities that had been introduced at Grosse Île. Any passengers declared unfit to travel would have been ushered to the well-equipped quarantine hospital, which had medical staff on hand to treat cases of typhoid, measles, dysentery, smallpox, scarlet fever, chicken pox, and other diseases.[62]

After leaving the immigration hall, Cameron carried his baggage to the railway office and boarded a train for the Prairies. Twenty years earlier most English immigrants would have headed for Upper Canada, with Toronto being a particularly strong magnet for those seeking urban employment. However, officials were caught off guard by this rapidly growing influx. Toronto's reception centre simply could not cope with the many frightened

Courtesy Library and Archives Canada, PA-148831.

Hospital quarantine station at Grosse Île, 1900–05.

and despairing immigrants who sought help. Scenes of bedlam ensued. In 1888, a Toronto resident wrote to his brother, who lived in Bedfordshire, describing how hordes of immigrants were living in squalor in Toronto's immigration sheds. Having been shocked by what he read, the man gave the letter wider coverage by sending it to his local newspaper:

> He says Toronto is a dumping hole for emigrants, who are flocking there daily in shoals of seven or eight hundred. When they get into what is known as the [immigration] sheds, he says they have no money, no fire is allowed, and they have nothing to eat … no bedding or blankets of any kind are furnished. [63]

A Canadian newspaper reporter described one of the sheds as a "long, foul-smelling and disgraceful hole, reeking with scents and crammed

Courtesy Library and Archives Canada, PA-021357.

Photograph of the immigration facilities at Louise Basin, Quebec, probably taken in the early 1900s. The main hall, about 250 feet (76 metres) long, could deal with up to a thousand passengers at one time. After being cleared by officials in the Immigration Arrival Hall, immigrants could walk to the nearby railway station and board a "colonist" sleeping car. The basin is now a marina for pleasure craft..

with strangers in a strange land. The air was full of the [blank] of angry men, the screams and cries of children and the pitiful wailing of infants."[64]

Needless to say, the Canadian government learned its lesson quickly and greatly improved the services that were made available to newly arrived immigrants. A crucial step forward was the establishment of a network of well-staffed immigration halls at towns and cities across Canada. Serving as reception centres, they were places where immigrants could find short-term accommodation and receive help in acquiring land or employment. By 1911 there were around fifty centres, most located in the Prairies.[65] The Winnipeg hall, which could accommodate up to five hundred immigrants, was the central receiving station for the whole of Western Canada.

While Quebec was the principal port of entry for people heading west, a substantial number of immigrants also landed at Halifax and a few at Saint John, New Brunswick, in either case transferring to railway cars for the completion of their journeys.[66] Elizabeth Strong's overland journey from Halifax to Prairie Creek, west of Red Deer, Alberta, had its challenges. As her ship headed for Pier 21 at Halifax,[67] they "stopped to take the Pilot on board; then there was excitement, everyone was in a hurry to get on deck, it was a most lovely evening, so clear and bright it was like going along a lovely river; it is 26 miles up the river to Halifax." After travelling by train to Montreal and transferring to another train for the next leg of the journey, her happy mood changed:

> We did not seem to be getting on at all quickly and could not make it out; but about midday Sunday we heard a dreadful rumour that they had put us on an Emigrant Train. We found this to be only too true, and then we were just crawling along all through Sunday night … then Monday morning about 6.30 a.m. our engine ran into a train of lorries; we do not have anything like this in our country, they are great trucks without tops but such a size (twice as big as ours).[68]

Upon reaching Calgary, Elizabeth and her children spent the night in a hotel, paying a dollar each for bed and breakfast. The next morning they caught the train to Innisfail, and were met later in the day by someone with a wagon who took them on to their final destination:

> I never saw such roads all through forest lands. Trees just cut down, stumps left in the ground and such hills and vales to go up and down.... I do not think there was a bit of level road all the way and the mud about eight inches deep with sometimes an extra dip into a sort of pond; then the hills we went down. I just shut my eyes and held on to the back and sides ... some places we went down sideways, like a crab, then getting up — it seemed as if the horses would never get us up.[69]

When Clara Williams and her parents reached Quebec in 1904 they had a much more testing time in reaching their final destination. Travelling by railway in "a colonist car" to Edmonton, they "slept on some straw in the cattle sheds under the grandstand at the exhibition grounds." They were heading for the Barr Colony at Lloydminster in Saskatchewan:

> We waited for a scow[70] to take us down the Saskatchewan River to Fort Pitt [a former Hudson's Bay Company fort due north of the colony site].... We all had to help steer the scow when the Pilot would take the punt and disappear for days.... There was a heavy oar that went through the scow from end to end.... We would pitch our tents every night along the river bank and chop enough wood to last another day for the tin stove [that] we used to cook meals on board the scow.[71]

After reaching Fort Pitt, the small group travelled by wagon to Lloydminster, where they "spent a few nights in the immigration hall; then Mr. and Mrs. Parr let us pitch a tent in their yard in the village and we lived in the tent and slept on our packing cases until Dad and

Mr. Parr built us a log house with a lumber shingle roof on Dad's farm. We moved into the house before winter, although the house was not finished. It had no floor just earth packed down."[72]

Unlike Elizabeth Strong, who recoiled at the thought of travelling on an "emigrant train," Jack Cameron was delighted to be travelling in the "new type of coach specially built for emigrants, labelled Colonist Car." In his letter home, he noted:

> The seats hold two [people] and face each other. Our party of three had one little nook all to ourselves. There are no cushions but we had rugs. The seats pull out and make comfortable beds, while above is an arrangement that pulls down and makes another bed.[73]

Major H.R. Davies, travelling to Vancouver, commented further on the size and layout:

> The first class carriages are about 80 feet long and will hold 24 passengers. They are very broad and have a passage down the middle and seats on each side.... At night the two lower seats are pulled together so as to form one bed and a berth is let down from the top as an upper berth. A curtain is then drawn across the berths and central corridor, and a piece of wood fits in to divide the berths off from the other berths in front or behind them.[74]

Despite his relative comfort, Cameron complained about the length and monotony of the journey:

> The scenery of western Ontario is one long succession of river, lake, hill, rock and forest — a country fit for nothing but hunting. Frequent stoppages were made at towns, that is, collection[s] of wooden huts, with deeply rutted dusty streets and side paths built

> of wood. It was lucky we took provisions, for the twenty five cent meals of the emigration books are not to be had.[75]

Upon reaching Winnipeg, he spent the night in a hotel. The following evening he was accommodated in a hotel at Elkhorn, west of Brandon, Manitoba: "The conductor put me down there because there was a decent hotel, while there was none at the proper junction."[76] The following morning he boarded a train for Lipton, Saskatchewan, his final destination.

The arrival of steamships and railways made crossing the Atlantic and travelling overland in Canada much less of an ordeal than was the case in the sailing-ship era. That said, immigrants were far less concerned about their creature comforts than would be the case today. Safety was a prime consideration, and to that end they were served well in that competition between shipowners to get their fares meant that they were generally offered the best shipping available.[77] However, what probably mattered to them even more was the ability to go back to Britain should the need arise. The poignant departure scene depicted on the front cover of this book shows a family coming to terms with the fact that they would never again see England, or their loved ones who remained behind. Returning home in the sailing-ship era was impractical for cost reasons. However, once steamships and the railways arrived, people could travel large distances by sea and land relatively easily and cheaply.[78] After 1870, the decision to emigrate was reversible. The heartache and grief of leaving one's native land for good was now a thing of the past.

CHAPTER 10

Canada's English Immigrants

We are proud of our Devon descent.[1]

Despite being Canadian-born, N.W. Hoyles, principal of the Osgoode Hall Law School in Toronto, identified strongly with his family's Devon roots. His letter was one of many responses to Sir Roper Lethbridge's circular of 1901 calling for "Devonians" living in Canada to reveal their family backgrounds.[2] Lethbridge took this initiative after being appointed president of the Devonshire Association, presumably in the hope that the thousands of Devon people living abroad would breathe new life into the organization.

Three large boxes of correspondence now housed in the Devon Record Office reveal the depth of feeling that was evoked in Canada. W.L. Wickett, a barrister living in St. Thomas, Ontario, spoke for many when he said that "there are a great number of Devonshire people in this locality and no matter where you go in Canada, particularly in Ontario, you find native Devonians."[3] First and foremost they were Devonians. They were also English, but what that meant is more difficult to define.

The English had come to a country that had adopted many of their customs and traditions. But, what they stood for was interchangeably

English and British. Britain has a national anthem, but not England. Thus an English person's patriotic feelings formed part of a wider British identity. However confusing this dual identity may have seemed to others, their love of home was and is unequivocal. The English strongly identified with the parish, town, county, or region in which they lived. When they emigrated, this bond intensified. Thus Lethbridge's initiative had recognized that England was a country of regions. That was why so many Devon people felt inspired to respond. Once settled in Canada, their English county background was far more important than the generality of being English.

When people from Tintagel in British Columbia relocated a stone from Tintagel Castle in Cornwall, the legendary birthplace of King Arthur, to their community in 1967 to mark the anniversary of Confederation, they were commemorating their Cornish links.[4] Similar associations with home motivated the many Clitheroe people who were living in Canada to put pen to paper in 1948. That was the year when this Lancashire town celebrated its eight-hundredth anniversary. To celebrate this momentous occasion, the mayor had sent out notices across the dominions asking Clitheroe people to provide details of themselves and where they were living. A folder bulging with letters, now residing in the Lancashire Record Office, reveals the heartfelt stories of the many who responded.

Most of the ex-Clitheroe people were living at the time in the cities and towns of Ontario, Quebec, and British Columbia. Writing from Oshawa, Mrs L.L. Fowler recalled that she had "lived in Jubilee Terrace and worked as a weaver after I left school," and that her "grandparents kept the fish and chip shop and tripe business in the market place." Alice and Jim Parker each said that despite having lived in Canada for twenty-five years — more recently in Hudson near Montreal — their "heart is still in Clitheroe." Herbert Chew of Montreal had many happy memories of cycling and walking in Clitheroe, and, like many others who responded, he still read the *Clitheroe Advertiser*. Mr. and Mrs. R. Flack, writing from Vancouver, said that despite living "in this part of the world for 38 years," they still "have fond memories of Old Clitheroe. There are quite a few of us from Clitheroe around here," they continued, "including Jim Foster and wife, Bill Grundy, Rosie Foster, Charles Landles, Edward Langford and wife.... Of course they do not have Morris Dancers in the parades here, like some we remember from Clitheroe."[5]

People from the town of Wellington, in Somerset, who were living in Vancouver at the turn of the twentieth century, had also been motivated by nostalgia. In 1910 they formed the "Wellingtonians," whose members ran social events and helped one another in times of need.[6]

Another group from this same Somerset town founded the Toronto-based Wellingtonians three years later.[7] Similarly, Winnipeg's Cumberland Association was established to help new arrivals from that county come to terms with their homesickness: "They wanted to associate with people that they could talk about the old country to."[8]

Toronto had a Devonian Society in 1907, the Ottawa and Victoria Devonian societies followed five years later, Edmonton had a West of England Association soon after, while the Devon, Cornwall and Somerset Society of Manitoba "fostered the study of these three counties and promoted the spirit of fraternity among our countrymen abroad."[9] There were many more groups like these. In each case their primary function was to help English people overcome the traumas and hardships of being newly arrived immigrants.

Courtesy Glenbow Archives, NA-4780-5.

English settlers photographed outside their sod-roofed homestead shack (no date). Sod roofs had to be able to resist heavy rain in the summer and blizzards in the winter.

The English experienced real cultural differences when they arrived in Canada, although they had less of an adjustment to make in the cities, where lifestyles were essentially British, if not English. When he visited Saint John and Fredericton in 1847, Abraham Gesner observed that, while most people had adopted what he called "American ways," he wrote that "the fashions are British with an occasional mixture brought in from the United States.... In summer there are races at Saint John and Fredericton, steamboat excursions, picnics, regattas, shooting, angling and a variety of amusements for those who are not engaged in active business."[10]

Twenty years later, Juliana Ewing, wife of an English army officer, attended a governor's lunch and croquet party in Fredericton, and looked forward to yet another picnic on the following day, when she and her husband would join another couple and go upriver in a canoe.[11] Also Charlottetown, with its amateur theatre, "picnic parties, common in summer and winter," together with its "public subscription library," offered a similar home away from home for its privileged English inhabitants.[12] English lifestyles had been transferred and adapted to meet the demands of the climate, terrain, and local customs.

Having been founded by the English in the mid eighteenth century, Halifax retained a strong English presence, both numerically and culturally. Merchants, military officers, government officials, and businessmen formed the Halifax elite, and, together with their families, lived in great opulence. At Queen Charlotte's birthday celebrations in 1786, "ladies, with their hair powdered and curled over a frame adorned with feathers, ribbons, lace, flowers and jewels, danced in their high-heeled, buckled slippers peeping out from the folds of rich brocades," as did the men, "in their white breeches, embroidered waistcoats, with lace frills at wrists."[13]

Balls were said to be almost daily occurrences in nineteenth-century Halifax: "The dazzling white shoulders of the Archdeacon's daughters, the bright eyes and elegant figures of the four Miss Cunards, the fair complexions and sweet expressions of the four Miss Uniackes all whirled ... orbiting happily with the arm of a red-coated or blue-jacketed gallant encircling their waist."[14] With its Victorian Public Gardens and regular British Army parades, Halifax certainly had the outward appearance of an English city. The good life was also available to those who could pay for it in Montreal, Toronto, and Quebec. The very well-off lived in elegant houses, dined out regularly, danced at balls, wore stylish clothing, and employed servants, much as their equivalents would have done at the time in London, Bristol, or Bath.

The English brought their love of fox hunting with them to Canada, but failed to win support for the sport from the wider population. Fox hunting had been highly fashionable in Charlottetown in the early nineteenth century, but opposition from farmers and the heavy expense of keeping hounds during long winters brought it to a swift end.[15] The sight of baying hounds and English gentlemen in their full regalia in Woodstock, Ontario, attracted comment, but here also the sport was a passing phenomenon:

> There were more aristocrats, "genteel" and cultured people, and other comparatively well-to-do settlers from England than from other parts of the British Isles; and not a few of them came to this country as to a combined fox-hunt and conversazione, accompanied by dogs, rigged out in loud tweeds, patent leather shoes and even monocles.[16]

However, the English were more successful when it came to importing horse racing. The British garrison stationed at Halifax had built the city's first racetrack by 1768, and a century later British soldiers did the same at Quebec City. And with the arrival in the 1850s of Colonel Francis Fane, a Lincolnshire-born army officer, the sport received an added boost in Quebec, since he raised funds for the track, helped to organize the races, and appointed the judges.[17]

Like horse racing, the quintessentially English sport of cricket was first introduced to Canada by the military, with the first recorded game being played in Montreal in 1785. From these small beginnings the sport grew in popularity, particularly in Toronto. The York (Toronto) Cricket Club, founded in around 1829, is the oldest in Canada, while the Upper Canada College Cricket Club, also located in Toronto and formed seven years later, was its main rival. By 1840, Guelph, Kingston, and Woodstock each had their own cricket club, with the

Bytown (Ottawa) Cricket Club emerging nine years later. Working as a government official in Kingston, Francis Howell reported with some excitement to his father in Devon that he had actually witnessed a cricket match played in August 1843 between civilians and the military personnel who were based at the garrison.[18]

The Charlottetown Cricket Club was formed in 1850 and "became a popular game and local teams often competed against teams from visiting naval vessels," while the Saint John, New Brunswick, Cricket and Athletic Club, founded in 1886, played matches regularly in Toronto, Montreal, New York, Boston, Baltimore, and Philadelphia.[19] A year later, cricket teams were established at Winnipeg, Regina, Brandon, Vancouver, and Victoria.[20] However, despite Sir John A. Macdonald's declaration at the time of Confederation that cricket was to be Canada's national sport, it steadily lost its popularity and succumbed in the end to American baseball.[21]

Courtesy Glenbow Archives, PB-227-12.

Central Collegiate Institute rugby team in Calgary, Alberta, 1919–20. An Edmonton team played against a Calgary team in 1891, marking the first time that the game was played in the province.

Rugby, yet another English sport, found favour in the Maritimes, the Prairies, and British Columbia, especially at colleges and private schools, but struggled for support in Ontario and Quebec.[22] Its Canadian roots date back to a match played in 1864 in Montreal, when British artillery men organized themselves into teams. The Montreal Rugby Club was formed four years later and rugby games were played in Toronto soon after. The Wanderers Amateur Club in Halifax formed its first rugby team twenty years later, with members being drawn mainly from the young professionals who had graduated from local universities. The Manitoba Rugby Union appeared in 1892, followed by the British Columbia Rugby Union seven years later, while the North West Mounted Police introduced the game to Alberta and Saskatchewan in the 1890s. Rugby's pulling power improved with the large English influx of the early twentieth century, but its popularity was short-lived. Once again the American version of the game (football) won out.

For climatic, cost, and class-based reasons, English sports had limited appeal in Canada. In any case, English immigrants were far more interested in attending social events than watching rugby and cricket matches. In addition to the county and regional groups already mentioned, many turned to the St. George's societies, which formed in cities across Canada. Their purpose was to commemorate England's patron saint on St. George's Day (April 23), promote loyalty to the Crown, and assist English people in financial distress.

The Halifax society was first to appear, doing so in 1786, and it still remains active today.[23] The Saint John's society followed in 1802, while Toronto and Montreal each had a St. George's Society by 1834. Quebec followed suit one year later and Ottawa did the same ten years later.[24] However, because these societies were essentially a social club for businessmen, they often seemed elitist to ordinary people. Thus, in Montreal, which had attracted a large number of English tradesmen and factory workers, the local St. George's Society lost many of its members to the more down-to-earth English Workingmen's Benefit Society.[25] By the late nineteenth century, the Workingmen's Society also celebrated St. George's Day, and, like the St. George's societies, did so by toasting Queen Victoria at a gala supper.[26]

A St. George's Club appeared in Sherbrooke, Quebec, in 1890, and soon after Edmonton had its first St. George's Society, but it faltered.[27] In later years, when the Edmonton Heritage Festival commemorated its residents' ethnic origins, forty countries were represented, but not England. This omission was rectified at the festival held in 1982 when the Alberta St. George's Society was established.

The lapsed members of the Edmonton St. George's Society may have been wondering what they were supposed to be commemorating. Although the St. George's societies were meant to be banging the drum for England, they actually shied away from any public displays of anything remotely English. Pompous and tight-lipped declarations of nationality were acceptable, but nothing more. The Reverend Henry Scadding's observation in his 1860 address to Toronto's St. George's Society that "the English … when transplanted from their native homes, do not see any especial need for asserting their nationality" summed up the position very nicely.[28] So, while the Irish revelled in their shamrocks

Courtesy Library and Archives Canada, LAC PA-029713.

St. George's Society of Toronto 75th Annual Dinner at St. George's Hall, April 25, 1910. Photograph by Frank W. Micklethwaite.

and St. Patrick's Day parades and the Scots did the same with their tartans, pipe bands, Burns' suppers, and St. Andrew's celebrations, the English elite in Canada simply raised a discreet glass to the monarch on St. George's Day. For that matter, there were never any parades or public holidays in England either. The day continues to escape notice in England today, although it is a provincial holiday in Newfoundland.

The Sons of England, another support group for the English, seemed to at least enjoy celebrations of Englishness. It was first established in Toronto in 1874 by George's Brooks, a Nottingham immigrant. Having witnessed the St. George Society's Christmas Day distribution of food to Toronto's poor, he decided to found a new group:

> Two things connected with the distribution pained him. First, the somewhat Poor-Law-Guardian haughtiness with which the goods were given in several cases. Second, the fact that Englishmen in Toronto were then the only

Courtesy City of Ottawa Archives/CA023060/Newton.

St. George's Society of Ottawa Ladies Auxiliary social event held in 1959. The empty seats reveal an organization in decline by this stage. However, the St. George's Society in Toronto was reported to be recruiting members at this time.

> people out of all the nationalities who had to parade their wants and sufferings to the gaze of others and be made the recipients of charity in a public manner.[29]

The first branch appeared in the Maritimes in 1891, and by 1913 the Sons of England Society had forty thousand members across Canada. Usually led by affluent Englishmen with military or professional backgrounds, it founded lodges which provided social activities, some being modelled on the English Music Hall. At such gatherings, people heard rousing songs, "wept at the evocations of England's green and pleasant land," and savoured the unique pleasure of drinking warm, dark ale.[30] There was a philanthropic side, as well, in that the Sons of England furnished its members with economic support and held out a helping hand to newly arrived English immigrants.[31]

The Anglican Church of Canada offered yet another medium for proclaiming pride in Empire and finding one's way in a strange country. With the rapid growth in British immigration in the first two decades

Courtesy Glenbow Archives, PB-165-1.

Sons of England Benefit Society, Calgary Lodge no. 240, 1903. This was one of three Sons of England lodges to be formed in Calgary between 1890 and 1911. In 1929, Manitoba had 2,500 members who mostly belonged to Winnipeg lodges.

of the twentieth century, church congregations grew rapidly. Between 1901 and 1921, Anglican Church membership in Canada nearly doubled, rising from 681,494 to 1,407,994 and far surpassing the growth rate of other religions. Anglican numbers in British Columbia quadrupled during this period, making it the province's principal religion, and by 1921, Anglicans were the second largest denomination in Ontario and Manitoba as well as being very well-represented in Saskatchewan and Alberta.[32]

A factor in Anglicanism's success was the proactive role undertaken by the Anglican Church in England in promoting emigration. It even advised people who were intending to emigrate to take letters of introduction from their local clergy to give to Anglican ministers once they reached their new abodes in Canada. This form of Anglican networking made it easier for new arrivals to find their bearings and it also had practical spinoffs, such as offering help in finding jobs.[33]

While the English had these various support groups that reminded them of their homeland, they still had to become Canadians. That was easier said than done. While they grabbed Canada's economic opportunities with both hands, they were far less keen to relinquish their English culture and lifestyles. Those who moved to the cities and towns had less of an adjustment to make; but the ones who opted for the flat prairie wildernesses, where hedges, bushes, and trees were a rarity, experienced an incredible shock. Those who faced the vast impenetrable forests of mid and eastern Canada were similarly challenged. Whether they had come from the long-established urban or rural parts of England, what they saw around them must have seemed strange and threatening. Then there were the isolation, the constant grind of back-breaking work, and the rigorous climate to be endured. Nevertheless, as Letitia Fraser, living near Prince Albert, Saskatchewan, pointed out, many English immigrants "did break the land, establish farms, and raise families in spite of the hardships. A lot of them, chiefly the older ones, managed to reproduce some of the patterns of social life that they had in England." However, some conceded defeat: "One [English] family on a chicken farm just picked up and left one morning after breakfast, leaving the dishes on the table, the food in the cupboard and the chickens in their coop."[34]

At the other extreme were the well-to-do English who had the resources to re-create their former lifestyles. When Claude Gardiner visited Mr. and Mrs. Berry's "nice little house" in Alberta, he remarked that "the room we were in was well furnished and looked like an English drawing room. Mrs. Berry is English."[35] Some wealthy families who relocated to British Columbia revelled in their afternoon teas and always dressed for dinner. A woman living near the Cowichan Valley recollected that each evening "her brother came down [for dinner] in his fresh white flannels and old school tie."[36] However, apart from these living-in-the-past eccentrics, most English immigrants adapted to Canadian ways, although, as Letitia Fraser observed, most did so by preserving some aspects of their previous lifestyles.

The Staffordshire miners who were recruited by the Hudson's Bay Company in 1854 to work at the Nanaimo colliery on Vancouver Island exchanged their modest brick-built terraced houses in England for company-built log houses. The houses were "dreary on the outside" and not much better on the inside, but the miners were glad to have them:

> Photographs of loved ones were displayed on the walls, or illustrations from newspapers. Despite the simple home, visitors were always made welcome. When a white tablecloth materialized and was spread over a painted board, it showed a measure of warm hospitality extended to the visitor.[37]

The tablecloth was simply an expression of the English talent for ceremony. Similarly, a linen tablecloth meant a great deal to Jack Cameron, an English homesteader in Saskatchewan who lived with his brother. When a couple from "up country" stayed the night at their house, Jack made it clear that anyone who loved him would have to love his tablecloth:

> The wife washed our dishes and was amazed to find we used linen table-cloths. We paralyzed her by producing a brand-new clean one. She said that when I get a woman (the Canadians refer to their wives as women), I

> would have to use an oil-cloth for a [Canadian] woman would not wash linen ones, but I remarked that such was not the woman for me.[38]

When they left England for their homesteading life in Saskatchewan, the wives of the urban workers who would go on to found the Barr Colony dressed as they might have done for a shopping excursion or social event back home, not realizing how inappropriate this would be in their new life:

> The occasional woman had chosen comfort and common sense over convention by wearing a wrapper, whose loose fit gave her more freedom of movement, and a man's wide-brimmed hat. But the majority of women wore crisp white shirtwaists, the necks high, the sleeves long and the fronts ruffled and decorated to cover modesty, bosoms thrust stylishly forward by whalebone corsets. They wore dark-coloured serge skirts with extra fullness in the back to accommodate a small bustle and petticoat or two to add volume and rustle as they swept the ground. High-laced boots with little heels crunched on the prairie wool. Only the hairdos had adapted to present conditions, the wind having won the battle over fashionable rolls and pompadours.[39]

By the time they experienced their first winter, they also learned "that their English coats would not keep out the wind, that mere gloves were useless, and that feet would freeze in five minutes in their English boots."[40]

Ontario historian Dr. Edwin Guillet gave the English credit for "assimilating themselves more speedily," and for being "less clannish than the Scots and Irishmen," but thought that "some of them arrived with no small amount of self-conceit, bounce and John Bullism, which was quickly taken out of them by their experiences and with the help often of rough-and-ready neighbours."[41]

Fur trader and author Edward Ermatinger also referred to the "John Bullism" of the English and their tendency to criticize Canadian ways: "They had grumbled themselves out of England, and the same spirit accompanied them to Canada."[42] Clearly, the fictional John Bull, depicted in cartoons as an energetic, brash, and insensitive Englishman, was regarded as an insufferable snob.[43] Nor was his perceived arrogance a question of class. All English immigrants, from the lowliest labourer to the country squire, arrived with the feeling that they were somehow special. When he settled near Lake Erie in 1823, the Cumberland-born Thomas Priestman soon overcame these feelings, but others around him had not: "Some of the old English people are a little self-willed and think they could do better but it is necessary to conform to the customs of the country.... This country is peopled from all nations and everyone has something of their own country plans, so this is a mixture of many nations ..."[44]

England's long history of military conquest and prosperity left its people with a strong sense of self-belief that sometimes came across as arrogance. However, their alleged reputation for grumbling and comparing Canada unfavourably with their homeland was blown all out of proportion. At the height of the "No English Need Apply" furor of the early 1900s, newspapers reported what was essentially a baseless hate campaign against the English. It had been orchestrated by Canada's labour movement in a desperate bid to stop the flood of English tradesmen, craftsmen, and labourers into the country, fearing that they would take jobs away from Canadian workers. Thus, while great scorn has been poured on a few suave and distinguished English, the majority have been comprehensively ignored. The English actually dominated the influx to Canada. In 1921, some two and a half million Canadians claimed English ancestry, more than the Scots and Irish put together.[45]

Thomas Douglas, from Newcastle-upon-Tyne, and therefore probably an ex-coal miner, was typical of the many thousands of Englishmen who sought a new life in Canada. He and his wife first settled in Weston, near Toronto, in the 1870s; ten years later they moved to Alberta, after Thomas had learned about farming and built their log house.

Courtesy Glenbow Archives, NA-3959-22.

Photograph taken circa 1914–19 of the English-born Mr. and Mrs. Thomas Douglas, who established a homestead at Pine Creek (De Winton area), Alberta.

The unassuming miners, carpenters, tailors, labourers, domestic servants, farmers, steel workers, shoemakers, and other workers were all part of the invisible immigrant stream that furnished Canada with a large part of its population. They did not wave flags or sing anthems. What national identity they felt was buried deep in their heads. When Luke Harrison wrote to his cousin from Nova Scotia in 1774 saying that "in my mind, I oftimes visit Rillington," he was expressing both his longing to be back in Yorkshire and his Englishness.[46] People like Luke had no sense of mission other than the desire to better themselves, and normally succeeded beyond their wildest dreams. The English brought their much-valued skills and knowledge with them, made a huge contribution to Canada's development, but left few outward signs of their Englishness along the way. They were the silent majority who simply faded into the background.

NOTES

Chapter 1: Ignored but Not Forgotten

1. Bernard Bailyn, *Voyagers to the West: Emigration from Britain to America on the Eve of the Revolution* (New York: Alfred A. Knopf, 1986), 411.
2. NSARM MG 1, vol. 427 (m/f 14920) Harrison family papers, no. 188: Luke to William Harrison, June 30, 1774; no. 190: Luke to William Harrison, January 1, 1803.
3. The "Introduction," written by Philip Buckner in *British Journal of Canadian Studies*, vol. 16 (1) 2003, 1–15, discusses the lack of recognition given to English settlement in Canada.
4. The colonies did not all join Confederation at the same time. Ontario, Quebec, Nova Scotia, and New Brunswick joined in 1867, British Columbia and Manitoba joined in 1871, Prince Edward Island in 1873, Alberta and Saskatchewan in 1905, while Newfoundland delayed joining until 1949.
5. Between 1904 and 1914 the British accounted for 41 percent of the immigration to Canada, the majority of it English, with the European proportion being 28 percent and the United States 31 percent. See Lloyd G. Reynolds, *The British Immigrant: His Social and Economic Adjustment in Canada* (Toronto: Oxford University Press,

1935), 299. N.H. Carrier and J.R. Jeffrey, *External Migration: A Study of the Available Statistics, 1815–1950* (London: HMSO, 1953), 96.

6. The English also formed a majority of the British immigrants who came to Canada during the 1920s and after the Second World War.
7. GRO D3549/13/1/P25: Peters to Granville Sharp, January 19, 1789.
8. GRO D3549/13/3/41: Moseley to Sharp, November 5, 1788.
9. PP 1831–2 (724) XXXII.
10. The payments were organized and administered at a local level by elected boards of guardians and overseen by Poor Law commissioners.
11. BEA DDX/1408/7/1: *Rockingham and Yorkshire and Lincolnshire Gazette*, September 1, 1830. The group could not have been assisted by their parish to go to the United States at this time since this would have been disallowed by the Poor Law commissioners.
12. Maude Frances Davies, *Life in an English Village: An Economic and Historical Survey of the Parish of Corsley in Wiltshire* (London: T. Fisher Unwin, 1909), 80–81.
13. BL Fox-Talbot Collection. Henrietta Gaisford (née Fielding) to William Henry Fox-Talbot, May 8, 1832.
14. Ibid., Elizabeth Fielding to William Henry Fox-Talbot, May 7, 1832.
15. DHC PE/Pl/OV 3/30 (Poole): Indenture, March 8, 1737.
16. DHC PE/PUD/OV7/2 (Puddletown).
17. The Overseers of the Poor Account Books (Wimborne) quoted in W. Gordon Handcock, *So Longe as There Comes Noe Women: Origins of English Settlement in Newfoundland* (St. John's, NL: Breakwater, 1989), 191–93.
18. DHC PE/WM/OV/11/1/181: April 20, 1801 (Wimborne Minster).
19. Lucille H. Campey, *Seeking a Better Future: The English Pioneers of Ontario and Quebec* (Toronto: Dundurn, 2012), 139–41, 160–61.
20. GRO D3549/13/3/41: A list of slaveholders in New Brunswick, circa 1789. Peters's list ends with "and many others." Granville Sharp (1733–1813), to whom he wrote his letter, was a biblical scholar and one of the first of the English reformers to push for the abolition of slavery.
21. LRO FANE/ 6/12/3: Journal of Mary Chaplin, 1840.
22. Abraham Gesner, *New Brunswick with Notes: For Emigrants, Comprehending the Early History, Settlement, Topography, Statistics, Natural History, etc.* (London: Simmonds & Ward, 1847), 329.

23. Lilian Francis Gates, *Land Policies in Upper Canada* (Toronto: University of Toronto Press, 1968), 303–07.
24. J.M. Bumsted, *The Peoples of Canada: A Pre-Confederation History*, vol. 1 (Toronto: Oxford University Press, 1992), 236–57.
25. For example, William Daubeny decided to leave Upper Canada for the United States, claiming that "I am almost broken hearted, for Canada is in such distress not to be equalled in any other part of the Globe." See SORO DD\X\OSB/7 #64: Sparks family papers. William Daubeny in Westminster, Upper Canada, to his cousin in Beaminster, Dorset, June 8, 1837.
26. J.I. Little, ed., *Love Strong as Death: Lucy Peel's Canadian Journal, 1833–1836* (Waterloo, ON: Wilfred Laurier University Press, 2001), 8.
27. Carrier, and Jeffery, *External Migration*, 95–96.
28. Stephen Constantine, ed., *Emigrants and Empire: British Settlement in the Dominions Between the Wars* (Manchester: Manchester University Press, 1990), 153.
29. For example, the Hornby scheme of 1937 proposed to settle British families across Canada with British government assistance under renewed Empire settlement legislation, but it never came to fruition. See LAC MG26-K #241656-8 (m/f M-1072): "British Community Settlements" in Ontario, Quebec, the Maritimes, Manitoba and Saskatchewan, October 9, 1933, and Montague Leyland Hornby, *A Plan for British Community Settlements in Canada* (Lethbridge, AB: Lethbridge Herald Print, 1931).

Chapter 2: The English Influx to Atlantic Canada

1. LAC MG23-J3: Narrative of a voyage on board the *Elizabeth* from England to the Island of St. John, 1775–1777, 30.
2. The New London (Lot 21) settlement was being organized by Robert Clark, a devout Quaker who found most of his recruits in London. The settlement struggled from crisis to crisis and eventually Lot 21 became largely Scottish. See Lucille H. Campey, *Planters, Paupers, and Pioneers: English Settlers in Atlantic Canada* (Toronto: Dundurn, 2010), 159–65.
3. Britain had laid claim to Newfoundland in the late sixteenth century. The Newfoundland Company was founded by English businessmen in 1610 to promote colonization, but progress was slow.

4. The Treaty of Utrecht (1713) confirmed Britain's possession of Nova Scotia and Newfoundland. France was forced to relinquish all sovereign rights in Newfoundland, in return for maintaining its fishing rights in the south, on what would become known as the "French Shore."
5. Peter L. McCreath and John G. Leefe, *A History of Early Nova Scotia* (Tantallon, NS: Four East Publications, 1990), 196–203.
6. Around 45 percent of the 2,547 settlers who arrived in 1749 were reported to have left the area. Esther Clark Wright, *Planters and Pioneers* (Wolfville, NS: published by author, 1982), 8–11.
7. The German immigrants founded the town of Lunenburg.
8. In 1752 the Acadian population was estimated to be between 10,000 and 15,000. Philip Buckner and John G. Reid, eds., *The Atlantic Region to Confederation: A History* (Toronto: University of Toronto Press, 1993), 131, 144, 164–65, 198–99.
9. Some Acadians escaped deportation in 1755 by fleeing to Île Royale (renamed Cape Breton) and the Island of St. John (renamed Prince Edward Island), then still under French control. But when Britain acquired these islands, another round of deportations followed in 1758. With the ending of hostilities in 1763 many Acadians returned to the eastern Maritimes, although they were confined to mainly remote areas and to relatively poor land. W.S. MacNutt, *The Atlantic Provinces: The Emergence of Colonial Society 1712–1857* (London: McClelland & Stewart, 1965), 62–63, 113; Buckner and Reid, *Atlantic Region*, 144–47, 164–65, 198–99.
10. The Mi'kmaq declared war on Britain in 1749, in retaliation for the creation of a British military presence and settlement at Halifax. Despite attempts by the British to bring this war to an end by treaty, the conflict continued until 1760, when a series of treaties brought peace. Meanwhile, with the defeat of the French at Louisbourg in 1758, the Mi'kmaq had been forced to surrender to British control, and from then on they were progressively removed from their hunting and fishing grounds to make way for European settlers and to accommodate Britain's defence needs.
11. *Planter* is an old English term for colonist.
12. Buckner and Reid, *Atlantic Region*, 151–52, 162–63; Bumsted, *The Peoples of Canada*, 140–44.

13. Cumberland was settled first in 1759 by families from Connecticut. Sackville had its first New England settlers by 1761. In addition to the New Englanders, the isthmus also attracted disbanded soldiers who had served in the large British garrison at Fort Cumberland. W.C. Milner "The Records of Chignecto," *Collections of the Nova Scotia Historical Society*, vol. 15 (1911): 1–40.
14. In 1767 the isthmus had 868 settlers: Amherst had 125 (85 Irish, 29 Americans), Cumberland had 334 (28 Irish, 269 Americans), Moncton had 60 (49 Germans), and Sackville had 349 (343 Americans). John Bartlet Brebner, *The Neutral Yankees of Nova Scotia: A Marginal Colony During the Revolutionary Years* (New York: Columbia University Press, 1937), 60–66. Louise Walsh Throop, "Early Settlers of Cumberland Township, Nova Scotia," *National Genealogical Society Quarterly* 67 (September 1979): 182–92.
15. JRL GB133 Eng MS 615: Journals of John Salusbury in "Nova Scotia Journal," no. 4: 36. Salusbury became a member of the new council of Nova Scotia in 1749. He was responsible for supervising the allocation of land in Halifax to the English settlers. *DCB*, John Salusbury, vol. III.
16. James Snowdon, "Footprints in the Marsh Mud: Politics and Land Settlement in the Township of Sackville, 1760–1800," University of New Brunswick, Fredericton: unpublished MA thesis, 1974: 53–62, 89–107.
17. *DCB*, Michael Francklin, vol. IV. Francklin had amassed a fortune during the Seven Years' War (1756–1763) by supplying troops to the British and privateering.
18. Advertisement placed by Michael Francklin in the *York Courant*, May 19, 1772. Only Protestants could apply for land and families had to bring £50 capital to invest in their farms.
19. Bailyn, *Voyagers to the West*, 373–74, 376, 379.
20. There is no surviving passenger list for the *Duke of York* crossing, but a partial list can be found in Campey, *Planters, Paupers, and Pioneers*, 385.
21. NAB T/47/9 and /10 contain passenger lists for the crossings of the *Two Friends*, *Albion*, *Thomas and William*, *Mary*, *Jenny*, and *Providence*. They are printed in Campey, *Planters, Paupers, and Pioneers*, 284–302. No passenger list survives for the *Prince George* crossing.

22. For biographical details of the Yorkshire settlers who came to Nova Scotia between 1772 and 1775, see Howard Trueman, *The Chignecto Isthmus and Its First Settlers* (Toronto: William Briggs, 1902), 217–59.
23. Legge to Dartmouth, May 10, 1774, in Brebner, *Neutral Yankees*, 102.
24. Snowden, *Footprints in the Marsh Mud*, 53–60.
25. John Robinson and Thomas Rispin, *A Journey Through Nova Scotia: Containing a Particular Account of the Country and Its Inhabitants; with Observations on the Management in Husbandry, the Breed of Horses and other Cattle, and Every Thing Material Relating to Farming; To Which Is Added an Account of Several Estates for Sale in Different Townships of Nova-Scotia, with Their Number of Acres and the Price at Which Each Is Set* (York: Printed for the authors by C. Etherington, 1774), 6, 8, 14, 15.
26. Ibid., 17.
27. Ibid., 32–34.
28. William Black was the son of a devout and very wealthy linen draper from Huddersfield, *DCB*, vol. VI.
29. They were known later as United Empire Loyalists in recognition of their loyalty to the Crown after the British defeat.
30. Just over 60 percent of the New Brunswick Loyalists originated from New York and New Jersey, but people from these two colonies represented only a slim majority in Nova Scotia. New Brunswick had a higher proportion of Loyalists from Connecticut (13 percent) but Nova Scotia had more southerners (about 25 percent), who came principally from North and South Carolina. A full 10 percent of Nova Scotia Loyalists were black, mainly runaway slaves who came from Virginia and South Carolina. Neil MacKinnon, *This Unfriendly Soil: The Loyalist Experience in Nova Scotia 1783–1791* (Montreal: McGill-Queen's University Press, 1986), 57–66. Esther Clark Wright, *The Loyalists of New Brunswick* (Fredericton, NB: 1955), 155–56, 159.
31. Around half of the 35,000 Loyalists who came to the Maritime region were civilian refugees and the other half were disbanded British soldiers and provincial soldiers who had served in regiments raised in North America. Most civilians went to Nova Scotia while the military Loyalists were mainly sent to New Brunswick.

32. Only about 600 Loyalists were allocated land in Prince Edward Island, but, because of great difficulty in obtaining grants, many left. It was a similar situation in Cape Breton, which became a separate colony in 1785. Having acquired about 400 Loyalists initially, it probably only had around 200 in 1786.
33. Buckner and Reid, *Atlantic Region*, 184–209.
34. Marion Gilroy, *Loyalists and Land Settlement in Nova Scotia* (Halifax: PANS Publication no. 4, 1937).
35. Wright, *Planters and Pioneers*, 12–16.
36. Graeme Wynn, "A Region of Scattered Settlements and Bounded Possibilities: North Eastern America 1775–1800," *Canadian Geographer* 31 (1987): 319–38.
37. MacKinnon, *This Unfriendly Soil*, 89–117, 158–79.
38. Men from the Duke of Cumberland Regiment went as far as asking the government for help in getting wives, since there were few eligible women in the district in which they lived. Solving this severe gender imbalance was a pressing concern in many parts of the Maritimes. MacKinnon, *This Unfriendly Soil*, 43.
39. Wynn, "A Region of Scattered Settlements," 321–25.
40. MacKinnon, *This Unfriendly Soil*, 27–36.
41. A partial passenger list for the *Trafalgar* crossing appears in NAB CO 384/1, 127–33. For further details of the crossing see Campey, *Planters, Paupers, and Pioneers*, 129–31. On April 20, 1816, the *Hull Advertiser* reported that "thirty-five individuals" who came from Marshland near Howden in Yorkshire "embarked last week for Saint John New Brunswick"; joining them were "several from Crowle in the Isle of Axholme, Lincolnshire."
42. A partial passenger list appears in Nelda Murray, ed., *The "Valiant" Connection — A History of Little York* (Charlottetown: York History Committee, 1993), 5–21. For further details of the crossing, see Campey, *Planters, Paupers, and Pioneers*, 166–68.
43. PP 1836 (567) XVII: Report of the 1836 Select Committee appointed to inquire into the causes of shipwreck.
44. The ill-fated crossing is described in Al Short, "The 1817 Journey of the Brig *Trafalgar* with Its Immigrants," *Generation — Journal of the New Brunswick Genealogical Society* (Spring 2006): 12–16.

45. PAPEI Acc 2277: Benjamin Chappell's diary, July 15, 1817.
46. Murray, *The "Valiant" Connection*, 6–7, 8.
47. The island's land had been divided and sold off by lottery in 1767 to various people who generally leased their land rather than offering freeholds. Andrew Hall Clark, *Three Centuries and the Island: A Historical Geography of Settlement and Agriculture in Prince Edward Island, Canada* (Toronto: University of Toronto Press, 1959), 48–52; F.W.P Bolger, ed., *Canada's Smallest Province: A History of Prince Edward Island* (Halifax: Nimbus, 1991), 38–42; J.M. Bumsted, *Land Settlement and Politics in Eighteenth-Century Prince Edward Island* (Kingston: McGill-Queen's University Press, 1987), 16–26.
48. Some Yorkshire people went to the Charlottetown area while others settled at Covehead (Lot 34) and Tryon (Lot 28).
49. John MacGregor, *Historical and Descriptive Sketches of the Maritime Colonies of British America* (London: Longman, Rees, Orme, Brown and Green, 1828), 480.
50. A.B. Warburton, *History of Prince Edward Island* (Saint John, NB: Barnes & Co., 1923), 347.
51. BEA DDX 1408/1/16: Marty Lund papers, Norman Creaser collection.
52. William Lund travelled in the *Valiant*, while David Cook travelled in the *Trafalgar*.
53. The 1841 Census of Great Britain, which recorded the extent of emigration by county, reveals that Cornwall and Devon lost large numbers in that one year. However, although Atlantic Canada acquired a relatively large number of immigrants from these two counties, they were only a small fraction of the number who went to the United States and Upper Canada. Charlotte Erickson, *Leaving England: Essays on British Emigration in the Nineteenth Century* (Ithaca, NY: Cornell University Press, 1994), 37–38.
54. For details of the island's shipbuilding industry, see Campey, *Planters, Paupers, and Pioneers*, 158–89.
55. John Bradley, *Letter-Books of John and Mary Cambridge of Prince Edward Island, 1792–1812* (Devizes: The Stationery Cupboard, 1996), 278–79, 322.
56. Basil Greenhill and Anne Giffard, *Westcountrymen in Prince Edward's Isle* (Toronto: University of Toronto Press, 1967), 101. Bruce S. Elliott,

"English Immigration to Prince Edward Island," *The Island Magazine*, part 1, no. 40 (1996): 9–11; part 2, no. 41 (1997): 4.

57. Queens County's sizable intake from Devon and Cornwall is revealed in tombstone inscriptions contained in Peter Gallant and Nelda Murray, *From England to Prince Edward Island* (Charlottetown: PEI Genealogical Society, 1991).
58. Elliott, "English Immigration to Prince Edward Island," part 2: 4.
59. Sherreall Branton Leetooze, *A Corner for the Preacher* with the introductory chapter by Elizabeth Howard; and a preface by Colin Short (Bowmanville, ON: L. Michael-John Associates, circa 2005), 18–22, 27–28, 31, 36.
60. The Bible Christian movement attracted small numbers, having only 369 members in 1855. Wesleyan Methodism attracted three times as many members. See Cameron, "P.E.I. Methodist Prelude." in Charles H.H. Scobie and John Webster Grant, eds., *Contribution of Methodism to Atlantic Canada* (Montreal: McGill-Queen's University Press, circa 1992), 129–30.
61. JRL MAW MS 91.11: Cephas Barker, *Notes by the Way: Papers and Addresses: In Memoriam* (Bowmanville, ON: H.J. Nott, 1882).
62. The Reverend Barker was transferred to Ontario in 1865. D.W. Johnson, *History of Methodism in Eastern British America, Including Nova Scotia, New Brunswick, Prince Edward Island* (Sackville, NB: Tribune Printing, 1925), 239–40.
63. The Census of 1657 reveals that, of the British population living in Newfoundland at that time, 80 percent originated from the West Country.
64. WORO 705:1059/9600/26(i)/ 3: Bishop of Newfoundland, December 4, 1866.
65. The importance that West Country merchants placed on being able to exercise total control over Newfoundland's affairs is discussed in David J. Starkey, "Devonians and the Newfoundland Trade," in *The New Maritime History of Devon*, Michael Duffy, et al., eds. (London: Conway Maritime Press in association with University of Exeter, 1992), vol. 1, 163–71.
66. Keith Matthews, "A History of the West of England-Newfoundland Fishery," (unpublished Ph.D. thesis, University of Oxford, 1968), 14.
67. DRO 2565A/P051/5 (Kingsteignton); DRO 3419A/P09/30 (Combeinteignhead).
68. DRO 3419A/P19/45 (Combeinteignhead).

69. Jean M. Murray, ed., *The Newfoundland Journal of Aaron Thomas, Able Seaman in HMS Boston: A Journal Written During a Voyage from England to Newfoundland and from Newfoundland to England in the Years 1794 and 1795, Addressed to a Friend* (London: Longmans, 1968), 173, quoted in Handcock, *So Longe As There Comes Noe Women*, 256.
70. DHC PE/WM/OV/11/1/181: April 20, 1801 (Wimborne Minster).
71. STRO D3388/23/3: William Dyott to his brother Richard in Lichfield, Staffordshire, July 1787.
72. The "Old English Shore" extended between Trepassey on the south to Greenspond on the north. By the early 1800s, new arrivals from the West Country were forced to look to territory in the more outlying areas along the north and south coasts to accommodate their communities.
73. SOAS LMS, Jacket B, Folder 2 /45, March 4, 1818.
74. DRO 5592Z/Z/4 Extracts of letters, March 4–31, 1817.
75. Ibid.
76. However, serious problems being caused by the decline in trade and rising poverty of the people still had to be addressed. See DRO 5592Z/Z/6: "Brief Considerations on the Nature, Importance and Existing Difficulties of the Newfoundland Trade Presented by a Deputation of Merchants to Lords Liverpool and Bathurst at the Board of Trade, 1817."
77. John J. Mannion, ed., *The Peopling of Newfoundland: Essays in Historical Geography* (St. John's: Institute of Social and Economic Research, Memorial University of Newfoundland, 1978), 1–13.
78. The distinctive English settlement patterns that were created by the West Country trade are described in Handcock, *So Longe As There Comes Noe Women*, 145–53.
79. Joseph Bouchette, *The British Dominions in North America: A Topographical and Statistical Description of the Provinces of Lower and Upper Canada, New Brunswick, Nova Scotia, the Islands of Newfoundland, Prince Edward Island and Cape Breton* (London: Longman, Rees, Orme, Brown, Green and Longman, 1832), vol. II, 184–85, 187.
80. However, poor people had been assisted to immigrate to British North America by parishes, local organizations, and private individuals long before 1834 without approval from Parliament. The Poor Law Act of 1834 was merely legitimizing a practice that was already widespread.

81. SROI FC 131/G14/1: Benhall Parish records, 1831. John Birt had six children, John Cook also six, William Smith two, while Charles Gibbs and Samuel Mayhew each had one child.
82. For example, the cost of maintaining John Cook's family was calculated to be £26 11s. 6d. The final emigration bill was expected to be £150.
83. They sailed in the *Minerva* (80), *Venus* (80), and *Rosa* (50). See Elliott, "English Immigration to Prince Edward Island," part 2, no. 41, 4–6.
84. PAPEI Acc4362#2: Mark Butcher fonds.
85. Elliott, "English Immigration to Prince Edward Island," in *Island Magazine*, part 2, no. 41: 5.
86. The increasing poverty of farm workers stimulated much assisted emigration from Wiltshire during the 1830s, but it was mainly directed at Upper and Lower Canada. It would appear that those who went to Prince Edward Island paid their own expenses.
87. Gallant and Murray, *From England to PEI.* Shipping and customs data provides evidence of a substantial influx from the North of England during the early 1820s. See Campey, *Planters, Paupers, and Pioneers*, 170.
88. For details of Nova Scotia's coal mining industry and the employment of English miners, see Campey, *Planters, Paupers, and Pioneers*, 98–109. Also see Bruce Elliott, "The English," in Paul Magosci, ed., *The Encyclopedia of Canada's Peoples* (Toronto: Published for the Multicultural History Society of Ontario by the University of Toronto Press, circa 1999), 468.
89. *Acadian Recorder*, June 16, 1827. In 1827, the *Margaret* brought eighty miners and the *Mary* brought forty miners. In 1838, the *Mary Ann* brought one hundred miners from Liverpool. The larger than average number of English passenger arrivals from Liverpool between 1827 and 1832, in 1838, and again between 1842 and 1847 suggest that a steady stream of men from the North of England came to work in the mines during these years. See J.S. Martell, *Immigration to and Emigration from Nova Scotia 1815–1838* (Halifax, NS: NSARM, 1942), 57–90; Susan Longley Morse, "Immigration to Nova Scotia 1839–51" (Halifax: Dalhousie University, unpublished M.A., 1946, 115–20).
90. *SPG Annual Report*, 1866: 55.

91. Nova Scotia's gold mines were located mainly in Guysborough, Halifax, and Queens Counties. Cornishmen found jobs at the Londonderry iron mines in Colchester County.
92. LAC RG17, vol. 139, no. 14579. The Cornish miners were organized by Nicholas Bryant of St. Agnes and his son Captain John Bryant. Edward Jenkins, the Agent General in London for the Dominion of Canada, organized some financial help for the Cornish group.
93. The New Brunswick and Nova Scotia Land Company was one of two land companies that became operational in 1834, the other being the British American Land Company, which strove to convert the wilderness of the Eastern Townships in Lower Canada into a settled landscape. Both were modelled on the Canada Company, established eight years earlier. The New Brunswick and Nova Scotia Land Company was never profitable and by 1872 had finished trading. For details of the company's prospectus, see NAB CO 384/41, 319–20. The land company published extensive publicity. See, for example, New Brunswick and Nova Scotia Land Company, *Practical Information Respecting New Brunswick for the Use of Persons Intending to Settle Upon the Lands of the New Brunswick and Nova Scotia Land Company* (London: Pelham Richardson, 1843).
94. *British Colonist* article reprinted in the *Berwick Advertiser*, August 21, 1836. The Berwick settlers who went to Stanley sailed to Saint John in the *D'Arcy* of Sunderland.
95. They had been promised lots of one hundred acres, with five acres cleared, and a log house (NAB CO 188/60 ff. 147–48).
96. NAB CO 188/61, 147–48, 388–89: Petition, dated April 1838. The Stanley petitioners' names are printed in Campey, *Planters, Paupers, and Pioneers*, 146.
97. NAB CO 188/60, 149–50: Petition to R. Haynes, Commissioner, New Brunswick and Nova Scotia Land Company, June 15, 1838.
98. *New Brunswick Courier*, July 15, 1837, quoted in Bruce Elliott, "Emigrant Recruitment by the New Brunswick Land Company," *Generations* (Summer 2005), 11–17. The Berwick settlers who went to Harvey sailed in the *Cornelius* of Sunderland.
99. PANB RG 637 26d: Records of the Surveyor General. A Harvey settler list produced by the company in 1837 is printed in Campey, *Planters, Paupers, and Pioneers*, 149–53.

100. PANB RS 24 1839 re/5: Assembly Sessional Papers, 1839: Report of the commissioners for locating the Northumberland emigrants, March 5, 1839.
101. PANB RG 637 #26d: Records of the Surveyor General.
102. PANB RS 24 1838 re/1: Assembly Sessional Papers, 1838.
103. From the 1840s, New Brunswick, Nova Scotia, and Prince Edward Island not only experienced a steady drop in the numbers arriving from Britain, they also lost some of their already-established British settlers to Upper Canada and the United States.
104. Most of the Customs Records were lost in 1877 in the great fire of Saint John (they only survive for 1815, 1832, 1833–34, and 1837–38).
105. Lucille H. Campey, *With Axe and Bible: The Scottish Pioneers of New Brunswick, 1784–1874* (Toronto: Dundurn, 2007), 3–94.
106. W.F. Ganong, "Monograph of the Origins of Settlements in the Province of New Brunswick," *Transactions of the Royal Society of Canada*, 2nd series (10), sections 1–2 (1904): 73–94. Immigrant numbers peaked in 1847 at 14,879, the overwhelming number being Irish.
107. Little is known about the regional origins of the English who settled in New Brunswick. Surviving passenger lists for 1833–34 reveal that most immigrants in those years sailed either from the West Country ports of Falmouth and Plymouth or from Liverpool and London. See New Brunswick Genealogical Society, *Passengers to New Brunswick: Custom House Records — 1833, 34, 37, 38* (Saint John, 1987).
108. In 1871, the Scots accounted for 14 percent of the total New Brunswick population and the Acadians 16 percent.
109. Canadian census-takers insisted that a person's ethnicity should be defined by the ethnicity of the first antecedent from Europe on the male side to have set foot on North American soil.
110. The Channel Island influx began in 1806. In 1881, 53 percent of Lot 64's population claimed English ancestry.
111. Generally, people of English origin had settled in those areas of the island where agriculture was most intensive and where shipbuilding operations were the best-developed. This, plus the fact that they were more inclined to own land and businesses, probably explains the English tendency to stay.

112. Clark, *Three Centuries and the Island*, 120–32.
113. Elliott, "The English," 463–65. In 1991, 49.5 percent of the population of Prince Edward Island claimed at least one English ancestor, while the comparable figures for Nova Scotia and New Brunswick were 54 percent and 43 percent respectively.
114. Marjorie Whitelaw, ed., *The Dalhousie Journals* (Ottawa: Oberon, 1978–82) vol. I, 83–84.

Chapter 3: Growing Numbers Who Headed for Quebec and Ontario

1. BEA DDX 1408/7/1: letter from Francis Jackson printed in the *Hull, Rockingham, and Yorkshire and Lincolnshire Gazette*, April 2, 1831.
2. J. M. Bumsted, "The Consolidation of British North America, 1783–1860," in Philip Buckner, ed., *Canada and the British Empire* (Oxford: Oxford University Press, 2008) 43–47.
3. Fernand Ouellet, *Le Bas Canada 1791–1840: Changements structuraux et crise* (Ottawa: Ottawa University, 1976) [Translated and adapted: Patricia Claxton, *Lower Canada, 1791–1840: Social Change and Nationalism* (Toronto: McClelland & Stewart, 1980)], 22–36.
4. Approximately 80 percent of the Loyalists settled in what were known as the Royal Townships: Charlottenburg, Cornwall, Osnabruck, Williamsburgh, Matilda, Edwardsburgh, Augusta, and Elizabethtown. Angela E.M. Files, "Loyalist Settlement along the St Lawrence in Upper Canada," in *Grand River Branch (U.E.L. Association of Canada) Newsletter*, vol. 8 (no. 1) February 1996, 9–12.
5. These Loyalists settled in what were known as the Cataraqui townships: Kingston (Frontenac County), Ernestown (Addington County), Fredericksburg and Adolphustown (Lennox County), and Marysburgh (Prince Edward County).
6. The Loyalists also included the Iroquois and other Native Americans who, wishing to maintain their loyalty to the king, fled from New York to Fort Niagara during the Revolutionary War. Numbering almost two thousand, most were granted land to the west of Lake Ontario, but a smaller number went to the Bay of Quinte region.
7. John Clarke, "A Geographical Analysis of Colonial Settlement in the

Western District of Upper Canada, 1788–1850" (unpublished Ph.D. thesis, University of Western Ontario, 1970), 37.

8. Bouchette, *The British Dominions in North America*, vol. II, 235.
9. Wilbur Henry Siebert, "American Loyalists in the Eastern Seigneuries and Townships of the Province of Quebec," in *Transactions of the Royal Society of Canada*, 3rd series (1913) vol. VII, 3–41.
10. Although Loyalists were initially unwelcome in much of Quebec, a concerted effort was made to establish small numbers of them in the Gaspé Peninsula. Around four hundred Loyalists were sent to the north side of Baie-des-Chaleurs, along the border between Lower Canada and New Brunswick, although many left. Wilbur Henry Siebert, "Loyalist Settlements in the Gaspé Peninsula," in *Transactions of the Royal Society of Canada*, 3rd Series (1914) vol. VIII, 399–405. Also see Campey, *Seeking a Better Future*, 45–47.
11. Gates, *Land Policies of Upper Canada*, 12–23.
12. Following later boundary changes, Foucault (renamed Caldwell Manor) is now in the state of Vermont.
13. Siebert, "American Loyalists in the Eastern Seigneuries and Townships," 32–37.
14. Initially, England lost fewer people to British North America than did Scotland or Ireland.
15. For details of the Scottish schemes, see Lucille H. Campey, *The Scottish Pioneers of Upper Canada, 1784–1855: Glengarry and Beyond* (Toronto: Natural Heritage, 2005), 35–68. For details of the Irish schemes, see Bruce S. Elliott, *Irish Migrants in the Canadas: A New Approach.* (Kingston, ON: McGill-Queen's University Press, 1988), 61–81.
16. DRO 152M/C1817/OH/109: Duke of Beaufort to Henry Addington (Viscount Sidmouth) at the Home Office, October 10, 1817.
17. Campey, *Seeking a Better Future*, 154.
18. Some of this land had probably belonged to French seigneurs who returned to France after the British conquest of Quebec. Lacolle seigneury had previously belonged to David Lienard de Beaujeu, after whom it had been named. Following Beaujeu's death in the Seven Years' War, his heirs sold the seigneury to Christie.

19. Serge Courville [translated by Richard Howard], *Quebec: A Historical Geography* (Vancouver: UBC Press, 2008), 105–06.
20. Lieutenant-General Napier Christie Burton (1755–1832) spent little time in Canada and was effectively an absentee landlord. In 1799 he was made lieutenant-governor of Upper Canada but returned to England in 1802 following the death of his wife. He frittered away most of his wealth and was imprisoned for having excessive debts in 1812. Despite this, he was promoted to the rank of general in 1814.
21. Some of the Lacolle settlers also came from the North Riding of Yorkshire and a few came from other northern counties. For a fuller description of the Lacolle settlement, see Campey, *Seeking a Better Future*, 53–67.
22. The geographical origins of the English families who settled in Lacolle can be found on the "History of English Settlement in Lacolle" website: *www.angelfire.com/home/lake/lacolle/hist.html.*
23. Robert Hoyle had various business interests. He owned carding and fulling mills for processing wool in nearby Huntingdon County and a store opposite Îsle aux Noix. By 1825 he was operating the ferry service across the Richelieu River to Noyan.
24. Having been a timber merchant in New York State before this, Hoyle understood the intricacies of the timber trade. During the War of 1812–1814, Hoyle and a business associate were said to have made large profits from selling American cattle to troops at the British garrison at Île aux Noix.
25. *DCB*, vol. VIII (Robert Hoyle). Hoyle played an active role in the Townships militia. His brother Henry arrived from New York in 1824 and later acquired the Lacolle seigneurial manor house and estate. He was elected to the House of Assembly in 1830.
26. The tariffs gave Canadian timber a considerable cost advantage and the trade with Britain soared. In spite of widespread and repeated complaints within Britain over the high cost of timber, the protective tariffs remained in place until 1860. Ralph Davis, *The Industrial Revolution and British Overseas Trade* (Leicester: Leicester University Press, 1979), 48–49. Duties increased from 25s. per load in 1804 to 54s. 6d. per load in 1811.
27. The Hudson River could be reached from Lake Champlain by 1819 following the completion of the Champlain Canal.

28. Odelltown was named after Joseph Odell, who originated from Poughkeepsie, New York. He and his wife and family arrived in 1788 and settled in the southern end of Lacolle seigneury. However, they left the area, as did many other Americans.
29. Published under the pseudonym of "An immigrant farmer," *Memoranda of a Settler in Lower Canada; or the Emigrant in North America, Being a Useful Compendium of Useful Practical Hints to Emigrants ... Together with an Account of Every Day Doings Upon a Farm for a Year* (Montreal: 1842), Rev. Abbott revealed his enthusiastic support for emigration and belief that Canada was superior to the United States as a destination for British immigrants.
30. Some Cumberland people emigrated to the Maritimes. Shipping data reveals that just over one hundred people arrived at Charlottetown between 1820 and 1822 from the Cumberland port of Whitehaven, although many would have originated from the Scottish Borders. Also, in 1819, the *Dumfries and Galloway Courier* (April 13) reported on the continuing loss of people to New Brunswick from Cumberland and the Scottish Borders.
31. Abbott's comments as quoted in John Thompson, *Hudson: The Early Years, Up to 1867* (Hudson, QC: Hudson Historical Society, 1999), 8.
32. Thompson, *Hudson: The Early Years*, 1–14, 78–97. The book includes an updated list of settlers provided by Shirley Lancaster. Thompson's material was first published in 1967 as the author's thesis: "The Evolution of an English-Speaking Community in Rural French Canada, 1820–1867."
33. The families mainly originated from parishes to the east of Penrith. A few came from the area to the west of Penrith and from the northern stretches of Westmorland County.
34. Thompson, *Hudson: The Early Years*, 78–80.
35. Ibid., 8.
36. James Emerson, "Emerson Family History — From Durham Co., England to Durham Co., U.C.," *Families* 29, no. 4 (1983): 229–39.
37. For Sunderland ship crossings to Quebec from 1817 to 1820, see Campey, *Seeking a Better Future*, 303–08. For example, in 1817 the *Amphitre* left Sunderland with twenty-three passengers, the *Curlew* with eighty-eight, the *Clio* with fifty, and the *Newbiggin* with

forty-seven. In 1818, the *Fame* left Sunderland with forty passengers, *Horsely Hill* with 113, the *Majestic* with thirty-two, and the *Amphitre* with sixty-nine people.

38. NAB CO 384/1 710, 715, 719, 733: William Peacock to Lord Bathurst, May 27, 1817. Richard Shackelton, Sr., Robert Millner, Thomas Waind, Thomas Caile, Henry Hendly, John Martindale, William Coultas, Thomas Easby, John Pennaby to sail in the *Brave*; Peacock to Bathurst, May 31, 1817. John Martindale, Joseph Trotter, Matthew Haigh, John Robson, William Murwood, John Story have sailed in the *Brave* (William Frost, master); Peacock to Bathurst, June 10, 1817. Robert and John Emmerson, Henry Allen, Leon Fryer to sail in the *Cleo* (Samuel Davison, master). Peacock to Bathurst, July 9, 1817. George Alder, wife and four children, Thomas Dale, John Chipchase, wife and four children, Laurence Lord, wife and five children, Thomas Baker, Joseph Baker, William Gowland, wife and child, Thomas Smith, wife and child, John Miller, William Miller and family of eight to sail in the *Newbiggin* (Thomas Foster Wills, master).
39. The group leader paid a £10 deposit for each emigrant (repayable once they settled) for which the group received its land grants free of charge.
40. CAS D/WAL/7/D. People in the second Alston group were assisted by their parish. The group included twenty families with children and a total of £311 was spent.
41. LAC MG24 I59: John Langton and family fonds, letters to his father, June 16, 28, August 12, 1835. Peter Robinson's Irish settlers were mostly Roman Catholics, mainly from County Cork, who had arrived in the Peterborough area in 1825.
42. NAB CO 384/5: 771, 835, 887: Captain Francis Spilsbury to the Colonial Office, January 27. The Newark group sailed in the *Fame* (Thomas Minnett, master) in May, 1819. The group included Benjamin Heard, Thomas Noon, and George Wilson.
43. NTRO PR7347: Carlton on Trent parish records. In 1845, Mary Vernon from Warsop Parish in Nottinghamshire requested aid from her parish to join her husband, already settled in Vespra Township (Simcoe County), but this was refused. See NAB MH 12/9361/36, 53–54, /185, 285.
44. By 1824 the English settlement was renamed the "Telfer settlement," after the many Telfer families who lived there. J.E. McAndless,

"Telfer Cemetery (English Settlement), London Township" *Families* 14, no. 3 (1975): 71–78; also see Jennifer Grainger, *Vanished Villages of Middlesex* (Toronto: Natural Heritage, 2002), 143–46.

45. *Montreal Gazette*, July 9, 1827.
46. *Quebec Gazette*, May 19, 1828.
47. H.J.M Johnston, *British Emigration Policy 1815–1830: Shovelling out Paupers* (Oxford: Clarendon Press, 1972), 91–108.
48. *The Third Emigration Report from the Select Committee on Emigration from the United Kingdom*, June 29, 1827. Appendix: Abstracts of English petitions and memorials, 477–83.
49. NAB CO 384/15, 703–06. Twenty-four heads of household petitioned the Colonial Office: Moses Kinsela, James Lawler, Dennis Lyons, Patrick Sennett, Edwin O'Brien, Miles Byrns, Michael Synnall, Michael Mullin, Hugh McCourt, Charles Toole, Richard Nowlan, John Doyle, David Ryan, George Hollin, Thomas Reartins, Thomas Rushton, William Wilson, Michael Handritten [*sic*], Peter McConnel, James Hall, Constantine Dougherty, Charles Webster, John Fagan, William Hughes.
50. NAB CO 384/15, 712–13. The heads of household were: Joseph Hartington, John Whittle, Peter Grene, Thomas Massey, William Whittle, Richard Warburton, Isaac Johnson, Charles Parr, James Johnson, Richard Adamson, William Johnson, Hamlet Wall.
51. NAB CO 384/15, 681–82. The heads of household were: John Gorman, James Richardson, Tom Gorman, William Colline, Peter McDermott, Thomas Richardson, James McDermott, James Killian, William McCallum, Robert Cheney, John Moore Molloy.
52. NAB CO 384/15, 135, 701–02. The petitioners were: William Stockdale (president), James Edye, William Campsley (secretary), Thomas Aspinall, William Tennant, Thomas Ormorod, Griffith Ormorod, John Young, James McConnell, Thomas Ainsworth, James Hargraves, William Ducket, Thomas Edmundson, William Ryley, Joseph Cumfistry. The Blackburn Society of Emigrants had sixty family heads as members in 1827.
53. Campey, *Seeking a Better Future*, 154.
54. A poor rate existed in Scotland but its nature varied from location to location, while Ireland had no poor rate at all.

55. By 1840, Australia and New Zealand were the preferred destinations of most parish-assisted immigrants, although their overall numbers were far lower than in the previous decade.
56. Robert Montgomery Martin, *History, Statistics and Geography of Upper and Lower Canada* (London: Whittaker, 1838), 344–52. The British American Land Company offered settlers land at attractive rates and provided an overall infrastructure of log houses, roads, churches, and schools.
57. The St. Francis Tract consisted of the following townships: Garthby, Stratford, Whitton, Weedon, Lingwick, Adstock, Bury, Hampden, Marston, Ditton, Chesham, Emberton, and Hereford.
58. For an analysis of the British American Land Company's role as a settlement promoter, see John Irvine Little, *Nationalism, Capitalism and Colonization in Nineteenth-Century Quebec, the Upper St. Francis District* (Kingston, ON: McGill-Queen's University Press, 1989), 36–63.
59. *Report from the Select Committee Appointed to Inquire into the Expediency of Encouraging Emigration from the United Kingdom*, 1826, A1861.
60. PP 1841 Session I (298) XV. Just under five thousand people arrived at Quebec from East Anglian ports in 1835–36. This would suggest that 80 percent of those who left from Norfolk and Suffolk in these two years had been assisted.
61. *The Second Annual Report of the Poor Law Commissioners for England and Wales* (London: HMSO, 1836) 571–74. A total of 3,068 Norfolk and 787 Suffolk paupers had received assistance to emigrate between June 1835 and July 1836, accounting for 73 percent of those assisted from England and Wales. The funds raised for the Norfolk group amounted to £15,198 10s, while £4,198 was raised for the Suffolk group.
62. *Quebec Gazette*, July 8, 1836.
63. For details of the parishes in Norfolk and Suffolk from which the people originated, their sea crossings, and places of settlement in the Eastern Townships, see Campey, *Seeking a Better Future*, 83–97, 336–43.
64. *Sherbrooke Daily Record*, March 16, 1957, quoted in Little, *Nationalism, Capitalism and Colonization*, 57.
65. For example, Charles Francis and Dennis Tite, who had both emigrated from Banham (Norfolk) in 1836, established themselves

and their families successfully in Brookbury. See Leonard Stewart Channell, *History of Compton County and Sketches of the Eastern Townships of St. Francis and Sherbrooke County* (Belleville, ON: Mika Publishing, 1975 [first published 1896]), 248–55. Also see Scott Frederick Surtees, *Emigrant Letters from Settlers in Canada and South Australia Collected in the Parish of Banham, Norfolk* (London: Jarrold and Sons, 1852). One letter (page 3) refers to the former Norfolk labourers in the Eastern Townships who "now have well-stocked farms of their own and write about the rates of wages *they* give *their* labourers."

66. RHL USPG Series E, 1854–55 (LAC m/f A-223); *SPG Annual Report*, 1855, xlvii–l. The Reverend Kemp had been sent to the area by the Society for the Propagation of the Gospel.
67. For details of the early settlements of the Eastern Townships and the Protestant missionaries who organized religious worship, see Françoise Noël, *Competing for Souls: Missionary Activity and Settlement in the Eastern Townships, 1784–1851* (Sherbrooke, QC: University of Sherbrooke, 1988), 7–41, 56–62.
68. The English came second numerically to French Canadians in this latter group of townships.
69. RHL USPG Series E, 1854–55 (LAC m/f A-223).
70. For further details of the Loyalist/American influx to the Eastern Townships, see Campey, *Seeking a Better Future*, 72–97.
71. Rainer Baehre, "Pauper Emigration to Upper Canada in the 1830s," *Social History* 14, no. 28 (1981): 349–67.
72. PP 1833(141)XXVII. The Quebec immigration agent reported that the paupers arriving in 1832 mostly came from Yorkshire, Norfolk, Suffolk, Bedfordshire, Northamptonshire, Kent, Sussex, Hampshire, Somerset, and Gloucestershire.
73. George Poullet Scrope, *Extracts of Letters from Poor Persons Who Emigrated Last Year to Canada and the United States for the Information of the Labouring Poor in This Country* (London: J. Ridgeway, 1831), 28–29. Scrope was MP for Stroud.
74. Ibid., 14–15.
75. Davies, *Life in an English Village*.

76. Alan G. Brunger, "The Geographical Context of English Assisted Emigration to Upper Canada in the Early Nineteenth Century," in *British Journal of Canadian Studies* 16, no. 1 (2003): 7–31.
77. A Frome sprouted just to the west of St. Thomas and a Corsley (renamed Sheddon) formed a short distance away. Both names were reminders of transferred English origins. For further details of the Corsley/Frome settlements see Campey, *Seeking a Better Future*, 135–39, 165–70. For details of the role played by Thomas Talbot in supervising the colonization of the area, see ibid., 162–68, 173–74.
78. Samuel Strickland, *Twenty-Seven Years in Canada West, or, The Experience of an Early Settler* (Edmonton: M.G. Hurtig Ltd., 1970), 138–39.
79. Dummer Assessment Roll of 1839, quoted in Terry McDonald, "A Door of Escape: Letters Home from Wiltshire and Somerset Emigrants to Upper Canada, 1830–1832, in *Canadian Migration Patterns*, edited by Barbara J. Messamore (Toronto: University of Toronto Press, 2004), 101–19.
80. Scrope, *Extracts of Letters from Poor Persons*, 11–12, 14–15.
81. Helen Cowan, *British Emigration to British North America: The First Hundred Years* (Toronto: University of Toronto Press, 1961), 204–05.
82. Audrey Saunders Miller, ed., *The Journals of Mary O'Brien* (Toronto: Macmillan of Canada, 1968), 152–53. Mary came to Vaughan Township (York County) to stay with her brother for a couple of years but ended up remaining in the Lake Simcoe area permanently.
83. GRO D1833/F4/20/1: William Frederick Hill Rooke to his parents, November 18, 1835. In 1973, Rama Township was transferred from Ontario to Simcoe County.
84. WHC 1306/105: Downton Parish, receipts for money paid on behalf of the 1835 group of emigrants.
85. For further details of the Downton and Whiteparish settlers, see Campey, *Seeking a Better Future*, 170–74.
86. GRO D637/IV/5: papers of Messrs. Vizard & Son, solicitors. W. Heurk to Alexander Gibbon, August 1852.
87. CKS P348/8/1: Stockbury parish records.
88. Helen Allinson, *Farewell to Kent: Assisted Emigration in the Nineteenth Century* (Sittingbourne, Kent: Synjon Books, 2008), 72–73. Poor people from the parishes of Lenham and Ulcomb in Kent were also assisted to

emigrate to Upper Canada in 1836–37, while another parish-assisted group from Ulcomb went to Upper Canada in 1841–42. See Poor Law Commissioners, *Third and Seventh Annual Reports*. On June 26, 1832, the *Montreal Gazette* had reported the arrival of seventy-five immigrants in the *Niagara* ("more than half English"), who included paupers from Lenham. Most were due to settle in the Newcastle District (Northumberland, Peterborough, Durham, and Victoria Counties).

89. Allinson, *Farewell to Kent*, 72–73.
90. PP 1843(109)XXXIV. The Kent paupers were well funded, having "received a free passage to Montreal with two day's provisions, and 20 s. to each adult on leaving the ship." A passenger list survives for the crossing of the *Sisters* in 1843. The ship carried 163 parish-assisted emigrants who came mainly from Kent — see NAB MH/12/13080/251, 393–94.
91. Elliott, "Regional Patterns of English Immigration and Settlement in Upper Canada," 72–73.
92. Ibid.
93. Ibid., 89.
94. Wendy Cameron, "English Immigrants in 1830s Upper Canada: The Petworth Emigration Scheme," in *Canadian Migration Patterns*, edited by Barbara J. Messamore (Toronto: University of Toronto Press, 2004), 91–100.
95. Wendy Cameron, Sheila Haines, and Mary McDougall Maude, eds., *English Immigrant Voices: Labourers' Letters from Upper Canada in the 1830s* (Montreal: McGill-Queen's University Press, 2000), 30–31 (Wright's letter to his father, 1832).
96. Ibid., 49–50 (Spencer's letter to his parents, 1832).
97. Cameron, *English Immigrant Voices*, 305, 319, 333.
98. Ibid., 187–88 (Mellish's letter to his parents, 1835).
99. Ibid., 208–09 (Ayling's letter to his parents, 1836).
100. Another son had immigrated to Upper Canada in 1832.
101. Cameron, *English Immigrant Voices*, 251–55 (Mann's letter to her sons, January 2, 1837).
102. Ibid., 165–66 (Carver's letter to his parents, June 30, 1834).
103. The Chelsea Pensioners name derives from their association with the Royal Hospital in Chelsea. They were mainly English.

104. At least four thousand Chelsea Pensioners commuted their pensions for cash. Of these, some 3,200 immigrated to British America, with most going to Upper Canada.
105. Chelsea Pensioners received between one hundred and two hundred acres of free land in Upper Canada.
106. J.K. Johnson, "The Chelsea Pensioners in Upper Canada," *Ontario History* 53, no. 4 (1961): 273–89.
107. A.B. Jameson, *Winter Studies and Summer Rambles in Canada* (London: Saunders & Otley, 1838), quoted in Johnson, "Chelsea Pensioners in Upper Canada," 279–80. Anna, wife of Attorney General Jameson, was one of the most celebrated female writers of her time.
108. For further details of the resettlement of Chelsea Pensioners in Upper Canada, see Campey, *Seeking a Better Future*, 139–41, 160–61.
109. John George Lambton, Earl of Durham, headed an investigation that looked at the causes of the 1837 rebellions and suggested reforms.
110. Johnson, "Chelsea Pensioners in Upper Canada," 282–88. A table of the 654 names has been compiled. See Barbara B. Aitken, "Searching Chelsea Pensioners in Upper Canada and Great Britain," *Families* 23, no. 3 (1984) [Part I]: 114–27; and no. 4 (1984) [Part II]: 178–97.
111. Letter written by John Graham in Weardale to his brother Joseph in North America, August 1, 1854, published in "Nineteenth-Century Emigration from Weardale," *Northumberland and Durham Family History Society* 21, no. 3 (Autumn 1996): 94.
112. Initially, Hull and Liverpool vied with each other as the most popular emigrant ports for North of England passengers, but Liverpool soared ahead after 1836.
113. NAB MH 12/11198/155, 243 /201, 311–12: Wolstanton Union, September 1849, January 24, 1850. The Burslem people sailed to Quebec in the *Elphinstone* in August 1849. They included: John, Samuel, Joseph and Henry Barker, Simpson Baggaley, Henry Bath, Joseph Caton, John Cartwright, John Ray, James Riley, Elijah Goodwin, Richard and Thomas Glover, Mary and Elizabeth Barker, Emma, Rachel and Naomi Cartwright, Hannah Ray, Mary and Mary Ann Riley.
114. Cornwall's copper mines began to decline from the 1840s as a result of foreign competition.

115. Rev. Barry Kinsmen, *Fragments of Padstow's History* (Padstow Parochial Church Council, 2003), 26–27.
116. PP w/e May 23, 1840.
117. PP w/e September 19, 1840.
118. See Campey, *Seeking a Better Future*, 347–51, for details of passengers carried on ship crossings from Padstow to Quebec.
119. CRO AD2183/3: Jacob Jenkings to William Brock in Torpoint, Cornwall, April 9, 1843.
120. PP w/e June 1, 1839.
121. PP w/e May 30, 1840. Twenty in the group were going to settle in Ohio and Indiana.
122. HCA DMJ/415/37–40: Bravender letters, November 30, 1846, December 11, 1846.
123. Ibid., May 15, 1847.
124. LAC MG24-H71: R. Kay diary, 58, 62.
125. *Yorkshire Gazette*, April 5, 19, 1851.
126. *Beverley Guardian*, April 24, 1858.
127. Poor Law Commissioners, *Ninth and Tenth Annual Reports*. NAB MH12/1528/240: Letter from Truro Poor Law Union, June 23, 1842. The parishes of St. Merryn, St. Eval, St. Issey, Mawgan, and St. Columb Major, lying to the south of Padstow, form a distinct cluster suggesting that emigration from one parish stimulated interest in its neighbours.
128. PP w/e May 23, 1846. A large number of the arrivals required financial assistance to enable them to proceed west. In 1846, Colyton Parish in Devon assisted nine people to emigrate to Upper Canada. See NAB MH12/2099/64, 115: Axminster Union, April 21, 1847; Poor Law Commissioners, *Thirteenth Annual Report*, 248.
129. RIC Cornish Memorial Scheme: Women's Institute survey of Cornish people who have emigrated.
130. Upper Canada Census, 1881.
131. Durham County had 2,772 Bible Christians in 1861, more than any other county. However, when considered in the context of its population of 39,115, the Bible Christian numbers were miniscule.
132. JRL MAW MS 91.11: "Notes by the Way," by Cephas Barker, "Papers and Addresses in Memoriam" (Bowmanville: H.J. Nott, 1882).

133. Neil Semple, *The Lord's Dominion: The History of Canadian Methodism* (Montreal: McGill-Queen's University Press, circa 1996), 7, 110–11, 180–86. The Methodist New Connexion could not compete with the mainstream Wesleyan Methodist or Episcopal Methodist movements. It eventually faltered, and in 1874 became subsumed with the Canadian Wesleyans.
134. Brome Township in the Eastern Townships had a substantial number of Methodist New Connexion followers in 1861. They were probably mainly settlers from East Anglia, and their offspring, who first arrived in the mid 1830s.
135. JRL MNC William Cooke Collection, Box 1, Correspondence on Canadian Mission: John Thornhill to William Cooke, August 4, 1841, "Money spent for the Canada mission in my account"; Box 2, John Addyman to William Cooke, June 25, 1841.
136. The Canada Company's remaining holdings, consisting of 1.4 million acres of Crown Reserves, were scattered widely across the province.
137. For the background to the setting up of the company, its operations, and the key people who promoted and directed it, see Robert C. Lee, *The Canada Company and the Huron Tract, 1826–1853* (Toronto, Natural Heritage, 2004). For details of the terms under which it offered land to immigrants, see Bouchette, *The British Dominions in North America*, vol. 1, "Instructions to Emigrants," 478–82.
138. Lee, *The Canada Company*, 205–12.
139. Biddulph Township was in Huron County until 1865, after which time it became part of Middlesex County.
140. Susan Muriel Mack, *The History of Stephen Township* (Crediton, ON: Corporation of the Township of Stephen, 1992), 17–19, 201. James Scott, *The Settlement of Huron County* (Toronto: Ryerson Press, 1966), 166–67.
141. Scott, *The Settlement of Huron County*, 62; Elliott, *Irish Migrants in the Canadas*, 131, 133–34.
142. Alan E. Richards, "Devonians in Canada," *Devon Family Historian* 40 (October 1986): 24–28. Among the Devon people who came to Centralia were: James Willis, Thomas Trivett, John Oliver, John Snell, and John Essery, the latter establishing the first sawmill in the district.
143. While the Balkwills and Snells were well-resourced, many of the others were short of funds, although the plentiful jobs on offer from

the Canada Company meant that any hardship was temporary.

144. Scott, *The Settlement of Huron County*, 62. Other Devon people who settled in the area included George Webber, Lewis Holman, Richard Bissett, Thomas Friend, William Greenway, Thomas Rowcliffe, and Richard Stanlake.
145. Isaac Carling was the son of Thomas Carling from Yorkshire, founder of the Carling brewing company. Thomas opened a brewery in London, producing a beer that was based on a recipe from his native Yorkshire.
146. *DCB*, Sir John Carling, vol. XIV.
147. DRO Z19/29/22, no.137: Roper-Lethbridge letters: Devonshire families resident abroad.
148. Mack, *The History of Stephen Township*, 254–56.
149. CRO FS/3/1168: Dairy of the Reverend Stephen Henry Rice. Rice moved to Upper Canada in 1871 and went initially to Bowmanville.
150. H.J. M. Johnston, "Immigration to the Five Eastern Townships of the Huron Tract," *Ontario History* vol. LIV (1962): 207–24.
151. Anon, *Emigration: Extracts from Various Writers on Emigration, with Authentic Copies of Letters from Emigrants from Norfolk, Suffolk, and Sussex, now Settled in Upper Canada, Containing Useful Information Respecting that Country* (Norfolk: Bacon and Kinnebrook, 1834), 11–15.
152. Wawanosh Township was divided into east and west in 1866.
153. BEA DDX406: Stephen C. Young, "They Went West: The Founding of a Family in Canada," *Canadian Genealogist* 8, no. 4 (December, 1986): 214–26.
154. In 1906, Mary's s son, Matthew, sold his farm and moved to the tiny hamlet of Findlater, Saskatchewan, joining other members of the family who had already relocated there. In 1921, Findlater had a population of ninety-three, of whom fifty-five were English.
155. For details of the groups whose departures were organized by Cattermole, and their sea crossings, see Campey, *Seeking a Better Future*, 203–05, 222–23.
156. NAB CO 384/74: Letter dated March 24, 1843, from the governor general.
157. In 1835, the adjoining parish of Widdington St. Mary the Virgin assisted fifteen people to emigrate. This group included John Franklin — Susannah's brother. That year, Debden Parish was reported to be in the process of assisting its paupers to emigrate. See ERO D/P12/12.

158. Norman Robertson, *History of the County of Bruce* (Toronto: William Briggs, 1906), 281.
159. Dean Wheaton, *Letters from Bruce County Written by Pioneers Joseph Bacon, 1705–1882* (Indiana: Author House, 2006), 1–2, 28–33.
160. Land in Manitoulin was opened up to settlers in 1866, having before this been reserved for the First Nations peoples. Land was made available to settlers at a cost of fifty cents per acre. The Parkin and Legge families eventually settled in Carnarvon Township.
161. BEA DDX632/1: Parkin and Legge family newsletter.
162. DRO 6105M/F/5/2/3: Ella Tanner to the Reverend Thomas Coombe Tanner in Bishop's Lydeard (Somerset) March 1939.
163. Ibid.
164. DRO 6105M/F/5/2/6: Ella Tanner to the Reverend Thomas Coombe Tanner, May 31, 1939.
165. It was claimed that "an industrious man may expect to make about one dollar a day throughout the year." STRO D615/P(L)/6/9: Open letter from Sir John Young, Governor General of Canada, printed in the *Pall Mall Gazette*, May 28, 1870.
166. LAC RG17 vol. 120, #11766: Henry Verrall to Immigration Department, October 16, 1874.
167. Anon., *Emigration to Canada: The Province of Ontario, Its Soil, Resources, Institutions, Free Grant Lands … for the Information of Intending Emigrants* (Toronto: Hunter, Rose, 1871), 21–25.
168. Anon., *Handbook of Information Relating to the District of Algoma in the Province of Ontario, Letters from Settlers and Others and Information also Land Regulations* (Minister of the Interior, Government of Canada, London: McCorquodale & Co., 1894).
169. With the demise of the Cornish copper industry, Cornishmen mobilized their own resources, regarding the world's mining centres as mere places from which they could extract success and profit.
170. The faltering of the Cornish tin industry in the 1870s made a bad situation worse and contributed to the increasing numbers of miners and their families who decided to emigrate. About 250,000 people left Cornwall for overseas destinations between 1815 and 1914. This is an extraordinarily large number given that the population of Cornwall at

no time reached half a million during this period. For further details, see Philip Payton, "Reforming Thirties and Hungry Forties: The Genesis of Cornwall's Emigration Trade," in *Cornish Studies Four*, edited by Philip Payton (Exeter: University of Exeter Press, 1996), 107–27; also see Philip Payton, "Cornish Emigration in Response to Changes in the International Copper Market in the 1860s," in *Cornish Studies Three*, edited by Philip Payton (Exeter: University of Exeter Press, 1995), 60–82.

171. Merrium Clancy, et al., *Cornish Emigrants to Ontario* (Toronto: Toronto Cornish Association, 1998), 13–20. Cornishmen frequently moved jobs. For example, Andrew Angwin, a Cornish mining surveyor, visited the Long Lake gold mines in Quebec in July 1911, then moved on a month later to Sudbury, where he spent several days "sampling." See CRO AD 706/5: Diary of Andrew Angwin (1854–1919).

172. RHL USPG E Series, vol. 37 (1882) 1581–599. The Reverend Compton reported on progress being made with Anglican churches and stations at Lancelot, Aspdin, and Seguin Falls in the Muskoka District, and Midlothian, Magnetawan, Pearceley, Burk's Falls, Emsdale, and Dufferin Bridge in the Parry Sound District.

173. Ibid.

174. Primarily an English phenomenon, remittance men received regular payments from a family member or friend, usually on condition that they moved to a stipulated overseas destination. Often, in such cases, there was a hint of scandal and a general desire to be rid of the person in question. For further details of Muskoka remittance men, see Campey, *Seeking a Better Future*, 236–38.

175. RHL USPG E Series, vol. 37 (1882) 1605–609. Burk's Falls already had a large hotel, two stores, and a number of houses. The new church had been built with funds from private donations and the Society for the Propagation of the Gospel.

176. RHL USPG E Series, vol. 37 (1882) 1581–599.

177. *SPG Annual Report* (1886), 97. English people came in substantial numbers to the Muskoka and Parry Sound districts. The Census of 1921 reveals that people with English ancestry accounted for 52.5 percent of the population of Muskoka and 39.5 percent of the population of Parry Sound.

Chapter 4: Westward to Manitoba and Saskatchewan

1. LAC MG30-C210: May Louise Jackman fonds, Letitia Fraser, daughter of May Jackman, "Prince Albert — 1904," 4.
2. May Newnham, daughter of the third Bishop of Saskatchewan, graduated from McGill University in 1917. Over the next two years she taught German at the University of Saskatchewan. Afterward, she spent a year in Paris teaching English and taking classes at the Sorbonne before obtaining a master's degree at McGill in 1921, a year before she married Noel. After her husband's death in 1947, she taught languages at McMaster University for several years.
3. LAC MG30-C210: Letitia Fraser, "Saskatchewan — 1922," 1.
4. LAC MG30-C210: May Jackman, "Farming in Saskatchewan Forty Years Ago," 1.
5. W.L. Morton, *Manitoba: A History* (Toronto: University of Toronto Press, 1967), 156.
6. Morton, *Manitoba*, 151–87. Robert England, *Colonization of Western Canada: A Study of Contemporary Land Settlement* (1896–1934) (London: P.S. King & Son, 1936) 53–62, 279–87.
7. Anon., *North-West Canada* (London: Society for the Propagation of the Gospel, 1882), 15–16.
8. England, *Colonization of Western Canada*, 279–81. Ethnic group figures are taken from the 1926 Census, which recorded people from Britain who were engaged in farming.
9. Settler locations have been identified using Robert England's maps (LAC MG30-C181). In particular, see "Origins of the population, 1911, Manitoba," and "Origins of the population, 1911, Saskatchewan."
10. Métis were of mixed-race extraction, being the offspring of French-Canadian males and their First Nation wives.
11. Riel and his followers organized a "National Committee" in 1869 and formed a provisional government to negotiate directly with Canada. Bumsted, *The Peoples of Canada*, vol. 1, 371–76.
12. Riel fled to the United States in 1870. He led the Métis in the North West Rebellion of 1885, and, following defeat, was hanged for treason.
13. Between 1868 and 1930 the federal government sold Crown lands directly to homesteaders, but after 1930, jurisdiction over land

transactions passed to the provincial governments of Manitoba, Saskatchewan, and Alberta.

14. England, *Colonization of Western Canada*, 200–78.
15. By 1911 the British element of the population of the Prairies declined to around 50 percent, with other ethnic groups (French, German, Austro-Hungarian, Ukrainian, Dutch, and Scandinavian) and American immigration accounting for the rest.
16. For details of the CPR's promotional activities, see James B. Hedges, *Building the Canadian West: The Land and Colonization Policies of the Canadian Pacific Railway* (New York: The MacMillan Company, 1939), 94–125.
17. Rapid City was formerly called Ralston's Colony. It was renamed in 1873.
18. John Ralston's obituary in the *Rapid City Reporter*, May 29, 1919.
19. See entry for Creasey J. Whellams (1842–1918) contained in the "Memorable Manitobans" section of the Manitoba Historical Society website: *www.mhs.mb.ca/docs/people*. See Morton, *Manitoba*, 180.
20. "Memorable Manitobans." In 1879, Armstrong became the Anglican minister for the town of Emerson while promoting the benefits of immigration to the province through letters and various publications. In 1880, he became a Dominion Land Commissioner, and the following year was appointed agent for the South Western Colonization line of the Canadian Pacific Railway.
21. The 1911 Census reveals that people of English descent in Rapid City were dominant and accounted for 40 percent of the population.
22. "Memorable Manitobans." Greenway served as premier of Manitoba from 1888 to 1900.
23. Sherrell Branton Leetooze, *Bible Christians of the Canadian Conference: The Bible Christians of North America (Ontario, PEI, Manitoba, Ohio, Michigan, Wisconsin) between 1831 and 1884* (Bowmanville, ON: Lynn Michael-John Associates, 2005). The only church to be erected in the area by the Bible Christians in 1881 was near Thornhill. It was replaced by the larger Zion church in 1896.
24. W.H. Brooks, "The Bible Christians in the West," *Prairie Forum* 1, no. 1 (1976): 59–67. Semple, *The Lord's Dominion*, 190, 278. During the 1870s and 1880s, the Methodist Episcopal Church made a concerted effort to develop missions in newly settled regions of Manitoba. By

1882, missions were formed in Winnipeg, Emerson, Morris, Carman, Nelsonville, Portage la Prairie, and Moosomin.

25. LAC RG17 vol. 167, #17397: Mr. Cole re: English Immigration to Manitoba.
26. 1891 Census of Canada. Bible Christians had settled at Glendale, Lansdowne, Odanah, and Minnedosa.
27. History Book Committee at Neepawa Manitoba, *Heritage — A History of the Town of Neepawa and District as Told and Recorded by Its People, 1883–1983* (Neepawa, MB: Neepawa Centennial Book Committee, 1983), 1–8. F.L. David, "Settlements and Arrivals of Pioneers," *Neepawa Press*, June 27, 1933.
28. Joseph H. Metcalfe, *The Tread of the Pioneers, Under the Distinguished Patronage of the Government of the Province of Manitoba, the Corporation of the City of Portage La Prairie, the Council of the Rural Municipality of Portage La Prairie* (Portage La Prairie, MB: Old Timers' Association, 1932), 65, 82.
29. Immigrant letter quoted in Alice E. Brown, "Early Days in Souris and Glenwood," *Manitoba Historical Society Transaction*, series 3, (10) 1953–54.
30. "Memorable Manitobans."
31. BEA DDX 1408/1/16: *Sackville Tribune*, March 24, 1904.
32. "Memorable Manitobans."
33. DRO Z19/29/22a-c #185.
34. "Memorable Manitobans." Brown, "Early Days in Souris and Glenwood."
35. "Memorable Manitobans." James Hoskin later spent three years at another rapidly growing Bible Christian stronghold in Thornhill, near Crystal City.
36. LAC RG76-1-A-1, vol. 426, #630756 (m/f C-10309): J. Obed Smith to W.D. Scott, Superintendent of Immigration, May 26, 1909.
37. USPG Series E, vol. 41a (1886) 741–43.
38. Immigration halls/sheds gave immigrants temporary accommodation and access to advice on where to find work or land. By 1872, immigration halls had been built in Quebec, Montreal, Ottawa, Kingston, Toronto, and Hamilton, and were under construction in London, while Winnipeg's first immigration shed was built soon after.

39. SORO DD\X\CXO/1: Ernest Smith to his father, June 29, 1883.
40. Ibid., Ernest Smith to his father, September 14, 1883.
41. Ibid., Octavius Cole to Ernest's parents, November 9, 1883; ibid., R. Walker to Mr. Yates, December 23, 1883.
42. J.G. Moore, *Fifteen Months Round about Manitoba and the North-west: A Lecture by J.G. Moore* (Stratford-upon-Avon: Simpkin, Marshall & Co., 1883), 24.
43. For details of the founding of the Red River Colony by Lord Selkirk and his Scottish Highland recruits, see Lucille H. Campey, *The Silver Chief: Lord Selkirk and the Scottish Pioneers of Belfast, Baldoon, and Red River* (Toronto: Natural Heritage, 2003), 77–142.
44. Prior to coming to Rupert's Land, the Reverend Taylor had served for eight years in Newfoundland. Parishioners from Clent, his native parish in Worcestershire, furnished the communion vessels when St. James Anglican Church was first built.
45. WORO 11777: William Henry Taylor papers, "Old St James Church, Manitoba." Taylor's letter of July 29, 1851, quoted in Anita E. Schmidt, *On the Banks of the Assiniboine, A History of the Parish of St. James* (Winnipeg, MB: L.F. Schmidt, 1975), 49–51.
46. MAA M107/2/5/8, Margaret Ashton to her parents, September 13, 1884. At the time of writing she was staying at the Queen's Hotel in Winnipeg.
47. Richard E.W. Goodridge, *A Year in Manitoba: Being the Experience of a Retired Officer in Settling his Son* (London: W & R Chambers, 1882), 96.
48. Ibid., 97.
49. Richard E.W. Goodridge, *The Colonist at Home Again; or, Emigration not Expatriation* (London: William Dawson & Sons, 1889), 14.
50. "Memorable Manitobans."
51. Gordon Skilling, *Canadian Representation Abroad: From Agency to Embassy* (Toronto: Ryerson Press, 1945), 14–20.
52. The £1 bonus was introduced in 1906. The original bonus, first introduced in 1893, was 7s. per adult.
53. Independent Labour Party of Ontario, *Industrial Banner* (London, Ontario: 1892–1922), February 1908, quoted in David Goutor, *Guarding the Gates: The Canadian Labour Market and Immigration, 1872–1934* (Vancouver: University of British Columbia Press, 2007), 115.

54. LAC RG76-1-A-1 vol. 135, #32959 (m/f C-4798): Department of Interior Memorandum, December 30, 1896.
55. Ibid. McMillan's letters to *The Canadian Gazette*, *Times*, and other newspapers, February 11, 1897. The cost of a steerage fare in the *Numidian*, which sailed in May, was £7 14s. 4d.
56. Ibid. McMillan to Clifton Sifton, Minister of the Interior, March 18, March 23, 1897.
57. Ibid. W.F. McCreary, Immigration Commissioner in Winnipeg, to James Smart, Deputy Minister of the Interior in Ottawa, May 25, 1897.
58. LAC RG76-1-A-1 vol. 252, #185950 (m/f C-7400): Willans to Superintendent of Immigration, February 3, 1902, May 31, 1905.
59. "Memorable Manitobans."
60. Hun's Valley takes its name from the Hungarian families who, having left the mining areas of Pennsylvania where they had previously settled, made a new beginning for themselves near Minnedosa in 1885. See Hedges, *Building the Canadian West*, 118–19.
61. GLA M3225: Ernest Baxter fonds: letter to his mother in Exeter, June 11, 1899.
62. LAC MG29-C38: My four-year experience in the northwest of America.
63. Ibid., 1, Introduction.
64. Ibid., 3, Introduction.
65. Mrs. Cecil Hall, *A Lady's Life on a Farm in Manitoba, 1882* (London: W.H. Allen, 1884) 64, 94–95. Her letters back home had not been intended for publication.
66. 1921 Census of Canada.
67. The site is now preserved in the Cannington Manor Provincial Historic Park, where a number of the original buildings have been reconstructed.
68. Mark Zuehlke, *Scoundrels, Dreamers, and Second Sons: British Remittance Men in the Canadian West* (Vancouver: Whitecap Books, 1994), 98–113.
69. Ibid., 99.
70. Ibid., 100.
71. Pierce acted as the local justice of the peace and co-founded a trading company.
72. Saskatchewan Archives Questionnaire x2/2 1885 reported on page 34 of Marjory Harper, "Probing the Pioneer Questionnaires: British Settlement in

Saskatchewan, 1887–1914," *Saskatchewan History* 52: 2 (Fall 2000): 28–46.

73. Zuehlke, *Scoundrels, Dreamers, and Second Sons*, 102.
74. LAC MG31-H13: English settlement at Cannington Manor, 31.
75. Ibid., ii–iii.
76. Anon., *Farming and Ranching in Western Canada: Manitoba, Assiniboia, Alberta, Saskatchewan* (Ottawa: Canadian Institute for Historical Micro Reproductions, 1982), 12.
77. Saskatchewan Archives Questionnaire x2/2 1894, quoted in Harper, "Probing the Pioneer Questionaires," 2, 34.
78. Zuehlke, *Scoundrels, Dreamers, and Second Sons*, 109.
79. Norman MacDonald, *Canada, Immigration and Colonization, 1841–1903* (Aberdeen: Aberdeen University Press, 1966), 250–51.
80. *DCB*, vol. XIII, Grace Fletcher (1850–1907). Grace Fletcher was one of Saskatoon's early entrepreneurs, making money as a merchant, bone dealer, and in running a livery stable.
81. MacDonald, *Canada, Immigration and Colonization*, 244.
82. Clifton F. Carbin, *Deaf Heritage in Canada: A Distinctive, Diverse and Enduring Culture* (Toronto: McGraw Hill, 1996), 236–37.
83. Ibid., 237.
84. MacDonald, *Canada, Immigration and Colonization*, 249–50.
85. The Bell Farm was marketed as the Albany Settlement in 1886. Anon., *The Albany Settlement: Qu'Appelle Valley, Canada N.W.T.: Colonial Profits with Home Comforts* (London: G. Kenning, 1886) 3, 4.
86. For details of the Barr colonists' sea crossing, onward travel to Battleford, and their initial settlements, see Lynne Bowen, *Muddling Through: The Remarkable Story of the Barr Colonists* (Vancouver: Douglas & McIntyre, 1992).
87. LAC MG30-C16: Saskatchewan Homesteading Experiences, vol. 2, item 28, 433–34.
88. Bowen, *Muddling Through: The Remarkable Story of the Barr Colonists*, 15.
89. The Alberta Family Histories Society Barr Colony website lists occupations.
90. GLA M6657: Alfred and Clara Causley fonds.
91. CRO AD362/1: Joe Hurrell to Mrs. S.M. Hoaking, St. Ives, Cornwall, March 2, 1951. Joe wrote a letter each year to acknowledge receipt of "Old Cornwall," an annual publication.

92. A buddleboy operated apparatus that flushed out impurities from crushed ore.
93. CRO AD362/1.
94. CRO AD362/2, October 20, 1957.
95. CRO AD362/4, n.d. As Joe pointed out, most Cornish tin miners died early because of the dust and damp.
96. CRO AD362/2, October 20, 1957. The Caradon copper mines were located in Bodmin Moor, in southeast Cornwall. Arthur Bater later became the Liberal MP for Battleford.
97. James M. Minifie, *Homesteaders: A Prairie Boyhood Recalled* (Toronto: MacMillan of Canada, 1972), 30–31. James became an eminent journalist.
98. The photograph of the Cheltenham group reveals a large extended family of Pearces, including spouses, children, and grandchildren. See *Cheltenham Chronicle and Gloucestershire Graphic*, July 6, 1912.
99. Hazlet Historical Society, *Hazlet Saskatchewan and its Heritage* (Hazlet Saskatchewan: Hazlet Historical Society, 1987), 2–4.
100. The *Cheltenham Chronicle and Gloucestershire Graphic*, July 27, 1912, contains a photograph of the group taken at Cheltenham railway station. They sailed from Southampton for Canada later that evening.
101. Saskatchewan Gen Web Project: English Saskatchewan Genealogy Roots website. The families initially settled at Rockglen near the American border, but moved later to be near North Battleford. However, by 1937 only six families remained.
102. The results of pioneer questionnaires sent out by the Saskatchewan Archives Board in the 1950s reveal that many respondents from Britain had an urban/industrial background. See Harper, "Probing the Pioneer Questionnaires," 28–45.
103. LAC MG-30-C16: Saskatchewan Homesteading Experiences, vol. 3, item 48: "A Green Englishman's Homestead Experience" (1903), 704–05.
104. NORO (typed manuscript), 1–3: Paul Frederick Groome, "My Life Story: Homesteading in Saskatchewan."
105. LAC RG17 vol. 1336, #266018: Superintendent of Immigration (W.D. Scott) to the Deputy Minister, Dept. of Agriculture, March 26, 1919.
106. GRO D4467/18: Charles Best to Frank Cookley, 1917.

107. USPG Series E, vol. 61a (1906), 8.
108. 1921 Census of Canada.

Chapter 5: Even Farther West to Alberta and British Columbia

1. Dinton Women's Institute, *Gladys and Dinton Through the Years: A History of Gladys and Dinton Districts and the Biographies of the Men and Women Who Pioneered the Area* (Calgary, AB: Dinton and Gladys Women's Institutes, 1965), 302.
2. Ibid., 305.
3. Edward Brado, *Cattle Kingdom: Early Ranching in Alberta* (Vancouver: Douglas & McIntyre, 1984), 81–98.
4. Ibid., 146–48.
5. Alberta Pioneer Profiles (website). Douglass later ranched at Bassano to the east of Calgary. Both of the Cufflings homesteaded near Okotoks.
6. GLA M7988: Edward F.J. Hill letters.
7. GLA M4180–31: Southern Alberta Pioneers and their Descendants fonds. The M4180 collection is a vast store of genealogical records that were first gathered by the Calgary Rotary Club in 1920.
8. Brado, *Cattle Kingdom: Early Ranching in Alberta*, 51–53. *DCB*, vol. XV (William Roper Hull). William purchased the six-thousand-acre Oxley Ranch in 1892.
9. Dinton Women's Institute, *Gladys and Dinton Through the Years*, 9, 29. Alfred and Caroline Stuart had eleven children. Alfred died at Okotoks in 1932.
10. The Wyndham land at Carseland was granted to the province of Alberta by Bill and Betty Wyndham, thus creating the Wyndham Provincial Park.
11. Jane Seymour, "The Canada I Knew," *Maclean's Magazine*, November–December, 1925.
12. Claude Gardiner, *Letters from an English Rancher* (Calgary: Glenbow Museum, 1988), vii.
13. Ibid. Claude to his mother, no date, 32–33.
14. Ibid. March 4, June 6, 1895, 34–35, 40–41.
15. Ibid. October 27, 1895, 50–51.

16. MAA GB127 M474/1/5/1: Wilfrid T. Ecroyd papers. Ancell to friends, May 11, 1906.
17. GLA M9004: January 5, 1911.
18. GLA M745: George Machon fonds.
19. GLA M4180–22: Thomas's sons became prominent businessmen. The site, now known as Edworthy Park, was purchased by the city of Calgary in 1962.
20. MAA GB127 M474/1/5/1: Wilfrid T. Ecroyd papers. Ancell to friends, May 11, 1906. Ecroyd was a leading figure in the Society of Friends' Adult School in Manchester.
21. GLA M4180: Southern Alberta Pioneers and their Descendants fonds.
22. GLA M4180–15.
23. GLA M4180–6.
24. GLA M4180–42.
25. GLA M4180–53.
26. GLA M8047: Joseph Tyas fonds, "Early Settlers in the Calgary Area," by Philip E. Tyas, his son, August 1988. Joseph Tyas apparently only remained in the district for a few years since he was buried in Pickering, Ontario.
27. Ibid.
28. GLA M4180–98.
29. GLA M4180–117, –140, –159: James Lambert joined the Yukon gold rush in 1898.
30. GLA M4180–66: Having first settled with his family in Guelph circa 1864, Robert arrived in Winnipeg five years later, where he worked for his father in a stone quarry. He prospered as a Lethbridge stonemason and later established a homestead and became a prominent public figure.
31. Alberta Pioneer Profiles (website).
32. GLA M4180–174.
33. GLA M9004: Martin W. Holdom fonds, February 5, March 11, 1912. Holdom's letters simply refer to the coal mine. Given that he was based at Castor, he was almost certainly referring to Drumheller rather than the more distant Lethbridge mines (Map 26).
34. Hedges, *Building the Canadian West*, 92, 154, 310–11.
35. Utah and Idaho lie directly south of Alberta.
36. GLA M7886: John B. Merrill fonds.

37. GLA M4180–239.
38. GLA M4180–236.
39. GLA M6583: Dawson family fonds, Campion Dawson, Jr., to Hugh Dempsey, March 12, 1983. The Dawsons were neighbours of Richard Bright.
40. Syson Lake near Sullivan Lake was named after Richard Syson.
41. GLA M8528: Richard Mackley Syson fonds, 28. Syson had originally immigrated to South Africa. He later homesteaded near Ponoka.
42. Ibid., 25a, 25b. 25c.
43. Ibid., 25e.
44. GLA M4180–77, –82.
45. USPG Series E, vol. 61a (1906), 4.
46. GLA M4180–80.
47. Born in Buckinghamshire, the Reverend Holdom later moved to British Columbia.
48. GLA M9004: Martin W. Holdom fonds, March 11, 1912.
49. Ibid., September 5, 1910.
50. GLA M9223: Morgan family fonds (letters home to family). Letter from Charles Morgan to his mother, July 7, 1898, 54–69.
51. Ibid., March 12, 1899, 134–41. The Atlin Gold Rush, starting in 1899, was one of the major offshoots of the Klondike Gold Rush in the Yukon, which began two years earlier.
52. Ibid., May 28, 1899, 146–48.
53. Charles Morgan also developed a homestead. Their younger brother Edwin joined John and Charles in 1904, building a house on land adjacent to his brothers' homesteads.
54. Ibid. Charles Morgan to his mother, November 17, 1901, 288–92.
55. Ibid. John Morgan to his mother, July 26, 1901, 223–27.
56. Ibid., September 30, 1901, 265–72.
57. Ibid., July 19, 1903, 365–68.
58. Edmonton's population grew from just over 2,500 in 1901 to nearly sixty thousand in 1921.
59. GLA M8857: Eric Holmgren fonds, "William Newton and the beginning of the Anglican Church at Edmonton," n.d. (probably 1981), 3.
60. Ibid., 7.
61. Ibid., 4.

62. John Gough Brick's achievements are recorded in a plaque located in front of the Peace River post office.
63. Various members of the Ottewell family, who originated from Derbyshire, immigrated to Upper Canada in the 1850s. See Campey, *Seeking a Better Future*, 220.
64. *www.sherwoodparknews.com*, article June 16, 2011, on "The Unveiling of a Sculpture Recognizing the Pioneering Contributions of Richard Philip Ottewell." His mansion burnt down in 1972, but his original log house has been preserved and is now located in Fort Edmonton Park. I wish to thank Brian McCormick for drawing my attention to the Ottewell monument.
65. James MacGregor, *A History of Alberta* (Edmonton: Hurtig Publishers Ltd., 1981), 167.
66. In 1921, the English were the dominant ethnic group in Parry Sound, representing around 40 percent of its population. The Beverley place name near Edmonton suggests that some of the arrivals from Parry Sound could trace their origins back to the East Riding of Yorkshire.
67. GRO D5049/2: Eva Martin to her mother, January 14, 1916.
68. Ibid., May 10, 1916.
69. The 1921 Census reveals that 67 percent of people having English ancestry lived in urban centres. Overall, around 40 percent of British Columbia's entire population was concentrated in the cities and towns in the southwest of the province.
70. Margaret A. Ormsby, *British Columbia: A History* (Vancouver: Macmillan, 1958), 101.
71. Stephen Hume, "A Shaft of Sunlight 150 Years Ago," *Vancouver Sun*, November 27, 2004. Hubert Howe Bancroft, *A History of British Columbia, 1792–1887* (San Francisco: The History Publishers, 1887), 193–95.
72. The Staffordshire miners on board the *Princess Royal* included George Baker, John Baker, Matthew Miller, John Meaking, William Incher, Joseph Webb, Richard Turner, Richard Richardson, John Richardson, Thomas Jones, Elijah Ganner, John Thompson, Thomas Lowands, Thomas Hawks, Joseph Bevilockway, Thomas York, John Malpass, John Biggs, and Edwin Gough. Others included William Harrison and Daniel Dunn, who assisted the cook; George Bull, who assisted the steward; and Jesse Sage, who attended the stock.

73. Jan Peterson, *Black Diamond City, Nanaimo – The Victorian Era* (Victoria: Heritage House Publishing Company, 2002), 56–62.
74. Ibid., 65.
75. Dorothy Mindenhall, "Choosing the Group: 19th Century Non-Mining Cornish in British Columbia," in *Cornish Studies Eight*, edited by Philip Payton (Exeter: University of Exeter Press, 2000), 40–53.
76. In 1862, when the Vancouver Coal Mining and Land Company purchased the coal mines, operations were expanded, and from then on Nanaimo's population grew rapidly.
77. *Victoria Daily Chronicle*, 1863, quoted in Mindenhall, "Choosing the Group," 46.
78. CRO AM923/2: William Gryllis Adams to his wife, Mary, September 6, 1897.
79. GRO D6368/1: testimonial for Charles Page from Gloucester.
80. *DCB*, vol. XIV (Edgar Dewdney). In 1865, Dewdney completed what became known as the Dewdney Trail, the principal route into the interior. He was elected to the British Columbia Legislative Council in 1869 and was the lieutenant-governor of British Columbia from 1892 to 1897.
81. Philip Payton, *The Cornish Overseas: A History of Cornwall's Great Emigration* (Fowey, UK: Alexander Associates, 1999), 328.
82. *DCB*, vol. XIII (John Teague). Teague had gone to the California in 1856, where they were also experiencing a gold rush. He found work as a general contractor, erecting buildings for mining companies, before setting off for British Columbia two years later.
83. Payton, *The Cornish Overseas*, 328. Quesnel was another important town created by the Cariboo Gold Rush. For details of the Golden River, Quesnelle Company prospectus, see WORO 705:775/6385/7/ii.
84. Mindenhall, '"Choosing the Group," 44.
85. Patrick Dunae, *Gentlemen Emigrants: From the British Public Schools to the Canadian Frontier* (Vancouver: Douglas & McIntyre, 1981), 39–40.
86. Silver, copper, lead, and iron were also mined in Kootenay (in addition to gold), making it the province's most important mining region.
87. The Marquis of Lorne (9th Duke of Argyll) was governor general of Canada from 1878 to 1883.

88. GLA M-2371: William A. Baillie–Groham fonds, "The Kootenay Company Ltd. Prospectus."
89. See the Balfour, Canada website: *www.balfourcanada.com*.
90. *Victoria Colonist*, August 16, 1903, quoted in J. Barman, *Growing Up British in British Columbia: Boys in Private School* (Vancouver: University of British Columbia Press, 1984), 19.
91. John Gordon, the seventh Earl of Aberdeen, was governor general of Canada from 1893 to 1898.
92. Jean Barman, "Unpacking English Gentlemen Emigrants' Cultural Baggage: Apple Orchards and Private Schools in British Columbia's Okanagan Valley," *British Journal of Canadian Studies* 16, no. 1 (2003): 140.
93. Census of 1911; Census of 1921.
94. Census of 1921.
95. John Thomas Bealby, *Fruit Ranching in British Columbia* (London: A & C Black, 1909), 36.
96. Barman, *Growing Up British in British Columbia*, 5–17.
97. Barman, "Unpacking English Gentlemen Emigrants' Cultural Baggage," 141–42.
98. Barman, *Growing Up British in British Columbia*, 19–20.
99. GRO D3355/7: Diary of Canon Rowen Ernest Grice-Hutchinson, vol. I, 14–16 (June 30, 1913).
100. Ibid., 73 (January 22, 1914).
101. Ibid., 2 (May 18, 1913).
102. Ibid., 8 (June 8, 1913), 80 (February 16, 1914).
103. The Gloucestershire-born Grice-Hutchinson had been based in Sorrento, north of Salmon Arm, from 1913 to 1916. Having served as an army chaplain to the British forces in the First World War, he returned once again to Sorrento when the war ended in 1918. That same year he was awarded the Military Cross. He resumed his role as Sorrento's Anglican minister from 1919 to 1923, after which time he moved back to Gloucestershire.
104. J. Barman, "British Columbia's Gentlemen Farmers," *History Today* 34 (April 1984): 11.
105. Hilda Glynn-Ward, *The Glamour of British Columbia* (London: Hutchinson, 1926), 214.

106. N. Riis, "The Walhachin Myth: A Study of Settlement Abandonment," *British Columbian Studies* 17 (Spring 1973): 3–25.
107. Jack Philips came from a London family who had been grain and coal merchants, but in recent years had fallen on hard times, while Daisy originated from Windsor, England. R. Cole Harris and Elizabeth Phillips, eds., *Letters from Windermere 1912–1914* (Vancouver: University of British Columbia Press, 1984), xiv, xv.
108. Harris and Phillips, eds., *Letters from Windermere*, 81: August 30, 1912. Daisy's letters were sent either to her mother or sister in Windsor.
109. Ibid., 208: May 19, 1914.
110. Jack died in an army hospital in 1915.
111. Edward Roper, *By Track and Trail: A Journey through Canada* (London: W.H. Allen, 1891), 248.
112. *The Times* of London, October 10, 1908, quoted in Barman, *Growing up British in British Columbia*, 18.
113. Mindenhall, "Choosing the Group," 42–43.
114. The coal mining town of Wellington, established in the 1870s and later becoming incorporated in the city of Nanaimo, had no connection with the people from Wellington in Somerset who settled in Vancouver.
115. SORO DD/HP/18: Wellington (Somerset) newspaper cuttings. Wellington, Somerset, had been a major cloth-making centre since 1731. Wellington people also formed a similar society in Toronto in 1913.
116. *Wellington Weekly News*, August 21, 1910.
117. Ibid., January 17, 1912.
118. Ibid., May 7, 1913.
119. CRO PIC/TIN/3/45: Centenary correspondence of the Confederation of Canada.

Chapter 6: The Great Twentieth-Century Exodus from England to Canada

1. Bristol *Times and Mirror*, January 30, 1907.
2. Carrier and Jeffrey, *External Migration*, 96. The figures shown in Table 1 reveal immigration from Britain to Canada. However, the actual British immigrant population is less owing to the fact that some died and or did not remain in Canada. See Reynolds, *The British Immigrant*, 26–27.

3. Carrier and Jeffrey, *External Migration*, 96.
4. OA F1009 MU1724: George T. Denison fonds (letter book), 35–65.
5. Ibid., 60–64. Letter to McKellar, March 17, 1873.
6. Ibid., 97–100. Letter to McKellar, April 19, 1873.
7. Ibid., 97–100, 104.
8. Pamela Horn, "Agricultural Trade Unionism and Emigration," *The Historical Journal* 15, no. 1 (March 1972): 95. One large group who arrived in London, Ontario, in 1874 were almost all provided with employment "within twenty-four hours of their arrival."
9. An agent could only claim a bonus from the government for farm labourers and their families, and female domestic servants.
10. Horn, "Agricultural Trade Unionism and Emigration," 87–102. Incentives offered by the Australia and New Zealand governments were even greater since they provided free passages.
11. *Driffield Times and General Observer*, April 29, 1882.
12. Miller's recruits may well have been attracted to emigrate by David Plewes, who had been lecturing in the Beverley area. Having relocated from Beverley to Brantford in southwestern Ontario in 1851, he could speak forcibly about "the desirability of young people with a little capital, and who are willing to work, going to that country [Canada], where he said there was room for all and to spare." (*Beverley Guardian*, July 17, 1880).
13. *Beverley Guardian*, April 26, 1882.
14. STRO D593/V/10/474: "The Visit of the Tenant-Farmer Delegates to Canada in 1890," 53–54. Colonel Francis Fane was an officer in the British Army who served in Canada during the 1850s with the 54th Regiment and returned to Canada in 1864 with the 25th Regiment.
15. Ibid., 101–02.
16. Hawkes immigrated to Canada when only eighteen years of age, taking up employment as a farm labourer and railway worker. After homesteading for six or seven years, he devoted much of his life to journalism and public service, ending his days as the official legislative librarian for Saskatchewan. He was credited with having established the province's travelling libraries.
17. LAC RG76-1-A-1 vol. 362, #449896 (m/f C-10264): John Hawkes, emigration agent. W.D. Scott, Superintendent of Immigration, to the

Hon. Frank Oliver, Minister of the Interior, January 4, 1906. Scott to Hawkes, October 25, 1906. Hawkes's lecture tour in 1906 took him to Bearsted and Maidstone in Kent and Hastings in Sussex.

18. LAC RG76-1-A-1 vol. 404, #589887 (m/f C-10294): Appointment of Rice Shepherd of Strathcona, Alberta, as farm delegate to England, 1906–09. Wilbert McIntyre, M.P. to the Superintendent of Immigration, April 16, 1907. Rice Sheppard served on Edmonton City Council for many years and was an executive member of the United Farmers of Alberta.
19. Donald F. Harris, "The Canadian Government's Use of Newspapers to Encourage Immigration in the Twenty Years Before the First World War, As Demonstrated in the Newspapers of Shropshire" (The 5th annual lecture of the Friends of Shropshire Records and Research, Shrewsbury, 3 November, 1999).
20. Donald F. Harris, "The Promotion in Shropshire of Emigration to Canada in 1914 with Particular Reference to the Period from 1890." Unpublished Ph.D. thesis, University of Birmingham, 1998, 170–192 in ETRC P997/001.04/009: Edward William Brewster papers.
21. Donald F. Harris, "The Role of Shropshire Local Shipping Agents in Encouraging Emigration to Canada, 1890–1914," *Local Historian* 30, no. 4 (November 2000): 239–59.
22. Harris, "The Promotion in Shropshire of Emigration to Canada in 1914," 184.
23. LAC RG76-1-A-1 vol. 431, #642590 (m/f C-10312): E.M. Murray to J. Obed. Smith, Immigration Branch, February 25, 1906.
24. LAC RG76-1-A-1 vol. 418, #605754 (m/f C-10303): H.M. Murray, Canadian government emigration agent, in Exeter. There were two booking agents in the region: Mark Whitwell in Bristol (see LAC RG76-1-A-1 vol. 426, #630677 [m/f C-10309]), and J.H. Stevens, who was based in Torrington in Devon (see LAC RG76-1-A-1 vol.440, #662692 [m/f C-10318]).
25. LAC RG76-1-A-1 #670688 (m/f C-10318): W.D. Scott, superintendent of immigration, to Albert Wilkinson, November 30, 1912.
26. The Girls' Friendly Society, founded in 1875 and run in conjunction with the Church of England, offered training and religious instruction for young girls working abroad as domestic servants or

in factories. See Joyce Ellen, ed., *Girls Friendly Society: Report of the Department for Members Emigrating, 1883–1897* (Winchester: Girls' Friendly Society, 1897) 12–13, 24–27, 32–41.

27. In 1911, the surplus of males expressed, as a percentage of the total male population, was around 44 percent in British Columbia, just over 30 percent in Saskatchewan and Alberta, and around 18 percent in Manitoba. By 1921, the male/female surplus ratio in these provinces had roughly halved. In Quebec and Ontario the male/female difference was miniscule in both years. See 1921 Census, Volume I, Table 25, 358–59, and 1911 Census, Volume II, Table 12, 368–69.
28. John Hawkes, "Where a Woman has a Chance," *The Woman's Magazine*, n.d. (circa 1905).
29. The economic and social upheavals of the late nineteenth and early twentieth centuries in Britain brought grief to many middle- and upper-class women. They were normally poorly qualified, and, at a time when women greatly outnumbered men, many failed to find a husband. In such circumstances, they endured low wages and financial embarrassment.
30. There is an extensive literature on female emigration to the British colonies during the late nineteenth and early twentieth centuries, with much of it relating to the special difficulties faced by middle- and upper-class women. For example, see Julia Bush, *Edwardian Ladies and Imperial Power* (London: Leicester University Press, 2000), 146–69, and A.J. Hammerton, *Emigrant Gentlewomen: Genteel Poverty and Female Emigration 1830–1914* (London: Croom Helm, 1979), 187–94. Female emigration to the Canadian West has also been extensively studied. For example, see C.A. Cavanaugh and R.R. Warne, eds., *Telling Tales: Essays in Western Women's History* (Vancouver: University of British Columbia Press, 2000).
31. Susan Jackal, *Flannel Shirt and Liberty: British Emigrant Gentlewomen in the Canadian West, 1880–1914* (Toronto: University of Toronto Press, 1996) (3 vols.) Volume 3, 187–216.
32. Ibid., 204.
33. Ibid.
34. Marilyn Barber, *Immigrant Domestic Servants in Canada* (Ottawa: Canadian Historical Association, 1991), 8–12. The subsidized fares

were on offer from 1872 to 1888. After this, agents were paid a bonus for recruiting domestic servants.

35. For further details of the various female emigration societies, see Lisa Chilton, *Agents of Empire: British Female Migration to Canada and Australia, 1860s–1903* (Toronto: University of Toronto Press, 2007), 118–25.
36. LAC RG17, vol. 328, no. 33825: Henry H. Martin to the Society for the Organisation and Protection of Female Immigrants, October 22, 1881. A copy of his letter was sent by G.H. Mussen to the Hon. J.H. Pope, Minister of Agriculture. November 26, 1881.
37. Bush, *Edwardian Ladies and Imperial Power*, 87, 151.
38. WORO 850 HANBURY 7584/9/2: "Report of a Visit to Canada," 1904, 100–02.
39. Ibid., 101.
40. WORO 850 HANBURY 7584/9/9: Miss Vernon's notebook, 1904, 43, 47–48.
41. Ibid., 79.
42. Ibid., 84, 86.
43. WORO 850 HANBURY/ 8919/2/i/25: "The Leaton Colonial Training Home," by Miss Vernon (1898), 5.
44. Middle- and upper-class women called themselves "home helps," a more delicate appellation than domestic servants.
45. Joyce House, in Kelowna, British Columbia, purchased by the British Women's Emigration Association (BWEA) in 1913, was used to house "educated women workers" seeking employment. It was later renamed "Brides House" by locals when they realized that most of the women hoped to find husbands. See *www.joycehouse.ca.*
46. Bush, *Edwardian Ladies and Imperial Power*, 151.
47. Some English women even ended up as ranchers. In 1912, the Colonial Intelligence League, an offshoot of the BWEA, opened the Princess Patricia Ranch on Lord Aberdeen's estate in British Columbia's Okanagan Valley to genteel English ladies who put their training into practice and became ranchers. Andrew Yarmie, "'I had always wanted to farm': The Quest for Independence by English Female Emigrants at the Princess Patricia Ranch, Vernon, British Columbia, 1912–1920," *British Journal of Canadian Studies* 16, no. 1 (2003): 102–25.

48. In 1921, males in British Columbia outnumbered females by just over 60,000 — representing just under half of the male surplus in 1911. See 1921 Census, Volume I, Table 25, 358–59, and 1911 Census, Volume II, Table 12, 368–69.
49. The 1921 Census reveals that Ontario's population was nearly three million and Quebec's just under 2.5 million. Together they accounted for just over 50 percent of Canada's population.
50. 1921 Census, Volume I, Table 28, 542–43.
51. As is shown in Table 6, the English proportion of the population fell in Quebec City between 1911 and 1921. It rose most dramatically during this decade in Vancouver, Victoria, Saint John, Edmonton, Hamilton, Halifax, and Calgary.
52. 1921 Census, Volume I, Table 51, 303–10.
53. 1921 Census, Volume I, Table 23, 354–55.
54. Reynolds, *The British Immigrant*, 63–88. Between 1902 and 1930, British immigrant adult workers (of whom the English would have been a majority) had mainly been employed in urban jobs. Those employed as agricultural workers represented only 38 percent of the total. See Reynolds, ibid., 306.
55. Carter F. Hanson, *Emigration, Nation, Vocation: The Literature of English Emigration to Canada, 1825–1900* (East Lansing: Michigan State University Press, 2009), 119–20.
56. BEA DDX 1408/1/15: Norman Creaser collection, papers of Joyce Tremblay of Tilbury.
57. *Bristol Times and Mirror*, January 30, 1907.
58. Bush, *Edwardian Ladies and Imperial Power*, 155–56.
59. Joy Parr, "The Skilled Emigrant and Her Kin: Gender, Culture and Labour Recruitment," in *Immigration in Canada: Historical Perspectives*, edited by Gerald Tulchinsky (Toronto: Copp Clark Longman Ltd., 1994), 334–52.
60. BEA DDX7/43: Tom Morfitt to his father, June 22, 1913.
61. Ibid., December 1914.
62. Ibid., June 22, 1913.
63. Goutor, *Guarding the Gates*, 88–151. For details of how Canada's labour movement developed and the negative stance adopted by Canadian trade unions toward immigration see ibid., 11–31.

64. Legislation was passed by the Canadian government in 1905 to outlaw the false representation of jobs by immigration agents.
65. Goutor, *Guarding the Gates*, 108.
66. Social reformers had long been calling for public subsidies to be made available to paupers, to assist them to emigrate; but they were always rebuffed by the government of the day, which feared it would be saddled with unacceptably high expenditure. An example was J.F. Boyd, who, during the 1880s, advocated that government-backed loans should be given to the unemployed in English cities. But like so many others he failed to win government support. See JRL BCS1/12/7: Boyd, J.F. "State Directed Emigration" (Manchester: John Heywood, 1883). Under Boyd's scheme, paupers were to be advanced funds that they would have to pay back.
67. In addition to the city council schemes, there were also instances of people being assisted through locally based groups. An example was the Beverley and East Riding Emigration Committee, which worked with the Church Army, an Anglican organization, to raise funds to enable fifty impoverished farm labourers from the area to emigrate to Ontario in 1906. They received a great send-off in Beverley Minster, which "was filled in every part with people."(*Hull Daily Mail*, April 6, 1906.)
68. Arthur Smith was a shoe finisher, Wallis Watson a bricklayer, Charles S. Sidebottom was a rough cutter, while Frank Harvey was a tailor's presser. William and John Dunderdale and William Lister had no stated occupation, while Herbert Barker was a labourer. LAC MG40-M62: Leeds City Council Treasurer's Department Distress Committee, 6–16.
69. Thomas Johnstone was going to Perth, Ernest Barlow to Caledonia, Robert Richards to Cornwall, George Thompson to Carleton Junction, Albert Wormald to Lancaster, Patrick McAndrew to Mallorytown, Hiram Holstead and Walter Pattison to Brockville, and John Hughes to Belleville. Harry Clough was heading for Bowmanville and John Jackson was going to the Lake Erie region; Joseph Townend and Henry Hoare were going to Toronto; Alfred Edward Brown went to Montreal. WYAS LLD3/719 [197]: Records of all persons aided to emigrate, 1906–1912. They travelled in the *Dominion*.

70. Simon Fowler, "0950 to Toronto: The Emigration of the Unemployed from Norwich to Ontario in 1906," *Families* 37, no. 3 (August 1998): 149.
71. Ibid., 146–52.
72. WIA B/031: Birkenhead Distress Committee records, November 1904–December 1910.
73. GLRO CUB/162: Emigration to British Columbia, 1914–1917. For further details see the Central Unemployed Body for London Minutes of the Emigration Committee, 1905–1917.
74. To receive assistance, the London unemployed applied through local distress committees in the various London boroughs. Each person needed a guarantor for the loan of their passage money, which had to be repaid. Funds were also raised by the East End Emigration Fund and the Charity Organisation Society.
75. *The Spectator*, March 14, 1908. Letter to the editor from a spokesman for the Charity Organisation Society.
76. *Bristol Times and Mirror*, January 30, 1907.
77. Ring spinning was the drawing out of fibres to make cotton yarn, while the fibres were disentangled before spinning through carding.
78. LAC MG40-M10: Bolton and District Card and Ring Room Operatives Association (originals held by Bolton Archive Service, Greater Manchester).
79. The British Women's Emigration Association mainly sponsored middle- and upper-class women who wished to settle overseas. Working-class women generally put their trust in the unpretentious Salvation Army.
80. By 1930, the Salvation Army had organized the departure of around two hundred thousand people, who mainly went to Canada. Marjory Harper, "Rhetoric and Reality: British Migration to Canada, 1867–1967," in *Canada and the British Empire*, edited by Philip Buckner (Oxford: Oxford University Press, 2008), 160–80. Also see Anon., *Empire Reconstruction: The Work of the Salvation Army Emigration-Colonization Department, 1903–1921 and After* (London: n.d.), 17–19.
81. The women who agreed to enter domestic service received loans to finance their sea crossings and were guaranteed placements through one of the Salvation Army's domestic lodges. Barber, *Immigrant Domestic Servants in Canada*, 12.

82. Goutor, *Guarding the Gates*, 106.
83. *Manchester Guardian*, October 21, 1924. In his letter, John Muir bemoaned the fact that Canadians were leaving in droves for the United States to take advantage of its lower taxes, higher wages, and better standard of living.
84. CRO FS/3/1374: Henry Jenkin to Benjamin Treloar in Penponds near Camborne September 12, 1921.
85. GRO D3471/251: Olwin Payne to Mr. H. Payne in Snugborogh Mill, Blockley, Worcestershire, October 15, 1928. Payne reported that he had bought another house and was busy painting it.
86. The Empire Settlement Act followed on the heels of the Soldier Settlement Scheme, 1919–1924, which offered government-sponsored emigration schemes for ex-service personnel and their families. However, they were a disappointment, since their soldiers' urban backgrounds made them unsuitable for farming challenges. See Kent Fedorowich, "The Assisted Emigration of British Ex-Servicemen to the Dominions, 1914–1922," in *Emigrants and Empire: British Settlement in the Dominions Between the Wars*, edited by Stephen Constantine (Manchester: Manchester University Press, 1990), 45–71.
87. *Manchester Guardian*, February 18, 1926.
88. In 1925, Canada supported the 3,000 Families Scheme under which three thousand British families were invited to take up land that had been originally earmarked for soldier settlement. This venture was one of the few carried out under the Empire Settlement Act that proved to be successful. John A. Schultz, "'Leaven for the Lump': Canada and Empire Settlement, 1918–1939," in *Emigrants and Empire: British Settlement in the Dominions Between the Wars*, edited by Stephen Constantine (Manchester: Manchester University Press, 1990), 150–73. Harper, "Rhetoric and Reality: British Migration to Canada, 1867–1967," 175–76.
89. Between 1923 and 1929, one-third of all emigrants to Canada were assisted, as were two-thirds of those who went to Australia. Eric Richards, *Britannia's Children: Emigration from England, Scotland, Wales and Ireland Since 1600* (London: Hambledon and London, 2004), 244–48.

90. The original intention was to recruit ten thousand men, but the number was later reduced to 8,500. The 1828 scheme was a rerun of a 1923 venture whereby around twelve thousand unemployed Britons had been hired by the British and Canadian governments to help with the prairie harvest that year. Around 80 percent of the Britons employed as harvesters had remained in western Canada where they were said to be successfully assimilated.
91. W.J.C. Cherwinski, "'Misfits,' 'Malingerers' and 'Malcontents': The British Harvester Movement of 1928," in *The Developing West: Essays on Canadian History in Honour of Lewis H. Thomas*, edited by John E. Foster (Edmonton: The University of Alberta Press, 1983), 273–302.
92. Ibid., 289, 292.
93. MAA M270/9/12/3: Edith Baker to Uncle Ernest in Manchester, August 16, 1933. Eburne became a ghost town.
94. Ibid., August 20, 1934.
95. Reynolds, *The British Immigrant*, 74, 298.
96. Ibid., 308.
97. The Anglican Church's missionary work in western Canada, concentrated mainly in the cities and towns, had only limited success. David Smith, "Instilling British Values in the Prairie Provinces," *Prairies Forum* 6, no. 2 (1981): 134–39.
98. Vera K. Fast, *Missionary on Wheels: Frances Hatton Eva Hasell and the Sunday School Caravan Mission* (Toronto: The Anglican Book Centre, 1979), 20–45.
99. Ibid., 27.
100. Donald Harris's study of the Church of England clergy in Shropshire reveals the extent to which the Anglican Church encouraged emigration to Canada. Together with the Society for the Propagation of Christian Knowledge, the Shropshire church produced emigration booklets, giving details of foreign destinations. Donald F. Harris, "The Church of England and Emigration to Canada: Rural Clergy in the County of Shropshire," *Journal of the Canadian Church Historical Society*, vol. XLI (1999): 5–26.
101. 1901 Census, Volume I, Table XVI, 450-51; 1921 Census, Volume II, Table 36, 240–41.

102. The near doubling of the English-born population in Nova Scotia between 1901 and 1911 partly reflects the industrial expansion that had taken place in the province, especially in the coal mining districts of Cape Breton and in Colchester and Halifax Counties.
103. 1921 Census, Volume I, Table 23, 354–55.
104. Ibid.

Chapter 7: Child Immigration

1. *Manchester Guardian*, April 15, 1910.
2. Ibid.
3. The philanthropists who organized the emigration of the children were swept along by strong moral convictions. Glowing reports of happily settled children issued by them and the immigration authorities in Canada spoke only of success. However, when social worker Phyllis Harrison solicited letters from former home children and their descendents in 1979 (published in her book *The Home Children*), she provided first-hand accounts of the suffering endured by some. Joy Parr's doctoral thesis, completed a year later, examined the case papers of every tenth child sent by Thomas Barnardo, and reached the conclusion that placements were determined mainly by economic criteria rather than emotional or other needs. See Joy Parr, *Labouring Children* (London: Croom Helm, 1980), 11–14.
4. Stephen Constantine, "Empire Migration and Social Reform, 1880–1950," in *Migrants, Emigrants and Immigrants: A Social History of Migration*, edited by Colin G. Pooley and Ian D. Whyte (London: Routledge, 1991), 62–83.
5. Parr, *Labouring Children*, 39–40.
6. Ibid., 45–61.
7. Marjorie Kohli, *The Golden Bridge — Young Immigrants to Canada, 1833–1939* (Toronto: Natural Heritage, 2003), 71–104. In 1870, Miss Rye organized the relocation of 253 children, who went mainly to Ontario. Annie Macpherson brought over 2,500 children to Ontario and Quebec between 1870 and 1875, establishing three reception homes in Canada that offered training in farming.

8. Upon arriving in Canada, children were brought to receiving homes, from which the final placements were determined. Rye's, Our Western Home at Niagara-on-the-Lake, and Macpherson's Marchmont Home at Belleville were the first to be established in Ontario, with many others sprouting to the east as far as Ottawa and to the west as far as London. See Parr, *Labouring Children*, 49, for the location of the distributing homes established between 1869 and 1924.
9. Andrew Doyle first alerted the British and Canadian authorities to the scandalous treatment of children he observed during a visit to Ontario and Quebec in 1875. Despite his recommendation that reforms were needed to ensure that child placements were properly supervised, little action was taken to remedy the situation until the early twentieth century.
10. Kohli, *The Golden Bridge*, 119–31.
11. Having emigrated from England, Laurie had acquired a large estate at Oakfield, near Halifax, by the early 1870s.
12. For details of the placements of Mrs Birt's children in Nova Scotia, see Campey, *Planters, Paupers, and Pioneers*, 229–43.
13. RG18 Ser I, Vol 1, #1: List of adults and children brought to Nova Scotia by Louisa Birt and Colonel Laurie, 1873–75. Jimmy was only four years old, Thomas and Stephen were aged five, Henry was aged eight, while George was ten.
14. Kohli, *The Golden Bridge*, 123–26. The Church of England Waifs and Strays Society joined Birt in the Eastern Townships, establishing their homes for boys and girls at Sherbrooke. Kohli, *The Golden Bridge*, 158–62.
15. BCL MS 517/20 Annual reports, 1897–1902; MS 517/107 Letters from the Halifax manager; MS 517/262 Settlements and Reports of Children sent to Canada. A large ledger was kept for each child recording parental consents, progress reports, and other snippets of information. Detailed information was recorded of each child's placements. Judging from the cryptic nature of some managers' reports, there were many instances when visits had taken place but the children had not been seen. Presumably visits were informal and unannounced in advance.

16. It is estimated that between 1873 and 1932 a total of five thousand children were brought to various parts of Canada by John Middlemore. Kohli, *The Golden Bridge*, 131–37.
17. For further details of the placement of Middlemore children in the Maritime provinces, see Campey, *Planters, Paupers, and Pioneers*, 244–48.
18. The Poor Law Act had been amended in 1850 to allow Poor Law Guardians to send orphaned and deserted children abroad. Parr, *Labouring Children*, 27–44.
19. Kohli, *The Golden Bridge*, 173–74.
20. The records are kept in the London Metropolitan Archives. For children sent by Camberwell see CABG/200 and CABG /206; for Fulham see FBG/117; for Greenwich see GBG/218 and GBG/219; for Hampstead HPBG/098; for Holburn HOBG/534/1-2; for Islington see ISBG/308; for Lambeth LABG/186/001; for Poplar POBG/280; and for Westminster WEBG/CW/065.
21. WYAS PL 3/7/4: *Emigration of Children from the Leeds Union, Report upon the Scheme* (Leeds: Joseph Rider, 1891), 2–6. The Catholic Protection Society in Liverpool dealt with the Catholics. "The Birmingham Institution," probably John Middlemore's Emigration Home, was also involved.
22. WYAS PL 3/7/5: Leeds Board of Guardians Register of Emigrant Children, 1888–95.
23. Ibid., 2–5.
24. WYAS PL 3/7/4: *Emigration of Children from the Leeds Union*, 6–10.
25. Kohli, *The Golden Bridge*, 112–19.
26. MAA M4/60/2: Chorlton Union Register of Children who emigrated to Canada. For details of the Catholic agencies, see Kohli, *The Golden Bridge*, 246–64, 338.
27. The Chorlton Union children sent to Ontario between 1875 and 1903 went to the following locations: Port Hope, Roslin, Thurso, Monaghan, Galloway, Bethany, Ballantrae Station, Kingston, Adolphustown, Campbellford, Seymour, East Flamborough, Cornwall, Glengarry, Carleton, Renfrew, Foxboro, Wilstead, Peterborough, Durham County, Lennox County, Milford, Wellington, Gananoque, Hastings County, Frontenac County, Nipissing, and Sudbury. Few children were sent to Quebec after 1903.

28. MAA M4/60/2: Chorlton Union Register of Children who emigrated to Canada.
29. Ibid.
30. *Manchester Guardian*, April 19, 1910. British House of Commons, *Hansard*, Debate, July 27, 1910, vol. 19, cc 2108–9.
31. William Edmondson, *Making Rough Places Plain, Fifty Years' work of the Manchester and Salford Boys' and Girls' Refuges and Homes, 1870–1920* (Manchester: Sherratt and Hughes, 1921), 90–91.
32. Ibid., 89.
33. Ibid., 93.
34. Parr, *Labouring Children*, 146–47.
35. For details of the Cottage Homes see Tom Percival, *Poor Law Children* (London: Shaw & Sons, 1912), 35–40.
36. Although he was not in Barnardo's league in promoting child emigration, James Fegan also dedicated himself to helping boys find a new life in Canada. Opening refuges for orphaned and destitute boys in London in 1882, Fegan began sending them two years later to Ontario and Manitoba, where he had built receiving homes. By 1939 Fegan had brought around 3,000 boys to Ontario. See Kohli, *The Golden Bridge*, 164–68.
37. Gail H. Corbett, *Nation Builders: Barnardo Children in Canada* (Toronto: Dundurn Press, 2002), 15–36.
38. Kohli, *The Golden Bridge*, 143–68. The number of children sent to Canada by the various agencies is shown in Wagner, *Children of the Empire*, 259.
39. Corbett, *Nation Builders: Barnardo Children in Canada*, 65–76.
40. Ibid., 62–81. Later, some children made contact with their families in England and a few returned to England permanently.
41. Parr, *Labouring Children*, 67–69.
42. SORO D\G\W/57/12: Wellington Guardians to Barnardo Home, January 11, 1913.
43. Ibid., August 1912.
44. Ibid., October 20, 1914.
45. Ibid., Barnardo Home to Wellington Guardians, June 1915.
46. Charles Tanner was in Colorado by 1872. WHC WSA 1743/1: Wiltshire Reformatory Committee Minute Books, February 2, 1870, July 27, 1871,

March 11, 1872; *Warminster Herald*, 1873. I am indebted to Ivor Slocombe for providing me with the extracts from the Minutes and the newspaper. For further details, see Ivor Slocombe, *Wiltshire Reformatory for Boys, Warminster, 1856–1924* (East Knoyle, Salisbury: Hobnob Press, 2005).

47. Kohli, *The Golden Bridge*, 294–95. All costs associated with relocating the children abroad were borne by the schools.
48. Ibid., 379–95. The Birkdale Farm Reformatory located in Southport, near Liverpool, sent about 193 boys to Canada between 1854 and 1894, although around a quarter returned to England. The Feltham Reformatory School in Middlesex sent 112 children to Ontario, Manitoba, and Quebec between 1885 and 1893. The Red Hill Reformatory Farm School in Surrey sent its boys to Canada from 1862. In 1889 a small number went to Waterville in the Eastern Townships of Quebec. By the 1890s the destination of most of the boys was the northwest, with about eighty-two going there between 1900 and 1904.
49. Kohli gives examples of schools, such as the Bedfordshire Reformatory School, the Boys' Home, Frome (Somerset), and St. Swithin's Industrial School, which sent their children to the Eastern Townships at this time. See *The Golden Bridge*, 297.
50. HRO D/EHts/Q39: Register Hertfordshire Reformatory School for Boys, a register of boys discharged or released on licence, 1883–1887, #282.
51. Ibid., #328.
52. Ibid., #308.
53. Ibid., #303.
54. Ibid., #276.
55. Ibid., #254.
56. Ibid., #271, #300.
57. By this time the regulations had been tightened, with boys being admitted only at the discretion of the Canadian High Commissioner in London.
58. HRO D/EHts/Q39: Hertfordshire Reformatory School for Boys, register of boys discharged or released on licence, 1904–1910. After leaving Copper Cliff in 1906, Thomas Wells had two other jobs before settling down in 1907 at the Larose mine in Cobalt. He had worked briefly at Bruce Mines as a labourer then had moved to Victoria Mines hoping to find work in the gold mines there.

59. The stipulation that children sent to Canada needed to be of school-leaving age put an end to the concerns expressed earlier about whether children of school age were failing to get a proper education. See Parr, *Labouring Children*, 142–53.
60. MAA M189/7/6/1: "Boy Scout Farm Learners for Ontario" pamphlet. *Wilmslow Advertiser*, April 8, 1926.
61. OA PAMH 1926 #72: A boy farm learner's life in Ontario, Canada: letters to his mother in England, 1922.
62. LAC R11550-8-E: Richard Robertson, arrived in New Brunswick from Ontario in the 1930s as "a boy farm labourer."
63. Goutor, *Guarding the Gates*, 206–07.
64. Kohli, *The Golden Bridge*, 194–97.
65. Parr, *Labouring Children*, 144
66. LAC RG76-1-A-1 vol. 615, file 911684 (m/f C-10435): Young English emigrants sent to Dakeyne Training Farm. The children staying at the farm at the time of Mr. Smart's inspection were: William Banham, William Bennett, Fred Cutler, Albert Glover, William Eaton, William Easton, Frank Porter, Cyril Potts, Perry Starbuck, Cyril Sunderland, Sydney J Dayton, and David Wilkinson.
67. LAC RG76-1-A-1: Cutting from Halifax newspaper, no date, but probably May 1924.
68. LAC MG26-K 241414 -241427 (m/f M-1072): R.B. Bennett (prime minister of Canada) to Bishop Farthing of Montreal, February 3, 1932; Minister of Immigration and Colonization to Bennett, February 19, 1932; A. MacLaren (United Church of Canada) to Bennett, March 10, 1932.
69. Ibid., J. Cuppello, International Association of Machinists to R.B. Bennett, March 10, 1932.
70. WYAS Pl/3/7/1-3: *Liverpool Daily Post*, May 14, 1887.
71. Parr, *Labouring Children*, 53; Roy Parker, *The Shipment of Poor Children to Canada 1867–1917* (Bristol: The Policy Press, University of Bristol, 2008), 277–82.

Chapter 8: How the English Were Regarded in Canada

1. Mary Inderwick, "A Lady and Her Ranch," *Alberta Historical Review*

15, no. 4 (1967), 6. Extract from a letter written by Mary in 1883 to her sister-in-law in Ontario.

2. Goodridge, *A Year in Manitoba*, 70.
3. London *Globe*, April 28, 1910.
4. Barry Broadbent, *The Immigrant Years from Britain and Europe to Canada, 1945–67* (Vancouver: Douglas & McIntyre, 1986), 121.
5. "Hints to Settlers: Don'ts for Englishmen," in Howard Palmer, ed., *Immigration and the Rise of Multiculturalism* (Toronto: Copp Clarke, 1975), 120.
6. GLA M9004: Martin W. Holdom fonds, July 5, 1911. Holdom's letters are published in Paul Voisey, ed., *A Preacher's Frontier: The Castor, Alberta Letters of Rev. Martin W Holdom, 1909–1912* (Calgary: Historical Society of Alberta, 1996).
7. Ibid., August 24, 1910.
8. John J. Rowan, *The Emigrant and Sportsman in Canada: Some Experiences of an Old Country Settler: With Sketches of Canadian Life, Sporting Adventures, and Observations on the Forests and Fauna* (London: E Stanford, 1876), 3–9.
9. Edward Folkes, *Letters from a Young Emigrant in Manitoba, 1883* (Winnipeg: University of Manitoba Press, 1981), 48.
10. Gardiner, Claude, *Letters from an English Rancher* (Calgary: Glenbow Museum, 1988), 40–41: Gardiner to his mother, June 6, 1895.
11. GLA M9004: July 14, 1910.
12. Voisey, *A Preacher's Frontier*, 217.
13. *Canadian Courier* (Toronto), January 11, 1913.
14. GLA 9004: Martin W. Holdom fonds, February 28, 1912.
15. MAA GB127 M474/1/5/3: Ancell to Wilfred Ecroyd, July 16, 1906, 6–7.
16. *Canadian Courier*, January 11, 1913.
17. *Morning Citizen*, September 4, 1907. The article was reprinted from a St. Catharines newspaper.
18. *Southport Visitor*, February 11, 1907.
19. Basil Stewart, *"No English Need Apply": Or, Canada as a Field for the Emigrant* (London: G. Routledge & Sons, Ltd., 1909), 83–84.
20. Ibid., 75.
21. *Labour Leader*, October 4, 1907, quoted in Basil Stewart, *The Land of the Maple Leaf* (London: G. Routledge & Sons, Ltd., 1908), 209.

22. LAC RG76-1-A-1 vol. 463, #708666 (m/f C-10402): Rufus Burriss correspondence, 1907–22. Burriss, an immigration agent based in Port Arthur, Ontario, supplied immigration officials in Ottawa with a dossier outlining why the English were so unpopular in Canada. The material had been collected by Robert Skene, who lived in Oxdrift, east of Kenora.
23. LAC RG76-1-A-1 vol. 463, #708666 (m/f C-10402): J. Obed. Smith, Assistant Superintendent of Emigration, London, England, to W.D. Scott, Superintendent of Immigration, Ottawa, August 9, 1909.
24. Ibid., W.D. Scott to J. Obed. Smith, January 3, 1914.
25. Ibid., April 8, 1914.
26. *Southport Visitor*, February 11, 1907.
27. LAC RG76-1-A1 vol. 46, #70866: W.D. Scott to J. Obed. Smith, August 24, 1909.
28. Ibid., W.D. Scott to G.J. Stewart, Immigration Agent, Toronto; W.D. Scott to J. Obed. Smith, 1909.
29. LAC RG76-1-A1 vol. 46, #70866: D.C. McIntyre to W.D. Scott, December 4, 1907.
30. Stewart, *"No English Need Apply,"* 92.
31. LAC RG76-1-A1 vol. 46, #70866: Will Hunter, manager, Banner Print Co., Caledonia, Ontario, to Immigration Department, London, November 12, 1912.
32. Mrs. Lloyd-Jones's article, entitled "On a Canadian Farm," was published in *National Review*, vol. 55, no. 328, June 1910.
33. LAC RG76-1-A1 vol. 46, #70866: article entitled "The Englishman in Canada: Facts versus Fiction," in an unspecified Toronto newspaper, September 20, 1910.
34. Ibid., August 22, 1910.
35. Ibid.
36. John Foster Fraser, *Canada As It Is* (London: Cassel, 1911), 90.

Chapter 9: Getting There: Sea Crossings and Journeys Beyond

1. GLA M6657: Alfred and Clara Causley fonds, "The Story of My Life," 2. Clara later married Alfred Causley. They settled at the Barr colony in Saskatchewan.
2. LCA 920 MD 289: "All our Yesterdays: To Canada by Sailing Ship," by Edgar Andrew Collard, undated newspaper article (1854).

3. William Fulford's diary, quoted in Alison Grant and Peter Christie, *The Book of Bideford* (Buckingham, UK: Barracuda Books Ltd. 1987), 38–39.
4. Many immigrants bound for the United States travelled to Quebec, since this was a cheaper option than sailing to New York.
5. CRO J/3/5/203: Frederick Grigg to John Hawkins, Petworth, July 16, 1821.
6. CRO CF/2/715: Journal of Sophy Caldwell, 1840.
7. LAC MG24 I131 (m/f M-5567): Elizabeth Peter's diary, 7, 12, 16.
8. Roger Inkerman, *Ships and Shipyards of Bideford Devon, 1568–1938* (Bideford: author, 1947), 28.
9. CRO FS/3/1114: Diary of Francis Coleman, April 29, 1834. A total of 117 passengers travelled in the *Priam*. Francis and his family joined other members of his family in Darlington Township (Durham County) in Upper Canada. See Campey, *Seeking a Better Future*, 147, 442.
10. In 1832, the price of a passage from London and east coast ports was around £3, but around £2 if the vessel left from Liverpool and other principal ports on the west coast. If the ship owner provided provisions, London and east coast crossings generally cost around £6, while Liverpool charges were lower, between £4 and £5. Anon., *Information Published by His Majesty's Commissioners for Emigration Respecting the British Colonies in North America* (London: Charles Knight, publisher to the Society for the diffusion of useful knowledge, 1832), 5.
11. Ibid., 7.
12. The Passenger Act of 1817 specified a space allocation of one and one half tons per person in the steerage, while the 1828 act required a passenger to tonnage ratio of three passengers for every four tons. These regulations were meant to limit over-crowding, but the setting of a minimum height of only 5 ½ feet between decks reveals that, despite these safeguards, people still had to tolerate very cramped conditions until 1842.
13. Oliver MacDonagh, *A Pattern of Government Growth 1800–1860: The Passenger Acts and Their Enforcement* (London: MacGibbon & Kee, 1961), 150–51. Oliver MacDonagh, "Emigration and the State, 1833–55: An Essay in Administrative History," *Transactions of the Royal Historical Society*, Fifth Series, vol. 5 (London: The Royal Historical Society, 1955): 133–59. Edwin C. Guillet, *The Great Migration: The Atlantic Crossing by Sailing Ships Since 1770* (Toronto: University of Toronto Press, 1963), 13–19.

14. Samuel Pedlar and Charles Wethey, "From Cornwall to Canada in 1841," *Families* 22, no. 4 (1983): 244–53.
15. CRO FS/3/1114: April 22, 1834.
16. Ibid., April 25, 1834.
17. Ibid., May 1, May 3, 1834.
18. The *Hebe* passengers were taken in a sloop to Sydney, Cape Breton, where they boarded a Liverpool vessel that carried them to Quebec.
19. LAC MG24-H15: Journal of a voyage from London to Quebec, 1833, by Francis Thomas, 2, 5–7, 11.
20. The *Lloyd's Shipping Register* reveals that the *Princess Royal* was a newly constructed "A1" vessel.
21. The Staffordshire miners were to be employed at the coal mines being opened up at Nanaimo on Vancouver Island. E. Blanche Norcross, ed., *Nanaimo Retrospective: The First Century* (Nanaimo, BC: Nanaimo Historical Society, 1979), 28–30.
22. Ibid., 60–62. After reaching Esquimalt Harbour, the passengers disembarked and transferred to the *Recovery* for the final leg of their voyage to Nanaimo. They came ashore at Pioneer Rock, near Cameron Island.
23. Peterson, *Black Diamond City*, 55–65. Details of the voyage were kept in a log by the first mate, Charles Gale. Much to Captain Wishart's annoyance, he did not confine his entries to the weather and the ship's navigation, but also described the crew's behaviour and comments made by various passengers.
24. *Quebec Gazette*, October 23, 1820.
25. NAB CO 384/4, f. 29: Special Meeting of the Quebec Emigration Society, October 11, 1819.
26. The Nova Scotia Legislature introduced a head tax of 5 shillings in 1832, payable by all overseas passengers. See Martell, *Immigration, Nova Scotia*, 23–29.
27. The Fredericton Emigrant Society, formed in 1820 to help destitute immigrants, was the first institution of its kind in the province.
28. Two thousand of the 1846–47 arrivals died later. See W.S. MacNutt, *New Brunswick: A History, 1784–1867* (Toronto: Macmillan of Canada, 1984), 303–04.
29. Letter published in the *Berwick Advertiser*, September 24, 1836.

30. The proceeds of the immigrant tax were divided into fourths, between the Quebec Emigrant Hospital, the Montreal General Hospital, the Quebec Emigrant Society, and the Montreal Emigrant Society. Cowan, *British Emigration*, 56–57, 152–53.
31. Carrier and Jeffrey, *External Migration*, 95.
32. John A. Dickinson and Brian Young, *A Short History of Quebec*, 2nd edition (Toronto: Longman, 1993), 113–14; Ouellet, *Le Bas Canada*, 215.
33. Cameron, *English Immigrant Voices*, 43–45: Capling's letter to his brother, August 28, 1832.
34. Robina Lizars and Kathleen MacFarlane Lizars, *In the Days of the Canada Company: The Story of the Settlement of the Huron Tract and a View of the Social Life of the Period 1825–1850* (Toronto: W. Briggs, 1896), 400–17.
35. Cameron, *English Immigrant Voices*, 135–37: Daniels to his brothers and sisters, July 14, 1833.
36. CRO FS/3/1114: May 13, 1834.
37. Merna M. Forster, "Quarantine at Grosse Île," *Canadian Family Physician*, vol. 41 (May 1995): 841–48.
38. Campey, *Seeking a Better Future*, 348–50.
39. Around eighteen percent of the 98,649 emigrants, mainly from Ireland, who boarded ship for Quebec in 1847 died before reaching their destination. Andre Charbonneau and Andre Sevigny, *1847 Grosse Île: A Record of Daily Events* (Ottawa: Canadian Heritage, 1997), 1–32.
40. Irish immigrants predominated from at least 1825, when official figures first became available (see Carrier and Jeffrey, *External Migration*, 95–96).
41. The Petworth immigrants mainly took the Ottawa River/Rideau Canal route. Although the barges they were on were towed by a succession of steamboats, they could remain in the same craft throughout the journey. See Wendy Cameron and Mary McDougall Maude, *Assisting Emigration to Upper Canada: The Petworth Project, 1832–37* (Montreal: McGill-Queen's University Press, 2000), 121–22.
42. CRO FS/3/1114, May 23, 1834.
43. Francis Thomas described the Rideau Canal as "a dismal course, when nothing for miles could be seen but wood and water" (see LAC

MG24-H15: Journal of a Voyage from London to Quebec, 1833, by Francis Thomas, 11–12).

44. Immigrants could halve their journey time to Hamilton by taking road transport from Montreal to Prescott, but this cost nearly six times the amount payable when the entire journey was made by river. Anon., *Information Published by His Majesty's Commissioners for Emigration*, 7–8.
45. Jackson's diary quoted in Cheryl MacDonald, *Norfolk Folk: Immigration and Migration in Norfolk County* (Delhi, ON: Norfolk Folk Book Committee, 2005), 39–40. George Jackson and his family had sailed to Quebec from Berwick-upon-Tweed, Northumberland, in the *Good Czar* in 1834. See Campey, *Seeking a Better Future*, 177, 265, 267, 278, 332.
41. Immigrants going to the Talbot settlements in Elgin County would have gone through the Welland Canal, linking Lake Ontario with Lake Erie, and disembarked at Port Stanley.
42. NTRO DD/H/151/202: Henry Rastall in Toronto to Edward Buck in Nottinghamshire, February 2, 1830.
43. Cowan, *British Emigration*, 57.
44. The Allan Line, founded in 1819 by Captain Alexander Allan of Saltcoats, Ayrshire, became the world's largest privately owned shipping concern. The line first established regular steamship services between Britain and Canada in 1854, operating from offices in Glasgow, Liverpool, and Montreal. See Thomas E. Appleton, *Ravenscrag: The Allan Royal Mail Line* (Toronto: McClelland & Stewart, 1974).
45. By the 1880s the average crossing time from Liverpool to Halifax was only nine days. Passenger numbers can be compared in Campey, *Seeking a Better Future*, "Appendix I: Emigrant Ships Crossings from England to Quebec, 1817–64," 301–415.
46. LAC MG29-C66: Henry Welch and family fonds, 3.
47. Ibid., 42–43.
48. CRO AM499/1: John Adams to George Adams in Saltash, Cornwall, August 15, 1884.
49. WORO 705/385 Acc. 4283/2: Journal of Major H.R. Davies describing a tour across Canada in 1906. Having sailed to New York, he travelled overland to Montreal where he boarded a Canadian Pacific Railway

train that would take him to Vancouver. Along the way the train called at Ottawa, Port Arthur, Thunder Bay, Winnipeg, Calgary, and Banff.

50. When a steamship rolled at sea, one propeller paddle would be lifted out of the water while the other was deeply submerged, thus putting a tremendous strain on the engine.
51. GLA M7907: Strong family fonds, Elizabeth Strong to her daughters, April 14, 1909. The fonds include a photocopy of William Strong's diary of his voyage from Liverpool to Prairie Creek, west of Red Deer, in Alberta, in the previous year. He had visited various friends in Montreal and later travelled to Calgary, staying at the Royal Hotel.
52. The Canadian Pacific Railway Steamship Services operated the Canadian Pacific Line. It acquired the Beaver Line fleet of ships in 1906 and the Allan Line fleet in 1916. For further details, see Peter Pigott, *Sailing Seven Seas: A History of the Canadian Pacific Line* (Toronto: Dundurn, 2010).
53. The *Empress of Ireland* sank in 1914 following a collision with another vessel in heavy fog when heading down the St. Lawrence River. Owing to difficulties in lowering the lifeboats in time, some 1,012 lives were lost with only 465 passengers being rescued.
54. GLA M9004: Martin W. Holdom fonds, October 11, 1909.
55. BEA DDX1062/1: Diary (unidentified author) of a voyage across the Atlantic in 1914. Dick intended to settle in Edmonton.
56. GLA M177 File #7: Cameron Family fonds, Jack Cameron to his mother, August 27, 1905.
57. Forster, "Quarantine at Grosse Île," 847–48.
58. BRO CRT 150/166: *Bedfordshire Times and Independent*, June 22, 1888.
59. Ibid.
60. Robert Vineberg, *Responding to Immigrants' Settlement Needs: The Canadian Experience* (London: Springer, 2012) 1–17, 70.
61. Because Halifax and Saint John were both ice-free ports, they could be used as ports of entry in the winter. Quebec was only accessible in the summer.
62. Pier 21 has been preserved as a heritage site. For further details see *www.pier21.ca*.
63. GLA M7907: Strong family fonds, Elizabeth Strong to her daughters, April 14, 1909.

64. Ibid. The rail service from Halifax to Montreal was operated by the Canadian National Railway. The line went north from Halifax to the Matapedia Valley in New Brunswick and afterward followed the south side of the St. Lawrence to Quebec and Montreal.
65. A scow is a flat-bottomed boat, having no roof and it therefore was open to the elements.
66. Clara, who was born in London, England, married Alfred Causley, also a Barr colonist. He probably arrived the previous year with the main group of colonists who sailed in the *Lake Manitoba* to Saint John, New Brunswick. Their train journey by Canadian Pacific Railway brought them through Maine to Montreal and later to Saskatoon. See Bowen, *Muddling Through: The Remarkable Story of the Barr Colonists*, 69–77.
67. GLA M6657: Alfred and Clara Causley fonds, 2–4.
68. GLA M177 File #7: Cameron Family fonds, Jack Cameron to his mother, August 27, 1905. The Canadian Pacific Railway Company ran two trains a day from Montreal to Vancouver in summer and one train a day in winter.
69. WORO 705/385 Acc. 4283/2: Journal of Major H.R. Davies, 13–14.
70. GLA M177 File #7: Jack Cameron to his mother, August 27, 1905.
71. Ibid.
72. Convincing evidence of the high quality of shipping used by immigrants can be found in the *Lloyd's Shipping Register*. This documentary source, dating back to the late eighteenth century, records the overall quality of ships that were in use in a particular year. For the sailing ships that brought English immigrants to Atlantic Canada, see Campey, *Planters, Paupers, and Pioneers*, 253–71, 303–80. For the sailing ships that brought English immigrants to Ontario and Quebec see Campey, *Seeking a Better Future*, 261–87, 301–415.
73. Since a sailing ship's hold on journeys to Britain was normally filled with Canadian timber, travelling in the steerage was not usually an option for passengers. Only people able to pay the much higher cabin fares could realistically think of returning.

Chapter 10: Canada's English Immigrants

1. DRO Z19/29/22a-c #136. Mr. Hoyles's grandfather had settled in Newfoundland, becoming one of the leading merchants in St. John's.
2. Lethbridge's circular was published in Canada, Australia, and the United States, as well as in other British dominions. Over three hundred families of Devon descent responded, most living in Canada. For a list of the Canadian letters, see Jean Harris, "Devonians in the Colonies: Canada Letters to the Devonshire Association in 1900 & 1901," *Families* 36, no. 3 (1997): 216–18.
3. DRO Z19/29/22a-c #137.
4. CRO PIC/TIN/3/45: Centenary correspondence of the Confederation of Canada.
5. LARO DDX 1357 2/1/10: Clitheroe.
6. *Wellington Weekly News*, August 21, 1910.
7. Ibid., May 7, 1913.
8. Ross McCormack, "Networks Among British Immigrants and Accommodation to Canadian Society: Winnipeg, 1900–1914," in *Immigration in Canada: Historical Perspectives*, edited by Gerald Tulchinsky (Toronto: Copp Clark Longman Ltd., 1994), 215.
9. R. Pease Chope, ed., *The Devonian Year Book, 1913* (London: The London Devonian Association, 1913), 127–34.
10. Gesner, *New Brunswick with Notes for Emigrants*, 330–32.
11. Margaret Howard Blom and Thomas E. Blom, eds., *Canada Home: Juliana Horatio Ewing's Fredericton Letters 1867–69* (Vancouver: University of British Columbia Press, 1983), 194–95.
12. Warburton, *History of Prince Edward Island*, 348.
13. Ibid., 64–65.
14. Mrs. W.T. Hallam, *When You Are in Halifax: Sketches of Life in the First English Settlement in Canada* (Toronto: Church Book Room, 1937), 73. Joseph Cunard had a great shipbuilding empire, while Richard Uniacke was the Nova Scotia attorney general.
15. Lorne C. Callbeck, *The Cradle of Confederation: A Brief History of Prince Edward Island from Its Discovery in 1534 to the Present Time* (Fredericton, NB: Brunswick Press, 1964), 164–65.
16. Edwin C. Guillet, *The Pioneer Farmer and Backwoodsman*, vol. 1 (Toronto: University of Toronto Press, 1963), 225.

17. Colonel Fane raised funds from civilians and members of the 54th regiment. LRO FANE 6/8/1/4 Francis Fane's Diary (1851): October 22, November 2. Horse racing was also introduced at the garrison cities of Halifax and Kingston by British Army officers. Colin D. Howell, *Blood, Sweat and Cheers: Sport and the Making of Modern Canada, Themes in Canadian Social History* (Toronto: University of Toronto Press, 2001), 17–18.
18. CRO DD.HL(2) 331/1-4: Francis Howell to David Howell, August 11, 1843.
19. Callbeck, *The Cradle of Confederation*, 164–65. Anon., *The Cricketer* (Saint John, NB: George A. Knodell, 1886).
20. John E. Hall and R.O. McCulloch, *Sixty Years of Canadian Cricket* (Toronto: Bryant Printing & Publishing Co., 1895), 24, 128, 180–81, 403.
21. Neil Tranter, *Sport, Economy and Society in Britain, 1750–1914* (Cambridge: Cambridge University Press, 1998), 13–31.
22. Howell, *Blood, Sweat and Cheers*, 47–49. Rugby also attracted support from English coal miners and their descendents who lived in Pictou County, Nova Scotia, and Cape Breton.
23. The Halifax St. George's Society commemorated its bicentenary by planting an English oak tree at the entrance to the city's Victorian Public Gardens.
24. A St. George's Society was established in London, Ontario, in 1867, and in Barrie in 1875. Elliott, "The English," 483–84.
25. Gillian I. Leitch, "The Importance of Being English: English Ethnic Culture in Montreal c.1800–1864," in *Locating the English Diaspora, 1500–2010*, Tanja Bueltmann, David T. Gleeson, and Donald M. MacRaild, eds. (Liverpool: Liverpool University Press, 2012), 100–17.
26. *Montreal Daily Star*, April 25, 1887. Membership of the English Workingmen's Benefit Society was restricted to Englishmen aged between eighteen and forty-five years.
27. ETRC P129/002/001: Philip Harry Scowen fonds.
28. Rev. Henry Scadding, the Address to the St George's Society in the Cathedral of St. James, Toronto, April 23, 1860 (Toronto: Rowsell & Hutchison Printers, 1860), 5.
29. John S. King, *The Early History of the Sons of England Benevolent Society: Including Its Origins, Principles and Progress* (Toronto: Bros. Thos. Moore & Co., 1891), 11.

30. Ross McCormack, "Cloth Caps and Jobs: The Ethnicity of English Immigrants in Canada," in *Ethnicity, Power and Politics in Canada*, edited by Jorgen Dahlie and Tissa Fernando, Toronto: Methuen, 1981, 38–55.
31. The Daughters of England first established a lodge in Hamilton in 1890. By 1952 there were a total of 117 lodges across Canada. Elliott, "The English," 483–84.
32. 1921 Census, Volume I, Table 31, 568–69.
33. A booklet produced in 1914 by the Society for the Propagation of Christian Knowledge lists all serving Anglican clergy in Canada. See WORO 850NEWLAND/9199/7/xii/5: List of clergy in the Colonies.
34. LAC MG30-C210: May Louise Jackman fonds, "Prince Albert — 1904," 4.
35. Gardiner, *Letters from an English Rancher*, Claude to his mother, no date, 24.
36. Alice Ravenhill, *The Memoirs of an Educational Pioneer* (Toronto: J.M. Dent, 1951), 177, quoted in Barman, *Growing Up British in British Columbia*, 20–21.
37. Peterson, *Black Diamond City*, 65.
38. GLA M177 File #7: Cameron Family fonds, Jack Cameron to his mother, September 24, 1905.
39. Bowen, *Muddling Through: The Remarkable Story of the Barr Colonists*, 108–09.
40. Ibid., 182–83.
41. Guillet, *The Pioneer Farmer and Backwoodsman*, vol. 1, 224–25.
42. Edward Ermatinger, *Life of Col. Talbot and the Talbot Settlement* (St. Thomas, ON: A. McLachin's Home Journal Office, 1859), 194–96.
43. John Bull was invented in 1712 by John Arbuthnot, a Scot. He was meant to be a cloth-trader and went through many modifications. By the twentieth century he was usually depicted wearing a Union Jack waistcoat and having a bulldog by his side.
44. CAS DX 1065/60/3: Thomas Priestman to his brother in Cumberland, September 7, 1823.
45. Census of Canada, 1921, Table 29, 560.
46. Bailyn, *Voyagers to the West*, 411.

BIBLIOGRAPHY

PRIMARY SOURCES (MANUSCRIPTS)

Archives of Ontario (AO)

F1009 MU1724: George T. Denison fonds (letter book).

PAMH 1926#72: A boy farm learner's life in Ontario, Canada: letters to his mother in England, 1922.

Bedfordshire Record Office (BRO)

CRT150/166: Newspaper article re: emigrants from Tingrith.

Beverley (East Riding of Yorkshire) Archives (BEA)

DDX7/43: Morfitt family.

DDX406: The Young family of Aughton.

DDX632/1: Parkin and Legge family newsletter.

DDX1062/1: Diary (unidentified author) of a voyage across the Atlantic in 1914.

DDX1408: Norman Creaser collection, emigration from Yorkshire to North America.

Birmingham Central Library (BCL)
MS 517: Middlemore Home Children Archive.

British Library, London (BL)
Fox Talbot correspondence.

Centre for Kentish Studies (CKS)
P348/8/1: Stockbury Parish.

Cornwall Record Office (CRO)
AD 706/5: Diary of Andrew Angwin.
AD362/1-4: Letters from Joe Hurrell of North Battleford, Saskatchewan.
AD2183/3: Jacob Jenkings, to William Brock, 1843.
AM499/1 John Adams to George Adams (his brother), 1884.
AM923/2: William Gryllis Adams to his wife, Mary 1897.
CF/2/715: Journal of Sophy Caldwell, 1840.
FS/3/1114: Diary of Francis Coleman, 1834.
FS/3/1168: Dairy of the Reverend Stephen Henry Rice.
FS/3/1374: Henry Jenkin to Benjamin Treloar, 1921.
HL/2: Howell family of Trebursye and Ethy.
J/3/5/203: Frederick Grigg to John Hawkins, 1821.
PIC/TIN/3/45: Tintagel British Columbia, 1967.

Cumbria Archive Service (CAS)
D/WAL/7/D: Emigration of Alston's poor.
DX 1065/60/1-6: Letters from Thomas Priestman in Upper Canada.

Devon Record Office (DRO)
152M/C1817/OH/108,109,110: Correspondence of Henry Addington (Viscount Sidmouth) regarding emigration, 1817.
2565A/P051/5: Parish of Kingsteignton.
3419A/P09/30, 3419A/P19/45: Parish of Combeinteignhead.
5592Z/Z/4: Extracts of letters, 4–31 March 1817, from St Johns Newfoundland concerning extreme poverty.
5592Z/Z/6: Brief Considerations on the nature, importance and

existing difficulties of the Newfoundland trade presented by a deputation of merchants to Lords Liverpool and Bathurst at the Board of Trade, 1817.
6105M/F/5/2: Ella Tanner to the Reverend Thomas Coombe Tanner, 1939.
Z19/29/22a-c: Roper Lethbridge papers.

Dorset History Centre (DHC)
PE/Pl/OV 3/30: Parish of Poole.
PE/PUD/OV7/2: Parish of Puddletown.
PE/WM/OV/11/1/181: Parish of Wimborne Minster.

Eastern Townships Resource Centre (ETRC)
P129/002/001: Philip Harry Scowen fonds.
P997/001.04/009: Edward William Brewster papers.

Essex Record Office (ERO)
ERO D/P12/12: Widdington parish.

Glenbow Archives, Calgary (GLA)
M177 File #7: Cameron Family fonds.
M745: George Machon fonds.
M2371: William A. Baillie-Grohman fonds.
M3225: Ernest Baxter fonds.
M4180: Southern Alberta Pioneers and their Descendants fonds.
M6583: Dawson family fonds.
M6657: Alfred and Clara Causley fonds.
M7886: John B. Merill fonds.
M7907: Strong family fonds.
M7988: Edward F. J. Hill letters 1883–85.
M8047: Joseph Tyas fonds.
M8528: Richard Mackley Syson fonds.
M8857: Eric Holmgren fonds.
M9004: Martin W. Holdom fonds.
M9223: Morgan family fonds.

Gloucestershire Record Office (GRO)
D3471/251: Letter to Mr H. Payne in Blockley, Worcestershire from his son Olwin in Calgary, 1928.
D637/IV/5: Papers of Messrs. Vizard & Son, solicitors.
D6368/1: Testimonial for Charles Page who is emigrating to B.C., 1913.
D1833/F4: Rooke family papers.
D3355: Diaries of Canon Rowen Earnest Grice-Hutchinson.
D3549: Granville Sharp papers.
D4467/18: Charles Best, letter to Frank Cookley, 1917.
D5049/2: Letters from Eva Martin, 1916.

Greater London Record Office (GLRO)
CUB/162: Emigration to British Columbia, 1914–1917.

Hertfordshire Record Office (HRO)
D/EHts/Q39: Register Hertfordshire Reformatory School for Boys.

Hull City Archives (HCA)
DMJ/415/37-40: Bravender letters, 1846–7, 1860

John Rylands Library, University of Manchester (JRL)
BCS1/12/: Pamphlets on trade union concerns and emigration.
GB133 Eng MS 615: Journals of John Salusbury, 1749–50.
MAW Ms 91.11: Pamphlet concerning the Reverend Cephas Barker.
MNC Cooke Collection (Boxes 1 and 2): Correspondence on Canadian Mission.

Lancashire Record Office (Preston) (LARO)
DDX 1357 2/1/10: Clitheroe 800th anniversary celebrations.

Library and Archives Canada (LAC)
MG23-J3: Narrative of a voyage on board the *Elizabeth* from England to the Island of St. John, 1775–1777.
MG24 H15: Journal of a voyage from London to Quebec, 1833, by Francis Thomas.

MG24-H71: R. Kay diary.
MG24 I59: John Langton and family fonds.
MG24 I131 (m/f M-5567): William Peters and family fonds.
MG26-K (m/f M-1072): 20th century child emigration and British community settlements.
MG29-C38: My four year experience in the north west of America.
MG29-C66: Henry Welch and family fonds.
MG30-C16: Saskatchewan homesteading experiences (3 vols.).
MG30-C181: Robert England maps.
MG30-C210: May Louise Jackman fonds.
MG31-H13: English settlement at Cannington Manor.
MG40-M10: Bolton and District Card and Ring Room Operatives Association.
MG40-M62: Leeds City Council Treasurer's Department Distress Committee.
RG 17: Records of the Department of Agriculture.
RG 76: Records of the Immigration Branch.

Lincolnshire Record Office (LRO)
FANE 6/8: Fane family papers.
FANE/ 6/12/3: Journal of Mary Chaplin.

Liverpool City Archives (LCA)
920 MD 289: 'All our Yesterdays: To Canada by Sailing Ship,' by Edgar Andrew Collard, undated newspaper article (1854).

London Metropolitan Archives (LMA)
CABG/200, /206: Camberwell Board of Guardians.
FBG/117: Fulham Board of Guardians.
GBG/218, /219: Greenwich Board of Guardians.
HOBG/534/1–2: Holburn Board of Guardians.
HPBG/098: Hampstead Board of Guardians.
ISBG/308: Islington Board of Guardians.
LABG/186/001:Lambeth Board of Guardians.
POBG/280: Poplar Board of Guardians.
WEBG/CW/065: Westminster Board of Guardians.

Manchester Archives (MAA)

GB127 M474/1/5: Wilfrid T. Ecroyd papers.

M4: Chorlton Union Records.

M107/2/5/5: Ashton family of Hyde.

M189/7/6/1: Boys and Girls' Welfare Society.

M270/9/12/3: Edith Baker of Eburne, British Columbia.

National Archives of Britain (NAB)

CO 188: New Brunswick original correspondence.

CO 384: Colonial Office papers on emigration containing original correspondence concerning North American settlers.

MH 12: Records of the Poor Law Commission.

T/47/9 and /10: Register of emigrants, 1773–1776.

Northamptonshire Record Office (NORO)

(Typed manuscript), 1–3: Paul Frederick Groome, "My Life Story: Homesteading in Saskatchewan."

Nottinghamshire Record Office (NTRO)

DD/H/151/202: Henry Rastall in Toronto to Edward Buck in Nottinghamshire, February 2, 1830.

PR7347: Carlton-on-Trent Parish.

Nova Scotia Archives and Records Management (NSARM)

MG 1 Vol. 427 (m/f 14920): Harrison family papers.

RG18 Ser I, Vol. 1, #1: List of adults and children brought to Nova Scotia by Louisa Birt and Col. Laurie, 1873–75.

Oxford University: Rhodes House Library (RHL)

USPG Series E (LAC m/f A-223): United Society for the Propagation of the Gospel, Reports from Missionaries.

Public Archives of New Brunswick (PANB)

RG 637 26d: Records of the Surveyor General.

RS 24: Legislative Assembly Sessional Records.

Public Archives and Records Office of Prince Edward Island (PAPEI)
AC 2277: Benjamin Chappell fonds.
Acc4362#2: Mark Butcher fonds.

Royal Institution of Cornwall (RIC)
Cornish Memorial Scheme (W.I. survey).

Somerset Record Office (SORO)
D\G\W/57/12: Child returned to Dr Barnard's Homes, 1914.
DD/HP/18: *Wellington Weekly News* newspaper cuttings.
DD\S\ST/23: Stradling family papers.
DD\X\CXO/1: Correspondence concerning Ernest Smith of Weston-Super-Mere, 1883.
DD\X\OSB/7: Sparks family papers.

Staffordshire County Record Office (STRO)
D593/v/10/474–475: The visit of the tenant-farmer delegates to Canada in 1890.
D615/P: Anson family papers.

Suffolk Record Office (Ipswich) (SROI)
FC 131: Benhall Parish.

University of London, School of Oriental and African Studies (SOAS)
MMS: Methodist Missionary Society Papers.

West Yorkshire Archive Service (WYAS)
LLD3/719 [197]: Records of all persons aided to emigrate, 1906–1912.
PL 3/7/4: *Emigration of Children from the Leeds Union, Report upon the Scheme* (Leeds: Joseph Rider, 1891).
PL 3/7/5: Leeds Board of Guardians Register of Emigrant Children, 1888–95.

Wiltshire History Centre (WHC)
1306/105: Downton Parish.
1743/1: Wiltshire Reformatory Committee Minute Books.

Wirral Archives (WIA)

B/031: Birkenhead Distress Committee records, November 1904–December 1910.

Worcestershire Record Office (WORO)

705/385 Acc. 4283/2: Journal of Major H.R. Davies.

705:775/6385/7/ii: Papers concerning Golden River, Quesnelle Ltd., B.C.

705:1059/9600/26(i)/ 3: Letter from Bishop of Newfoundland, 1866.

850 HANBURY 7584/9: Notebook, Miss A.L. Vernon.

850 HANBURY/ 8919/2/i/25: United British Women's Emigration Association reports by Miss Vernon.

850NEWLAND/9199/7/xii/5: List of clergy in the Colonies.

11777: William Henry Taylor papers, Old St. James Church, Manitoba.

PRINTED PRIMARY SOURCES AND CONTEMPORARY PUBLICATIONS

An English Farmer. *A Few Plain Directions to Persons Intending to Proceed as Settlers to His Majesty's Province of Upper Canada in North America.* London: Baldwin, Cradock & Joy, 1820.

"An immigrant farmer" (pseudonym of Rev. Abbott). *Memoranda of a Settler in Lower Canada; or the Emigrant in North America, Being a Useful Compendium of Useful Practical Hints to Emigrants … Together with an Account of Every Day Doings Upon a Farm for a Year.* Montreal: 1842.

Anon. *A Statement of the Satisfactory Results Which Have Attended Emigration to Upper Canada from the Establishment of the Canada Company until the Present Period.* London: Smith, Elder & Co., 1841.

————. *Emigration: The British Farmers and Farm Labourer's Guide to Ontario.* Toronto: Blackett Robinson, 1880.

————. *Emigration: Extracts from Various Writers on Emigration, with Authentic Copies of Letters from Emigrants from Norfolk, Suffolk, and Sussex, Now Settled in Upper Canada, Containing Useful Information Respecting That Country.* Norfolk: Bacon and Kinnebrook, 1834.

———. *Emigration to Canada: The Province of Ontario, Its Soil, Resources, Institutions, Free Grant Lands ... .for the Information of Intending Emigrants.* Toronto: Hunter, Rose, 1871.

———. *Handbook of Information Relating to the District of Algoma in the Province of Ontario, Letters from Settlers & Others & Information, also Land Regulations.* Minister of the Interior, Government of Canada. London: McCorquodale & Co., circa 1894.

———. *Information Published by His Majesty's Commissioners for Emigration Respecting the British Colonies in North America.* London: Charles Knight, publisher to the Society for the diffusion of useful knowledge, 1832.

———. *North-West Canada.* London: Society for the Propagation of the Gospel, 1882.

———. *The Albany Settlement: Qu'Appelle Valley, Canada N.W.T.: Colonial Profits with Home Comforts.* London: G. Kenning, 1886.

———. *The Cricketer.* Saint John, NB: George A. Knodell, 1886.

Bancroft, Hubert Howe. *A History of British Columbia, 1792–1887.* San Francisco: The History Publishers, 1887.

Barker, Cephas. *Notes by the Way: Papers and Addresses: In Memoriam.* Bowmanville, ON: H.J. Nott, 1882.

Bouchette, Joseph. *The British Dominions in North America: A Topographical and Statistical Description of the Provinces of Lower and Upper Canada, New Brunswick, Nova Scotia, the Islands of Newfoundland, Prince Edward Island and Cape Breton*, vols. I and II. London: Longman, Rees, Orme, Brown, Green and Longman, 1832.

Cattermole, William. *Emigration: The Advantages of Emigration to Canada: Being the Substance of Two Lectures Delivered at the Town-Hall, Colchester, and the Mechanics' Institution, Ipswich.* London: Simpkin & Marshall; Woodbridge: J. Loder, 1831.

Census of Canada, 1901, 1911, 1921.

Census of Great Britain, 1841.

Census of Ontario, 1881.

Champion, Thomas Edward. *The Anglican Church in Canada.* Toronto: Hunter, Rose, 1898.

Cobbett, William. *The Emigrant's Guide in 10 Letters Addressed to the Taxpayers of England; Containing Information of Every Kind, Necessary for Persons About to Emigrate; Including Several Authentic and Most Interesting Letters from English Emigrants, Now in America, to Their Relations in England.* London: author, 1829.

Ermatinger, Edward. *Life of Col. Talbot and the Talbot Settlement.* St. Thomas, ON: A. McLachin's Home Journal Office, 1859.

Fraser, John Foster. *Canada As It Is.* London: Cassel, 1911.

Gesner, Abraham. *New Brunswick with Notes for Emigrants, Comprehending the Early History, Settlement, Topography, Statistics, Natural History, etc.* London: Simmonds & Ward, 1847.

Goodridge, Richard E.W. *A Year in Manitoba: Being the Experience of a Retired Officer in Settling His Son.* London: W & R Chambers, 1882.

Goodridge, Richard E.W. *The Colonist at Home Again; or, Emigration not Expatriation.* London: William Dawson & Sons, 1889.

Hall, John E., and R.O. McCulloch. *Sixty Years of Canadian Cricket.* Toronto: Bryant Printing & Publishing Co., 1895.

Hall, Mrs. Cecil. *A Lady's Life on a Farm in Manitoba, 1882.* London: W.H. Allen, 1884.

Jameson, A.B. *Winter Studies and Summer Rambles in Canada*, London: Saunders & Otley, 1838.

Joyce, Ellen, ed. *Girls Friendly Society: Report of the Department for Members Emigrating, 1883–1897.* Winchester: Girls' Friendly Society, 1897.

King, John S. *The Early History of the Sons of England Benevolent Society: Including Its Origins, Principles and Progress.* Toronto: Bros. Thos. Moore & Co., 1891.

Lizars, Robina, and Kathleen MacFarlane Lizars. *In the Days of the Canada Company: The Story of the Settlement of the Huron Tract and a View of the Social Life of the Period 1825–1850.* Toronto: W. Briggs, 1896.

Lloyd's Shipping Register, 1775–1855.

MacGregor, John. *Historical and Descriptive Sketches of the Maritime Colonies of British America.* London: Longman, Rees, Orme, Brown and Green, 1828.

Martin, Robert Montgomery. *History, Statistics and Geography of Upper and Lower Canada.* London: Whittaker, 1838.

Moore, J.G. *Fifteen Months Round about Manitoba and the Northwest: A Lecture by J.G. Moore*, Stratford-upon-Avon: Simpkin, Marshall & Co., 1883.

New Brunswick and Nova Scotia Land Company. *Practical Information Respecting New Brunswick for the Use of Persons Intending to Settle upon the Lands of the New Brunswick and Nova Scotia Land Company.* London: Pelham Richardson, 1843.

Robinson, John, and Thomas Rispin. *A Journey Through Nova Scotia: Containing a Particular Account of the Country and Its Inhabitants; with Observations on the Management in Husbandry, the Breed of Horses and Other Cattle, and Every Thing Material Relating to Farming; to Which Is Added an Account of Several Estates for Sale in Different Townships of Nova-Scotia, with Their Number of Acres and the Price at Which Each Is Set.* York: Printed for the authors by C. Etherington, 1774.

Roper, Edward. *By Track and Trail: A Journey Through Canada.* London: W.H. Allen, 1891.

Rowan, John J. *The Emigrant and Sportsman in Canada: Some Experiences of an Old Country Settler: with Sketches of Canadian Life, Sporting Adventures, and Observations on the Forests and Fauna.* London: E. Stanford, 1876.

Scadding, Rev. Henry. *The Address to the St. George's Society in the Cathedral of St. James, Toronto, April 23rd, 1860.* Toronto: Rowsell & Hutchison Printers, 1860.

Scrope, George Poullett. *Extracts of Letters from Poor Persons Who Emigrated Last Year to Canada and the United States for the Information of the Labouring Poor in this Country.* London: J. Ridgeway, 1831.

Surtees, Scott Frederick. *Emigrant Letters from Settlers in Canada and South Australia Collected in the Parish of Banham, Norfolk.* London: Jarrold & Sons, 1852.

OFFICIAL BRITISH GOVERNMENT PUBLICATIONS

PP 1836 (567) XVII: Report of the 1836 Select Committee appointed to inquire into the causes of shipwreck.

British Parliamentary Papers: Annual Reports of the Immigration Agent at Quebec (1831–61).

British Parliamentary Papers: Colonial Land and Emigration Commissioners, Annual Reports (1841–72).

Annual Reports of the Poor Law Commissioners for England and Wales. London: Charles Knight & Co., 1836–54.

Reports from the Select Committee Appointed to Inquire into the Expediency of Encouraging Emigration from the United Kingdom, 1826, IV, 1826–27, V.

Official reports of debates in Parliament (Hansard).

CONTEMPORARY NEWSPAPERS

Acadian Recorder
Bedfordshire Times and Independent
Berwick Advertiser
Beverley Guardian
Bristol Times and Mirror
Canadian Courier
Canadian Gazette
Cheltenham Chronicle and Gloucestershire Graphic
Clitheroe Advertiser
Driffield Times and General Observer
Dumfries and Galloway Courier
Free Press
The Globe
Hamilton Spectator
Hull Advertiser
Hull Daily Mail
Industrial Banner
Labour Leader
Lloyd's List
Manchester Guardian
Manitoba Daily Free Press
Maclean's Magazine
Montreal Daily Star
Montreal Gazette
Morning Citizen

National Review
Neepawa Press
New Brunswick Courier
Quebec Gazette
Rapid City Reporter
Reynolds Weekly Newspaper
Rockingham and Yorkshire and Lincolnshire Gazette
Sackville Tribune
Sherbrooke Daily Record
Southport Visitor
The Spectator
The Times
The Woman's Magazine
Toronto Evening Telegram
Toronto Globe
Vancouver Sun
Victoria Colonist
Victoria Daily Chronicle
Warminster Herald
Wellington Weekly News
Wilmslow Advertiser
York Courant
Yorkshire Gazette

CONTEMPORARY MATERIAL OF LATER PRINTING

Anon. *Farming and Ranching in Western Canada: Manitoba, Assiniboia, Alberta, Saskatchewan*. Ottawa: Canadian Institute for Historical Micro Reproductions, 1982.

Channell, Leonard Stewart. *History of Compton County and Sketches of the Eastern Townships of St. Francis and Sherbrooke County*. Belleville, ON: Mika Publishing, 1975 [first published 1896].

Cobbett, William, and Ian Dyck (ed.). *Rural Rides, Rural Rides in the Counties of Kent, Sussex, Hampshire, Wiltshire, Gloucestershire,*

Herefordshire, Worcestershire, Somerset, Oxfordshire, Berkshire, Essex, Suffolk, Norfolk, and Hertfordshire. London: Penguin Books, 2001.

Murray, Jean M., ed. *The Newfoundland Journal of Aaron Thomas, Able Seaman in HMS Boston: A Journal Written During a Voyage from England to Newfoundland and from Newfoundland to England in the Years 1794 and 1795, Addressed to a Friend.* London: Longmans, 1968.

Whitelaw, Marjorie, ed. *The Dalhousie Journals.* Ottawa: Oberon, 1978–82.

SECONDARY SOURCES

Aitken, Barbara B. "Searching Chelsea Pensioners in Upper Canada and Great Britain." *Families* 23, no. 3 (1984) [Part I]: 114–27; and no. 4 (1984) [Part II]: 178–97.

Allinson, Helen. *Farewell to Kent: Assisted Emigration in the Nineteenth Century.* Sittingbourne, Kent: Synjon Books, 2008.

Anon. *Empire Reconstruction: The Work of the Salvation Army Emigration-Colonization Department, 1903–1921 and After* (London: n. d.).

————. "Nineteenth Century Emigration from Weardale." *Northumberland and Durham Family History Society* 21, no. 3 (Autumn 1996): 94.

Appleton, Thomas E. *Ravenscrag: The Allan Royal Mail Line.* Toronto: McClelland & Stewart, 1974.

Baehre, Rainer. "Pauper Emigration to Upper Canada in the 1830s." *Social History* 14, no. 28 (1981): 339–67.

Bailyn, Bernard, *Voyagers to the West; Emigration from Britain to America on the Eve of the Revolution.* New York: Alfred A. Knopf, 1986.

Barber, Marilyn. *Immigrant Domestic Servants in Canada.* Ottawa: Canadian Historical Association, 1991.

Barman, J. "British Columbia's Gentlemen Farmers." *History Today* 34 (April 1984) 9–15.

————. *Growing Up British in British Columbia: Boys in Private School.* Vancouver: UBC Press, 1984.

Barman, Jean. "Unpacking English Gentlemen Emigrants' Cultural Baggage: Apple Orchards and Private Schools in British Columbia's

Okanagan Valley." *British Journal of Canadian Studies* 16, no. 1 (2003) 137–49.

Bealby, John Thomas. *Fruit Ranching in British Columbia*. London: A & C Black, 1909.

Bean, P. & J. Melville. *Lost Children of the Empire*. London: Unwin Hyman, 1989.

Blake, George. *Lloyd's Register of Shipping 1760–1960*. London: Lloyd's, 1960.

Blom, Margaret Howard, and Thomas E. Blom, eds. *Canada Home: Juliana Horatia Ewing's Fredericton Letters 1867–69*. Vancouver: UBC Press, 1983.

Bolger. F.W.P., ed. *Canada's Smallest Province: A History of Prince Edward Island*. Halifax: Nimbus, 1991.

Bowen, Lynne. *Muddling Through: The Remarkable Story of the Barr Colonists*. Vancouver: Douglas & McIntyre, 1992.

Bradley, John. *Letter-Books of John and Mary Cambridge of Prince Edward Island, 1792–1812*. Devizes, Wiltshire: The Stationery Cupboard, 1996.

Brado, Edward. *Cattle Kingdom: Early Ranching in Alberta*. Vancouver: Douglas & McIntyre, 1984.

Brebner, John Bartlet. *The Neutral Yankees of Nova Scotia: A Marginal Colony During the Revolutionary Years*. New York: Columbia University Press, 1937.

Broadbent, Barry. *The Immigrant Years from Britain and Europe to Canada, 1945–67*. Vancouver: Douglas & McIntyre, 1986.

Brooks, W.H. "The Bible Christians in the West." *Prairie Forum* 1, no. 1 (1976): 59–67.

Brown, Alice E. "Early Days in Souris and Glenwood." *Manitoba Historical Society Transaction*, Series 3, no. 10 (1953–54).

Brunger, Alan G. "The Geographical Context of English Assisted Emigration to Upper Canada in the Early Nineteenth Century." *British Journal of Canadian Studies* 16, no. 1 (2003): 7–31.

Buckner, Phillip. "Introduction." *British Journal of Canadian Studies* 16, no. 1 (2003), 1–5.

Buckner, Philip, ed. *Canada and the British Empire*. Oxford: Oxford University Press, 2008.

Buckner, Phillip, and John G. Reid, eds. *The Atlantic Region to Confederation: A History*. Toronto: University of Toronto Press, 1993.

Bumsted, J.M. *Land Settlement and Politics on Eighteenth-Century Prince Edward Island*. Kingston: McGill-Queen's, 1987.

————. *The Peoples of Canada, a Pre-Confederation History*, vol. 1. Toronto: Oxford University Press, 1992.

Bush, Julia. *Edwardian Ladies and Imperial Power*. London: Leicester University Press, 2000.

Callbeck, Lorne C. *The Cradle of Confederation: A Brief History of Prince Edward Island from Its Discovery in 1534 to the Present Time*. Fredericton, NB: Brunswick Press, 1964.

Cameron, Wendy, and Mary McDougall Maude. *Assisting Emigration to Upper Canada:The Petworth Project, 1832–37*. Montreal: McGill-Queen's University Press, 2000.

Cameron, Wendy. "English Immigrants in 1830s Upper Canada: The Petworth Emigration Scheme." In *Canadian Migration Patterns*, edited by Barbara J. Messamore, 91–100. Toronto: University of Toronto Press, 2004.

Cameron, Wendy, Sheila Haines, and Mary McDougall Maude, eds. *English Immigrant Voices: Labourers' Letters from Upper Canada in the 1830s*. Montreal: McGill-Queen's University Press, 2000.

Campey, Lucille H. *Planters, Paupers, and Pioneers: English Settlers in Atlantic Canada*. Toronto: Dundurn, 2010.

————. *The Scottish Pioneers of Upper Canada, 1784–1855: Glengarry and Beyond*. Toronto: Natural Heritage, 2005.

————. *Seeking a Better Future: The English Pioneers of Ontario and Quebec*, Toronto: Dundurn, 2012.

————. *The Silver Chief: Lord Selkirk and the Scottish Pioneers of Belfast, Baldoon, and Red River*. Toronto: Natural Heritage, 2003.

————. *With Axe and Bible: The Scottish Pioneers of New Brunswick, 1784–1874*. Toronto: Dundurn, 2007.

Carbin, Clifton F. *Deaf Heritage in Canada: A Distinctive, Diverse and Enduring Culture*. Toronto: McGraw-Hill, 1996.

Carrier, N.H., and J.R. Jeffrey. *External Migration: A Study of the Available Statistics 1815–1950*. London: HMSO, 1953.

Cavanaugh, C.A., and R.R. Warne, eds. *Telling Tales: Essays in Western Women's History*. Vancouver: UBC Press, 2000.

Charbonneau, Andre, and Andre Sevigny. *1847 Grosse İsle: A Record of Daily Events*. Ottawa: Canadian Heritage, 1997.

Cherwinski, W.J.C. "'Misfits,' 'Malingerers,' and 'Malcontents': The British Harvester Movement of 1928." In *The Developing West: Essays on Canadian History in Honour of Lewis H. Thomas*, edited by John E. Foster, 273–302. Edmonton: The University of Alberta Press, 1983.

Chilton, Lisa. *Agents of Empire: British Female Migration to Canada and Australia, 1860s–1903*. Toronto: University of Toronto Press, 2007.

Chope, R. Pease, ed. *The Devonian Year Book, 1913*. London: The London Devonian Association, 1913.

Clancy, Merrium, et al. *Cornish Emigrants to Ontario*. Toronto: Toronto Cornish Association, 1998.

Clark, Andrew Hill. *Three Centuries and the Island: A Historical Geography of Settlement and Agriculture in Prince Edward Island, Canada*. Toronto: University of Toronto Press, 1959.

Clarke, John. "A Geographical Analysis of Colonial Settlement in the Western District of Upper Canada, 1788–1850." (Unpublished Ph.D. thesis, University of Western Ontario, 1970).

Clark, Samuel Delbert. *Church and Sect in Canada*. Toronto: University of Toronto Press, 1948.

Constantine, Stephen, ed. *Emigrants and Empire: British Settlement in the Dominions Between the Wars*. Manchester: Manchester University Press, 1990.

Constantine, S. "Empire Migration and Social Reform." In *Migrants, Emigrants and Immigrants: A Social History of Migration*, edited by C.G. Pooley and I.D. Whyte, 62–83. London: Routledge, 1991.

Corbett, Gail H. *Nation Builders: Barnardo Children in Canada*. Toronto: Dundurn, 2002.

Courville, Serge [translated by Richard Howard]. *Quebec: A Historical Geography*. Vancouver: UBC Press, 2008.

Cowan, Helen. *British Emigration to British North America: The First Hundred Years*. Toronto: University of Toronto Press, 1961.

Davis, John F. "From Eastern Canada to Western Canada: Illustrations." In *Canadian Migration Patterns from Britain and North America*, edited by Barbara J. Messamore, 171–81. Ottawa: University of Ottawa Press, 2004.

Davies, Maude Frances. *Life in an English Village: An Economic and Historical Survey of the Parish of Corsley in Wiltshire.* London: T. Fisher Unwin, 1909.

Davis, Ralph. *The Industrial Revolution and British Overseas Trade.* Leicester: Leicester University Press, 1979.

Dinton Women's Institute. *Gladys and Dinton Through the Years: A History of Gladys and Dinton Districts and the Biographies of the Men and Women Who Pioneered the Area.* Calgary, Alberta: Dinton and Gladys Women's Institutes, 1965.

Dickinson, John A., and Brian Young. *A Short History of Quebec.* 2nd edition. Toronto: Longman, 1993.

Dictionary of Canadian Biography. Toronto: University of Toronto Press, 1979–85.

Dunae, Patrick. *Gentlemen Emigrants: From the British Public Schools to the Canadian Frontier.* Vancouver: Douglas & McIntyre, 1981.

Edmondson, William. *Making Rough Places Plain, Fifty Years' Work of the Manchester and Salford Boys' and Girls' Refuges and Homes, 1870–1920.* Manchester: Sherratt and Hughes, 1921.

Elliott, Bruce. "Emigrant Recruitment by the New Brunswick Land Company: The Pioneer Settlers of Stanley and Harvey." *Generations,* the journal of the New Brunswick Genealogical Society (Winter 2004), 50–54; (Spring 2005), 34–40; (Summer 2005), 11–17.

Elliott, Bruce. "Regional Patterns of English Immigration and Settlement in Upper Canada." In *Canadian Migration Patterns from Britain and North America,* edited by Barbara J. Messamore, 51–90. Ottawa: University of Ottawa Press, 2004.

————. "The English." In *The Encyclopedia of Canada's Peoples,* edited by Paul Robert Magosci, 462–88. Toronto: Published for the Multicultural History Society of Ontario by the University of Toronto Press, circa 1999.

Elliott, Bruce S. "English Immigration to Prince Edward Island." *The Island Magazine* Part One, no. 40 (1996), 3–9; Part Two, no. 41 (1997), 3–9.

————. *Irish Migrants in the Canadas: A New Approach.* Kingston, ON: McGill-Queen's University Press, 1988.

Emerson, James. "Emerson Family History — From Durham Co., England, to Durham Co., U.C." *Families* 29, no. 4 (1983): 229–39.

England, Robert. *Colonization of Western Canada: A Study of Contemporary Land Settlement (1896–1934).* London: P.S. King & Son, 1936.

Erickson, Charlotte. *Leaving England: Essays on British Emigration in the Nineteenth Century.* Ithaca, NY: Cornell University Press, 1994.

Fast, Vera K. *Missionary on Wheels: Frances Hatton Eva Hasell and the Sunday School Caravan Mission.* Toronto: The Anglican Book Centre, 1979.

Fedorowich, Kent. "The Assisted Emigration of British Ex-Servicemen to the Dominions, 1914–1922." In *Emigrants and Empire: British Settlement in the Dominions Between the Wars*, edited by Stephen Constantine, 45–71. Manchester: Manchester University Press, 1990.

Folkes, Edward. *Letters from a Young Emigrant in Manitoba, 1883.* Winnipeg: University of Manitoba Press, 1981.

Files, Angela E.M. "Loyalist Settlement along the St. Lawrence in Upper Canada." *Grand River Branch (U.E.L. Association of Canada) Newsletter* 8, no. 1 (February 1996): 9–12.

Forster, Merna M. "Quarantine at Grosse Îsle." *Canadian Family Physician* 41 (May 1995): 841–48.

Fowler, Simon. "0950 to Toronto: The Emigration of the Unemployed from Norwich to Ontario in 1906." *Families* 37, no. 3 (August 1998): 146–52.

Gallant, Peter, and Nelda Murray. *From England to Prince Edward Island.* Charlottetown: PEI Genealogical Society, 1991.

Ganong, W.F. "Monograph of the Origins of Settlements in the Province of New Brunswick." *Transactions of the Royal Society of Canada*, 2nd series (10), sections 1–2 (1904): 1–185.

Gardiner, Claude. *Letters from an English Rancher.* Calgary: Glenbow Museum, 1988.

Gates, Lilian Francis. *Land Policies in Upper Canada.* Toronto: University of Toronto Press, 1968.

Gilroy, Marion. *Loyalists and Land Settlement in Nova Scotia.* Halifax: PANS Publication No. 4, 1937.

Glynn-Ward, Hilda. *The Glamour of British Columbia.* London: Hutchinson, 1926.

Goutor, David. *Guarding the Gates: The Canadian Labour Market and Immigration, 1872–1934*. Vancouver: UBC Press, 2007.

Grainger, Jennifer. *Vanished Villages of Middlesex.* Toronto: Natural Heritage, 2002.

Grant, Alison, and Peter Christie. *The Book of Bideford.* Buckingham, UK: Barracuda Books Ltd., 1987.

Greenhill, Basil, and Anne Giffard. *Westcountrymen in Prince Edward's Isle*. Toronto: University of Toronto Press, 1967.

Guillet, Edwin C. *The Great Migration: The Atlantic Crossing by Sailing Ships Since 1770*. Toronto: University of Toronto Press, 1963.

———. *The Pioneer Farmer and Backwoodsman*. Toronto: University of Toronto Press, 1963.

Hallam, Mrs. W.T. *When You Are in Halifax: Sketches of Life in the First English Settlement in Canada*. Toronto: Church Book Room, 1937.

Hammerton, A. J. *Emigrant Gentlewomen: Genteel Poverty and Female Emigration, 1830–1914*. London: Croom Helm, 1979.

Handcock, W. Gordon. *So Longe As There Comes Noe Women: Origins of English Settlement in Newfoundland.* St. John's, NL: Breakwater, circa 1989.

Hanson, Carter F. *Emigration, Nation, Vocation: The Literature of English Emigration to Canada, 1825–1900*. East Lansing, MI: Michigan State University Press, 2009.

Harper, Marjory. "Probing the Pioneer Questionnaires: British Settlement in Saskatchewan, 1887–1914." *Saskatchewan History* 52:2 (Fall, 2000): 28–46.

Harper, Marjory. "Rhetoric and Reality: British Migration to Canada, 1867–1967." In *Canada and the British Empire*, edited by Philip Buckner, 160–80. Oxford: Oxford University Press, 2008.

Harris, Donald F. "The Canadian Government's Use of Newspapers to Encourage Immigration in the Twenty Years before the First World War, As Demonstrated in the Newspapers of Shropshire" (The fifth annual lecture of the Friends of Shropshire Records & Research, Shrewsbury, November 3, 1999).

———. "The Church of England and Emigration to Canada: Rural Clergy in the County of Shropshire." *Journal of the Canadian Church Historical Society*, Vol. XLI (1999): 5–26.

————. "The Promotion in Shropshire of Emigration to Canada in 1914 with Particular Reference to the Period from 1890." (Unpublished Ph.D. thesis: University Of Birmingham, 1998).

————. "The Role of Shropshire Local Shipping Agents in Encouraging Emigration to Canada, 1890–1914." *Local Historian* 30, no. 4 (November 2000).

Harris, R. Cole, and Elizabeth Phillips, eds. *Letters from Windermere 1912–1914.* Vancouver: UBC Press, 1984.

Harrison, Phyllis, ed. *The Home Children: Their Personal Stories.* Winnipeg: Watson & Dwyer Publishing Ltd., 1979.

Hawkes, John. "Where a Woman has a Chance." *The Woman's Magazine*, n.d. (circa 1905).

Hazlet Historical Society. *Hazlet Saskatchewan and Its Heritage.* Hazlet,SK: Hazlet Historical Society, 1987.

Hedges, J. *Building the Canadian West: The Land and Colonization Policies of the CPR* (New York: The MacMillan Company, 1939).

History Book Committee at Neepawa Manitoba. *Heritage: A History of the Town of Neepawa and District As Told and Recorded by Its People, 1883–1983.* Neepawa, MB: Neepawa Centennial Book Committee, 1983.

Horn, Pamela. "Agricultural Trade Unionism and Emigration." *The Historical Journal* 15, no. 1 (March 1972), 87–102.

Hornby, Montague Leyland. *A Plan for British Community Settlements in Canada.* Lethbridge, AB: Lethbridge Herald Print, 1931.

Howell, Colin D. *Blood, Sweat and Cheers: Sport and the Making of Modern Canada.* Toronto: University of Toronto Press, 2001.

Howells, Gary. "Emigration and the New Poor Law: Norfolk Emigration Fever of 1836." *Rural History* 11, no. 2 (October 2000): 145–64.

————. "On Account of Their Disreputable Characters': Parish-Assisted Emigration from Rural England, 1834–1860." *History* 88, no. 292 (October 2003): 587–605.

Hume, Stephen. "A Shaft of Sunlight 150 Years Ago." *Vancouver Sun*, November 27, 2004.

Inderwick, Mary. "A Lady and Her Ranch." *Alberta Historical Review* 15, no. 4 (1967): 1–9.

Inkerman, Roger. *Ships and Shipyards of Bideford Devon, 1568–1938.* Bideford: author, 1947.

Jackal, Susan. *Flannel Shirt and Liberty: British Emigrant Gentlewomen in the Canadian West, 1880–1914.* Toronto: University of Toronto Press, 1996 (3 volumes.).

Johnson, D.W. *History of Methodism in Eastern British America Including Nova Scotia, New Brunswick, Prince Edward Island.* Sackville, NB: Tribune Printing, 1925.

Johnson, J.K. "The Chelsea Pensioners in Upper Canada." *Ontario History* 53, no. 4 (1961): 273–89.

Johnston, H.J.M. *British Emigration Policy 1815–1830: Shovelling Out Paupers.* Oxford: Clarendon Press, 1972.

———. "Immigration to the Five Eastern Townships of the Huron Tract." *Ontario History*, Vol. LIV (1962): 207–24.

Kinsmen, Rev. Barry. *Fragments of Padstow's History.* Padstow: Padstow Parochial Church Council, 2003.

Kohli, Marjorie. *The Golden Bridge: Young Immigrants to Canada, 1838 – 1939.* Toronto: Natural Heritage, 2003.

Lee, Robert C. *The Canada Company and the Huron Tract, 1826–1853.* Toronto: Natural Heritage, 2004.

Leetooze, Sherreall Branton. *A Corner for the Preacher*: introductory chapter by Elizabeth Howard; preface by Colin Short. Bowmanville, ON: L. Michael-John Associates, circa 2005.

———. *Bible Christians of the Canadian Conference: The Bible Christians of North America (Ontario, PEI, Manitoba, Ohio, Michigan, Wisconsin) between 1831 and 1884* (Bowmanville, ON: Lynn Michael-John Associates, 2005).

Leitch, Gillian I. "The Importance of Being English: English Ethnic Culture in Montreal c.1800–1864." In *Locating the English Diaspora, 1500–2010*, edited by Tanja Bueltmann, David T. Gleeson, and Donald M. MacRaild, 100–17. Liverpool: Liverpool University Press, 2012.

Little, John Irvine. *Nationalism, Capitalism and Colonization in Nineteenth-Ccentury Quebec: The Upper St. Francis District.* Kingston, ON: McGill-Queen's University Press, 1989.

Little, J.I., ed. *Love Strong as Death: Lucy Peel's Canadian Journal, 1833–1836.* Waterloo, ON: Wilfred Laurier University Press, 2001.

MacDonagh, Oliver. *A Pattern of Government Growth 1800–1860: The Passenger Acts and Their Enforcement*. London: MacGibbon & Kee, 1961.

———. "Emigration and the State, 1833–55: An Essay in Administrative History." *Transactions of the Royal Historical Society*, fifth series, vol. 5 (London: The Royal Historical Society, 1955): 133–59.

MacDonald, Cheryl. *Norfolk Folk: Immigration and Migration in Norfolk County*. Delhi, ON: Norfolk Folk Book Committee, 2005.

MacDonald, Norman. *Canada, Immigration and Colonization, 1841–1903*. Aberdeen: Aberdeen University Press, 1966.

———. *Canada, Immigration and Settlement 1763–1841*. London: Longmans & Co., 1939.

MacGregor, James. *A History of Alberta*. Edmonton: Hartig Publishers Ltd., 1981.

Mack, Susan Muriel. *The History of Stephen Township*. Crediton, ON: Corporation of the Township of Stephen, 1992.

MacKinnon, Neil. *This Unfriendly Soil: The Loyalist Experience in Nova Scotia 1783–1791*. Montreal: McGill-Queen's University Press, 1986.

MacNutt, W.S. *New Brunswick: A History, 1784–1867*. Toronto: Macmillan, 1984.

———. *The Atlantic Provinces; the Emergence of Colonial Society 1712–1857*. London: McClelland & Stewart, 1965.

Magosci, Paul Robert, ed. *The Encyclopedia of Canada's Peoples*. Toronto: Published for the Multicultural History Society of Ontario by the University of Toronto Press, circa 1999.

Mannion, John J., ed. *The Peopling of Newfoundland: Essays in Historical Geography*. St. John's: Institute of Social and Economic Research, Memorial University of Newfoundland, 1978.

Martell, J.S. *Immigration to and Emigration from Nova Scotia 1815–1838*. Halifax: PANS 1942.

Matthews, Keith. "A History of the West of England-Newfoundland Fishery." University of Oxford: Unpublished Ph.D. thesis, 1968.

McAndless, J.E. "Telfer Cemetery (English Settlement) London Township." *Families* 14, no. 3 (1975): 71–78.

McCormack, Ross. "Networks Among British Immigrants and Accommodation to Canadian Society: Winnipeg, 1900–1914." In

Immigration in Canada: Historical Perspectives, edited by Gerald Tulchinsky, 203–23. Toronto: Copp Clark Longman Ltd., 1994.

————. "Cloth Caps and Jobs: The Ethnicity of English Immigrants in Canada." In *Ethnicity, Power and Politics in Canada*, edited by Jorgen Dahlie and Tissa Fernando, 38–55. Toronto: Methuen, 1981.

McCreath, Peter L., and John G. Leefe. *A History of Early Nova Scotia.* Tantallon, NS: Four East Publications, 1990.

McDonald, Terry. "A Door of Escape: Letters Home from Wiltshire and Somerset Emigrants to Upper Canada, 1830–1832." In *Canadian Migration Patterns*, edited by Barbara J. Messamore, 101–19. Toronto: University of Toronto Press, 2004.

Metcalfe, Joseph H. *The Tread of the Pioneers, Under the Distinguished Patronage of the Government of the Province of Manitoba, the Corporation of the City of Portage La Prairie, the Council of the Rural Municipality of Portage La Prairie.* Portage la Prairie, MB: Old Timers' Association, 1932.

Miller, Audrey Saunders, ed. *The Journals of Mary O'Brien.* Toronto: Macmillan, 1968.

Milner W.C. "The Records of Chignecto." *Collections of the Nova Scotia Historical Society* 15 (1911): 1–86.

Mindenhall, Dorothy. "Choosing the Group: 19th Century Non-Mining Cornish in British Columbia." In *Cornish Studies, Eight*, edited by Philip Payton, 40–53. Exeter: University of Exeter Press, 2000.

Minifie, James M. *Homesteaders: A Prairie Boyhood Recalled.* Toronto: Macmillan, 1972.

Murray, Nelda, ed. *The Valiant Connection: A History of Little York.* Charlottetown: York History Committee, 1993.

Morse, Susan Longley. "Immigration to Nova Scotia, 1839–51." Halifax: Dalhousie University, unpublished M.A., 1946.

Morton, W.L. *Manitoba: A History.* Toronto: University of Toronto Press, 1967.

New Brunswick Genealogical Society, Passengers to New Brunswick: Custom House Records — 1833, 34, 37, and 38. Saint John, NB: 1987.

Noël, Françoise. *Competing for Souls: Missionary Activity and Settlement in the Eastern Townships, 1784–1851.* Sherbrooke, QC: University of Sherbrooke, 1988.

Norcross, E. Blanche, ed. *Nanaimo Retrospective: The First Century*. Nanaimo, BC: Nanaimo Historical Society, 1979.

Ormsby, Margaret A. *British Columbia: A History*. Toronto: Macmillan, 1958.

Ouellet, Fernand, *Le Bas Canada 1791–1840; Changements structuraux et crise* (Ottawa: Ottawa University, 1976) [Translated and adapted: Patricia Claxton, *Lower Canada, 1791–1840: Social Change and Nationalism* (Toronto: McClelland & Stewart, 1980)].

Palmer, Howard, ed. *Immigration and the Rise of Multiculturalism*. Toronto: Copp Clarke, 1975.

Parker, Roy. *The Shipment of Poor Children to Canada, 1867–1917*. Bristol: University of Bristol, the Policy Press, 2008.

Parr, Joy. *Labouring Children*. London: Croom Helm, 1980.

————. "The Skilled Emigrant and Her Kin: Gender, Culture and Labour Recruitment." In *Immigration in Canada: Historical Perspectives.*, edited by Gerald Tulchinsky, 334–52. Toronto: Copp Clark Longman Ltd., 1994.

Paxman, Jeremy. *The English: The Portrait of a People*. London: Michael Joseph, 1998.

Payton, Philip. "Cornish Emigration in Response to Changes in the International Copper Market in the 1860s." In *Cornish Studies Three*. Edited by Philip Payton. Exeter: University of Exeter Press, 1995: 60–82.

————. "Reforming Thirties and Hungry Forties: The Genesis of Cornwall's Emigration Trade." In *Cornish Studies Four*, edited by Philip Payton, 107–27. Exeter: University of Exeter Press, 1996.

————. *The Cornish Overseas*. Fowey: Alexander Associates, 1999.

Pedlar, Samuel, and Charles Wethey. "From Cornwall to Canada in 1841." *Families* 22, no. 4 (1983): 244–53.

Percival, Tom. *Poor Law Children*. London: Shaw & Sons, 1912.

Peterson, Jan. *Black Diamond City, Nanaimo — The Victorian Era*. Victoria: Heritage House Publishing Company, 2002.

Pigott, Peter. *Sailing Seven Seas: A History of the Canadian Pacific Line*. Toronto: Dundurn, 2010.

Ravenhill, Alice. *The Memoirs of an Educational Pioneer*. Toronto: J.M. Dent, 1951.

Reynolds, Lloyd G. *The British Immigrant: His Social and Economic Adjustment in Canada*. Toronto: Oxford University Press, 1935.

Richards, Alan E. "Devonians in Canada." *Devon Family Historian*, no. 40 (October 1986): 24–8.

Richards, Eric. *Britannia's Children: Emigration from England, Scotland, Wales and Ireland since 1600*. London: Hambledon and London, 2004.

Riis, N. "The Walhachin Myth: A Study of Settlement Abandonment." *British Columbian Studies* 17 (Spring 1973): 3–25.

Robertson, Norman. *History of the County of Bruce*. Toronto: William Briggs, 1906.

Rompkey, Ronald, ed. *Expeditions of Honour: The Journal of John Salusbury in Halifax, Nova Scotia, 1749–53*. Newark: University of Delaware Press; London, Toronto: Associated University Presses, circa 1982.

Rose, Michael E. *The English Poor Law 1780–1930*. Newton Abbott: David & Charles, 1971.

Rowse, A.L. *The Cornish in America*. London: Macmillan, 1969.

Schmidt, Anita E. *On the Banks of the Assiniboine: A History of the Parish of St. James*. Winnipeg, MB: L.F. Schmidt, 1975.

Schultz, John A. "'Leaven for the Lump': Canada and Empire Settlement, 1918–1939." In *Emigrants and Empire: British Settlement in the Dominions Between the Wars*, edited by Stephen Constantine, 150–73. Manchester: Manchester University Press, 1990.

Scobie, Charles H.H., and John Webster Grant, eds. *Contribution of Methodism to Atlantic Canada*. Montreal: McGill-Queen's University Press, circa 1992.

Scott, James. *The Settlement of Huron County*. Toronto: Ryerson Press, 1966.

Semple, Neil. *The Lord's Dominion: The History of Canadian Methodism*. Montreal, Buffalo: McGill-Queen's University Press, circa 1996.

Short, Al. "The 1817 Journey of the Brig *Trafalgar* with Its Immigrants." *Generations*, the journal of the New Brunswick Genealogical Society (Spring 2006), 12–16.

Siebert, Wilbur Henry. "American Loyalists in the Eastern Seigneuries and Townships of the Province of Quebec." *Transactions of the Royal Society of Canada*, 3rd series (1913) vol. VII: 3–41.

———. "Loyalist Settlements in the Gaspé Peninsula." *Transactions of the Royal Society of Canada*, 3rd Series (1914) vol. VIII, 399–405.

Skilling, Gordon. *Canadian Representation Abroad: From Agency to Embassy.* Toronto: Ryerson Press, 1945.

Slocombe, Ivor. *Wiltshire Reformatory for Boys, Warminster, 1856–1924.* East Knoyle, Salisbury: Hobnob Press, 2005.

Smith, David. "Instilling British Values in the Prairie Provinces." *Prairies Forum* 6, no. 2 (1981): 134–39.

Snell, K.D. *Annals of the Labouring Poor: Social Change and Agrarian England 1660–1900.* Cambridge: Cambridge University Press, 1985.

Snowdon, James. "Footprints in the Marsh Mud: Politics and Land Settlement in the Township of Sackville, 1760–1800." University of New Brunswick, Fredericton: unpublished MA thesis, 1974.

Starkey, David J. "Devonians and the Newfoundland Trade." *The New Maritime History of Devon*, vol. I, edited by Michael Duffy, et al. London: Conway Maritime Press in association with University of Exeter, 1992.

Stevenson, John. *Popular Disturbances in England, 1700–1832.* London: Longman, 1992.

Stewart, Basil. *"No English Need Apply": Or, Canada as a Field for the Emigrant.* London: Routledge, 1909.

———. *The Land of the Maple Leaf.* London: Routledge, 1908.

Strickland, Samuel. *Twenty-Seven Years in Canada West, or, The Experience of an Early Settler* (Edmonton: M.G. Hurtig Ltd., 1970).

Thompson, John. *Hudson: The Early Years, Up to 1867.* Hudson, QC: Hudson Historical Society, 1999. Thompson's material was first published in 1967 as the author's thesis, "The evolution of an English-speaking community in rural French Canada, 1820–1867."

Throop, Louise Walsh. "Early Settlers of Cumberland Township, Nova Scotia." *National Genealogical Society Quarterly* 67 (September 1979): 182–282.

Tranter, Neil. *Sport, Economy, and Society in Britain, 1750–1914.* Cambridge: Cambridge University Press, 1998.

Trueman, Howard. *The Chignecto Isthmus and Its First Settlers.* Toronto: William Briggs, 1902.

Vineberg, Robert. "Quebec City — The Forgotten Port of Entry." *Canadian Immigration Historical Society Newsletter*, Issue 59 (September 2010).

Voisey, Paul, ed. *A Preacher's Frontier: The Castor, Alberta Letters of the Reverend Martin W. Holdom, 1909–1912*. Calgary: Historical Society of Alberta, 1996.

Wagner, Gillian. *Children of the Empire*. London: Weidenfeld & Nicolson, 1982.

Warburton, A.B. *History of Prince Edward Island*. Saint John, NB: Barnes & Co., 1923.

Wheaton, Dean. *Letters from Bruce County Written by Pioneer Joseph Bacon, 1705–1882*. Indiana: Author House, 2006.

Wright, Esther Clark. *Planters and Pioneers*, Wolfville, NS: the author, 1982.

———. *The Loyalists of New Brunswick*. Fredericton, NB: 1955.

Wynn, Graeme. "A Region of Scattered Settlements and Bounded Possibilities: North Eastern America 1775–1800." *Canadian Geographer* 31 (1987): 319–38.

Yarmie, Andrew. "'I Had Always Wanted to Farm': The Quest for Independence by English Female Emigrants at the Princess Patricia Ranch, Vernon, British Columbia, 1912–1920." *British Journal of Canadian Studies* 16, no. 1 (2003): 102–25.

Young, Stephen C. "They Went West: The Founding of a Family in Canada." *Canadian Genealogist* 8, no. 4 (December 1986): 214–26.

Zuehlke, Mark. *Scoundrels, Dreamers, and Second Sons: British Remittance Men in the Canadian West*. Vancouver: Whitecap Books, 1994.

INDEX

ABOUT THE AUTHOR

Ottawa-born Dr. Lucille H. Campey began her career in Canada as a scientist and computer specialist, having previously obtained a degree in chemistry from Ottawa University. Following her marriage in 1967 to her English husband, Geoff, she moved to England. Lucille obtained a master's degree at Leeds University following research on medieval settlement patterns. She subsequently gained a doctorate at Aberdeen University following research on Scottish immigration to Canada. She then went on to write eight books on the Scots, all published by Dundurn. Lucille's first book on English immigration, *Planters, Paupers, and Pioneers: English Settlers in Atlantic Canada*, was published in 2010, while *Seeking a Better Future: The English Pioneers of Ontario and Quebec* followed in 2012. The first of the three books that she will be writing on Irish immigration to Canada will be published by Dundurn in 2016. Lucille and Geoff live near Salisbury in Wiltshire.